Proving Prophecy

Islamic Literatures

TEXTS AND STUDIES

Edited by

Jamal J. Elias (*University of Pennsylvania, Philadelphia*)
Feras Hamza (*University of Wollongong, Dubai*)
Walid Saleh (*University of Toronto*)
Roberto Tottoli (*Università degli Studi di Napoli L'Orientale*)

VOLUME 5

The titles published in this series are listed at *brill.com/ilts*

Proving Prophecy

Dalāʾil al-Nubūwa *Literature as Part of the Scholarly Discourse on Prophecy in Islam*

By

Mareike Koertner

BRILL

LEIDEN | BOSTON

Cover illustration: Designs for tiles in Islamic style c.1840–50. Pencil and watercolour. Owen Jones (1809–1874)

Library of Congress Cataloging-in-Publication Data

Names: Koertner, Mareike, author.
Title: Proving prophecy. Dala'il al-nubuwa literature as part of the scholarly discourse on prophecy in Islam / by Mareike Koertner.
Description: Leiden ; Boston : Brill, 2024. | Series: Islamic literatures, 2214-6601 ; volume 5 | Includes bibliographical references and index.
Identifiers: LCCN 2023045785 (print) | LCCN 2023045786 (ebook) | ISBN 9789004687332 (hardback) | ISBN 9789004687349 (ebook)
Subjects: LCSH: Muḥammad, Prophet, -632—Prophetic office. | Prophecy—Islam.
Classification: LCC BP76.6 .K64 2024 (print) | LCC BP76.6 (ebook) | DDC 297.6/3—dc23/eng/20231002
LC record available at https://lccn.loc.gov/2023045785
LC ebook record available at https://lccn.loc.gov/2023045786

Typeface for the Latin, Greek, and Cyrillic scripts: "Brill". See and download: brill.com/brill-typeface.

ISSN 2214-6601
ISBN 978-90-04-68733-2 (hardback)
ISBN 978-90-04-68734-9 (e-book)
DOI 10.1163/9789004687349

This book is printed on acid-free paper and produced in a sustainable manner.

To the memory of my mother
Ruth Sofia Körtner (1957–2021)

Contents

Acknowledgements XI
Abbreviations XII

Introduction 1
1 Historiography, Hagiography, and the Marginalization of *Dalāʾil al-Nubūwa* Literature 4
2 Are Miracles Categorically "Popular"? 10
3 Hagiology as an Analytical Tool 13

1 **The Scholar and the Storyteller?—*Quṣṣāṣ* in Early Islam** 18
1 ʿUrwa b. al-Zubayr and the "Authenticated" Traditions 23
2 Wahb b. Munabbih and the "Unauthenticated" Traditions 25
3 Comparative Analysis: The Accounts of the *Hijra* according to ʿUrwa b. al-Zubayr and Wahb b. Munabbih 28
3.1 *ʿUrwa b. al-Zubayr's Account of the* Hijra 28
3.2 *Wahb b. Munabbih's Account of the* Hijra 29
3.3 *A Detailed Comparison between the* Hijra *Accounts of ʿUrwa b. al-Zubayr and Wahb b. Munabbih* 32
3.4 *Miracles in the Corpus of ʿUrwa b. al-Zubayr* 35

2 **Biographies of the Earliest *Dalāʾil al-Nubūwa* Authors** 39
1 The First Generation 41
2 The Second Generation 46
3 The Third Generation 53
4 The Fourth Generation 55
5 The Evolution of Early *Dalāʾil al-Nubūwa* Authors 60

3 **Methodological and Structural Approaches in *Dalāʾil al-Nubūwa* Literature** 63
1 Methodologies of Authentication in Early *Dalāʾil al-Nubūwa* Works 64
1.1 *Al-Jūzajānī's "Amārāt al-Nubūwa"* 67
1.2 *Ibn Saʿd's "ʿAlamāt al-nubūwa"* 69
1.2.1 The Question of Unauthenticated Materials in Ibn Saʿd's *Ṭabaqāt* 71
1.2.1.1 *Muḥammad's Encounter with Umm Maʿbad* 72
1.2.1.2 *Muḥammad's Encounter with Surāqa* 75

1.2.1.3 *The Cobweb and the Pigeon* 77
1.2.2 "Popular" Materials in Ibn Saʿd's Chapters on the Signs of Prophecy 79
2 Methodologies of Authentication in Later *Dalāʾil al-Nubūwa* Works 84
2.1 *Al-Khargūshī's* Sharaf al-Nabī 85
2.2 *Abū Nuʿaym al-Iṣfahānī's* Dalāʾil al-Nubūwa 86
2.3 *Al-Bayhaqī's* Dalāʾil al-nubūwa 87
3 Structure and Arrangement of *Dalāʾil al-Nubūwa* Works 92
3.1 *Ibn Saʿd's "ʿAlamāt al-Nubūwa"* 93
3.2 *Al-Khargūshī's* Sharaf al-Nabī 97
3.3 *Abū Nuʿāym al-Iṣfahānī's* Dalāʾil al-Nubūwa 98
3.4 *Al-Bayhaqī's* Dalāʾil al-Nubūwa 99

4 Content Analysis of Early Extant *Dalāʾil al-Nubūwa* Works 103
1 Maʿmar b. Rāshid's "Bāb al-Nubūwa" 104
2 Ibn Saʿd's "ʿAlamāt al-Nubūwa" 105
2.1 *Announcement or Prediction of Prophecy* 106
2.1.1 Monotheistic Predictions 106
2.1.2 Previous Prophets 111
2.1.3 Predictions by Pagans 112
2.2 *Water- and/or Food-Related Incidents* 114
2.3 *Natural Phenomena* 117
2.4 *Events in the Prophet's Childhood* 120
2.5 *States of the Prophet* 126
2.6 *Interactions with the Divine* 126
2.7 *Hidden Knowledge* 129
2.8 *Material Transformation and Healing* 130
3 Al-Bukhārī's "ʿAlāmāt al-Nubūwa fī l-Islām" 133
4 Al-Jūzajānī's "Amārāt al-Nubūwa" 135
4.1 *Food-Related Incidents as "Proofs of Prophecy"* 135
4.2 *The Prophet's Character as "Proof of Prophecy"* 137
4.3 *Light as "Proof of Prophecy"* 138
4.4 *Interactions with the Divine* 139
5 Al-Tirmidhī's "Bāb mā jāʾ fī ayāt Nubūwa al-Nabī wa-mā qad khaṣṣa Allāh bihi" 140
5.1 *Food/Water Related Incidents* 140
5.2 *Natural Phenomena* 141

5 Ibn Saʿd's "Proofs of Prophecy" and Its Intellectual Landscape 144
1 Political and Religious Impulses on the Notion of Prophecy 145
2 Christian-Muslim Encounters in the Early ʿAbbāsid Period 150
3 Analysis: Approaches to Christian Apologetic Literature 157
3.1 *Christians Addressing Muḥammad's Prophetic Status and Islam's Role in Sacred History* 162
3.2 *Islam as a Vehicle for Muḥammad's Personal Gain or Immoral Behavior* 165
3.3 *Miracles* 167
4 Ibn Saʿd and Christian Apologetics 169
5 Muslim Discourse on Pre-Qurʾānic Annunciations of Muḥammad 170
5.1 *The* Kitāb al-Maghāzī *of Ibn Isḥāq (d. 150/767)* 177

6 Recurring Themes in Later *Dalāʾil al-Nubūwa* Literature 187
1 Al-Khargūshī's *Sharaf al-nabī* 187
2 Abū Nuʿaym al-Iṣfahānī's *Dalāʾil al-nubūwa* 191
3 Al-Bayhaqī's *Dalāʾil al-nubūwa* 196
4 Theology in Later *Dalāʾil al-Nubūwa* Works 198
4.1 *Theology in Abū Nuʿaym al-Iṣfahānī's* Dalāʾil al-Nubūwa 199
4.2 *Theology in al-Bayhaqī's* Dalāʾil al-Nubūwa 202
5 Conclusion 203

Epilogue: *Dalāʾil al-nubūwa* and the Promise of Comparative Hagiology 207
Appendix: A Detailed Comparison between ʿUrwa b. al-Zubayr and Wahb b. Munabbih 211
Bibliography 215
Index of Subjects 229
Index of People and Places 242
Index of Scriptures 249

Acknowledgments

This book has been many years in the making, starting with my interest in childhood narratives of Muḥammad that emerged during an undergraduate class. In the many years since, I have been lucky to have received guidance and support from many colleagues and friends. I am first and foremost indebted to those who taught me not only to examine the fine detail of Arabic texts but also to consider the history of the Islamic Middle East as a grand panorama; Beatrice Gruendler, Gerhard Böwering, Dimitri Gutas, Racha el-Omari, Verena Klemm, and Stefanie Brinkmann are certainly among these.

I am deeply grateful to Mushegh Astryan, Yousef Casewit, and Rick Colby who took the time to read drafts and offered profoundly helpful insights. I am also grateful to Ruggero Vimercati Sanseverino and Michael Pregill, with whom I shared deep conversations while researching the 'signs of prophecy.' I also benefited from Jonathan A. C. Brown's advice. The Comparative Hagiology Seminar at the AAR conference, with its co-chairs Brian Siebeking and Todd French, introduced me to rich works by scholars of hagiography who shaped the theoretical framework of my work. This book greatly benefited from their wisdom, while all of its mistakes and shortcomings are my responsibility alone. At Brill, I want to thank the series editors, Jamal Elias, Feras Hamza, Walid Saleh, and Roberto Tottoli, as well as Teddi Dols, for their patient support.

I have been fortunate to have many thoughtful and supportive friends over the years; they have certainly made this journey a joyous and rewarding one: Matteo DiGiovanni, Matt Melvin-Koushki, Martin Nguyen, and Samuel Ross. A special word of thanks is also due to my supportive colleagues at Trinity College, in particular Zayde Antrim, Janet Bauer, Elly Findley, Gabe Hornung, Tamsin Jones, Ron Kiener, and Timothy Landry.

Finally, I'm deeply grateful for the unwavering support of my husband and the delightful inspiration that my children give me every day.

Abbreviations

BSOAS	*Bulletin of the School of Oriental and African Studies*
EI[1]	*Encyclopaedia of Islam, First edition*. Edited by M. Th. Houtsma, T. W. Arnold, R. Basset and R. Hartmann. Leiden: Brill, 1913–1936.
EI[2]	*Encyclopaedia of Islam, Second Edition*. Edited by P. Bearman, Th. Bianquis, C. E. Bosworth, E. van Donzel, and W. P. Heinrichs. 12 vols. Leiden: Brill, 1960–2004. Brill Online.
EI[3]	*Encyclopaedia of Islam, THREE*. Edited by Kate Fleet, Gudrun Krämer, Denis Matringe, John Nawas, and Everett Rowson. Leiden: Brill, 2007–. Brill Online.
EQ	*Encyclopedia of the Qurʾān*. Edited by Jane McAuliffe Dammen. 6 vols. Leiden: Brill, 2001–2006. Brill Online.
EIr	*Encyclopaedia Iranica*. Edited by Ehsan Yarshater. New York: Columbia University. Online http://www.iranicaonline.org
JAOS	*Journal of the American Oriental Society*
JNES	*Journal of Near Eastern Studies*

Introduction

A shepherd was herding his flock when a wolf approached and stole one of his sheep. The shepherd threw stones at the wolf until it let go of its prey but the wolf turned toward the shepherd and began to scold him for depriving him of the sustenance that God had provided for him. The shepherd was dumbfounded at the animal's speech, yet the wolf countered that there are more important matters than an articulate beast of prey. He informed the shepherd about the Prophet preaching in Medina. The shepherd immediately drove his flock to Medina, told the Prophet and his Companions about his encounter with the wolf, and accepted Islam.[1]

It was this particular account that led the nineteenth-century scholar Tor Andrae (d. 1947) to declare *dalāʾil al-nubūwa* literature "fantastic legends" and "barbaric embellishments that veil the true historical figure of the Prophet."[2] Most scholars of the twentieth century followed Andrae's lead and dismissed this literature as a product of popular veneration of the Prophet and edification for ordinary believers. I, however, argue that it not only originated among scholars of *ḥadīth* but also that this literature was part of a wider scholarly discourse about prophethood, one that occurred in numerous religious sciences and reflected specific ideological purposes. After all, prophethood is a significant foundational concept in theological, political, and social realms in Muslim societies. It is an essential pillar of faith, as most Muslim scholars argue that the central belief in the existence and unity of God (*tawḥīd*) can only be achieved through His messengers. Based on the centrality of the notion of prophetic Sunna, prophethood also became the principal subject of political, social, and legal authority. Muḥammad's death brought an end to two vital sources of authority: the ongoing revelation of the Qurʾān and his unique ability to interpret and exemplify its message in his daily life. The resulting challenges to develop new rulings for the community led to the colossal scholarly efforts to collect his *sunna* and develop methodologies on how to center Muḥammad's

1 Qāḍī ʿIyād, *al-Shifāʾ*, 1:432.

2 Andrae, *Die Person Muhammeds*, 28, 92f.

 | DOI:10.1163/9789004687349_002

authoritative voice and establish guiding principles after his passing. The political authority vested in Muḥammad and in prophethood as a concept became an immediate matter of concern in early Islamic history when "false" prophets arose. Abū Bakr had to confront the threat of rival tribal figures who claimed prophethood for themselves in a bid for political power, and similar contenders emerged periodically throughout Islamic history. The expansion of Muslim political rule over Christian and Jewish populations, who held their own doctrines of prophethood and frequently sought to delegitimize the faith of their new rulers, further prompted Muslim thinkers to articulate uniquely Islamic concepts of prophethood. These intersecting aspects brought forth a broad scholarly discourse on prophethood that aimed at addressing Muslim and non-Muslim challenges in an attempt to define the nature of prophethood and distinguish between individuals who held legitimate claims and "false" contenders. As Robinson put it, "[p]recisely because Muhammad's prophecy lay at the heart of Islamic belief, he stood at the center of what might be called the early Islamic imaginary."[3]

Works of *dalāʾil al-nubūwa* do not simply cater toward a Muslim need for edification and veneration of Muḥammad, rather, these works should be seen as part of a larger discourse on prophecy, one that seeks to establish evidence of Muḥammad's prophetic mission in light of Muslim and non-Muslim challenges that changed over time, according to their intellectual and social historical contexts. While similar works were eventually found in all Abrahamic faith traditions, Stroumsa has argued that this type of literature seems to have originated in the circles of Muslim scholars because there is hardly any precedence of this type of literature in Judaism and Christianity prior to the advent of Islam.[4] Islamic tradition holds that the nascent Muslim community defended the prophetic status of Muḥammad in their day-to-day interactions with the People of the Book (*ahl al-kitāb*). In Medina it was mostly members of the Jewish tribes who challenged Muḥammad to prove his prophecy.[5] Naturally, interactions with the People of the Book expanded significantly during the Muslim conquests which brought a Muslim minority into a position of political and military control over a diverse non-Muslim majority. The emerging *dalāʾil al-nubūwa* literature during the early ʿAbbāsid period should be seen in the context of socio-political shifts that led learned men among the established Abrahamic traditions to maintain religious supremacy by challenging the legitimacy of Muḥammad's prophecy and the religious community it brought

3 Robinson, "History and Heilsgeschichte in Early Islam," 3.

4 Stroumsa, "The Signs of Prophecy"; cf. Stroumsa, *Freethinkers of Medieval Islam*, 22–36.

5 Rubin, "Jews and Judaism."

forth. The link between challenges to religious legitimacy and shifts in political power seems to be corroborated by the fact that there were no Jewish works directed against the Muslim faith in the first centuries after the rise of Islam, whereas Christian writings of this kind, either in epistles or reports of disputations, abound.[6]

However, the Islamic *dalāʾil al-nubūwa* literature should not be mistaken as a purely defensive attempt by Muslim scholars to justify their religion, rather it should be understood as a manifestation of an interactive process that also shaped theological notions of the other religious traditions through common and mutually posed questions. Over time some *dalāʾil al-nubūwa* works transcended religious boundaries as Jewish, Christian, and Muslim authorities debated the nature of prophecy. Stroumsa has shown that the general frame of the discussion as well as the particular "signs" offered in these works were very similar for the three religious traditions but that the literature of each tradition displayed individual characteristic components.[7] More immediately, these works played an active role in shaping doctrinal views and theological concepts in a variety of scholarly fields in the Islamic religious sciences which devoted attention to the question of prophecy and the parameters by which it might be evaluated. As such, we find Muʿtazilī works, such as *Kitāb Ḥujjaj al-nubūwa* by al-Jāḥiẓ (d. 255/868–869) or *Tathbīt dalāʾil al-nubūwa* by ʿAbd al-Jabbār al-Hamadhānī (d. 415/1025), Ismāʿīlī works like *Kitāb Ithbāt al-nubūwa* by Abū Yaʿqūb al-Sijistānī (d. after 360/971), works by Ashʿarī theologians, such as *Aʿlām al-nubūwa* by al-Māwardī (d. 450/1058), and *ḥadīth* anthologies by scholars such as Abū Nuʿaym al-Iṣfahānī (d. 430/1038) and al-Bayhaqī (d. 458/1066). Given this vast array of contributing scholars, Muslim literature on the "proofs of prophecy" displays variegated approaches to the subject. Dominating these approaches are (1) compilations of accounts from *ḥadīth* and *sīra* literature that relate supposedly evidentiary events or characteristics, (2) works substantiating the Qurʾānic claim that Muḥammad was foretold in previous scriptures by adducing relevant passages from the Hebrew Bible and New Testament, and (3) theological discussions on the necessity and nature of prophecy. While these various kinds of *dalāʾil al-nubūwa* works emerged as distinct methodological approaches, they should not be considered as mutually exclusive and later authors often employed more than one approach. For the most part, they have been studied separately based on their methodological context; while *ḥadīth*-based approaches have received the least scholarly

---

6 Adang, *Muslim Writers on Judaism*, 140; also see Griffith, "Answering the Call of the Minaret," and Griffith, "The Prophet Muḥammad."

7 Stroumsa, "The Signs of Prophecy," 106f.

attention. In this study, I seek to provide a more comprehensive view by contextualizing the *ḥadīth*-based works in broader methodological debates across the various emerging Islamic sciences and the larger discourses on prophecy that occurred across religious boundaries.

1 Historiography, Hagiography, and the Marginalization of *Dalāʾil al-Nubūwa* Literature

Despite its contribution to Islam's intellectual landscape, *ḥadīth*-based *dalāʾil al-nubūwa* literature has been under-utilized and mostly dismissed in Islamic studies. It has been categorized as a type of popular work, and this seems to have discouraged scholarly investigations because popular literature tends to be studied to establish a social history, but is rarely seen as part of or contributing to intellectual and doctrinal history. A number of factors led scholars throughout the nineteenth and twentieth centuries to misunderstand the provenance of this literature.

First, the view of early scholars of Islamic studies was, at least in part, informed by the limited sources available at the time; this prevented scholars from realizing the scope of this literature, its origins in circles of *ḥadīth* scholarship, and its wider contribution to the epistemological discourse on prophecy. Many important texts in the early history of this literature are no longer extant and were not known to early scholars of Islamic studies. Tor Andrae dedicated a chapter of his 1918 work *Die Person Muhammeds in Lehre und Glaube seiner Gemeinde* to legends and miracles attributed to the Prophet;[8] this provided a tentative outline for the development of *ḥadīth*-based *dalāʾil al-nubūwa* literature. When Andrae first considered the nature of this literature, his study was based on two chapters in the *Ṭabaqāt* of Ibn Saʿd (d. 230/845) as well as works by Abū Nuʿaym al-Iṣfahānī and al-Bayhaqī, written almost 200 years later. The scarcity of accessible primary sources and their historical distance made an accurate characterization of this literature virtually impossible. Based on these three works, it is not surprising that scholars did not link them to the circles of *ḥadīth* scholars as Ibn Saʿd presents the "signs of prophecy" in his biographical dictionary, and Abū Nuʿaym al-Iṣfahānī and al-Bayhaqī were both scholars of *ḥadīth*, but their respective *dalāʾil al-nubūwa* works were closer to prophetic biographies with regard to their sources, content, and structure. While Meir Jacob Kister indicated in 1983 that Ibn Saʿd may have benefited from his predecessor Maʿmar b. Rāshid (d. 153/770) and added a few more, mostly later, works

8 Andrae, *Die Person Muhammeds*, 26–91.

to the list of *dalāʾil al-nubūwa* authors,[9] scholars of Islamic studies remained unaware of the full scope of this literature. Even more recent scholars, like Tilman Nagel in his major publication from 2008, still name Abū Nuʿaym and al-Bayhaqī as two of the earliest authors of this genre.[10] Biographic and bibliographic evidence, however, shows that *ḥadīth*-based works that were intended to validate and defend Muḥammad's claim to prophecy sprawl across the entirety of Islamic history, from thematic chapters in early *ḥadīth* compilations by scholars such as Maʿmar b. Rāshid and the earliest independent works of al-Ḥumaydī (d. 219/834) and al-Madāʾinī (d. between 224 and 231/839 and 845) to scholars of the twentieth century, such as ʿAbd al-Ḥalīm Maḥmūd (d. 1980). The lack of awareness of earlier texts that are no longer extant led to a late dating of the literature and to misconceptions regarding the authorship of the literature.

Furthermore, when modern scholars of Islamic studies dismissed these works as popular literature, it reflected their own intellectual framework rather than the views of these texts' authors and their contemporaries. Andrae's examination was not based on a thorough study of numerous Islamic sources, rather it focused on very few versions and considered them phenomenologically in the context of various other faith traditions. A key example is the account of a shepherd's encounter with a speaking wolf mentioned at the beginning of this introduction. Andrae refers to an account he found, not in *ḥadīth* collections or the early *dalāʾil al-nubūwa* compilations, but in *al-Shifāʾ* by Qāḍī ʿIyāḍ (d. 543/1149).[11] Thus, Andrae's point of departure was one relatively late text. His methodology and a priori assumptions about the origins and contents of this literature also played a significant role in his dismissal of it. His judgment was primarily based on a comment Qāḍī Iyāḍ made in reference to this *ḥadīth*; he states, "This hadith contains *qiṣṣa*" (والحَدِيثُ فيه قِصَّةٌ). Tor Andrae read this statement as an indication that Qāḍī ʿIyāḍ suspected that it had a folkloristic origin going back to *quṣṣāṣ* rather than a scholarly origin.[12] The mostly negative views of Muslim *quṣṣāṣ* became common among modern scholars of Islamic studies since the work of Ignaz Goldziher (d. 1921), who described them primarily as embellishers and fabricators of religious stories that were meant to steer the masses toward religious devotion but who were also suspected of personally enriching themselves in the process.[13] For

---

9 Kister, "The Sirah Literature," 356.

10 Nagel, *Allahs Liebling*, 103–110.

11 Qāḍī ʿIyād, *al-Shifāʾ*, 1:432.

12 Andrae, *Die Person Muhammed*, 27.

13 Goldziher, *Schools of Koranic Commentators*, 36–38; Goldziher, *Muslim Studies II*, 149–159.

Western scholars of Andrae's time, these storytellers were therefore synonymous with charlatans who freely invented stories about the Prophet in order to please their mostly illiterate audiences. More recently, Jonathan Berkey and Lyall Armstrong have shown that these early *quṣṣāṣ* were, for the most part, properly trained in the prophetic tradition and Islamic law, and that they were often hired by the caliph or other high-ranking officials to spread basic knowledge of Islam among the newly converted population of the expanding Muslim empire.[14] The profession only later came to be associated with dubious characters who entertained the masses with imaginary tales and Isrāʾīliyyāt (stories of the prophets), and were frequently criticized by the authorities. Andrae's reliance on one late text combined with his general notion of *quṣṣāṣ* as untrustworthy sources led him to dismiss the entire *dalāʾil al-nubūwa* literature without investigating the occurrence of this account in other texts. The narrative of the speaking wolf, in fact, appears in a number of early and often prominent *ḥadīth* collections, such as the *Musnad* of the famous legal scholar Ibn Ḥanbal (d. 241/855),[15] the two canonical *ḥadīth* collections of al-Bukhārī (d. 256/870)[16] and Muslim (d. 261/875),[17] the *Ṭabaqāt* of Ibn Saʿd, and in later compilations, such as the *dalāʾil al-nubūwa* works of al-Bayhaqī,[18] Abū Nuʿaym al-Iṣfahānī,[19] and *al-Sīra al-nabawiyya* of Ibn Kathīr[20] (d. 774/1373). It is noteworthy that the same *ḥadīth* was related—at the same time and sometimes even in the same collections—in shorter and longer versions. The core of the story—a wolf speaking to a shepherd to inform him about Muḥammad's prophetic mission in Medina—was central in all the versions; the differences only

14 Berkey, *Popular Preaching*.

15 Ibn Ḥanbal, *Musnad*, 3:203f. (no. 8049; this is a shorter account only relating the shepherd's encounter with the wolf, and without many descriptive details), 4:210f. (no. 11814); 4:222 (no. 11863).

16 This *ḥadīth* is only partially related to the one in Ibn Saʿd's "signs of prophecy." Related in the book of cultivation and agriculture, it states, "While a man was riding a cow, it turned toward him and said, 'I have not been created for this purpose, I have been created for ploughing.' The Prophet added, 'I, Abū Bakr, and 'Umar believe in this story.' The Prophet said further, 'A wolf caught a sheep, and when the shepherd chased it, the wolf said, 'Who will be its guard on the day of wild beasts, when there will be no shepherd for it except I?' After narrating it, the Prophet said, 'I, Abū Bakr, and 'Umar, too, believe it.' Abū Salama said, 'Abū Bakr and 'Umar were not present'; cf. al-Bukhārī, *Ṣaḥīḥ*, 3:295 (no. 2324).

17 Muslim, *Ṣaḥīḥ*, 15:103 (no. 2388).

18 The *dalāʾil al-nubūwa* encompasses a chapter containing various versions of this narrative. Their *isnād*s vary in strength. Two of these accounts are very close to the one in Ibn Saʿd; cf. al-Bayhaqī, *Dalāʾil al-nubūwa*, 6:41–44.

19 Abū Nuʿaym's work also contains two versions of this account; cf. al-Iṣfahānī, *Dalāʾil al-nubūwa*, 222f.

20 Ibn Kathīr, *al-Sīra al-nabawiyya*, 4:183.

relate to descriptive details, such as what kind of leaves the sheep were feeding on. The narrative of the speaking wolf has, therefore, clearly been part of the scholarly discourse from the early third/ninth century onward. Given that the term *qiṣṣa* is generally associated with the notion of relating a piece of information, Qāḍī ʿIyāḍ probably meant that this particular version of the *ḥadīth* he listed was unusually detailed in its descriptions compared to other versions, not that its provenance was unreliable storytellers. Due to an insufficient body of texts and an over-generalization of the role of storytellers in early Muslim societies, Andrae failed to trace this account in other texts and thus was misled into believing that these texts were part of popular veneration.

In addition to having an incomplete textual foundation, early Orientalists held various inter-related views that were common among historians of the nineteenth and twentieth centuries. Their positivist view of history, which significantly impacted their evaluation of *dalāʾil al-nubūwa* literature, was certainly prominent. Ernest Renan infamously remarked that Muḥammad was "born in the full light of history,"[21] and a number of scholars confidently expressed their ability to distinguish historical and fictional accounts of his life. For instance, Ignaz Goldziher,[22] Giorgio Levi Della Vida (d. 1961),[23] Hamilton A. R. Gibb (d. 1971),[24] Josef Horovitz (d. 1931),[25] and Tor Andrae all viewed elements of the *sīra* as evidence of the increased veneration for the person of Muḥammad that led to the growth of a hagiographic legend. This view in particular shaped the way scholars categorized *dalāʾil al-nubūwa* as a popular, and, thus, historically inaccurate, sub-genre of *sīra* literature. As we noted at the outset of this chapter, Andrae viewed the *dalāʾil al-nubūwa* literature exclusively through the lens of Muḥammad's legends and miracles, and declared it "fantastic legends" and "barbaric embellishments that veil the true historical figure of the Prophet."[26]

At its core, these assumptions were grounded in the positivist approach to history prevalent at the time; this approach differentiated between historiography, i.e., "truthful" and "factual" accounts, and hagiography, i.e., falsified accounts that were aimed at crafting a particular image for ulterior purposes. Historiography was understood methodologically as empirical history and, thus, seen as "scientific" and "objective." This view of history, however, reflects the academic discourses of post-Enlightenment European scholars, not those

21 Reinhart, Review of *Juynbolliana*, 416.
22 Goldziher, *Muslim Studies II*, 255–262.
23 Della Vida, "Sīra."
24 Gibb, "Taʾrīkh."
25 Horovitz, "Zur Muḥammadlegende."
26 Andrae, *Die Person Muhammeds*, 28, 92f.

of early Muslim authors of the third/ninth and fourth/tenth centuries who did not categorically view accounts of the past as either sacred history or empirically verifiable history. Famous works of historiography like al-Ṭabarī's (d. 310/923) *Tārīkh al-rusul wa-l-mulūk* seamlessly blend the sacred history of the creation of the world and various prophets with the empirical history of rulers and conquests. Likewise, Ibn Isḥāq's (d. 150/767) prophetic biography, which preceded Ibn Hishām's edition, started with an account of the beginning of the world. This is not to say that Muslim scholars did not attempt to differentiate between acceptable and unacceptable contributions. Their discerning process, however, centered on modes of authentication that related to particular Islamic disciplines and their concrete applications, rather than on a positivist quest for "truthfulness" or historicity. As a foundation for Islamic law, for instance, *ḥadīth* were subjected to an elaborate and rigorous process of authentication. Other literature, such as *sīra* or historiographies, informed its audience of a sense of the past but did not have the same normative import, and accordingly, these works were not expected to uphold the same methodological scrutiny. Thus, these diverging methodologies were reflective of the texts' application rather than the audience's concern for historicity. Categorizing early Muslim texts based on the methodological assumptions of the nineteenth and twentieth centuries is, therefore, an anachronistic approach and does not contribute to our understanding of these texts in the historical consciousness of their own time period.

In an attempt to move beyond these binary assumptions of historiography and hagiography, contemporary scholars of European intellectual history have offered approaches that are better suitable to understanding these particular sets of texts holistically. Dominick LaCapra addressed the binary assumption of documentary texts, i.e., those that empirically record the past, and "work-like" types of texts, i.e., those that supplement empirical reality through interpretation or imagination.[27] He argued that privileging documentary approaches in the academic study of the past has led to reductionist readings, if not the complete exclusion of complex or literary texts from the relevant historical records.[28] Rather than considering documentary and "work-like" texts as entirely separate categories, he suggests that they be thought of as aspects or components of any given text that may be developed to different degrees.[29] As such, the historian ought to acknowledge that empirical documents possess "work-like" qualities and complex literary texts entail documentary elements

27 LaCapra, *Rethinking Intellectual History*, 30.
28 LaCapra, *Rethinking Intellectual History*, 33.
29 LaCapra, *Rethinking Intellectual History*, 30.

as well.[30] If all texts entail "work-like" elements, studying historical texts must inevitably consider the relationship between a documentary reconstruction of the past and an author's dialogue with that past.[31] A text cannot be seen as

> a simple illustration of either a long tradition or the specific time. Rather the problem becomes that of the way long tradition, specific time, and text repeat one another with variations, and the matter of elucidation becomes the degree of importance of these variations and how to construe it. The text is seen as a "place" where long tradition and specific time intersect, and it effects variations on both. But the text is not immobilized or presented as an autonomous node; it is situated in a fully relational network.[32]

These texts, then, must be understood in a set of interacting contexts, such as the author's intentions and motivations, the societal and cultural relation to the text, as well as the structure and corpus of the text.[33] Gabrielle Spiegel has argued, similarly, that

> [a]ll texts occupy determinate social spaces, both as products of the social world of authors and as textual agents at work in the world, with which they entertain often complex and contestatory relations. In that sense, texts mirror *and* generate social realities, are constituted by *and* constitute the social and discursive formations which they may sustain, resist, contest, or seek to transform, depending on the case at hand.[34]

The historian must look beyond the text and reconstitute the social world in question by "looking at the inextricably interrelated nature of social and discursive practices, of the material and linguistic realities that are interwoven into the fabric of the text, whose analysis as a determinate historical artifact in turn grants us access to the past."[35] Both LaCapra and Spiegel emphasize that all texts, including the ones that historians frequently valorize as "empirical" and, by extension, deem objective recordings of the past, entail an element of subjective interpretation based on the varying contexts in which the texts emerge and with which they interact.

30 LaCapra, *Rethinking Intellectual History*, 30f.
31 LaCapra, *Rethinking Intellectual History*, 27.
32 LaCapra, *Rethinking Intellectual History*, 44.
33 LaCapra, *Rethinking Intellectual History*, 36.
34 Spiegel, "History, Historicism," 77–78.
35 Spiegel, "History, Historicism," 84–85.

Taking the interactive dynamics between texts and their diverse contexts into account is particularly relevant with regard to those texts that aim to construct exemplary religious personae in their shifting imaginary frameworks. After all, exemplary figures constitute, as Pierre Delooz stated, constructed notions that reflect the discrete historical, geographic, social, and cultural factors of the communities that craft them.[36] But it is equally important to understand that these inter-related and interacting relations between so-called hagiographic texts and their intellectual and social environs are fundamentally the same as they are for other kinds of historical texts, as LaCapra and Spiegel have laid out. Felice Lifshitz argued, accordingly, that the notion of hagiography as a distinct form of medieval religious literature is problematic because such a distinction relies on obsolete historiographical suppositions about methodologically sound historiography, on the one hand, and fictional hagiography, on the other, that did not exist at the time they were written.[37] She continued, stating that in order to understand the function of these narratives in their own historical and intellectual contexts, the scholar must go beyond the anachronistic application of positivist theory and the concept of a "hagiographic" genre.[38] Rather than distinguishing the normative binary of "accurate" and "forged" accounts of the past, Lifshitz's approach appreciates competing imaginations of past figures and, thus, helps us study the particular functions of these texts in the historical conscience of their time. While LaCapra, Spiegel, Delooz, and Lifshitz all work in the realm of European intellectual history, their approaches can benefit the study of premodern Islamic intellectual history, as I discuss below.

2 Are Miracles Categorically "Popular"?

Another facet of many nineteenth- and twentieth-century scholars' approaches is their foundation in secularism and concomitant rejection of miracles. The dismissal of *dalāʾil al-nubūwa* literature as popular veneration is largely based on the assumption that the content of these collections consists primarily of miracle narratives. Tor Andrae, for instance, voiced this view as follows:

> Ziemlich früh scheint man auf den gedanken gekommen zu sein, die wunder des propheten in besondere werke zu sammeln. Schon Ibn Saʿd

36 Delooz, *Sociologie et Canonisations*.
37 Lifshitz, "Beyond Positivism and Genre," 98, 101.
38 Lifshitz, "Beyond Positivism and Genre," 95.

> hatte in der *sīra*, die sein klassenbuch einleitet, die "kennzeichen des prophetentums" in besonderen paragraphen behandelt. Diese anordnung gab den anlass, die wundererzählungen monographisch darzustellen. Solchen werken gab man den titel *dalāʾil al-nubūwa*, d.h. beweise für das prophetentum oder zeichen des prophetentum.[39]

Annemarie Schimmel, likewise, defined *dalāʾil al-nubūwa* as "biographies of the Prophet, studded with evidentiary miracles—those that happened before and after Muhammad's birth as well as before and after his call to prophethood, and those that pointed to his exalted status as the last Prophet."[40]

This understanding of *dalāʾil al-nubūwa* literature is problematic for a number of reasons. First, considering miracles generically as the defining characteristic of this literature poses an analytical challenge. On the one hand, scholars like Andrae excluded *dalāʾil al-nubūwa* from "acceptable" religious literature because these works include miracle narratives. On the other hand, core texts, such as the Qurʾān and *ḥadīth*, contain ample references to events that have been deemed "miraculous," such as Muḥammad's splitting of the moon, with the consent of Muslim scholars of various fields.[41] This would imply that premodern Muslim scholars distinguished between legitimate and illegitimate miracles. Such debates certainly existed, though they were mostly centered on questions of authenticating the narrative rather than accepting the historicity of the event. Understanding these discourses about how such narratives were differentiated requires in-depth examinations of the specific "miracles" related in each work, and examinations of the sources of their narratives and the various positions scholars have held regarding each "miracle." In the absence of such elaborate examinations, unspecified references to miracles alone do not suffice to classify *dalāʾil al-nubūwa* literature as popular hagiography rather than historiography.

This notion of *dalāʾil al-nubūwa*, furthermore, equates the epistemological concern for "proofs of prophecy" with the (mostly) theological notion of miracles without considering the complexity of these two approaches and their heterogeneity among various sectarian groups, intellectual disciplines, and theological schools of thoughts, nor does it take into account how these approaches evolved over time. It is, furthermore, incongruent with the content of extant works of *dalāʾil al-nubūwa*. As I show in chapter 3, earlier compilations list numerous events side by side without any systematic distinction or

39 Andrae, *Die Person Muhammeds*, 57.

40 Schimmel, *And Muhammad Is His Messenger*, 33.

41 Q. 54:1.

commentary. We might be tempted to label some of these accounts as miraculous based on their contents, but this would only project our interpretation onto the intellectual mindset of these authors, who did not distinguish or identify narratives as "miraculous" themselves. By contrast, later independent works, such as those of Abū Nuʿaym and al-Bayhaqī, also included a broad range of narratives but clearly classified some of them as miracles, listed them in separate chapters, and contextualized them in an Ashʿarī theological framework in introductions and commentaries. Thus, *dalāʾil al-nubūwa* literature reflects evolving epistemological notions of "proofs of prophecy" that at times encompasses prophetic miracles but are not limited or equal to them. In other words, the content of *dalāʾil al-nubūwa* collections is more diverse than previous scholars may have assumed. By the same token, not every compilation of "signs of prophecy" includes all miraculous accounts known by its author. Gabriele von Bülow studied "miraculous" *ḥadīth* in al-Bukhārī's *Ṣaḥīḥ* and found that in this collection the total of these is more extensive than those accounts he included in his chapter on "signs of prophecy in Islam."[42] As a consequence, the notions of "miracles" and "proofs of prophecy" occasionally overlap but are by no means interchangeable and the evolving discourses behind each of these notions require further research.

The incomplete textual basis, miscategorization as popular literature, and equation with miracles certainly played a major role for many Western scholars, such that they missed the connection between *dalāʾil al-nubūwa* literature in general to *ḥadīth* circles and to the broader discourse of proofs of prophecy. The boundaries of the field may have contributed as well. Most scholars of Islamic studies tend to examine *dalāʾil al-nubūwa* texts individually and in the context of separate disciplines or intellectual fields, such as *ḥadīth*, *fiqh*, *kalām*, philosophy, and *tafsīr*, rather than considering their interactions.[43] *Ḥadīth* studies, by contrast, were often subsumed under the field of Islamic law and were mostly considered with regard to aspects of authenticity, or they functioned as a *source* for the reconstruction of Islamic history as well as the history of religious ideas and institutions. The importance of *ḥadīth* to questions of theology as well as their formative role in the articulation of Sunnī Islam in

42 Bülow, "Hadithe über die Wunder des Propheten Muhammad," 109.

43 For biblical and pseudo-biblical approaches, see Lazarus-Yafeh, *Intertwined Worlds*, particularly 75–110; Adang, *Muslim Writers on Judaism*, particularly 139–191; Schmidtke, "The Muslim Reception of Biblical Materials"; Schmidtke, "Abū al-Ḥasan al-Baṣrī"; Schmidtke, "Biblical Predictions"; Adang, "A Rare Case of Biblical 'Testimonies'." For theological approaches, see Abū Ḥātim al-Rāzī (trans. Khalidi), *The Proofs of Prophecy*; Aminrazavi and Rowson, "Abū Ḥātim Rāzī"; Goodman, "Rāzi vs. Rāzī"; Talbani, "The Debate about Prophecy"; Reynolds, *A Muslim Theologian*, particularly 80f., 178–183.

general is rarely considered.[44] Yet the inclusion of chapters dedicated to *ʿalām al-nubūwa* or *dalāʾil al-nubūwa* in various *ḥadīth* compilations, including the canonical collections of al-Bukhārī and al-Tirmidhī, highlights the way epistemological questions such as the recognition and veracity of Muḥammad's prophetic mission were indeed addressed in *ḥadīth* compilations. Rather than being conceived as one or several genres defined by formal qualities, such as organizational structure, compositional rules, or methodological approaches, *dalāʾil al-nubūwa* literature should be viewed as part of a vast epistemological discourse on prophecy to which Muslim and non-Muslim scholars of various disciplines and schools of thought have contributed.

3 Hagiology as an Analytical Tool

This book is a study of *ḥadīth*-based *dalāʾil al-nubūwa* literature, particularly during the formative period up to the early fifth/eleventh century, with regard to the scholarly discourses and the social milieu that informed it. As such I am interested in positioning the analysis of this literature in the intellectual framework of its time and approaching the historically evolving notions of "proofs of prophecy" from the perspective of *ḥadīth* as a creative field that contributed to the articulation of doctrines, and, by extension, to the formation of Sunnī Islam. Therefore, it seems helpful to understand this kind of literature through the heuristic framework of hagiography. I do not mean by that to project the specifically Christian-based notion of "saints" and their "vitae" onto Islamic texts and realities nor do I assume an unscholarly origin of these texts. My intent is to apply the concept more broadly, following a recent attempt to redefine hagiography as a comparative and collaborative approach across religious traditions.[45] I adopt Rondolino's view of hagiography "as an analytical category for the taxonomy of sources that contribute to construct and promote the recognition of a given individual as a perfected being."[46] We then need to distance our understanding of the term from its etymologically defined nature because the individual under consideration is not ontologically imbued with

44 For the relationship between differing arrangements and theological truths among early Shīʿī *ḥadīth* scholars, see Newmann, *The Formative Period of Twelver Shīʿism*. For discussions about the role of authorial aspects in *ḥadīth* compilations, see Burge, "Myth, Meaning and the Order of Words"; and Burge, "Reading between the Lines."

45 See the special issue of *Religion*, "Comparative Hagiology: Issues in Theory and Method," particularly Rondolino, "Some Foundational Considerations on Taxonomy"; Hollander, "Comparison as Collaboration."

46 Rondolino, "Some Foundational Considerations on Taxonomy," 2.

something *hagios*, "sacred" or "holy." The exemplary status of perfection is crafted discursively among groups of followers. "There can be no saint, no being that is understood as embodying perfection, without a community that recognizes them as such, in light of a given interpretation of particular doctrines and theories of truth, which construct and preserve their memory and promote their cult and way of life."[47] Sociologist of religion Pierre Delooz pointed out in the 1960s that the exemplary figure in a religious community should be understood as a constructed notion, reflective of discrete historical, geographic, social, and cultural factors.[48] Consequently, the historiographical discourse among scholars today is no longer a quest for the most historically accurate account of an individual's life. In 1994, Felice Lifshitz argued that in order to understand the hagiographic narratives' function in the historical consciousness of their time periods, scholars must go beyond the anachronistic application of both positivist theory and the concept of a hagiographic genre.[49] She continued, stating that an examination of these texts should focus on the particular function that might be fulfilled by elevating an individual to the station of an exemplar, and on the processes involved in this elevation and how these relate to an individual or collective worldview. Similar approaches are centered in the emerging field of comparative hagiology, which first grew out of interlocking conversations of scholars of diverse disciplinary backgrounds at the meeting of the American Academy of Religion (AAR) in 2017. Similarly, more recent scholars of Islamic intellectual history have found that an examination of the various texts focusing on Muḥammad's life should be built on an appreciation of competing ideological interpretations and the agendas of various authors and their respective theological, political, and social realities.[50]

I understand *ḥadīth*-based *dalāʾil al-nubūwa* literature as part of this category of hagiographic texts because these authors each crafted particular theologically-imbued images of Muḥammad and his prophetic mission by selecting materials from *ḥadīth*, *sīra*, and auxiliary literatures. This literature, as part of a hagiographical discourse of constructing the distinct personae of the Prophet, can nevertheless be thought of as deeply historiographic texts in the sense that they contribute in concrete ways to the construction of the authors' own sense of historical identity. Works of *dalāʾil al-nubūwa* literature emerged at the nexus of inter-religious debates, the development of various religious sciences, and the religio-political events and social movements in the rising

47 Rondolino, "Some Foundational Considerations on Taxonomy," 6.

48 Delooz, "Pour une étude sociologique"; Delooz, *Sociologie et Canonisations*.

49 Lifshitz, "Beyond Positivism and Genre," 95.

50 For instance, Khalidi, *Images of Muhammad*; Ali, *The Lives of Muhammad*; Anthony, *Muḥammad and the Empires of Faith*; Frederick Colby, *Narrating Muḥammad's Night Journey;* Michael Muhammad Knight, *Muhammad's Body*.

Muslim empire, and were part of a larger epistemological discourse that often transcended divisions between various religious disciplines in the Islamic tradition as well as between the boundaries of religious traditions. Crucial moments in the intellectual history of Islam, such as the initial divide between the partisans of *ḥadīth* (*ahl al-ḥadīth*) and theologians (*mutakalimūn*), the short period of state intrusion into theology during the trials (*miḥna*) imposed by al-Maʾmūn, and the ensuing intellectual crisis, the rise of Ashʿarī theology, and finally the reconciliation of previously disjointed schools of thought all left their mark on *dalāʾil al-nubūwa* literature. The texts bear witness to these diverse political, social, and intellectual stimuli and enact a past that informs and gives meaning to the authors' context by providing a foundation for their ideological and doctrinal views.

In chapter 1, I challenge some of the crucial underlying assumptions that have led to various misconceptions about this literature and marginalized it. Based on comparative textual analyses of some of the earliest biographical sources as well as recent studies of the intellectual and social environment in which religious knowledge was disseminated during the early Islamic period, I question the clear-cut dichotomy between scholars and storytellers (*quṣṣāṣ*), on the one hand, and the equally common assumption that scholars of the prophetic biography rejected the notion of Muḥammad's miracles in its entirety, on the other. My comparative analysis is based on the accounts of the *hijra* by ʿUrwa b. al-Zubayr (d. 94/713) and Wahb b. Munabbih (d. between 109 and 113/728 and 732) and juxtaposes their methodological approaches and their contents. Understanding that one narrative is not representative of each author's corpus, I introduce these accounts, their compilers, and their respective transmitters in order to partially show the trajectory of narratives that occurred in these early texts and became well-established parts of the notion of "proofs of prophethood" in later *dalāʾil al-nubūwa* collections.

In chapter 2, I further demonstrate the scholarly origin of early *dalāʾil al-nubūwa* works by identifying twenty-four early authors who contributed to this literature, from Maʿmar b. Rāshid's (d. 153/770) short thematic chapter to the most well-known independent works by Abū Nuʿaym al-Iṣfahānī and al-Bayhaqī. I emphasize the scholarly provenance of the literature by establishing these authors' social networks and the intellectual and doctrinal environments in which they operated. In chapter 3, I study the methodological and structural approaches in eight extant works and explore how the shifts in these authors' works around the fourth/tenth century are mirrored in their organizational structures.

In the fourth chapter, I examine the contents of the earliest extant works of Maʿmar b. Rāshid, Ibn Saʿd, al-Bukhārī, al-Jūzajānī, and al-Tirmidhī, and their various thematic choices of "proofs of prophecy" in order to understand the processes by which these authors individually and collectively crafted the notion of "proofs of prophecy" through the narratives they selected.

I use the case of Ibn Saʿd in chapter 5 to examine why interest in "proofs of prophecy" may have expanded during his lifetime and to establish what influences might have shaped his selection processes. Ibn Saʿd's chapters on the proofs of prophecy provide an interesting test case for a number of reasons: While he is not the first known author to compile accounts thematically, the scope of his chapters is considerably larger than that of his predecessor Maʿmar b. Rāshid. Biographical dictionaries (*ṭabaqāt*), furthermore, indicate that in this period there was an overall increase in works written on the topic of "proofs of prophecy." As Ibn Saʿd's lifetime coincided with various Christian-Muslim debates and literary exchanges that may have triggered his own interest in the subject, I examine both the socio-historical circumstances in which Christian and Muslim scholars interacted as well as the polemical debates held in light of Christian challenges to the religious legitimacy of their new rulers. This chapter juxtaposes Christian theological positions regarding Muḥammad's claim to prophethood with Ibn Saʿd's main theme, in which the learned men of the *ahl al-kitāb* recognized and acknowledged Muḥammad's prophetic mission.

Finally, chapter 6 focuses on the later *dalāʾil al-nubūwa* works of the fourth/tenth and fifth/eleventh centuries which display an increasing degree of systematization with regard to their contents and structural organization; in addition, they frequently conform to the established discipline-based methodologies and theological discourses of their times.

Studying a group of texts in relation to the scholarly discourses and social milieus that informed them involves a number of challenges and requires some caveats. First, there is the selection of works to include. Due to my initial identification of works in biographical dictionaries, I was guided to include works with titles such as *Dalāʾil al-nubūwa*, *Amarāt al-nubūwa* or similar semantically related titles. Inevitably, a title-based selection process will not provide an exhaustive list of all the works that have contributed to epistemological debates about prophethood, but it grants insight into the various ways authors deliberately and distinctively conceptualized their particular notion of "proofs" or "signs of prophethood" in their respective works. Second, my own process of selection occurred on multiple levels, particularly the interpretative labeling of individual narratives and the subsequent attempts to contextualize them. While I tried to trace the possible factors that may have influenced authors' choices, this process inevitably occurred through my own subjective lens. In the absence of detailed personal commentary by the authors about their choices, I can only outline correlations between an author's choices and concurrent discourses and cannot claim causality between the two with any degree of certainty.

Finally, there were numerous restrictions beyond my control, as the final research for this work was severely impacted by the COVID-19 pandemic in 2020 that led to worldwide library closures, travel restrictions, and stay-at-home orders. I had initially planned on extending the historical reach of this work beyond the fifth/eleventh century but had to settle for what could be researched with a laptop from home. The resulting analysis of Ibn Saʿd's position in Christian-Muslim debates is deeply indebted to the work of colleagues focused on Christian intellectual history; this enabled me to include Jewish and Christian discourses that were otherwise inaccessible to me due to my lack of expertise and language skills. While my excursion into this sub-field was born out of necessity, I believe it vastly enriched my attempt to contextualize early *dalāʾil al-nubūwa* literature in various intellectual discourses of the time.

CHAPTER 1

The Scholar and the Storyteller?—*Quṣṣāṣ* in Early Islam

In the early twentieth century, Western views of *dalāʾil al-nubūwa* literature were significantly shaped by its perceived connection to unreliable biographical traditions of the *quṣṣāṣ* and the a priori assumptions scholars of Islamic studies held of its contents.* Their views were based on the notion that information on Muḥammad's life originated and circulated in two distinct circles, those of scholars who transmitted their accounts in study circles and those of laymen preachers who spread popular but inaccurate tales by word of mouth. This juxtaposition between critical scholarly texts and unreliable popular accounts of the Prophet's life is common among Muslim and Western scholars alike and is premised on the assumption that these two groups and the traditions they produced existed within well-defined boundaries. More recent scholarship on the early nature of the *quṣṣāṣ* has modified this clear-cut dichotomy in which the work of scholars is seen as a methodologically critical approach to Muḥammad's biography that catered to an equally critical scholarly audience, while the lay preachers were depicted as careless in their transmission of questionable materials and were frequently accused of fabricating narratives in order to entertain uneducated masses.[1] On the one hand, we need to keep in mind that scholarly approaches in any discipline that encompasses agreed-upon critical methodologies, including *ḥadīth* and *sīra*, only emerged over time. Prior to the development of a distinct "scholarly" tradition, Muḥammad's biography was preserved in the living memory of his Companions, particularly those who embraced Islam at later stages in their lives. Their children, by contrast, imbibed religious teachings from infancy and were regular consumers of preaching and religious acculturation. It was their generation's learned elite who embarked on the more structured promotion of religious teachings.[2] It was the generation that flourished between the years 80/700 and 122/744 that saw the increased evolution of specialized circles of

* An earlier version of this chapter has been published in Jamal Elias and Bilal Orfali, *Light upon Light. Essays in Early Islamic Thought in Honor of Gerhard Bowering* (Leiden: Brill, 2019), 3–24.

1 For studies on the positions of early *quṣṣāṣ*, see, for instance, Pedersen, "The Criticism of the Islamic Preacher"; Berkey, *Popular Preaching*; Armstrong, *The Quṣṣāṣ of Early Islam*.

2 Hallaq, *The Origins and Evolution of Islamic Law*, 42.

 | DOI:10.1163/9789004687349_003

learning known as *ḥalaqa*. Over time, these circles became fixed institutions that were usually held in the mosques of the major centers of the Umayyad Empire.[3] Gradually, specializations became separate disciplines, each with distinct methodologies and evolving qualifications.

Quṣṣāṣ, on the other hand, are difficult to subsume under one homogenous group identity, as their activities, skills, and social backgrounds varied greatly. Goldziher described the majority of *qāṣṣ* as primarily embellishers and fabricators of religious stories attempting to interpret the Qurʾān and promote religious devotion among the masses, though he did acknowledge that there were some early reputable scholars in their midst and they taught wider audiences and encouraged the Muslim armies in their pursuits.[4] His emphasis, however, remained on portraying *quṣṣāṣ* as unreliable sources. "This association between *quṣṣāṣ* and the fanciful stories led to their being identified by some scholars as a primary source of the fabrication both of the predominantly narrative-style exegetical material on the Qurʾān and of Prophetic *ḥadīth*."[5]

Much of this negative imagery and the devaluation of the *quṣṣāṣ* held by later Muslim and Western scholars were based on three works written by distinguished medieval scholars. The earliest and most important was *Kitāb al-Quṣṣāṣ wa-l-mudhakkirūn* (The book of the *quṣṣāṣ* and the admonishers) by Ibn al-Jawzī (d. 597/1200), followed by *Aḥādīth al-quṣṣāṣ* (The *ḥadīth* transmissions of the *quṣṣāṣ*) by Ibn Taymiyya (d. 728/1328), and the *Taḥdhīr al-khawāṣṣ min akādhīb al-quṣṣāṣ* (Warning the educated about the lies of the *quṣṣāṣ*) by al-Suyūṭī (d. 911/1505). There was some degree of inconsistency regarding the particular identity of the *quṣṣāṣ*. In the first/seventh century, they were known as *wāʾiẓ* (preacher; admonisher), *mudhakkir* (admonisher), or *qāṣṣ* (preacher), but the precise meaning of each of these terms at the time remains uncertain.[6] Even later texts that mostly criticized their activities and, thus, shaped the Western perception of these individuals, lack specificity as to whom their criticism refers. The Ḥanbalī jurist and theologian Ibn al-Jawzī began his treatise with definitions of each of these terms, but notes that *qāṣṣ* was most commonly associated with their practice. But while Ibn al-Jawzī seems to use all of these terms interchangeably, they do not appear to be fully synonymous, as only *qāṣṣ* appears to have gained the negative connotation of charlatanism.[7] It remains unclear what specifically distinguished the three terms in this early period and

3 Hallaq, *The Origins and Evolution of Islamic Law*, 63f.

4 Goldziher, *Schools of Koranic Commentators*, 36–38; Goldziher, *Muslim Studies II*, 149–159.

5 Armstong, *The Quṣṣāṣ of Early Islam*, 4f.

6 Pedersen, "The Criticism of the Islamic Preacher," 215.

7 Armstrong, *The Quṣṣāṣ of Early Islam*, 4.

later usage. This lack of clarity renders a universally applicable translation of the term *qāṣṣ* virtually impossible. Lyall Armstrong convincingly argued that the commonly used translations of "storyteller" and "preacher," with their implications of untrained individuals entertaining uneducated masses with wildly fabricated narratives, do not adequately reflect the activities, textual output, or social contexts of these individuals.

First, Armstrong showed that a large number of *quṣṣāṣ* held other positions and were engaged in other activities during the Umayyad period. Textual evidence across multiple types of literature suggests that those identified as *qāṣṣ* during this period, in fact, addressed a number of religious topics with various methodologies, including the theological question of divine will and human responsibilities,[8] the immanence of death and final judgment,[9] pre-Islamic prophets,[10] and the prophetic *sunna* as the exemplar for the Muslim community,[11] legal rulings,[12] statements related to military conquests,[13] and religio-political matters.[14] Their engagement in religious questions in particular required a thorough education in several areas of religious thought and that often also included non-religious expertise, such as history, biography, and Arabic grammar.[15] Furthermore, they appear to have been associated with individuals from numerous scholarly disciplines, including Qurʾān reciters and commentators, *ḥadīth* transmitters, jurists and judges, as well as narrators of Isrāʾīliyyāt, orators, admonishers, and ascetics.[16] The areas across which *quṣṣāṣ* and scholarly material was spread in the early period is further evidenced in the representation of *quṣṣāṣ* material in the works of commentary (*tafsīr*). Armstrong identified one hundred nine individuals that were specifically referred to as *qāṣṣ* in a broad array of Islamic sources prior to 132/750, and argued that *quṣṣāṣ* played a pivotal role in the *tafsīr* tradition.[17] An analysis of the *tafsīr* of ʿAbd al-Razzāq (d. 211/827), for instance, reveals that his commentary consisted overwhelmingly of exegesis by the early *quṣṣāṣ*,[18] and Heribert Horst has shown similar results in his analysis of al-Ṭabarī's *tafsīr*.[19] Armstrong

8 Armstrong, *The Quṣṣāṣ of Early Islam*, 15–21.
9 Armstrong, *The Quṣṣāṣ of Early Islam*, 21–33.
10 Armstrong, *The Quṣṣāṣ of Early Islam*, 33–38.
11 Armstrong, *The Quṣṣāṣ of Early Islam*, 39–41.
12 Armstrong, *The Quṣṣāṣ of Early Islam*, 41–45.
13 Armstrong, *The Quṣṣāṣ of Early Islam*, 49–70.
14 Armstrong, *The Quṣṣāṣ of Early Islam*, 70–74.
15 ʿAthamina, "Al-Qasas," 54.
16 Armstrong, *The Quṣṣāṣ of Early Islam*, 74–152.
17 Armstrong, *The Quṣṣāṣ of Early Islam*, 83.
18 Armstrong, *The Quṣṣāṣ of Early Islam*, 86f.
19 Horst, "Zur Überlieferung."

has demonstrated that the majority of *quṣṣāṣ* through the end of the Umayyad period were widely acknowledged religious scholars, whose ranks included reliable *ḥadīth* transmitters.[20] Furthermore, we should also refine the frequently held view that *quṣṣāṣ* targeted the uneducated and, thus, potentially gullible population as their audience. The sound reputation of the vast majority of early *quṣṣāṣ*, particularly as transmitters of *ḥadīth*, places them in the ranks of the religious establishment, alongside those whose pedagogy included transmitting *ḥadīth* in teaching sessions to their own students. While these sessions may have occurred in a number of locations and formats, they were not necessarily open to the uneducated "masses."[21] Their versatile intellectual engagement, social and professional interactions, and impact on scholarly disciplines such as Qurʾān commentary show that the early *quṣṣāṣ* were in no way isolated from scholarly circles but, more often than not, deeply rooted in them.

The fact that the majority of the early *quṣṣāṣ* had solid reputations is not to say that their activities were not subject to scrutiny, and criticism of a few individuals occurred early on. The earliest critics appear to have been Sufis, including Abū Ṭālib al-Makkī (d. 386/996), who perceived the *quṣṣāṣ* gatherings as inferior to their own *dhikr* circles.[22] Furthermore, he cites reports from Ḥasan al-Baṣrī (d. 110/728) who allegedly viewed the sessions of *quṣṣāṣ* as innovation (*bidʿa*).[23] Later, when preaching and storytelling became closely associated with Sufis themselves, critics complained of the wild emotionalism of the audiences in popular meetings.[24] Armstrong suggested that the involvement of a number of *quṣṣāṣ* in theological debates, particularly on the controversial issue of *qadar*, may have contributed to the eventual repudiation of the *quṣṣāṣ* as a class.[25] A more generic criticism of the profession's activities emerged in the fourth/tenth century, and took its most well-known form in Ibn al-Jawzī's *Kitāb al-Quṣṣāṣ wa-l-mudhakkirūn*.[26] In it, Ibn al-Jawzī criticized certain aberrant tendencies among the *quṣṣāṣ* and advised them to amend their conduct, but he did not outright censure them.[27] What earned his and other critics' disapprobation was not the contents of their preaching per se but certain practices of those who engaged in these activities.

---

20 Armstrong, *The Quṣṣāṣ of Early Islam*, 151; Hallaq, *The Origins and Evolution of Islamic Law*, 40.

21 Armstrong, *The Quṣṣāṣ of Early Islam*, 280f.

22 Berkey, *Popular Preaching*, 27f.

23 Armstrong, *The Quṣṣāṣ of Early Islam*, 142.

24 Berkey, *Popular Preaching*, 27f.

25 Armstrong, *The Quṣṣāṣ of Early Islam*, 279.

26 Pedersen, "The Criticism of the Islamic Preacher," 217.

27 Armstrong, *The Quṣṣāṣ of Early Islam*, 3.

> According to some reports, the *quṣṣāṣ* were censured for what was perceived to be their negative influence on Islamic society, exemplified in their personal conduct as well as the lack of proper comportment in their sessions. This was indicated by the pride *qaṣaṣ* fostered in the *qāṣṣ*, the unruliness, especially in terms of volume, of *qaṣaṣ* sessions and the breaking down of gender barriers by allowing men and women to participate in the same sessions.[28]

Some critics were also troubled that gatherings threatened the gender boundaries both among the audiences and because of female preachers.[29] Others were concerned that weak or untrustworthy materials were being transmitted. The authenticity of the material spread by *quṣṣāṣ* was only raised in relation to individual *quṣṣāṣ* rather than the entire group. It is noteworthy that this issue was only one of numerous complaints, and often not the predominant one. This stands in contrast to the common view among medieval and modern scholars that the *quṣṣāṣ* were generally lax and unreliable in *ḥadīth* transmission. Armstrong suggests that the pervasive notion of *quṣṣāṣ* as second-rate scholars that is found in medieval Islamic studies and in modern studies was a result of the ongoing categorization of the disciplines of Islamic thought (i.e., grouping scholars into categories such as *ḥadīth* transmitters, legal scholars, etc.) and the evolving methodological restrictions placed on *ḥadīth* transmission.[30] Emerging theological doctrines also appear to have played a role. For instance, as the doctrine of the protection (*ʿiṣma*) of the prophets developed, traditions and stories that tarnished their reputations were rejected and their transmitters marginalized.[31]

Later criticism of the *quṣṣāṣ* should not obscure the fact that the majority of early *quṣṣāṣ* were largely reputable scholars who were well-trained and active in many fields of religious learning, and thus played an important role in the articulation and diffusion of Islam in the first Islamic centuries. Even before the realms of political and legal authority had crystalized, they operated at the center of a network of individuals who shaped Islamic law by answering questions on ritual and correct behavior posed to them by members of their audiences; thus, they contributed to the process by which the nascent religion defined itself.[32] Therefore, I do not follow the common dichotomy of

28 Armstrong, *The Quṣṣāṣ of Early Islam*, 279.
29 Berkey, *Popular Preaching*, 27–31.
30 Armstrong, *The Quṣṣāṣ of Early Islam*, 278.
31 Armstrong, *The Quṣṣāṣ of Early Islam*, 278.
32 Berkey, *Popular Preaching*, 22–23.

"scholarly" vs. "popular" narratives but instead distinguish various strands of these traditions as "authenticated" and "unauthenticated" narratives in order to focus on the specific methodological approach chosen by these authors, rather than judging the authors' work and intellectual and social context in a generic sense. As recent scholarship has reevaluated the significance and role of *qāṣṣ* in early Islamic societies, it becomes clear that the origins, content, and social implications of *dalāʾil al-nubūwa* literature, which has long been viewed as a product of the *quṣṣāṣ*, should also be reconsidered on the basis of textual analyses and the intellectual landscape of its authors. Who contributed to this literature? Can we see any substantial differences in the materials transmitted by transmitters who followed the methodological approaches of authenticating individual accounts through *isnād*s and others who did not? In order to examine this question, I briefly introduce two figures: ʿUrwa b. al-Zubayr and some of his students who played key roles in spreading the authenticated narratives of Muḥammad's life; and Wahb b. Munabbih, as the earliest extant source for unauthenticated narratives. This lays the groundwork for a comparison between the two earliest textual bodies on the prophet's life that I examine in the second half of this chapter.

1 ʿUrwa b. al-Zubayr and the "Authenticated" Traditions

One of the first main figures to employ a critical approach to the prophetic tradition was ʿUrwa b. al-Zubayr (d. 94/713).[33] ʿUrwa was a leading legal specialist in Medina and a regular participant in the local teaching circles (*ḥalaqāt*).[34] He belonged to the generation of the "Followers" (*tābiʿūn*) and had direct family relations to some of the closest Companions of the Prophet: His mother was Asmāʾ, the daughter of Abū Bakr al-Ṣiddīq, his maternal aunt was Muḥammad's wife ʿĀʾisha, who served as his main informant; his grandmother Ṣafīya was the daughter of ʿAbd al-Muṭṭalib; his father al-Zubayr was one of the earliest Companions of the Prophet; and his paternal aunt was Khadīja, the Prophet's first wife.[35] These relationships enabled him to obtain firsthand accounts of the early days of Islam. He was generally held in high esteem among the scholars of *ḥadīth* and was considered one of the seven jurists (*fuqahāʾ*) of Medina. He lectured on *ḥadīth* in a family setting and in public at a mosque, and is said

33 For references to Western scholars holding this view, see Schoeler and Görke, *Die ältesten Berichte*, 10.

34 Hallaq, *The Origins and Evolutions of Islamic Law*, 64.

35 Horovitz, *Earliest Biographers*, 15f.

to have attracted large crowds.[36] Based on the materials that have come down to us, it is evident that he transmitted accounts on all the significant events in Muḥammad's life after his call to prophecy.[37] Like other legal scholars of his time, his approach reflects the early stages of critical *ḥadīth* studies, in that he "supported" the material he transmitted with a chain of transmission (*isnād*). The inclusion of *isnād*s was not yet mandatory and there are indeed some accounts found in ʿUrwa's corpus that still lack the chain of transmission.[38]

ʿUrwa's student al-Zuhrī (d. 124/742) followed his teacher in his critical approach to the historical material, though there are instances in which he provides no *isnād* at all.[39] A study of those accounts that have survived suggests that he was the first to give the *sīra* a definite structure.[40] The systematization of the prophetic biography took further shape in the subsequent generation. Three of al-Zuhrī's students are known to us as the authors of books on the conquests (*maghāzī*): Mūsā b. ʿUqba (d. 140/758), Maʿmar b. Rāshid (d. 153/770), and Muḥammad b. Isḥāq (d. 150/767).[41] Maʿmar b. Rāshid employed the stricter standards of later *ḥadīth* scholars and used precise *isnād*s.[42] Other well-known pioneers of *sīra* literature were less rigorous in authenticating their accounts. Mūsā b. ʿUqba presented his material in long, continuous, and mostly anonymous reports, but he occasionally included authenticated traditions that were transmitted by acknowledged scholars of *ḥadīth*. Schoeler and Görke suggest that Mūsā b. ʿUqba did not provide specific *isnād*s for his longer reports because he compiled them from various and sometimes questionable sources, while the individual reports that are preceded by an accurate *isnād*

36 Schoeler, *Charakter und Authentie*, 29.

37 ʿUrwa compiled written notes on legal *ḥadīth* and legal opinions, but he is also said to have destroyed these notes at one point, something that he later regretted; cf. Schoeler, *Charakter und Authentie*, 29f. Later sources like Ibn Kathīr and Ḥājjī Khalīfa claimed that ʿUrwa authored a *Kitāb al-Maghāzī*, which, according to Schoeler, contradicts both the European scholarly view of the pace of the development of written traditions in Arabic as well as the Muslim tradition that the *taṣnīf* in general only emerged in the generation of Maʿmar b. Rāshid, Ibn Jurayj (d. 150/768), Mālik b. Anas (d. 179/796), and Ibn Isḥāq; cf. Schoeler, *Charakter und Authentie*, 31. Lawrence Conrad, however, states that scholars in the Arab world have recently inclined toward the view that ʿUrwa himself compiled such a work; cf. Horovitz, *Earliest Biographers*, 26 n. 106. ʿUrwa's correspondence with the caliph ʿAbd al-Malik and others regarding questions about the Prophet's life was preserved in al-Ṭabarī and by other historians; cf. Schoeler and Görke, *Die ältesten Berichte*.

38 Schoeler and Görke, *Die ältesten Berichte*, 270.

39 Schoeler and Görke, *Die ältesten Berichte*, 271; cf. Motzki, "Der Fiqh des–Zuhrī," 6.

40 Dūrī, *The Rise of Historical Writing among the Arabs*, 27f.

41 Horovitz, *Earliest Biographers*, 67.

42 Ibn Rāshid, *Expeditions*, xxii.

were taken from the lectures of known scholars.[43] Ibn Isḥāq mainly used collective *isnād*s at the beginning of a paragraph or section rather than providing individual ones for each account.[44] Peers criticized him for various methodological shortcomings, such as using questionable *isnād*s and accounts transmitted by the People of the Book (*ahl al-kitāb*), frequently citing fabricated poetry, referring to erroneous genealogies, and particularly for transmitting the works of contemporary scholars without having heard them.[45] Al-Wāqidī (d. 207/823) used all the sources available to him, including written versions of Ibn Isḥāq, Mūsā b. ʿUqba, and ʿAbd al-Razzāq, but presented partially fictitious collective *isnād*s rather than acknowledging these sources.[46] Al-Wāqidī was repudiated by *ḥadīth* scholars (*muḥaddithūn*), but respected with regard to his scholarship on *sīra*, the *maghāzī*, and jurisprudence (*fiqh*).[47] After Ibn Isḥāq, Ibn Saʿd (d. 230/845) is the earliest author of a *sīra* that has been preserved in its entirety. His biography of the Prophet is based, for the most part, on the materials of his teacher, al-Wāqidī, and to a lesser extent on Ibn Isḥāq, Abū Maʿshar (d. 170/787), and Mūsā b. ʿUqba.[48] Scholars who became central figures of the *sīra* literature felt a need to authenticate their material and developed distinct standards for this process that differed from those used by *ḥadīth* scholars.

2 Wahb b. Munabbih and the "Unauthenticated" Traditions

By contrast, the earliest written source containing "unauthenticated" traditions goes back to Wahb b. Munabbih (d. between 109 and 113/728 and 732). Fragments of his biography of the Prophet are preserved in one of the earliest Muslim papyri.[49] Despite this material evidence of Wahb's interest in the Prophet's life, a list of his works demonstrates that his main field of expertise

---

43 Schoeler and Görke, *Die ältesten Berichte*, 274.

44 Schoeler and Görke, *Die ältesten Berichte*, 274.

45 Dūrī, *The Rise of Historical Writing among the Arabs*, 35f.

46 Schoeler and Görke, *Die ältesten Berichte*, 121f., 142f., 183f., 276. Regarding the longstanding debate over whether al-Wāqidī in fact used Ibn Isḥāq's work, see Schoeler, *Charakter und Authentie*, 138–142.

47 Horovitz, *Earliest Biographers*, 116.

48 Horovitz, *Earliest Biographers*, 121.

49 Georges Khoury edited the papyri fragments of Wahb b. Munabbih, which are held at Heidelberg (PSR Heid Arab 23). Dated 229/844, these papyri constitute some of the earliest textual evidence of Muslim culture. They consist of two texts, the story of David and the biography of the Prophet. For a detailed description of the papyrus, see Khoury, *Wahb b. Munabbih*, 1:15–32.

was neither *ḥadīth* nor Islamic history. Wahb's work primarily covered the pre-Islamic heritage, such as the stories of the prophets (*qiṣaṣ al-anbiyā'*); indeed he is often cited as a source for pre-Islamic history by Ibn Isḥāq and others.[50] But while scholars frequently named him as a source for pre-Islamic history, his name was never linked with information on the Prophet's life, though some of his material eventually entered the *sīra* literature anonymously.[51]

As a contemporary of ʿUrwa b. al-Zubayr, Wahb also belonged to the generation of the Followers, but he lacked ʿUrwa's close connections to the Companions. Wahb was a native of Sanaa. Direct studies under the Companions would have required him to travel extensively, and we only know with certainty that he went on pilgrimage in 99/718.[52] Both Wahb and his brother Hammām b. Munabbih transmitted traditions on the authority of Abū Hurayra (d. 59/678) and ʿAbdallāh b. ʿAbbās (d. 68/687), but only Hammām maintained close relationships to these two Companions and specialized in *ḥadīth*.[53] From the few *isnād*s that he provided in his work, we assume that Wahb b. Munabbih was aware of the practice of authentication of accounts and occasionally employed them when possible.[54] However, the vast majority of his accounts do not include chains of transmission at all. This absence is probably due to his lack of personal interaction with these well-known scholars; Wahb did not belong to their circles and, therefore, did not utilize their methodology.

Wahb b. Munabbih is most frequently associated with the introduction of Isrāʾīliyyāt into the Islamic tradition.[55] Khoury has argued that his approach to biblical material suggests that he drew his information from oral Jewish traditions, not from his own study of the Bible.[56] In light of his very limited personal

---

50 The first book attributed to him bears the title *Kitāb al-Mubtada' wa-qiṣāṣ al-anbiyā'* (even though the title was assigned to the book by posterity and varies according to different authors). Furthermore, a *Kitāb al-Isrāʾīliyyāt* is attributed to Wahb b. Munabbih, but this does not seem to have been known in the first-/sixth-century literature; it probably relates to stories arising out of those in the preceding book; Khoury, "Wahb b. Munabbih"; cf. Khoury, *Wahb al-Munabbih*, 1:206, 208, 310f.

51 Khoury, *Wahb al-Munabbih*, 1:277.

52 Khoury, *Wahb al-Munabbih*, 1:211. However, he is also said to have visited his father's native Herat more than once; Khoury, *Wahb al-Munabbih*, 1:194.

53 Khoury, *Wahb b. Munabbih*, 1:211.

54 Ibn ʿAbbās was named about twenty times, Kaʿb al-Aḥbār was mentioned less than ten times, and Abū Hurayra about five times; other names occur less frequently; cf. Khoury, *Wahb al-Munabbih*, 1:211.

55 Khoury, *Wahb b. Munabbih*, 210–221; Khoury, "Wahb b. Munabbih."

56 Khoury suggests that Wahb (contrary to his own claims) had not actually read the Bible, because there were considerable differences between his material and actual biblical material; early Muslim scholars like Ibn Qutayba pointed this out as well. While the possibility of Wahb embellishing the materials cannot be ruled out, the parallels to Talmudic

interaction with Companions, it seems plausible that he took his Islamic material from the oral traditions that circulated in his vicinity but lacked formal authentication, then added the few properly authenticated traditions he had received to the oral traditions. Yet, his focus on pre-Islamic traditions and his engagement with unauthenticated materials should not automatically lead to the conclusion that he was, during his lifetime, considered a *qāṣṣ*. Despite his wide association with the *quṣṣāṣ* in modern studies, his name does not appear in connection with the term *qāṣṣ* until much later, and even biographers like al-Mizzī (d. 654/1256), al-Dhahabī (d. 748/1348), and Ibn Ḥajar (d. 852/1449), who all lived after Ibn al-Jawzī had written his critique and would have associated *quṣṣāṣ* with Isrāʾīliyyāt, did not specifically identify Wahb as a *qāṣṣ*.[57] He was only explicitly linked to the term in two relatively late sources, Ibn Samura al-Jaʿdī (d. 585/1190) and Yāqūt al-Ḥamawī (d. 696/1229),[58] which supports more recent views that the early engagement with Muḥammad's biographic material does not fall into a simple and clear-cut binary between *muḥaddith* and *qāṣṣ*. Because he did not utilize the field's methodology of supporting his reports with an *isnād*, Wahb was not accepted among the *ḥadīth* scholars (*muḥaddithūn*), but he was also not considered a *qāṣṣ*.

The main distinguishing factor between the "authenticated" and the "unauthenticated" traditions so far appears to have been their methodological approach, i.e., whether or not they provided chains of transmission. However, given that various scholars identified the *quṣṣāṣ* material as the potential origin of miracles in the *sīra*,[59] we should expect differences between the two traditions in terms of their content as well. A comparative look at the earliest available sources highlights similarities and differences between both strands of engagement with the prophetic biography. ʿUrwa b. al-Zubayr's corpus of traditions on the Prophet's life was reconstructed by Gregor Schoeler and Andreas Görke, who traced, in later works, *ḥadīth*s going back to ʿUrwa. The corpus includes accounts on the beginning of the revelation, the *hijra*, the battles of Badr and Uḥud, the incident of the lie surrounding ʿĀʾisha, the battle of al-Khandaq (trench) and the Banū Qurayẓa, the treaty of Ḥudaybiyya, and the conquest of Mecca.[60] Accounts of the *hijra* constitute the only common narrative found in both the corpus of ʿUrwa b. al-Zubayr and the papyri of

---

and Midrash traditions suggest otherwise. But even these materials do not suffice to explain the entirety of the differences; Khoury, *Wahb b. Munabbih*, 1:219f.

57 Armstrong, *The Quṣṣāṣ of Early Islam*, 94.

58 Armstrong, *The Quṣṣāṣ of Early Islam*, 301.

59 Dūrī, *The Rise of Historical Writing Among the Arabs*, 30.

60 Schoeler and Görke, *Die ältesten Berichte*.

Wahb b. Munabbih. Therefore, it serves as an example to establish the kinds of narratives circulating in the two traditions.

3 Comparative Analysis: The Accounts of the *Hijra* according to ʿUrwa b. al-Zubayr and Wahb b. Munabbih

ʿUrwa b. al-Zubayr's accounts of the *hijra* are recorded in numerous versions. There are two extended accounts that were handed down through ʿUrwa's main transmitters, Hishām b. ʿUrwa and Ibn Shihāb al-Zuhrī.[61] Both of these long versions describe the persecutions Muslims were facing in Mecca, and the emigrations to Abyssinia and Medina. Hishām b. ʿUrwa's recension is preserved in the form of a letter ʿUrwa sent to the caliph ʿAbd al-Malik.[62] The most extensive version of al-Zuhrī's transmission is narrated on the authority of Maʿmar b. Rāshid and recorded in ʿAbd al-Razzāq's *Muṣannaf*.[63] The traditions of Hishām and al-Zuhrī correspond in most central aspects but diverge in numerous details. In the following I provide a summary of those elements of ʿUrwa's account of the *hijra* that are common to the transmissions of both Hishām and al-Zuhrī. I then summarize Wahb's account as it is found in the papyri. After presenting general outlines of both narratives, I provide a more detailed juxtaposition of the differences between ʿUrwa and Wahb as well as various strands of transmission in ʿUrwa's corpus.

3.1 *ʿUrwa b. al-Zubayr's Account of the* Hijra

After the Prophet started speaking out against their deities, the Meccans began to oppress the Muslim community, which led many believers to revoke their faith. The Prophet advised his community to migrate to Abyssinia, a trading partner of the Quraysh ruled by a Christian ruler, the Negus. In the meantime, the number of Muslims in Mecca increased and some of the leaders of Quraysh converted to Islam. The pressure on the Muslim community lessened

61 In addition to these long versions, there is a tradition of medium length that was transmitted on the authority of Muḥammad b. ʿAbd al-Raḥmān and a number of shorter traditions that only relate to the *hijra* itself. For a detailed analysis of these traditions see Schoeler and Görke, *Die ältesten Berichte*, 38–77.

62 The letter is found in al-Ṭabarī, albeit not in a coherent account but interspersed with other traditions; cf. al-Ṭabarī, *Tārīkh*, 1:1180f., 1224f., 1234f. A continuous version of this letter is found in al-Ṭabarī, *Tafsīr*, 6:246f., 375; A shorter version of the same letter is found in Ibn Ḥanbal, *Musnad*, 6:212.

63 ʿAbd al-Razzāq, *al-Muṣannaf*, 5:384f.; cf. Schoeler and Görke, *Die ältesten Berichte*, 49f.

for a while.[64] The emigrants returned from Abyssinia and many of the people in Medina embraced Islam, leading the Quraysh to increase their pressure on the Muslim community. Seventy people from Medina met with the Prophet in Aqaba and guaranteed him protection.[65] The Prophet advised the Muslims to emigrate to Medina. Abū Bakr asked the Prophet for permission to emigrate with the others, but was, in turn, asked to stay. He purchased two camels and took care of them until God gave the Prophet permission to emigrate. ʿĀʾisha related that one day the Prophet came to their house during midday, which was contrary to his custom of coming in the morning or in the evening. Abū Bakr realized the unusual time and anticipated that something had happened. The Prophet asked other people to leave the house and Abū Bakr assured him that he was alone with his daughters. The Prophet related to him that he received permission to emigrate to Medina and confirmed that Abū Bakr was allowed to accompany him. Abū Bakr offered him one of the two camels and the Prophet insisted on buying it from him. At the time of the *hijra*, Abū Bakr owned a sheep. He ordered ʿĀmir b. Fuhayra[66] to drive the sheep to the cave of Thawr every night, where Abū Bakr and the Prophet could milk it. A man from the Banū ʿAbd b. ʿAdī took the camels and was hired as a guide despite being a pagan. ʿAbdallāh b. Abī Bakr brought news from Mecca every night and once the turmoil about the *hijra* subsided in Mecca, the Prophet and Abū Bakr, together with ʿĀmir b. Fuhayra and their guide from the Banū ʿAbd b. ʿAdī, set out. Abū Bakr and ʿĀmir b. Fuhayra took turns riding [the camel].[67] They reached the Banū ʿAmr b. Awf before noon and were said to have stayed with them for two days, though the Banū ʿAmr b. Awf claimed that it was longer. The Prophet then led his camel until he reached the residences of the Banū l-Najjār.[68]

3.2 *Wahb b. Munabbih's Account of the* Hijra

The Quraysh gathered to discuss how to treat the growing threat of Muḥammad and his community. Following the advice of Iblīs, the Quraysh decided to kill the Prophet. Gabriel came to Muḥammad and transmitted a Qurʾānic verse[69] and related to the Prophet what happened during the meeting of the

---

64 Al-Ṭabarī, *Tārīkh*, 1:1180f.

65 Al-Ṭabarī, *Tārīkh*, 1:1224f.

66 ʿĀmir b. Fuhayra, a maternal half-brother of ʿĀʾisha and ʿAbdallāh b. Abī Bakr, was previously a slave of Ṭufayl b. ʿAbdallāh but after embracing Islam he was bought and released by Abū Bakr.

67 The letter includes a detailed description of their route; cf. al-Ṭabarī, *Tārīkh*, 1:1224f.

68 Al-Ṭabarī, *Tārīkh*, 1:1234f.

69 Q. 8:30.

Quraysh.[70] Muḥammad went to Abū Bakr at midday and told him about the newly revealed verse, the meeting of the Quraysh and the presence of Iblīs, and their plot against him. Abū Bakr was then sent to spy on the Quraysh.[71] The Prophet then told Abū Bakr to prepare for their departure at night. Wahb then quotes ʿAlī[72] who related a first-person account of how the Prophet ordered him to sleep in the Prophet's place that night. The Prophet told ʿAlī that he will pass by the Quraysh and the latter expressed concern about Muḥammad's safety; he then assured ʿAlī of God's protection. ʿAlī followed the Prophet to see what would happen and Muḥammad told him to go to Abū Bakr and convey to him that Muḥammad will be waiting for him at the cave of Thawr. Muḥammad added that Gabriel is walking in front of him, spreading his wings to shield him from the eyes of the Quraysh. The Prophet took a handful of soil and scattered it over the Quraysh's heads. Then Abū Bakr came to ʿAlī who related to him what the Prophet had said.[73] Wahb then quoted Abū Bakr's first-person account, stating that he followed the Prophet's traces. The Prophet mistook him for one of his enemies, rushed, and stumbled, causing himself to bleed. Witnessing this, Abū Bakr identified himself to the Prophet by clearing his throat and the Prophet continued on his way at a slower pace until they both reached the cave of Thawr.[74] Inside the cave were twelve holes, ten of which Abū Bakr filled with pieces of cloth he tore from his garments. He covered the remaining two holes with his back but was stung by a scorpion. The Prophet noticed Abū Bakr in pain and placed his hands on his companion's leg, saying: "Through the breath of God, I will raise you up and God will heal you from everything that causes you pain." Abū Bakr was relieved of his pain.[75] The scene then shifts to a first-person account of ʿAlī relating that Abū Jahl and the Quraysh came that morning to kill the Prophet. He told them that Muḥammad passed them during the night while they were awake [and the Quraysh did not see him].[76] Abū Jahl sent messengers all the way to Yathrib to inform the people that Muḥammad and Abū Bakr had escaped and offered a reward of 100 camels for retrieving the fugitives.[77] Umayyya b. Khalaf and Abū Jahl sought Usāma b. Fāyiq to track their traces. At first he stated that all the traces look the same but

70 Khoury, *Wahb b. Munabbih*, 1:136.

71 Wahb supported these passages with two proper *isnād*s, the first going back to ʿĀʾisha and the second one stopping with himself; cf. Khoury, *Wahb b. Munabbih*, 1:136f.

72 For this, there is no *isnād* provided; cf. Khoury, *Wahb b. Munabbih*, 1:140f.

73 Khoury, *Wahb b. Munabbih*, 1:138.

74 Khoury, *Wahb b. Munabbih*, 1:142.

75 Khoury, *Wahb b. Munabbih*, 1:142.

76 This first-person account again lacks an *isnād*; Khoury, *Wahb b. Munabbih*, 1:142f.

77 Khoury, *Wahb b. Munabbih*, 1:144.

then he found the place where the Prophet had passed the Quraysh, but they denied that this had happened. He then found the place where the Prophet had started bleeding and followed the traces to the cave [called] Thawr.[78] The narrative again switches to Abū Bakr's first-person account, stating that he began to fear when he heard a noise but that the Prophet said: "Do not be afraid. God is with us." The narrative voice switched back to the third person, proclaiming that God sent a spider that, within an hour, through magic, made a cobweb that normally would have taken a year to spin. God also sent an angel to the cave in the form of a dove. Then Abū Bakr heard the voices of their pursuers who reached the cave but could not find any traces of them and so assumed that God was shielding the Prophet. The pursuers passed the cave and someone suggested that Muḥammad and Abū Bakr might have sought refuge in the cave but they quickly rejected the idea because the cobweb and the dove would not be in place if anyone had entered the cave.[79] ʿAlī and Asmāʾ bt. Abī Bakr brought food to the cave. On the third day, Muḥammad ordered ʿAlī to rent three camels and a guide. Muḥammad specified that the guide should be from ʿAbd al-Qays, a tribe that is said to have been Christian. ʿAlī hired ʿAbdallāh b. Urayqiṭ, and the account mentions that he was passionately reading books, which most likely indicates that he was familiar with Christian scripture. The guide saw the Prophet's "seal of prophecy" on his shoulder. He kissed it and embraced Islam.[80]

They set out, ʿAbdallāh b. Urayqiṭ leading the way, and passed the Banū Mudlij. One of them recognized the Prophet. Surāqa mounted his racing horse and followed them. Abū Bakr realized that they were being pursued and suggested that Muḥammad ask God to stop Surāqa. The Prophet followed his suggestion and the legs of Surāqa's horse were paralyzed and sank into the sand. Surāqa asked the Prophet to free his horse and promised not to follow them. The horse was set free and Surāqa talked to Muḥammad until he saw his father's men approach. Surāqa returned to them in order to divert them.[81]

Muḥammad continued to Medina and passed Umm Maʿbad al-Khuzāʿīya's camp. A third-person narrator praised her generosity and kindness. The Prophet and his Companions asked for food but she could not provide them with any because of a winter drought. Muḥammad saw a sheep and asked whether it had milk. When Umm Maʿbad denied this, he asked permission to try to milk

78 Khoury, *Wahb b. Munabbih*, 1:144.

79 Khoury, *Wahb b. Munabbih*, 1:144f.

80 This passage closes with verses of poetry (presumably recited by ʿAbdallāh b. Urayqiṭ) mentioning that "God protects His Messenger"; Khoury, *Wahb b. Munabbih*, 1:146f.

81 Khoury, *Wahb b. Munabbih*, 1:148f.

it and renamed it "Baraka." The milk satiated him and his men, and he milked it a second time for Umm Maʿbad. After a while Abū Maʿbad returned home and asked about the milk, indicating that all the sheep were out in the pastures grazing. Umm Maʿbad told him about "a blessed man" who came by, and she gave him a description of his appearance. Abū Maʿbad realized that it was the fugitive that the Quraysh were looking for and regretted not having met him.[82]

The next morning, the inhabitants of Mecca heard an unidentified voice relating that the Prophet stopped at Umm Maʿbad's camp. Muḥammad and his Companions were praised and the voice related that the Prophet drew milk from a barren sheep.[83] When Muḥammad and Abū Bakr reached Medina, Abū Bakr sent a letter to the Quraysh mentioning that the people—with the exception of Surāqa—still demanded proof of the Prophet's cause and so he related what happened to Surāqa's horse.[84] When the letter reached Mecca, Abū Jahl and the Banū Makhzūm went to Abū Usāma al-Fāyyiq to reproach him for his behavior toward Muḥammad but Abū Usāma stated that their inability to harm the Prophet was due to God's protection. The notables of the Quraysh also sought to reproach Abū Usāma. Abū Jahl sent a letter to the Banū Mudlij blaming Surāqa, who responded with a letter explaining the situation, that his horse's legs sank into the ground.[85]

The Prophet arrived at the oasis of Medina.[86] After staying in Qubāʾ for a couple of days, he offered Friday prayers in Medina. When various Anṣār invited him to stay with them, the Prophet asked them to return to their houses and he rode his camel with loose reins, because he wanted to leave the decision of his residence to God. People stopped him four times asking him to stay with them but the Prophet asserted his intention to wait until his camel kneeled somewhere. His camel finally chose a location, which the Prophet bought from two orphans and his residential complex was built there.[87]

3.3 *A Detailed Comparison between the* Hijra *Accounts of ʿUrwa b. al-Zubayr and Wahb b. Munabbih*

The juxtaposition of the accounts of the *hijra* by ʿUrwa b. al-Zubayr and Wahb b. Munabbih's (appendix) shows considerable differences in terms of their content, but little contradictory information. In most cases, the divergences

82 Khoury, *Wahb b. Munabbih*, 1:150f.

83 Khoury, *Wahb b. Munabbih*, 1:152f.

84 Khoury, *Wahb b. Munabbih*, 1:156f.

85 Khoury, *Wahb b. Munabbih*, 1:156f.

86 The dates of the *hijra* are given: the Prophet left Mecca on the first day of Rabīʿ al-Awwal and arrived at Qubāʾ on the fifteenth of that month; cf. Khoury, *Wahb b. Munabbih*, 1:160.

87 Khoury, *Wahb b. Munabbih*, 1:160f.

could simply be a result of the selective process by which the compiler omitted some aspects of an existing account. This is not only clear by comparing the accounts of ʿUrwa b. al-Zubayr to Wahb b. Munabbih, but it also occurs in the various recensions of ʿUrwa's account. Regarding the provisions for the Prophet and Abū Bakr, for instance, Wahb does not mention sheep being driven to the cave; recension (a) of ʿUrwa's account, by contrast, mentions the sheep but not the food preparations of Asmāʾ bt. Abī Bakr. Recension (b) includes an independent *ḥadīth* relating to Asmāʾ's food preparation, and recension (c) combines the two. Therefore, it is plausible that the two pieces of information are complementary but not always mentioned in the same tradition, since ʿUrwa sometimes only transmitted some passages relating to certain themes. For instance, in his letter to ʿAbd al-Malik, references to the emigration to Abyssinia are general, while the recension of al-Zuhrī focuses on Abū Bakr's encounter with Ibn al-Daghina and thus presents the Muslims' situation in Mecca and their desire to emigrate through the personal experience of Abū Bakr.

Schoeler and Görke have suggested that the circulation of longer and shorter accounts that contain varying degrees of details indicates that ʿUrwa himself presented the material in different ways, by combining a number of narrative elements and details.[88] The technique of combining various events into coherent narratives was, therefore, not restricted to the realm of "unauthenticated" narratives like that of Wahb b. Munabbih, who presented his entire *sīra* in one continuous narrative. We find longer accounts in ʿUrwa's corpus that combine the description of the Muslims' situation in Mecca, the emigration to Abyssinia, and the *hijra*, as well as shorter individual accounts of each of these events. Schoeler and Görke pointed to the fact that the independent recensions of Hishām b. ʿUrwa and al-Zuhrī are close enough in content to assume that ʿUrwa himself had combined various themes and elements into one narrative.[89] These acts of combining or separating the accounts indicate two trends among the "scholarly" tradition: (1) even critical scholars did not necessarily transmit their material verbatim but rather attempted to encapsulate the meaning, and (2) this process required them to select certain elements and omit others. This aspect of selectivity may explain the complete absence of certain elements in ʿUrwa's account.

The greatest divergence between the accounts of ʿUrwa and Wahb is the plethora of supernatural elements that are only included in the *sīra* of Wahb. As such, the presence of Iblīs among the Quraysh, the Prophet passing the

88 Schoeler and Görke, *Die ältesten Berichte*, 75.

89 Schoeler and Görke, *Die ältesten Berichte*, 74.

Quraysh unnoticed, the healing of Abū Bakr, the concealment of the cave's entrance with a cobweb, and the encounter with Surāqa are absent in all the recensions of ʿUrwa's account. The absence of these accounts in the earliest source led Schoeler and Görke to conclude that the "scholarly" tradition developed from the earliest traditions, such as the corpus of ʿUrwa b. al-Zubayr, and the later *maghāzī* works, such as those of Ibn Isḥāq, Ibn Hishām, or al-Wāqidī. They state that the distinguishing features of the later works are literary embellishments, dramatic additions to the narrative, the addition of miracle stories, and the increasing significance of certain people.[90] This conclusion is based on several observations: ʿUrwa focuses almost exclusively on the Medinan period; the only events he describes preceding the *hijra* are the first revelation and the situation of the Muslim community in Mecca that eventually led to the emigration to Medina.[91] Many events that form generally accepted aspects of the Prophet's life in later *sīra* works, such as his genealogy, stories about his grandfather ʿAbd al-Muṭṭalib and his father ʿAbdallāh, Muḥammad's birth, and the years of Muḥammad's childhood and adolescence are missing in ʿUrwa's traditions. Moreover, accounts of miracles do not play any important role.[92] But the absence from ʿUrwa's accounts of Muḥammad's pre-prophetic period and his alleged miracles is not necessarily proof of the development of *sīra* literature, which later incorporated these aspects. This view of an evolving "scholarly" tradition is built on two premises. First, it presupposes that ʿUrwa b. al-Zubayr's corpus is representative of the entire scholarly engagement with the Prophet's biography during ʿUrwa's lifetime. Second, and closely linked to this, is the premise that *sīra* literature underwent a linear development that began with the life story of the Prophet, which only encompassed his later life after his call to prophecy and did not contain any miracles. Later biographies were supplemented with narratives of the period prior to the beginning of revelation and with miracles throughout Muḥammad's life. Thus, the biography of the historical figure was transformed into hagiographical legends. *Quṣṣāṣ* material is usually considered to be the origin of the miraculous or folkloristic material added to the "factual" *sīra*. The period of these addenda is thought to have occurred in the generation after al-Zuhrī.[93] This view, therefore, assumes that the "scholarly" *sīra* tradition during ʿUrwa's lifetime generally did not include prophetic miracles. It is noteworthy that the compilers themselves did

---

90 Schoeler and Görke, *Die ältesten Berichte*, 264.

91 Schoeler and Görke, *Die ältesten Berichte*, 263.

92 Schoeler and Görke, *Die ältesten Berichte*, 264.

93 Dūrī, *The Rise of Historical Writing among the Arabs*, 30; Schoeler and Görke, *Die ältesten Berichte*, 275f.

not label these events as miraculous. This theological classification of miracles can be traced to the interpretation of Western scholars who, as I noted in the introduction, mostly relied on their own cultural framework rather than the framework contemporaneous to the early Muslim compilers. Even if we accept this anachronistic assessment, for the notion of a linear development of biographical literature to maintain its validity, we must assume that none of the miraculous narratives were in circulation prior to or contemporary with al-Zuhrī and are found exclusively in *quṣṣāṣ* materials. There are, however, numerous "miraculous" narratives that circulated among the earliest *sīra* scholars, including those of ʿUrwa himself.

3.4 *Miracles in the Corpus of ʿUrwa b. al-Zubayr*

Although ʿUrwa's account of the *hijra* does not include any miracles, his accounts of other events in the Prophet's life suggest that he did not deny the notion of prophetic miracles in general. ʿUrwa's account of the treaty of Ḥudaybiyya, for instance, recounts the Prophet's restoration of a dry well. The account is transmitted in numerous long versions by al-Zuhrī and in two long versions by Hishām b. ʿUrwa.[94] These accounts all include the narrative of the Prophet's men facing a scarcity of water at Ḥudaybiyya. The Prophet took an arrow from his quiver and ordered one of his Companions to stir the well with it. The formerly dry well then began to overflow with water.[95] In addition to the versions transmitted by al-Zuhrī and Hishām b. ʿUrwa, there are traditions going back to Abū l-Aswad independently from al-Zuhrī.[96] According to Abū l-Aswad's version, the Muslims reached Ḥudaybiyya during intense heat but could only access one well. The Prophet rinsed his mouth, poured the water back into the well, and stirred it with an arrow, and this led the well to overflow with water.[97] Görke has pointed out that this narrative may contain only certain elements of ʿUrwa's account, but not go back to him, given that it encompasses many elements that are not found in other *ḥadīth* collections or historiographical works. Nevertheless, the parallels to ʿUrwa's account are clear. Finally, there is a report going back to ʿUrwa b. al-Zubayr that is not part of the long versions of al-Zuhrī or Hishām b. ʿUrwa; this report is transmitted on the authority of Yazīd b. Rūmān and Ibn Isḥāq. According to this account Gabriel miraculously punished four people for ridiculing the Prophet. Gabriel threw a leaf into the

94 Schoeler and Görke, *Die ältesten Berichte*, 186.

95 Görke, "The Historical Tradition about al-Ḥudaybiya," 241; cf. Schoeler and Görke, *Die ältesten Berichte*, 188, 194, 202, 208, respectively.

96 Görke, "The Historical Tradition about al-Ḥudaybiya," 256f.; cf. Schoeler and Görke, *Die ältesten Berichte*, 186.

97 Görke, "The Historical Tradition about al-Ḥudaybiya," 256f.

face of Aswad b. al-Muṯṯalib and this caused him to become blind; he then pointed at the stomach of Aswad b. ʿAbd Yaghūth, it began to swell and he died of hydrops. Next, Gabriel pointed at the inside of al-ʿĀṣ b. al-Wāʾil's foot, and he stepped on a thorn and died from the wound. Finally, Gabriel pointed at the head of al-Ḥārith b. al-Ṭulāṭila, it festered, leading to his death.[98] The accounts transmitted by Abū l-Aswad and Yazīd b. Rūmān may not be traceable to ʿUrwa himself, given that they do not appear in any of the longer versions of ʿUrwa's main transmitters. However, the references to a water miracle at Ḥudaybiyya were transmitted independently by al-Zuhrī and Hishām b. ʿUrwa and, therefore, provide sufficient evidence that ʿUrwa b. al-Zubayr did not generally deny the possibility of miraculous events in the Prophet's lifetime.

Major *maghāzī* scholars, such as ʿĀṣim b. ʿUmar b. Qatāda, and Ibn Shihāb al-Zuhrī, in the generation after ʿUrwa include a number of references to supernatural events that occurred around the Prophet. A common motif in these early accounts is that of various people predicting or announcing Muḥammad's prophecy. Knowledge of his future prophecy was associated with soothsayers and astronomers,[99] sacrificial animals,[100] *jinn*,[101] and Jews who identified and confirmed Muḥammad based on their knowledge of Hebrew scriptures.[102] There are also a number of less frequent motifs, such as the water miracle that is found in all recensions of ʿUrwa's corpus. In al-Zuhrī's body of literature, this account of the water miracle is linked to the motif of the divine protection of the Prophet; that is, his camel's reluctance to proceed on a specific path is interpreted by Muḥammad as God's protection.[103] ʿĀṣim's account of Salmān al-Fārisī's manumission details how gold increased in weight after Muḥammad touched it with his tongue; this caused it to reach the negotiated

98 Al-Ṭabarī, *Tafsīr*, 7:550; Ibn Ḥishām, *al-Sīra al-nabawiyya*, 1:410; Ibn Kathīr, *al-Bidāya*, 3:106; cf. Schoeler and Görke, *Die ältesten Berichte*, 71f.

99 ʿAbd al-Razzāq, *al-Muṣannaf*, 5:343.

100 Al-Ṭabarī, *Tārīkh*, 1:1065f.

101 Ibn Saʿd, *Ṭabaqāt*, 1:141. The *jinn* announce the beginning of revelation or the *hijra* and their inability to access heaven to overhear the discourses of the angels as they used to. This account draws on the belief that, prior to Islam, *jinn* used to overhear the conversations of angels. However, from the advent of Islam onward, they were hindered from doing so and those *jinn* who still tried were chased away by shooting stars (*shihāb*), as is described in various verses of the Qurʾān (cf. Q. 15:17–18, 37:6–10, 67:5, 72:8–9).

102 Al-Ṭabarī, *Tārīkh*, 1:1065f.; Ibn Saʿd, *Ṭabaqāt*, 1:134; Ibn Isḥāq, *The Life of Muhammad*, 93. A very similar reference is found in Ibn Kathīr, *al-Sīra al-nabawiyya*, 1:291.

103 ʿAbd al-Razzāq, *al-Muṣannaf*, 5:332f.

price of Salmān's freedom.[104] Furthermore, ʿĀṣim related a story of the Prophet healing his grandfather's eyes during the battle of Uḥud.[105]

Such an increase in material among the scholars of al-Zuhrī's generation might be explained by assuming that the material was already in circulation at the time, but was not transmitted by ʿUrwa himself. The fact that ʿUrwa mentioned a miraculous event in passing, but related only a few such events himself may simply be a result of his selective choice rather than from a lack of such material in scholarly circles. A similar process occurred with regard to Muḥammad's life story prior to his call to prophecy. While ʿUrwa mostly restricted himself to events of the Medinan period, all three of the major *maghāzī* scholars of the subsequent generation, ʿAbdallāh b. Abī Bakr b. Muḥammad (d. ca. 120/738), ʿĀṣim b. ʿUmar b. Qatāda (d. ca. 119/737), and ʿUrwa's student al-Zuhrī, transmitted material on the Prophet's life, including his youth and early years. ʿAbd al-Razzāq's recension of al-Zuhrī's *maghāzī*, for instance, included many accounts of the Prophet's conception, birth, childhood, and adolescence, accounts that are usually related in later *sīra* works.[106] Prior to the beginning of the revelation, Muḥammad's life may not have been scrutinized and, therefore, was not as rigorously attested to as it was during the prophetic era. Yet the Followers (*tābiʿūn*), particularly ʿUrwa himself, certainly had direct access to the collective memory of the Meccan community and could draw information from them about the time before Muḥammad's call to prophecy. While ʿUrwa gained prominence as one of the earliest compilers of *maghāzī*, it should be borne in mind that he was primarily a scholar of *ḥadīth* and one of Medina's leading jurists (*fuqahāʾ*). Thus, his focus on the Medinan period could simply be a result of his professional interest as a scholar. Given that the life of the Prophet prior to his call to prophecy did not have legal implications, it might not have been of interest to him. The same might be true for supernatural events. Therefore, the rarity of miraculous accounts in ʿUrwa's corpus is not necessarily based on the scholars' general rejection of the notion of miracles as part of Muḥammad's biography as early Western scholars like Andrae have suggested. These kinds of narratives were already part of the scholarly discourse in al-Zuhrī's generation and possibly earlier. If these assumptions are accurate, then ʿUrwa's corpus might not necessarily be representative of all the accounts circulated by his generation of scholars and

104 Ibn Saʿd, *Ṭabaqāt*, 1:156. An extended version of this account is found in Ibn Kathīr, *al-Sīra*, 1:241.

105 Qāḍī Iyād, *al-Shifāʾ*, 1:321f.; Ibn Saʿd, *Ṭabaqāt*, 1:158.

106 ʿAbd al-Razzāq, *al-Muṣannaf*, 5:313–320.

supernatural events such as the ones Wahb recounted may have been part of the earliest discourse. Armstrong has shown that, while Wahb b. Munabbih came to be affiliated with stories of pre-Islamic prophets, the early sources rarely refer to him explicitly as a *qāṣṣ* and the earliest biographers did not view him as such.[107]

•••

The overlap between the corpora of ʿUrwa and Wahb on the prophetic biography are limited to the accounts of the *hijra*. Therefore, they are not sufficient to provide a general overview of the materials that were in circulation among the earliest "scholarly" and the "unauthenticated" traditions, nor do they allow us to trace the trajectory of individual narratives entering the *sīra* literature over time. They do show, however, that the two strands often contain very similar material and did not contradict, but rather complement, each other in many instances. Divergences in details occur not only between the accounts of ʿUrwa and Wahb, but also between various transmissions of ʿUrwa's material. The greatest divergence between the two narratives lies in the numerous supernatural elements that are only found in Wahb's corpus. This does not necessarily support the view that the "scholarly" tradition did not include such elements in its discourse, particularly given that ʿUrwa himself includes at least one such event in a different account and the scholars of the subsequent generation all included various supernatural accounts of Muḥammad in their collections. All of this suggests that the discourse on Muḥammad's biography continued to allow for flexibility in the material, depending on its intended audience or purpose, and also that there was not yet a clear-cut dichotomy between "scholarly" and "unauthenticated" traditions. Thus, this textual comparison corroborates more recent research about the religious and social roles *quṣṣāṣ* played in the first/seventh century and suggests that religious scholars and *quṣṣāṣ* operated in overlapping social circles. This more refined view of the networks in which early biographic accounts of Muḥammad may have emerged has significant implications for our re-evaluation of *dalāʾil al-nubūwa* literature since many of the premises regarding its origin in circles of *quṣṣāṣ* have been successfully questioned here.

107 Armstrong, *The Quṣṣāṣ of Early Islam*, 94.

CHAPTER 2

Biographies of the Earliest *Dalāʾil al-Nubūwa* Authors

Dalāʾil al-nubūwa compilations span a period from the mid-second/eighth century through to the twentieth and twenty-first centuries. Given that the literature was categorized as popular and subsequently marginalized by scholars of Islamic studies, in large part due to the significant gaps in its early textual history, I focus my study on the early and least studied texts, from the first specimen up to the most widely-known works of the fifth/eleventh century. Theodor Nöldeke and Tor Andrae have pointed out that this type of literature had its predecessor in the *sīra* section of Ibn Saʿd's *Ṭabaqāt*,[1] and Meir Jacob Kister indicated that Ibn Saʿd may have benefited from the antecedent in Maʿmar b. Rāshid;[2] however, these scholars were not aware of the scope of *dalāʾil al-nubūwa* works and still labeled the later *dalāʾil al-nubūwa* works of Abū Nuʿaym al-Iṣfahānī (d. 430/1038) and al-Bayhaqī (d. 458/1066) as among the earliest authors, without recognizing that there was a continuous tradition of these works that began more than two hundred years earlier.

In the following, I identify the authors of the earliest *ḥadīth* compilations specifically dedicated to the theme of *dalāʾil al-nubūwa* in order to show that this literature was squarely positioned in the scholarly works of their time. The compilations considered here are either independent works by an individual author that are entirely dedicated to the topic of the signs of prophecy or chapters in multi-themed *ḥadīth* collections. The majority of early book-length works seems to be no longer extant and, thus, do not allow for any examination of their contents or structure. Therefore, my decision to include them in this study is based on their titles, which are usually *dalāʾil al-nubūwa*, *ʿalām al-nubūwa*, *amarāt al-nubūwa*, or semantically related variations listed in biographical and bibliographical dictionaries. I am aware that using the titles as a selection paradigm carries inherent risks, as it is not uncommon for works to be known by various titles or for the works to have been (re)named by individuals other than the authors. In cases of extant works, both monographs and chapters in larger collections, these doubts can be addressed by studying their

1 Andrae, *Die Person Muhammeds*, 26–91. See also Horovitz, *Earliest Biographies*, 120; Nöldeke, *Geschichte des Qorāns*, 2:135.
2 Kister, "The Sīrah Literature," 356.

 | DOI:10.1163/9789004687349_004

content and structure and evaluating whether or not the author, in fact, used the signs of prophecy as a foundational notion around which to organize his compilation. Nevertheless, there is value in considering even those works for which we only have an entry in a bibliographical dictionary. The mere fact that these titles were associated with certain scholars shows that the theme itself was recognizable to a larger scholarly audience and was not a type of marginalized popular literature, and this holds true regardless of whether or not we can verify an individual work's existence and contents.

A few words must be said about the notion of authorship in this regard. Given that even the earliest scholars in question, such as Maʿmar b. Rāshid and Ibn Saʿd, drew on existing written sources and authenticated oral reports, the understanding of authorship should be expanded beyond the narrow sense of an individual composer of a literary work. The act of compiling works of *ḥadīth* may not require the same level of literary involvement as the composition of an original work of fiction, but it still necessitates a creative process of selecting, omitting, and arranging accounts in a particular way which, in this case, actively influences the molding of Muḥammad's life story. But here, the implications go beyond the articulation of a biographic narrative. The selection of these accounts and the way the compiler chose to organize and present them in his work may also have a theological and doctrinal importance with regard to the kinds of events he presents as having evidentiary value to Muḥammad's prophetic mission.[3] It is this particular act of creating theologically relevant epistemological paradigms of prophecy that I consider the most significant contribution of authors of *dalāʾil al-nubūwa* literature.

Given the large number of compilers, it is beyond the scope of this chapter to provide exhaustive biographies for each of them. Rather, I present short sketches of their lives that enable us to identify the individual authors of these works. In addition, these biographical sketches allow us to conduct a network analysis, by studying their interactions with one another; this, in turn, lays the groundwork for later chapters, in which I investigate whether authors who interacted closely with one another chose similar narratives for their notion of "proofs of prophecy." Finally, these biographical summaries include information about the scholars' legal and theological orientations, as available, in order to place them in a larger intellectual landscape. In subsequent chapters, this background provides us with an opportunity to contextualize their

3 Andrew Newmann has argued similarly that the early Shīʿī *ḥadīth* collections by al-Kulaynī, al-Ṣaffār, and al-Barqī differed in content and arrangement due to differing statements about theological truths in Twelver Shīʿism, see Newmann, *The Formative Period of Twelver Shīʿism*, particularly 193–201.

respective methodological approaches as well as their selective emphases and their notions of the "proof of prophecy" with regard to religious disciplines and particular legal or theological schools of thought.

With regard to the parameters of selecting authors and works for this chapter, I focus on *ḥadīth*-based *dalāʾil al-nubūwa* works. Accordingly, this chapter only includes authors whose works consist of accounts from *ḥadīth* or *sīra*, and does not include theologically oriented collections with similar titles, such as *Kitāb Ḥujjaj al-nubūwa* by al-Jāḥiẓ (d. 255/868–869) or *Tathbīt dalāʾil al-nubūwa* by ʿAbd al-Jabbār al-Hamadhānī (d. 415/1025). I have divided the authors of *ḥadīth*-based *dalāʾil al-nubūwa* works into four generations to establish a better sense of chronology. Given that many of these works are no longer extant, a chronological arrangement by composition is often not possible. Therefore, these works are arranged roughly based on the death dates of their authors. Note that this division is intended to provide a structure to orient readers and follow the literature's evolution. As such, these generational divisions are often approximated groupings rather than clear-cut distinctions based on essential characteristics of the authors' biographies or works.

1 The First Generation

The earliest compilations of "signs of prophecy" appear in the mid-second/eighth century, at a time when most religious sciences, including *ḥadīth* scholarship, were still in the process of articulating specific methodologies and boundaries between them were not always clear-cut. Therefore, it does not come as a surprise that *dalāʾil al-nubūwa* authors in this period have a variety of disciplinary backgrounds, though they are all part of scholarly circles.

The first author, Maʿmar b. Rāshid (d. 153/770), is a fixture in the early biographical tradition of the Prophet through his *maghāzī* work, one of the earliest surviving books on the subject. Originally a Persian slave from Basra, Maʿmar was deeply steeped in Arabic language and Islamic culture and learning, and allegedly sought knowledge from famous Basran scholars such as Qatāda b. Diʿāma (d. 117/735) and Ḥasan al-Baṣrī (d. 110/728).[4] Maʿmar traveled the Islamic world as a trader for his masters; this allowed him to expand his studies beyond the limits of his native city. He serendipitously became a student of the leading scholar Ibn Shihāb al-Zuhrī (d. 124/742) during his stay at the caliphal court in Ruṣāfā. Maʿmar's transmission of al-Zuhrī's materials was highly desirable in the eyes of other scholars, as Maʿmar was able to recite memorized traditions

4 Ibn Rāshid, trans. Anthony, *The Expeditions*, xxvi.

back to al-Zuhrī for review and correction.[5] Later, as Syria descended into the violence of the third civil war, Maʿmar settled in Sanaa for the last twenty years of his life. There he became part of what Scott Lucas called a brief efflorescence of *ḥadīth* scholarship;[6] he transmitted *ḥadīth* to major scholars, including ʿAbd al-Razzāq b. Hammām (d. 211/827), who claimed to have studied with Maʿmar for seven years and who was responsible for putting much of Maʿmar's work into writing. Among the texts preserved by ʿAbd al-Razzāq is Maʿmar's *al-Jāmiʿ*, which is included as an appendix in ʿAbd al-Razzāq's *Muṣannaf*.[7] *Al-Jāmiʿ* contains a short chapter entitled "Bāb al-nubūwa," which contains six *ḥadīth*s and which Kister identified as the earliest thematic compilation of what later developed into *dalāʾil al-nubūwa* literature.[8] Interest in compiling *ḥadīth* about signs of Muḥammad's prophecy increased significantly after Maʿmar's lifetime, as dedicated chapters in multi-thematic works grew in length and the first independent works on the subject began to emerge.

The second known compilation on the subject was penned by Ibn Saʿd (d. 230/845). Born in Basra around 167/784, he died in Baghdad. Only a little is known of his life: He studied with the leading scholars of Medina and later moved to Baghdad, where he became a scribe and transmitter of al-Wāqidī.[9] Among his teachers was ʿAbd al-Razzāq b. Hammām. While the majority of his teachers were praised as reputable scholars of *ḥadīth* in Sunnī biographical dictionaries, the eighth-/fourteenth-century Ḥanbalī scholar al-Dhahabī considered two of them, Hishām b. al-Kalbī (d. 206/822) and Muḥammad b. ʿUmar al-Wāqidī (d. 207/823), weak in *ḥadīth* but invaluable in historical traditions (*akhbār*).[10] Ibn Saʿd's famous biographical dictionary *Kitāb al-Ṭabaqāt al-kubrā* is his only work that has come down to us. The work opens with the biography of the Prophet, which constitutes the earliest fully extant *sīra* after Ibn Hishām's edition of Ibn Isḥāq.[11] Ibn Saʿd's biography of the Prophet includes two extensive thematic chapters describing the "signs of prophecy" (*ʿalāmāt al-nubūwa*); one is dedicated to "signs" preceding Muḥammad's call to prophecy, the other one presents "signs" subsequent to the first revelation.

5 Ibn Rāshid, trans. Anthony, xxvi.
6 Lucas, *Constructive Critics*, 71f.
7 Cf. ʿAbd al-Razzāq, *Muṣannaf*, 10:379–468, vol. 11.
8 Kister, "The Sirah Literature," 356.
9 Fück, "Ibn Saʿd," 3:922; for references in biographical dictionaries, cf. Horovitz, *Earliest Biographers*, 118 n. 129; Mūsā, *Ibn Saʿd wa-ṭabaqātuhu*, 17.
10 Al-Dhahabī, *Tadhkirat al-ḥuffāẓ*, 1:250 (Ibn al-Kalbī), and 254 (al-Wāqidī).
11 It has been debated whether this biographical account originally existed as an independent work entitled *Akhbār al-nabī*; see Loth, *Classenbuch*, 24–34; cf. Horovitz, *Earliest Biographers*, 120. For a succinct summary of the entire debate, including the reference to Arabic biographical dictionaries, see Mūsā, *Ibn Saʿd wa-ṭabaqāquhu*, 23f.

Their significance in Ibn Saʿd's biography is attested by the fact that these two chapters are the most voluminous ones of his entire *sīra* section, containing forty-seven and forty-two accounts respectively. Ibn Saʿd was a student of ʿAbd al-Razzāq, who, as noted, was Maʿmar b. Rāshid's student and wrote much of his teacher's materials. Thus Ibn Saʿd's interest in the signs of prophecy might have been influenced by Maʿmar's short chapter on the same subject. In chapter 3, I explore the issue of whether they compiled similar narratives in their respective chapters.

Around the same time Ibn Saʿd compiled his two extensive chapters, the first book-length *dalāʾil al-nubūwa* works emerged among contemporaneous *ḥadīth* scholars and early Muʿtazilī figures. As such, Ibn al-Nadīm ascribed a book entitled *Ḥujja fī ithbāt al-nabī* to the alleged founder of the Muʿtazilī school of Baghdad, Bishr al-Muʿtamir (d. 209–210/825–826), and a work of *aʿlām al-nubūwa* to the caliph al-Maʾmūn (r. 198–218/813–833), who famously enforced Muʿtazilism as the creed of the state.[12] The correlations between *ḥadīth*-based *dalāʾil al-nubūwa* compilations and other disciplines' interest in the subject is discussed in a later chapter; it is noteworthy that interest in the signs of prophecy during this period was not restricted to circles of *ḥadīth* scholarship. One of Ibn Saʿd's colleagues was Abū Bakr al-Ḥumaydī (d. 219/834), a *ḥadīth* scholar from Mecca who accompanied al-Shāfiʿī to Egypt and stayed there until al-Shāfiʿī's death in 204/820, then eventually returned to his native Mecca.[13] He transmitted from al-Shāfiʿī,[14] Sufyān b. ʿUyayna (d. 196/811),[15] and others. Al-Ḥumaydī studied with Sufyān for nineteen years,[16] and was in charge of transmitting his teacher's material.[17] Al-Ḥumaydī was generally considered a reliable transmitter[18] and his material was passed down by renowned *ḥadīth* scholars (*muḥaddithūn*) like al-Bukhārī (d. 256/870),[19] Muslim (d. 261/875), Ibn Mājah (d. 273/ 887), Abū Dāwūd (d. 275/889), al-Tirmidhī (d. 279/892), al-Nisāʾī (d. 302/915), Abū Zurʿa al-Rāzī (d. 264/878), and Abū Ḥātim al-Rāzī

12 Ibn al-Nadīm, *Fihrist*, 162 and 129, respectively. Neither book has been preserved.

13 Sezgin, *GAS*, 1:101f.

14 Sezgin, *GAS*, 1:101f.

15 Ibn Saʿd, *Ṭabaqāt*, 5:502; al-Bukhārī, *Kitāb al-Tārīkh al-kabīr*, 5:7f.; al-Dhahabī, *Tadhkirat al-ḥuffāẓ*, 413f.

16 Al-Bukhārī, *Kitāb al-Tārīkh al-kabīr*, 5:7 f.

17 Ibn Saʿd, *Ṭabaqāt*, 5:502.

18 Ibn Saʿd, *Ṭabaqāt*, 5:502.

19 Sezgin found excerpts of al-Ḥumaydī's books in direct transmission in thirty-three passages in al-Bukhārī's *Kitāb al-Tārīkh al-kabīr*, who also quotes him forty times via intermediaries; Sezgin, *GAS*, 1:101f.

(d. 322/934).[20] Ḥājjī Khalīfa/Kātib Çelebī mentions his *dalāʾil al-nubūwa*,[21] which has not been preserved.

The second author of an independent *dalāʾil al-nubūwa* work was Abū l-Ḥasan al-Madāʾinī (d. between 224 and 231/839 and 845), who was born 161/777 in Basra but lived in Madāʾin and later went to Baghdad.[22] Al-Madāʾinī authored *muṣannaf* works[23] and was considered one of the greatest *ḥadīth* scholars of his era and was praised for his expertise in criticizing *ḥadīth* narrations (*ʿilāl*).[24] As a student, he heard traditions from his father, Ḥammād b. Zayd, Hashīm, Sufyān b. ʿUyayna,[25] and ʿAbd al-Razzāq b. Hammām.[26] In addition to *ḥadīth* proper, he was learned in the traditions (*akhbār*) of the Arabs and their genealogies; the history of the conquests (*maghāzī*); and in the transmission of poetry.[27] The sources provide lists of his students. Al-Khaṭīb al-Baghdādī names al-Zubayr b. Bakkār, Aḥmad al-Khazzāz, al-Ḥārith b. Usāma, and al-Ḥasan b. ʿAlī b. al-Mutawakkil as people that related *ḥadīth* from him.[28] Al-Bukhārī and al-Dhahabī (d. 748/1348) also mention that Aḥmad b. Ḥanbal (d. 241/855) heard *ḥadīth* from him.[29] Furthermore, al-Dhahabī lists al-Dhahalī, Abū Dāwūd, Ismāʿīl al-Qāḍī, Abū Yaʿal, and al-Baghawī as his students.[30] Opinions diverge with regard to the year of al-Madāʾinī's death. According to Ibn Saʿd, al-Madāʾinī died in Samarra in 234/849.[31] Al-Khaṭīb al-Baghdādī states that he died in 224/839 or 225/840 aged 93.[32]

According to Ibn al-Nadīm, al-Madāʾinī authored some 200 books on various historical subjects such as the Quraysh, the caliphs, the Arabs, and poets, as well as works on the conquests and *ḥadīth*.[33] The list of al-Madāʾinī's works on the Prophet himself includes thirty titles covering aspects of the Muḥammad's life such as his ancestors, marriages, physical appearance, campaigns/conquests (*maghāzī*), his correspondence to rulers, his vows, pledges, and more.

20 Al-Dhahabī, *Tadhkirat al-ḥuffāẓ*, 413f.; Ibn Ḥajar al-ʿAsqalānī, *Tahdhīb al-tahdhīb*, 2:334f.
21 Kātib Çelebī/Ḥājjī Khalīfa, *Kashf al-ẓunūn*, 2:1418.
22 Sezgin, *GAS*, 1:108.
23 Al-Khaṭīb al-Baghdādī, *Tārīkh Baghdād*, 12:54f.
24 Sezgin, *GAS*, 1:108.
25 Al-Dhahabī, *Tadhkirat al-ḥuffāẓ*, 428f.
26 Sezgin, *GAS*, 1:108.
27 Al-Khaṭīb al-Baghdādī, *Tārīkh Baghdād*, 12:54f.
28 Al-Khaṭīb al-Baghdādī, *Tārīkh Baghdād*, 12:54f.
29 Al-Bukhārī, *Kitāb al-Tārīkh al-kabīr*, 6:113f.; al-Dhahabī, *Tadhkirat al-ḥuffāẓ*, 428f.
30 Al-Dhahabī, *Tadhkirat al-ḥuffāẓ*, 428f.
31 Ibn Saʿd, *Ṭabaqāt*, 7:308.
32 Al-Khaṭīb al-Baghdādī, *Tārīkh Baghdād*, 12:54f.
33 Ibn al-Nadīm, *Fihrist*, 2:315–323; cf. Ibn Ḥajar al-ʿAsqalānī, *Tahdhīb al-tahdhīb*, 7:357.

It also mentions one work dedicated to the Prophet's "signs" (*ayāt al-nabī*).[34] None of these books seems to be extant.

A picture emerges that clearly positions all the earliest authors of *dalāʾil al-nubūwa* works in the scholarly tradition, though their specific fields varied. Ibn Saʿd in particular contributed less to *ḥadīth* scholarship proper and more to its auxiliary field of investigating narrators (*ʿilm al-rijāl*). This first generation of *dalāʾil al-nubūwa* authors were, furthermore, linked in one way or another, and we find many sharing prominent teachers. All drew on the materials of Ibn Shihāb al-Zuhrī (d. 124/742), either directly or through his student Sufyān b. ʿUyayna (d. 196/811). Sufyān was a Qurʾān commentator, jurisprudent, and most prominently, a *ḥadīth* scholar[35] who had studied with al-Zuhrī and was considered one of his major transmitters.[36] The three authors who compiled more extensive material on the signs of prophecy, al-Ḥumaydī, al-Madāʾinī, and Ibn Saʿd, were not only contemporaries, they also shared several of their teachers. As such, all three studied with Sufyān b. ʿUyayna,[37] although it cannot be established whether or not they studied with him at the same time. Thus, theoretically, the compilations of Ibn Saʿd, al-Ḥumaydī, and al-Madāʾinī could offer a comparison as to whether they shared a corpus of accounts that could be traced back to their teacher Sufyān b. ʿUyayna. Unfortunately, the textual basis is insufficient for us to draw such conclusions, given that the only preserved work of al-Ḥumaydī is his *Musnad* and nothing remains of al-Madāʾinī's works. "Sufyān" is mentioned 1,252 times in al-Ḥumaydī's *Musnad*. Yet, there are no obvious parallels in the accounts of al-Ḥumaydī and Ibn Saʿd.[38] Even if the records in al-Humaydī's *Musnad* and Ibn Saʿd's chapters on the signs of prophecy overlapped, the assumption that al-Ḥumaydī also included these accounts in his *dalāʾil al-nubūwa* would be conjectural, as we have no textual evidence from al-Ḥumaydī's *dalāʾil* work itself.

While neither al-Zuhrī nor Sufyān seems to have written on signs of prophecy specifically, various *dalāʾil al-nubūwa* authors of this generation were connected to the earliest author of this literature, Maʿmar b. Rāshid. Ibn Saʿd

---

34 Ibn al-Nadīm, *Fihrist*, 2:316.

35 Spectorsky, "Sufyān b. ʿUyayna"; cf. Sezgin, *GAS*, 1:96; Kaḥḥāla, *Muʿjam al-muʾallifīn*, 4:235.

36 Spectorsky, "Sufyān b. ʿUyayna"; Juynboll has pointed out that there was debate whether al-Madāʾinī might have been too young to study with al-Zuhrī; cf. Juynboll, *Encyclopedia of Canonical Ḥadīth*, 568.

37 For al-Ḥumaydī and al-Madāʾinī, see above; for Ibn Saʿd, see Mūsā, *Ibn Saʿd wa-ṭabaqātuhu*, 19.

38 Furthermore, traditions on the authority of Sufyān in the six canonical collections rarely relate to the Prophet's life and there are no accounts of *dalāʾil al-nubūwa* or similar contents; cf. Juynboll, *Encyclopedia of Canonical Ḥadīth*, 568–621; cf. Wensinck, *Concordance*, 8:105f.

is indirectly linked with him through the intermediary ʿAbd al-Razzāq b. Hammām, from whom Ibn Saʿd received Maʿmar's material,[39] and al-Madāʾinī also studied with him. Given that the texts of al-Ḥumaydī and al-Madāʾinī are no longer extant, our knowledge of what the first generation of compilers gathered as "signs of prophecy" is restricted to the small chapter in Maʿmar's *al-Jāmiʿ* and the two chapters in Ibn Saʿd's *Ṭabaqāt*.

2 The Second Generation

The second generation of early contributors to *dalāʾil al-nubūwa* literature includes some of the most prominent *ḥadīth* scholars of the third/ninth century. Abū Isḥāq Ibrāhīm b. Yaʿqūb b. Isḥāq al-Saʿdī l-Jūzajānī (d. 259/873) was born toward the end of the second/eighth century, probably during the reign of Hārūn al-Rashīd (r. 169–183/786–809).[40] There are a number of uncertainties about his biography. It is not known where he was born, but his *nisba* suggests Jūzajān.[41] Even though al-Jūzajānī traveled widely in search of *ḥadīth*, information about his journeys tends to be scarce. Given that a number of his teachers who died before 210/826 were people from Jūzajān, Kufa, Basra, and Baghdad, it seems likely that he visited these places at a young age. It is attested that he traveled to Hamadhan in the year 230/845 or 232/847, and to Egypt in 245/860; we have no details about his trips to Mecca, al-Ramla, and Basra. His biographers agree that he eventually settled in Damascus, and during his time there, he corresponded frequently with Aḥmad b. Ḥanbal.[42] Some of his later biographers, such as Ibn Ḥibbān (d. 354/965), Ibn ʿAdī al-Jurjānī (d. 365/976), and al-Dāraquṭnī (d. 385/995), sought to discredit him among Sunnī scholars by claiming that he harbored ʿAlid tendencies. However, none of these scholars were al-Jūzajānī's students or otherwise in contact with him, and those who were in contact with him, including Aḥmad b. Ḥanbal, never mention any ʿAlid tendencies. Al-Jūzajānī died in Damascus in 259/873.

Al-Jūzajānī was clearly a well-established participant in the circles of *muḥaddithūn*. Biographical dictionaries list that he had a total of 137 teachers,

39 Horovitz, *Earliest Biographers*, 74.

40 The exact date of birth is not known. Based on the fact that some of his teachers died in 203/819, al-Bastawī estimated that al-Jūzajānī was born in the 180s/800s; cf. al-Bastawī, *al-Imām al-Jūzajānī*, 10f.

41 According to Yāqūt (*Kitāb Muʿjam al-buldān*), Jūzajān or Jūzajānān are the same, referring to a vast rural district in Khurasan between Balkh and Merv, with cities like Fāryāb, al-Anbār and Kilār. cf. al-Bastawī, *al-Imām al-Jūzajānī*, 11ff.

42 Al-Bastawī, *al-Imām al-Jūzajānī*, 39.

including Ibn Maʿīn (d. 233/848), Isḥāq b. Rahawayh al-Ḥanẓalī (d. 238/852 or 853), and Aḥmad b. Ḥanbal (d. 241/855).[43] He was a contemporary of al-Bukhārī, and Muslim (d. 261/875),[44] and his students included Abū Dāwūd (d. 275/889), al-Tirmidhī, al-Nisāʾī, Abū Zurʿa al-Rāzī, Abū Ḥātim Muḥammad b. Idrīs al-Rāzī (d. 277/891), Abū Zurʿa al-Dimashqī (d. 281/894), and al-Ṭabarī (d. 310/923).[45] Thus, the list of his teachers and students firmly positions him in the realm of *ḥadīth* scholarship. Indeed, al-Jūzajānī was a famously critical scholar who required that accounts be backed up with sound chains of transmission.[46]A total of seven books are attested to him. Four of these pertain to *ḥadīth* sciences, *Aḥwāl al-rijāl, al-Mutarjim, al-Jarḥ wa-l-taʿdīl, Kitāb al-Ḍuʿafāʾ*, one records his correspondence with Ibn Ḥanbal (*Masāʾil al-Imām Aḥmad*), one is a historical work (*al-Tārīkh*), and finally his work dedicated to the signs of prophecy (*Amārāt al-nubūwa*).[47] This last work is preserved in a unique unpublished manuscript fragment in the Ẓāhiriyya collection.[48]

The list of early *dalāʾil al-nubūwa* contributors also includes three compilers whose *ḥadīth* collections later became part of the six canonical *ḥadith* collections of Sunnī Islam, namely, those of al-Bukhārī, al-Tirmidhī, and Abū Dāwūd. The earliest of these three, al-Bukhārī, was a contemporary and student of al-Jūzajānī. Having finished his elementary studies in his native town of Bukhara at the age of eleven, al-Bukhārī immersed himself in the study of *ḥadīth* and started a series of journeys during which he passed through all the important centers of Islamic learning, including the major cities of Iraq, the Hijaz, and Egypt. Al-Bukhārī's educational journey continued for some four decades; among his numerous teachers, he counted al-Ḥumaydī,[49] al-Jūzajānī, and Isḥāq b. Rāhawayh al-Ḥanẓalī. Al-Ḥanẓalī allegedly mentioned to al-Bukhārī that he wished a scholar would compile a comprehensive book containing only sound *ḥadīth* and this is said to have inspired al-Bukhārī to compile his *Ṣaḥīḥ*.[50] Al-Bukhārī's magnum opus, in fact, contains a substantial chapter called "ʿAlāmāt al-nubūwa fī l-Islām" of more than sixty *ḥadīth*; this makes it the second most extensive chapter on *ʿalāmāt* of his generation.

43 For a complete list, please see al-Bastawī, *al-Imām al-Jūzajānī*, 16–26.
44 Al-Bastawī, *al-Imām al-Jūzajānī*, 9.
45 For a full list of his students, see al-Bastawī, *al-Imām al-Jūzajānī*, 27–30.
46 Al-Bastawī, *al-Imām al-Jūzajānī*, 40.
47 Al-Bastawī, *al-Imām al-Jūzajānī*, 35–37.
48 Damascus Asad Library, MS Majmūʿ 104, fols. 162–165; cf. al-Albānī, *Fihris*, 250.
49 Al-Dhahabī, *Tadhkirat al-ḥuffāẓ*, 413.
50 Ṣiddīqī, *Ḥadīth Literature*, 53f.

Another contemporary of al-Jūzajānī and al-Bukhārī who is said to have penned an independent *dalāʾil al-nubūwa* work was Abū Zurʿa al-Rāzī.[51] Together with his friend Abū Ḥātim al-Rāzī, he was considered one of the most influential *ḥadīth* scholars of his time.[52] He was also a student of al-Jūzajānī and on several occasions visited Baghdad,[53] where he frequently sat with Aḥmad b. Ḥanbal (d. 241/855).[54] Ibrāhīm b. Isḥāq al-Ḥarbī (d. 285/898) was among al-Rāzī's students in Baghdad.[55] His *dalāʾil al-nubūwa* work does not seem to be extant.

The well-known *ḥadīth* compiler Abū Dāwūd Sulaymān al-Ashaʿth al-Sijistānī is, of course, most famous for his *Sunan*, but he is also associated with an independent work entitled *Aʿlām al-nubūwa*,[56] though it is not extant. Following his elementary education in his native city of Sijistān, he studied under Muḥammad b. Aslam (d. 242/856),[57] and then traveled to Basra, where he acquired most of his *ḥadīth* training. In 242/838 he visited Kufa, from where he set out to travel to the Hijaz, Iraq, Iran, Syria, and Egypt. He met most of the foremost *ḥadīth* scholars of his time, including Aḥmad b. Ḥanbal,[58] al-Jūzajānī,[59] and al-Madāʾinī,[60] and acquired from them a profound knowledge of the *ḥadīth* that were available. His most celebrated book on *ḥadīth* and Islamic law is his *Sunan*, one of the six canonical *ḥadīth* collections of Sunnī Islam.

Another compiler whose collection later gained canonical status among Sunnī scholars was Abū ʿĪsā l-Tirmidhī. Born in Mecca in 206/821, he traveled extensively in his quest for *ḥadīth*, visiting the great centers of Islamic learning in Iraq, Iran, and Khurasan, where he associated with eminent scholars, such as al-Bukhārī, Muslim, Abū Dāwūd,[61] and al-Jūzajānī.[62] He died in Tirmidh in 279/892. Al-Tirmidhī's *al-Jāmiʿ al-ṣaḥīḥ* is recognized as one of the most important works of *ḥadīth* literature, and is unanimously included among the six canonical collections of Sunnī *ḥadīth*. This collection contains a chapter

---

51 Al-Sakhāwī, *al-Iʿlān*, 91; cf. al-Iṣfahānī, *Nayl*, 1:222.

52 Sezgin, *GAS*, 1:145. He is not to be confused with the Ismāʿīlī scholar Abū Ḥātim Aḥmad b. Ḥamdān al-Rāzī (d. 322/934).

53 Al-Khaṭīb al-Baghdādī, *Tārīkh Baghdād*, 10:326.

54 Sezgin, *GAS*, 1:145.

55 Sezgin, *GAS*, 1:145.

56 Al-Sakhawī, *Iʿlān*, 91.

57 Yāqūt, *Kitāb Muʿjam al-buldān*, 3:44.

58 Al-Dhahabī, *Tadhkira al-ḥuffāẓ*, 549.

59 Al-Bastawī, *al-Imām al-Jūzajānī*, 27.

60 Al-Dhahabī, *Tadhkira al-ḥuffāẓ*, 428.

61 Ṣiddīqī, *Ḥadīth Literature*, 61f.

62 Al-Bastawī, *al-Imām al-Jūzajānī*, 27.

entitled "Bāb mā jāʾa fī ayāt nubūwat al-nabī wa-mā qad khaṣṣa Allāh bihi" of nine *ḥadīth*.

Adding to the list of widely renowned authors of *dalāʾil al-nubūwa* works is Abū Isḥāq Ibrāhīm b. Isḥāq al-Ḥarbī (d. 285/898), who studied *ḥadīth* with Aḥmad b. Ḥanbal.[63] Among his teachers were the Basran Musaddad b. Musarhad, who was linked to the Ḥanbalī school;[64] ʿAffān b. Muslim, also a *muḥaddith*; al-Qāsim b. Sallām, an exegete and man of letters;[65] and Abū Nuʿaym al-Faḍl b. Dakīn,[66] who was also a teacher of Abū Zurʿa al-Rāzī. Later biographers disagree with regard to al-Ḥarbī's school of thought. Ibn Kathīr calls him a Ḥanbalī, while al-Subkī refers to him as a Shāfiʿī.[67] Whatever his legal affiliation may have been, in terms of theology al-Ḥarbī vigorously opposed Muʿtazilism, particularly the doctrine of the createdness of the Qurʾān. He was joined in his opposition to Muʿtazilī ideas by the famous *ḥadīth* scholars Ibn Abī Shayba, Ibn al-Munādī, Ibn Ṣāʿid, and Ibn Maʿīn, who viewed themselves as promoters of Sunnī Islam.[68] Books attributed to al-Ḥarbī include *Kitāb Manāsik al-ḥajj*, *Kitāb al-Hadāyā*, and *Kitāb al-Hammām*, twenty-four collections of *ḥadīth*,[69] as well as a *dalāʾil al-nubūwa work*.[70]

Abū Bakr al-Firyābī (d. 301/913) was another *dalāʾil al-nubūwa* author who moved in similar scholarly circles as did al-Ḥarbī. Having studied *ḥadīth* in Khurasan and Transoxania, as well as in Iraq, the Hijaz, Egypt, Syria, and Mesopotamia, al-Firyābī eventually took up residence in Baghdad. Among his numerous teachers was Aḥmad b. Ḥanbal's well-known protégé Isḥāq b. Rāhawayh al-Ḥanẓalī.[71] Al-Firyābī was considered reliable in his transmissions and his lectures attracted large crowds. He died in 301/913 at the age of 94.[72] He composed a *dalāʾil al-nubūwa* work that has been preserved and edited.[73]

63 Al-Dhahabī, *Tadhkira al-ḥuffāẓ*, 584f.

64 Brockelmann, *GAL*, Suppl. 1:310.

65 Vadet, "Ibrāhīm b. Isḥāḳ."

66 Al-Dhahabī, *Tadhkira al-ḥuffāẓ*, 584f.

67 Cf. Ibn Kathīr, *al-Bidāya*, 9:79; al-Subkī, *Ṭabaqāt al-Shāfiʿiyya al-kubrā*, 1:26.

68 Vadet, "Ibrāhīm b. Isḥāḳ."

69 Vadet, "Ibrāhīm b. Isḥāḳ."

70 Kātib Çelebī/Ḥājjī Khalīfa, *Kashf al-ẓunūn*, 1:860; al-Iṣfahānī, *Nayl*, 223.

71 Al-Khaṭīb al-Baghdādī, *Tārīkh Baghdād*, 7:200; for extensive lists of his teachers, see al-Khaṭīb al-Baghdādī, *Tārīkh Baghdād*, 7:199–202.; al-Firyābī, *Kitāb Dalāʾil al-nubūwa*, 1:10f.

72 Al-Khaṭīb al-Baghdādī, *Tārīkh Baghdād*, 7:199–202.

73 Al-Firyābī, *Kitāb Dalāʾil al-nubūwa*.

Abū Sulayman Dāwūd b. ʿAlī b. Khalaf al-Iṣbahānī l-Ẓāhirī (d. 270/884) was born in Kufa around 199/815.[74] His family was originally from Isfahan.[75] He went to Nishabur to study with Isḥāq b. Rahwayh al-Ḥanẓalī before going on to Baghdad, where he lived and authored his books.[76] Originally a Shāfiʿī, his tendency to reject human reason and to rely solely on the Qurʾān and *ḥadīth* eventually went beyond the Shāfiʿī practice and later became a pivotal approach of the *madhhab* that bore his name though it died out around the eighth/fourteenth century. Ibn al-Nadīm lists him as the author of a work entitled *Aʿlām al-nubūwa*, which seems to be lost.[77]

Being a scholar of *ḥadīth*, theology, and most famously a writer of *adab*, Abū l-ʿAbbās Muḥammad b. al-Ḥasan b. Qutayba (d. 276/889) was one of the great Sunnī polymaths of the third/ninth century. He was born in Kufa in 213/828, but little is known of his early life. Biographers have produced long lists of his teachers,[78] and Lecomte has identified Isḥāq b. Ibrāhīm b. Rāhawayh al-Ḥanẓalī as someone who greatly influenced the young Ibn Qutayba.[79] After the trials (*miḥna*) imposed by al-Maʾmūn, Ibn Qutayba found himself popular because of his literary works; he was appointed *qāḍī* of Dinavar around 236/851 and held the office for nearly twenty years. After 257/871, Ibn Qutayba devoted himself to teaching his works in a district of Baghdad until his death.[80] Ibn Qutayba authored a work called *ʿAlām al-nubūwa*, of which an incomplete and apparently unique manuscript was preserved in the Dār al-Kutub al-Ẓāhiriyya library in Damascus.[81] This work is not a *ḥadīth*-based collection, rather it consists of biblical and, mostly, pseudo-biblical passages that were used to buttress the Qurʾān's position that Muḥammad's prophetic mission was predicted in previous scriptures and therefore provides further evidence of the veracity of his prophecy. Despite this very different methodological approach, its contemporaneous existence with the *ḥadīth*-based *dalāʾil al-nubūwa* works gives us a sense of contemporary debates around prophecy in other Islamic disciplines.[82]

Abū Bakr ʿAbdallāh b. Muḥammad b. ʿUbayd b. Sufyān b. Qays (d. 281/894), commonly known as Ibn Abī l-Dunyā, was a teacher and author of

74 Brockelmann, *GAL*, 1:183; Suppl. 1:312; Sezgin, *GAS*, 1:312.

75 Al-Khaṭīb al-Baghdādī, *Tārīkh Baghdād*, 8:369.

76 Al-Khaṭīb al-Baghdādī, *Tārīkh Baghdād*, 8:369.

77 Ibn al-Nadīm, *Fihrist*, 272.

78 For instance, al-Dhahabī, *Tadhkirat al-ḥuffāẓ*, 1:764.

79 Lecomte, "Ibn Ḳutayba."

80 Cf. Lecomte, "Ibn Ḳutayba."

81 MS Majmuʿ 955/6; fols. 127a–159b. For a description of the manuscript, see al-Albānī, *Fihris*.

82 These debates are discussed in more detail in chapter 5.

muṣannaf works on asceticism[83] and edifying literature, such as those that preach patience, humility, penitence, trust in God, silence, frugality, and so forth.[84] He also authored an *ʿalām al-nubūwa* work,[85] though it seems to be lost. Ibn Abī Ḥātim was among those who transmitted *ḥadīth* on Ibn Abī Dunyā's authority and said that both he himself and his father wrote *ḥadīth* they had learned from Ibn Abī l-Dunyā;[86] this suggests that Ibn Abī l-Dunyā may have been in contact with the *ḥadīth* scholar Abū Ḥātim Muḥammad b. Idrīs al-Rāzī.

While the previously mentioned authors of this second generation were interconnected, Abū Isḥāq Ibrāhīm b. al-Haytham b. al-Muhallab (d. 278/891), a *ḥadīth* scholar in Baghdad who is said to have written a *dalāʾil al-nubūwa* work,[87] does not appear to have been connected to any of the other authors of this kind of literature at his time.[88]

Based on these biographies, we see some clear patterns among the authors of *dalāʾil al-nubūwa* work during the third/ninth century. First, like their predecessors, all the contributors to this literature in this generation are widely acknowledged scholars, not untrained storytellers or preachers. Their affiliation to *ḥadīth* scholarship increased as the vast majority of the authors primarily focused on the compilation and transmission of prophetic traditions. The only exceptions to this are Ibn Qutayba, who wrote on a variety of subjects, including, most prominently, *adab*, and whose *dalāʾil al-nubūwa* is not a *ḥadīth*-based compilation, and Ibn Abī Dunyā, whose works are devoted to ethics and piety.

The ongoing interconnections of *dalāʾil al-nubūwa* authors is, furthermore, a hallmark of the second generation. On the one hand, there are connections between members of this generation and the preceding one. Abū Zurʿa al-Rāzī and al-Bukhārī, for instance, were both students of al-Ḥumaydī, while al-Madāʾinī was a teacher of Abū Dāwūd. Abū Dāwūd and al-Ḥarbī both studied with Ibn Ḥanbal. Abū Dāwūd, al-Tirmidhī, al-Firyābī, al-Ẓāhirī, and Ibn Qutayba all studied with al-Ḥanẓalī. Al-Bukhārī, Abū Dāwūd, and al-Tirmidhī were all students of al-Jūzajānī, who authored works on *dalāʾil al-nubūwa*. The following chart visualizes the personal relationships between scholars involved in the transmission of *dalāʾil al-nubūwa* compilations. The dark blue boxes in this chart represent authors of self-contained works, boxes with

83 Al-Khaṭīb al-Baghdādī, *Tārīkh Baghdād*, 10:89.

84 Dietrich, "Ibn Abī al-Dunyā," 3:684. For an extensive list of works, see al-Dhahabī, *Siyar aʿlām al-nubulāʾ*, 13:401f.

85 Al-Dhahabī, *Siyar aʿlām al-nubulāʾ*, 13:401.

86 Al-Dhahabī, *Siyar aʿlām al-nubulāʾ* 13:399; al-Dhahabī, *Tadhkirat al-ḥuffāẓ*, 1:687.

87 Al-Sakhawī, *al-Iʿlān*, 91.

88 For a list of his teachers and students, see al-Khaṭīb al-Baghdādī, *Tārīkh Baghdād*, 6:206.

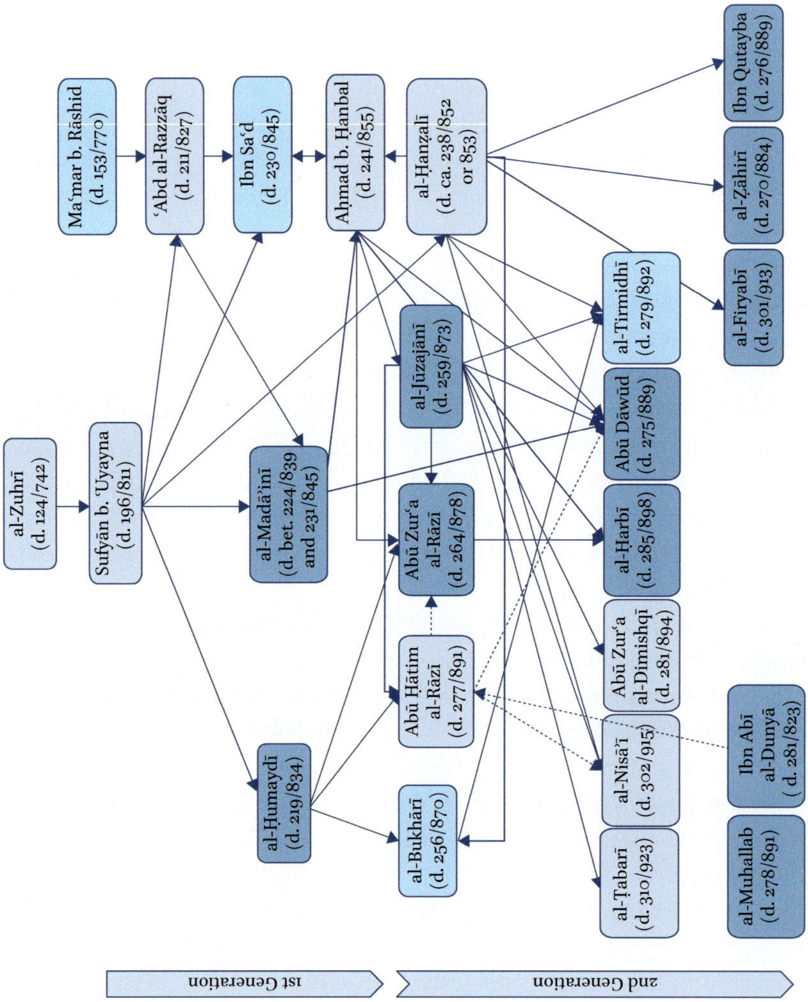

CHART 1 Network of early authors

diagonal stripes represent scholars who compiled "proofs of prophecy" as part of a multi-themed compilations, and light blue boxes identify scholars who did not author such works but are intermediary links between various authors of *dalāʾil al-nubūwa* compilations.

The chart above demonstrates that this network was centered around a circle of scholars who were associated with the *ahl al-ḥadīth* movement. Al-Jūzajānī, a central figure for the second generation of authors, was in frequent correspondence with Aḥmad b. Ḥanbal, who was in turn a student of al-Madāʾinī. A connection between these three authors and the Ḥanbalī circle is, furthermore, established through al-Bukhārī, who was a student of Ibn Ḥanbal's protégé Isḥāq b. Rāhwayh al-Ḥanẓalī. Aḥmad b. Ḥanbal's opposition to Muʿtazilī doctrine and his strict devotion to *ḥadīth* are well known. Al-Ḥanẓalī was an associate of Ibn Ḥanbal and shared his views on the pre-eminence of *ḥadīth*. Al-Ḥarbī was also known as a staunch proponent of *ḥadīth* who dismissed Muʿtazilī ideas, and al-Ẓāhirī's rejection of anything but tradition is apparent in the methodology of the *madhhab* that bears his name. While Ibn Qutayba's *Aʿlām al-nubūwa* was not a *ḥadīth* compilation but rather a collection of pseudo-biblical passages allegedly related to Muḥammad's prophecy, Sabine Schmidtke has suggested that his work mainly circulated among *ahl al-ḥadīth*. Her judgment is based on the reception of the text and the fact that the only extant manuscript of Ibn Qutayba's text is part of a *majmuʿ* that contains a total of twelve tracts by scholars belonging mostly to the *ahl al-ḥadīth*.[89] The only exceptions to this tightly knit network of scholars revolving around the *ahl al-ḥadīth* movement are Ibn Abī l-Dunyā who focused on religious ethics, and Ibn al-Muhallab who apparently had no direct relationship to any of the *dalāʾil al-nubūwa* authors I identify here, *ahl al-ḥadīth* or otherwise. This allows us to conclude that, while *dalāʾil al-nubūwa* literature was primarily centered around a network of scholars, it was not entirely restricted to this narrow group of like-minded scholars who all moved in the same intellectual circles.

3 The Third Generation

Various shifts occur among the circle of *dalāʾil al-nubūwa* authors during the fourth/tenth century that clearly distinguish the third generation from its predecessors. As such, Abū Bakr Muḥammad b. al-Ḥasan b. Muḥammad b. Ziyād al-Naqqāsh (d. 351/962) was mostly known as a Qurʾān exegete and was well-versed in the various readings of the Qurʾān. His works include an extensive

89 Schmidtke, "The Muslim Reception of Biblical Materials," 55.

tafsīr titled *Kitāb Qirāʾāt bi-ʿilaliha* and *Kitāb al-Ishāra fī gharīb al-qurʾān* as well as three *muʿjam* works.[90] He was criticized for his *ḥadīth* transmission: Abū Bakr al-Barqānī and al-Khaṭīb al-Baghdādī both stated that al-Naqqāsh's *isnād*s were unknown (*munkar*).[91] Ṭalḥa b. Muḥammad al-Shāhid said that al-Naqqāsh lied about *ḥadīth*, and the eighth-/fourteenth-century scholar al-Dhahabī labeled most of al-Naqqāsh's material as *qaṣṣāṣ*.[92] Al-Dhahabī's position may be derived from the fact that one of al-Naqqāsh's works was called *Kitāb Akhbār al-quṣṣāṣ*.[93] A work titled *Kitāb Ḍidd al-ʿaql* and a *dalāʾil al-nubūwa* were also attributed to him.[94] Hence, al-Naqqāsh was the first of the *dalāʾil al-nubūwa* authors whose reputation as a *ḥadīth* transmitter was called into question. Ibn Shāhīn, another author of a *dalāʾil al-nubūwa* work, was one of his transmitters.[95]

Abū l-Qāsim al-Ṭabarānī (d. 360/971) was a *ḥadīth* scholar who authored numerous *musnad* works, three *muʿjam* works, a *dalāʾil al-nubūwa*, and others.[96] His *dalāʾil al-nubūwa* work does not seem to be extant. Biographical dictionaries suggest that he was familiar with the material of al-Firyābī, who had also written a work on *dalāʾil al-nubūwa*, but there are contradicting views regarding whether he was a direct student of al-Firyābī or received his material through another scholar. In the *Tadhkirat al-ḥuffāẓ*, al-Dhahabī lists al-Ṭabarānī as al-Firyābī's student.[97] In the *Siyar aʿlām al-nubulāʾ*, however, al-Dhahabī does not mention al-Ṭabarānī's direct connection with al-Firyābī but rather links him with Ibrāhīm b. Abī Sufyān, who transmitted al-Firyābī's materials.[98] Al-Ṭabarānī was also linked to several authors of the subsequent generation of *dalāʾil al-nubūwa* authors, and among his students, we know of Ibn Mandah (d. 395/1005), Abū Nuʿaym al-Iṣfahānī (d. 430/1038), and al-Ṭabarānī's younger contemporary Abū l-Shaykh al-Iṣfahānī (d. 368/979).[99]

---

90 Al-Dhahabī, *Siyar aʿlām al-nubulāʾ*, 15:574f.

91 Al-Dhahabī, *Siyar aʿlām al-nubulāʾ*, 15:574f.

92 Al-Dhahabī, *Siyar aʿlām al-nubulāʾ*, 15:574f.; cf. al-Khaṭīb al-Baghdādī, *Tārīkh Baghdād*, 2:205.

93 Al-Dhahabī, *Siyar aʿlām al-nubulāʾ*, 15:574f.

94 Al-Dhahabī, *Siyar aʿlām al-nubulāʾ*, 15:574f.

95 Al-Khaṭīb al-Baghdādī, *Tarīkh Baghdād*, 2:205.

96 Al-Dhahabī, *Siyar aʿlām al-nubulāʾ*, 16:128.

97 Al-Dhahabī, *Tadhkirat al-ḥuffāẓ*, 2:315; cf. al-Firyābī, *Kitāb Dalāʾil al-nubūwa*, 10.

98 Al-Dhahabī, *Siyar aʿlām al-nubulāʾ*, 16:120.

99 Neither al-Dhahabī's *Tadhkirat al-ḥuffāẓ* nor his *Siyar aʿlām al-nubulāʾ* list Abū l-Shaykh directly as al-Ṭabarānī's student. However, the *Siyar aʿlām al-nubulāʾ* quotes Sulaymān b. Ibrāhīm al-Ḥāfiẓ relating that Abū Aḥmad al-ʿAsāl al-Qāḍī claimed to have heard 20,000 *ḥadīth* from al-Ṭabarānī, Abū Isḥāq b. Ḥamza heard 30,000, and Abū l-Shaykh heard

Abū Bakr Muḥammad b. ʿAlī l-Shāshī (d. 365/975) was a Shāfiʿī legal scholar and *muḥaddith* from the Central Asian city of Shāsh, that is, modern-day Tashkent.[100] He authored a *dalāʾil al-nubūwa* work and was in contact with two later authors of this literature. Ibn Mandah and al-Ḥākim Abū ʿAbdallāh Muḥammad b. ʿAbdallāh (d. 404/1014) relate material on his authority.[101]

This third generation of *dalāʾil al-nubūwa* authors differs significantly from the previous one with regard to its links to preceding generations. While the first two generations were interconnected through direct teacher-student relationships, we find almost no relation between the second and third generations. Only al-Ṭabarānī received *ḥadīth* material from al-Firyābī, either directly or through an intermediary. Al-Ṭabarānī was also a student of Abū Zurʿa al-Dimashqī, who did not author *dalāʾil al-nubūwa* literature himself, though he was al-Jūzajānī's student and may have been familiar with the latter's writings on the subject. Al-Naqqāsh and al-Shāshī seem unconnected to any of the previously mentioned *dalāʾil al-nubūwa* authors. In addition to their break with predecessors, we also notice a decline in the scholarly standing of these authors, as this generation features the first *ḥadīth* scholar of questionable reputation, al-Naqqāsh.

4 The Fourth Generation

Abū l-Ḥafṣ ʿUmar b. Aḥmad b. ʿUthmān b. Aḥmad al-Baghdādī (d. 385/995), commonly known as Ibn Shāhīn, studied with teachers in Syria, Iran, and Basra. He was said to be a prolific author who allegedly wrote 330 works, among them a large exegesis (*tafsīr*), a *musnad*, a history (*tārīkh*), and a work on asceticism (*zuhd*).[102] Kister also mentions a *dalāʾil al-nubūwa* work.[103] He was generally considered sound in his transmissions but was criticized for his flawed Arabic (*laḥn*) and his lack of knowledge of Islamic jurisprudence (*fiqh*).[104] It is worth noting that al-Dhahabī identifies him as a well-known preacher (*wāʿiẓ*). As we have seen, many nineteenth- and twentieth-century Western scholars commonly linked *dalāʾil al-nubūwa* works with popular preachers and storytellers, implying that they were untrained, unreliable in their transmissions, and

40,000; cf. al-Dhahabī, *Siyar aʿlām al-nubulāʾ*, 16:122; al-Dhahabī, *Tadhkirat al-ḥuffāẓ*, 3:945f.

100 Al-Dhahabī, *Siyar aʿlām al-nubulāʾ*, 16:284.

101 Al-Dhahabī, *Siyar aʿlām al-nubulāʾ*, 16:284.

102 Al-Dhahabī, *Tadhkirat al-ḥuffāẓ*, 3:988.

103 Kister, "The Sirah Literature," 355.

104 Al-Dhahabī, *Tadhkīrat al-ḥuffāẓ*, 3:988.

prone to fabrication. Ibn Shāhīn is actually the first *dalāʾil al-nubūwa* author who is directly identified as a preacher; this provides a much more nuanced insight into the intellectual context of preaching and this kind of literature. First, Ibn Shāhīn is a relatively late author in relation to the *dalāʾil al-nubūwa* works considered in this book. I have been able to identify eighteen authors of *dalāʾil al-nubūwa* works prior to Ibn Shāhīn who were not associated with or considered preachers. Furthermore, Ibn Shāhīn was labeled a preacher by an eighth-/fourteenth-century scholar al-Dhahabī, who may have been impacted by Ibn al-Jawzī's critique. But even if this were the case, it is noteworthy that Ibn Shāhīn's practice as a preacher (*wāʿiẓ*) did not impact al-Dhahabī's view of him as a reliable transmitter. Thus, Ibn Shāhīn's preaching activities do not conform to the assumptions of Orientalists' about the authors of *dalāʾil al-nubūwa* works.

Abū Muḥammad ʿAbdallāh b. Muḥammad al-Iṣfahānī (d. 368/979), known as Abū l-Shaykh, was a *ḥadīth* scholar. His works include the *Ṭabaqāt al-muḥaddithīn*, which is a biographical dictionary of *ḥadīth* scholars from Isfahan and an important source for Abū l-Nuʿaym's *Akhbār Iṣfahān*.[105] In addition, he authored a *tafsīr* (now lost), a mystical work called *Kitāb al-ʿAẓama*, and he wrote on questions of *fiqh*.[106] Al-Sakhawī attributes a work entitled *Dalāʾil al-nubūwa* to him, which—if it ever existed—has not been preserved.[107] His extant work *Akhlāq al-nabī wa-adabuhu* does not address proofs of prophecy, rather it describes the Prophet's physical appearance, mannerisms, character traits, and the numerous objects he possessed and thus is closer to the *Shamāʾil* work of al-Tirmidhī than the *dalāʾil al-nubūwa* works considered here. He was generally thought of as a critical and sound *ḥadīth* scholar. Some, however, found fault with him for being too inclusive. Al-Dhahabī, for instance, castigated him for padding his books with trivia.[108] Abū Nuʿaym was among those who transmitted Abū l-Shaykh's material.[109]

Abū ʿAbdallāh Muḥammad b. Mandah (d. 395/1005) was a highly respected *ḥadīth* scholar from Isfahan.[110] He first heard *ḥadīth* from his father, his father's uncle, and other scholars in his native town, before traveling widely in pursuit of his studies. His journeys led him to study in Nishabur, Samarqand, Mecca, Baghdad, as well as Syria and Egypt.[111] The number of teachers he studied with

105 McDermott, "Eṣfahānī, Abū'l-Šayk Abū Moḥammad ʿAbd Allāh."
106 Sezgin lists nine titles that exist at least in part; cf. Sezgin, *GAS*, 1:200f.
107 Al-Sakhawī, *al-Iʿlān*, 91.
108 Al-Dhahabī, *Siyar aʿlām al-nubulāʾ*, 279.
109 Al-Dhahabī, *Tadhkirat al-ḥuffāẓ*, 3:945f.
110 Al-Dhahabī, *Tadhkirat al-ḥuffāẓ*, 3:1031–1036.
111 Al-Dhahabī, *Tadhkirat al-ḥuffāẓ*, 3:1031–1036.

or heard *ḥadīth* from allegedly reached 1,700 and he is said to have authored so many books that it required forty mules to carry them.[112] However, none of these has survived. Al-Sakhawī lists Ibn Mandah as the author of a *dalāʾil al-nubūwa* work, which, like the rest of his works, appears to be lost.[113] Among those who transmitted *ḥadīth* from him were his teacher Abū l-Shaykh and Abū Nuʿaym al-Iṣfahānī.[114]

Another contributor to the *dalāʾil al-nubūwa* literature was Abū Saʿd ʿAbd al-Malik b. Abī ʿUthmān Muḥammad b. Ibrāhīm al-Nīsābūrī (d. 407/1016), commonly known as al-Khargūshī. He was Shāʿifī in law and Ashʿarī in theology, but was mainly devoted to promoting piety with his sermons; thus, he was referred to as a *wāʿiẓ*.[115] He was known for having built a hospital in Nishabur in which he and his followers dedicated themselves to menial nursing chores. He also built a madrasa and a Sufi convent in Khargūsh Street in Nishabur, where he lived most of his life.[116] In 392/1002, he went to Baghdad on his way to the pilgrimage, and resided in Mecca for a while before he returned to Nishabur where he died in 405/1015 or 406/1016.[117] Abū l-Ḥasan al-Masarjisī (d. 384/994?), with whom he studied Shāfiʿī law, considered him sound.[118]

His extant works include *Tahdhīb al-asrār*, a collection of Sufi sayings; the *Bishāra wa-l-nidhāra*, an interpretation of dreams; and the *Sharaf al-Muṣṭafā*, a long biography of the Prophet[119] that also circulated under different titles. Ḥājjī Khalīfa, also known as Kātib Çelebī, and al-Dhahabī mention a *dalāʾil al-nubūwa* by al-Khargūshī that may be an extract of *Sharaf al-Muṣṭafā*. Brockelmann identified *Sharaf al-Muṣṭafā* with *dalāʾil al-nubūwa* and Storey mentions an extant Persian translation with the alternative title *Dalāʾil al-nubūwa*. Melchert has suggested that Storey could be referring to a Persian abridgment. Finally, Kātib Çelebī listed a work under the title *Sharaf al-nubūwa*, and Melchert suggested that this may be an Arabic abridgment of *Sharaf al-Muṣṭafā*,[120] and an

112 Al-Dhahabī, *Tadhkirat al-ḥuffāẓ*, 3:1031–1036.
113 Al-Sakhawī, *al-Iʿlān*, 91.
114 Al-Dhahabī, *Tadhkirat al-ḥuffāẓ*, 3:1031–1036.
115 Melchert, *Khargūshi*, 29.
116 Al-Samʿānī, *Ansāb*, 5:101f.; al-Subkī, *Ṭabaqāt al-Shāfiʿiyya al-kubrā*, 3:369; cf. Bulliet, *The Patricians of Nishapur*, 251f.
117 Al-Khaṭīb al-Baghdādī, *Tārīkh Baghdād*, 10:432; al-Samʿānī adds Egypt to his itinerary, cf. al-Samʿānī, *Ansāb*, 5:101.
118 Melchert, "Khargūshi," 30.
119 *Sharaf al-Muṣṭafā* has recently been published by al-Ghamrī, *Manāḥil al-shifāʾ*. A 1967 Egyptian edition of the *Dalāʾil al-nubūwa* is mentioned by Ṭāhirī and Pūrjavādī, "Abū Saʿd-i Khargūshī-yi Nīshābūrī."
120 Cf. Kātib Çelebī/Ḥājjī Khalīfa, *Kashf al-ẓunūn*, 1045, 1047, 1569; al-Dhahabī, *Siyar aʿlām al-nubulāʾ*, 17:256; Storey, *Persian Literature*, 1:175f.; Brockelmann, *GAL*, Suppl. 1:361, no. 3; Melchert, "Khargūshi," 31.

existing Persian translation of the book has been published with yet another title, *Sharaf al-nabī*.[121] Al-Khargūshī was also linked to other authors of *dalāʾil al-nubūwa* works, such as al-Ḥākim and Abū Bakr al-Bayhaqī (d. 458/1066) transmitted on al-Khargūshī's authority.[122]

The most famous author of a *dalāʾil al-nubūwa* work was Aḥmad b. ʿAbdallāh b. Aḥmad b. Isḥāq b. Mūsā b. Mehrān, also known Abū Nuʿaym al-Iṣfahānī. He was a famous *ḥadīth* scholar and author of *Ḥilyat al-awlīyāʾ*, a collection of Sufi biographies; *Akhbār Iṣfahān*, a biographical dictionary of the city's religious scholars; and one of the most well-known *dalāʾil al-nubūwa* works to date.[123] He was born in Isfahan in 336/948[124] into an established family of the town. His maternal grandfather was a major figure in Iṣfahānī Sufism and his father Abū Muḥammad ʿAbdallāh (d. 365 /976) was a *ḥadīth* scholar who had traveled to Iraq and Syria in search of traditions.[125]

At the early age of eight, Abū Nuʿaym formally heard *ḥadīth* from the most noted scholars in Isfahan, including Abū l-Shaykh b. Khayyān and Sulaymān b. Aḥmad al-Ṭabarānī, then set out to study elsewhere. He traveled to various centers of Islamic learning in the provinces Khūzistān, Iraq, and Hijaz, including Wāsiṭ, Kufa, Baghdad, and Mecca. He probably also intended to visit Syria but was prevented from doing so by the upheavals accompanying the Fāṭimid invasion in 359/969–970. He briefly returned to Isfahan before traveling to the provinces Jurjān and Khurasan. In Nishabur he heard prophetic traditions from Ḥākim Aḥmad Muḥammad b. Muḥammad b. Isḥāq, Abū ʿAbd al-Raḥmān al-Sulamī, and many others. He is reported to have received permission to transmit *ḥadīth* from over 430 scholars, from some of whom he was the only known transmitter.[126] His reputation spread and he attracted a large numbers of students from far and wide. His teaching activity, however, became severely restricted when a feud broke out between him and another famous Iṣfahānī *ḥadīth* scholar and fellow author of a *dalāʾil al-nubūwa* work, the above-mentioned Muḥammad b. Isḥāq b. Mandah. The feud evolved from the division of Iṣfahānī scholars into Shāfiʿī and Ḥanbalī legal schools. Abū Nuʿaym was probably not formally trained in jurisprudence or theology but followed the Shāfiʿī school in legal and ritual matters and apparently approved of the Ashʿarī school, which he considered to be a form of *kalām* that was in

121 Al-Khargūshī, *Sharaf al-nabī*.
122 Al-Dhahabī, *Siyar aʿlām al-nubulāʾ*, 17:256.
123 For extant manuscripts, see Brockelmann, *GAL*, 1:446; Suppl. 1:617.
124 Variant dates are 334/946 or 330/942; Madelung, "Abū Noʿaym al-Eṣfahānī," 354f.
125 Madelung, "Abū Noʿaym al-Eṣfahānī," 354f.
126 Madelung, "Abū Noʿaym al-Eṣfahānī," 354f.

accordance with the doctrine of the *ahl al-sunna*.[127] Furthermore, he appears to have criticized the literalist Ḥanbalī reading of anthropomorphic expressions in the Qurʾān and *ḥadīth*. Because he held these views, he clashed with Ibn Mandah, the leader of the Hanbalī faction, who denounced Abū Nuʿaym's creed as unorthodox. Ibn Mandah's adjudication led pro-Ḥanbalī students of *ḥadīth* to ostracize Abū Nuʿaym, and he was expelled from the great mosque in Iṣfahan, which was dominated by the Ḥanbalī faction.[128] As a result of this feud, Abū Nuʿaym, who had studied *ḥadīth* with Ibn Mandah,[129] later accused his former teacher of becoming confused in his transmission of *ḥadīth* in his old age and of erroneously ascribing doctrines to people.[130] Abū Nuʿaym al-Iṣfahānī died in 430/1038.

Abū Nuʿaym's posthumous reputation is somewhat contested. Ḥanbalī scholars, such as Ibn al-Jawzī, rejected his legacy because of his Ashʿarī sympathies.[131] Furthermore, they accused him of irregularities in his transmission from Ḥanbalīs. These charges were refuted by Shāfiʿī scholars such as Ibn al-Najjār, al-Dhahabī, and al-Subkī.[132] Later Imāmī sources described Abū Nuʿaym as a crypto-Shīʿī, pointing particularly toward the biographies of early Shīʿī imams in *Ḥilyat al-awlīyāʾ* and in a collection of forty *ḥadīth* concerning the coming of the Maḥdī. According to Madelung, however, these *ḥadīth* do not reflect specifically Shīʿī doctrines.[133]

The other prominent author of an extant *dalāʾil al-nubūwa* work was Abū Bakr Aḥmad b. al-Ḥusayn b. ʿAlī b. Mūsā l-Khusrawjirdī (d. 458/1066), mostly known as al-Bayhaqī, who was a scholar of *ḥadīth* and Shāfiʿī law. He traveled extensively in pursuit of *ḥadīth* and is credited with having had one hundred teachers, including al-Ḥākim. Al-Bayhaqī was a prolific writer, and his *Kitāb al-Sunan al-kubrā* is perhaps his most notable book, and seems to have been held in high esteem. In theology he was an Ashʿarī. Toward the end of his life he went to Nishabur where he taught *ḥadīth* and transmitted his books. Even though he was a *ḥadīth* scholar of some note, he is reputed to have been unacquainted with the works of al-Tirmidhī, al-Nisāʾī, and Ibn Mājah, and it was suggested that he had not seen the *Musnad* of Aḥmad b. Ḥanbal.[134] Later scholars praised him for his skill in arranging his books rather than his

127 Madelung, "Abū Noʿaym al-Eṣfahānī," 354f.
128 Madelung, "Abū Noʿaym al-Eṣfahānī," 354f.
129 Al-Dhahabī, *Tadhkirat al-ḥuffāẓ*, 3:1032.
130 Madelung, "Abū Noʿaym al-Eṣfahānī," 354f.
131 Ibn al-Jawzī, *al-Muntaẓam*, 7:100; cf. Madelung, "Abū Noʿaym al-Eṣfahānī," 354f.
132 Madelung, "Abū Noʿaym al-Eṣfahānī," 354f.
133 Madelung, "Abū Noʿaym al-Eṣfahānī," 354f.
134 Al-Subkī, *Ṭabaqāt al-Shāfiʿiyya al-kubrā*, 3:9.

scholarship per se. Al-Dhahabī, for instance, said that the breadth of his *ḥadīth* was not great but that he was an adept at arranging it, being versed in the subdivisions and the men who appear in *isnād*s.[135] Al-Subkī declared that his *Sunan* was unparalleled in arrangement and excellence.[136] Al-Bayhaqī died in 458/1066 in Nishabur, and was buried in Khusrawjird.[137] Scholars of Islamic studies have frequently named al-Bayhaqī as the most prominent author of the entire *dalāʾil al-nubūwa* literature.

The fourth and final generation of *dalāʾil al-nubūwa* authors under consideration here are not only linked to the previous generation but are also closely intertwined with them. Despite the general connections, two strands appear to emerge in this generation. The first is a closely connected network of respected *ḥadīth* scholars, such as al-Ṭabarānī, al-Shāshī, Ibn Mandah, Abū l-Shaykh, and Abū Nuʿaym. Despite their interaction, this strand of authors was not free from conflict, as the feud between Ibn Mandah and Abū Nuʿaym shows. The second strand is a more loosely linked group encompassing Ibn Shāhīn and al-Khargūshī, and the latter's student al-Bayhaqī. Ibn Shāhīn's teacher, al-Naqqāsh, a scholar of the third generation, may also be included in this circle. None of these four men were of the same scholarly caliber with regard to Sunnī *isnād*-based *ḥadīth* methodology as the first and second generations. Al-Naqqāsh may have been well-versed in Qurʾānic readings but his reputation as a scholar of *ḥadīth* was tainted with accusations of weak *isnād*s, dishonesty, and corruption from *quṣṣāṣ*. Ibn Shāhīn and al-Khargūshī were better known as preachers and ascetics, though their scholarly merits were not entirely discredited. Finally, al-Bayhaqī is faulted with severe shortcomings in his expertise in *ḥadīth*, including his apparent unawareness of the major *ḥadīth* collections. It is important to note, however, that despite this decline in their scholarly reputations none of the authors discussed here correspond to Orientalist assumptions that this kind of literature is a direct output of or strongly influenced by untrained charlatans who produced fabrications in an attempt to entertain laymen.

5 The Evolution of Early *Dalāʾil al-Nubūwa* Authors

Abū Nuʿaym and al-Bayhaqī's *dalāʾil al-nubūwa* works have become almost synonymous with the literature as a whole. This fame has misled many scholars of Islamic studies to identify them with the earliest specimen of this literature.

135 Al-Dhahabī, *Tadhkira al-ḥuffāẓ*, 3:309f.
136 Al-Subkī, *Ṭabaqāt al-Shāfiʿiyya al-kubrā*, 3:3f.
137 Robson, "al-Bayhaḳī."

Having identified the authors of twenty-two *ḥadīth*-based *dalāʾil al-nubūwa* compilations prior to their works not only fills a gap in Western scholarship on the textual history of this literature but has also provides opportunities to observe its evolution between the mid-second/eighth and early fifth/eleventh centuries. The following chart illustrates the relations of all four generations.

While each of these scholars may have had scores of teachers and students who did not write on the subject, the identification of the earliest authors of *ḥadīth*-based *dalāʾil al-nubūwa* works demonstrates a network of continuous interactions between contributors to this literature. Establishing this network of authors also allows us to locate them in the intellectual landscape of their time. The first two generations are squarely positioned in the circles of respected *ḥadīth* scholars. Their ranks include *muḥaddithūn* who shaped their own field by compiling canonical collections or major contributions to the field's methodology. In the larger context of religious sciences, we can conclude that many of them sided with the *ahl al-ḥadīth* movement's opposition to Muʿtazilī views in particular, and *kalām* more generally. Al-Ḥarbī, for instance, was known for his opposition to the rationalist views of the Muʿtazila. Al-Jūzajānī and the majority of the second generation were directly associated with Aḥmad b. Ḥanbal or his protégé Isḥāq b. Rahawayh al-Ḥanẓalī.

A drastic shift at the end of the fourth/tenth century occurred between the second and the third generations of *dalāʾil al-nubūwa* authors, a shift both in terms of their connections and their scholarly profiles. First, few personal connections link the third generation to its predecessor: al-Ṭabarānī's unverified encounter with al-Firyābī would seem to be the only direct contact. Furthermore, from the third generation onward contributors to this kind of literature were no longer uniformly acclaimed as scholars of the prophetic tradition. Their reputations were built, instead, on their lives as preachers, ascetics, or scholars, whose lack of expertise in *ḥadīth* is noted. Even among the respected *muḥaddithūn* of the third and fourth generations, there is a noticeable change in their intellectual positions. The third generation was particularly marked by their rejection of speculative theology. This position seems to have lost its leverage among authors of *dalāʾil al-nubūwa* works in later generations, as Ibn Mandah seems to be the only one who still maintained his disapproval of theology. Others, like Abū Nuʿaym and al-Bayhaqī, openly identify as Ashʿarīs.

These shifts in the intellectual orientation of *dalāʾil al-nubūwa* authors are examined further in subsequent chapters. In chapter 3, I analyze extant works related to the structural and methodological approaches, while chapter 4 explores whether these interconnected authors held similar notions of what constituted "signs of prophecy" and how this is reflected in their selections of narratives.

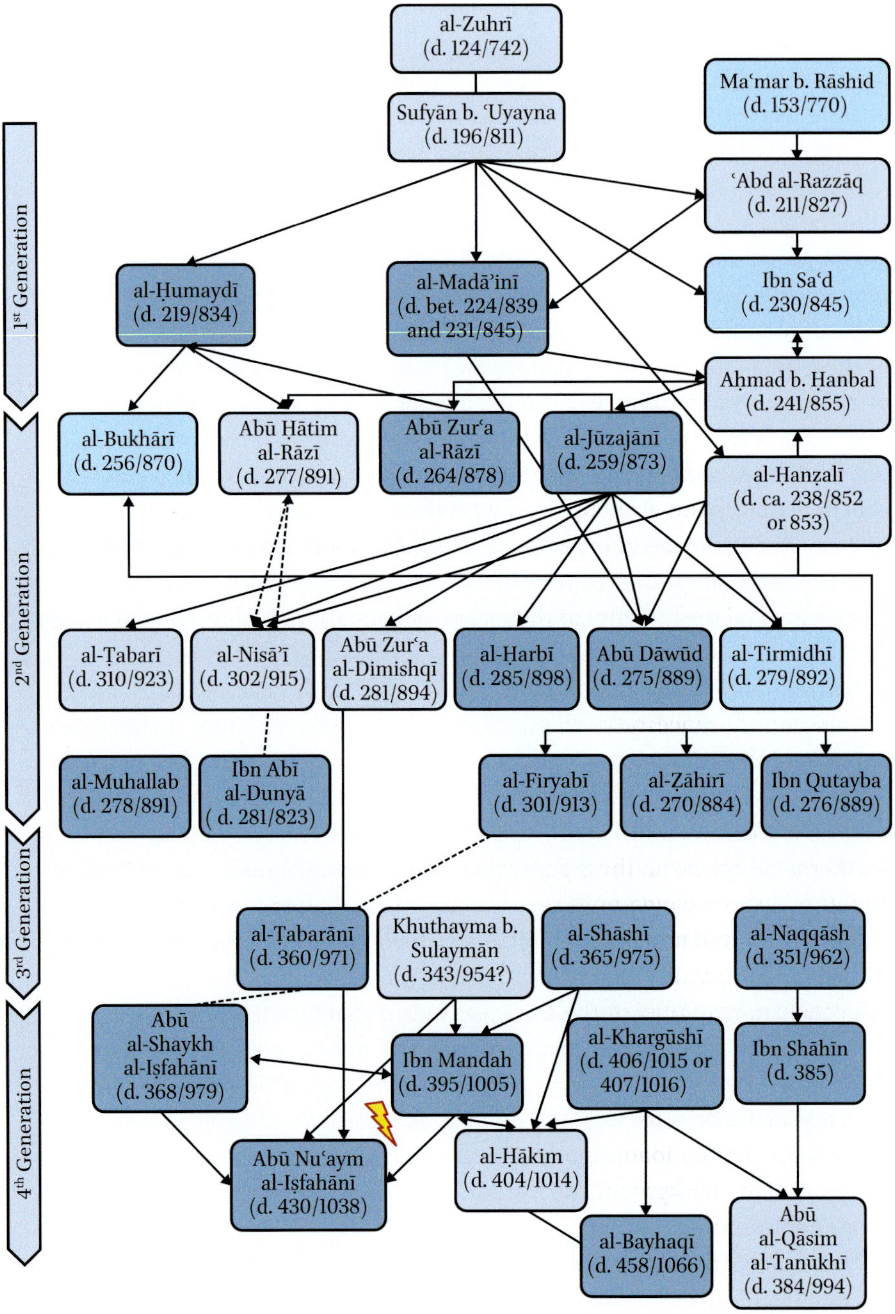

CHART 2 Network of authors

CHAPTER 3

Methodological and Structural Approaches in *Dalāʾil al-Nubūwa* Literature

Ḥadīth-based *dalāʾil al-nubūwa* works have been authored since the mid-second/eighth century, but only a few of the compilations that were written in the period up to the end of the third/ninth century have been preserved. The analysis of *dalāʾil al-nubūwa* authors in the previous chapter suggests that the evolution of this literature was marked by shifts in authorship from solidly reputable scholars of *ḥadīth* to authors who came from other fields of expertise or had less than perfect scholarly records. Based on the extant works of *dalāʾil al-nubūwa* literature, I examine how methodological and structural changes may reflect these shifts in authorship, and, more generally, the character of the literature, and ultimately reiterate my finding, that this literature clearly originated in the scholarly realm and was not the product of prophetic veneration by laymen.

The means of authentication that these authors employed lay, of course, at the center of this investigation of methodologies. Note that in this process the level of authenticity is based on the parameters of the compilers' respective environments and reflects the value that the compilers themselves ascribed to the accounts. Ultimately, my goal is to understand the intellectual processes that led these authors to craft their notions of the proofs of prophecy. Therefore, I try to avoid projecting later criteria onto the authors' methodological and structural approaches; by later criteria, I refer to the epistemological reliability attributed to particular accounts by later Sunnī legal theorists or the positivist concerns of early Orientalists with regard to the historicity of events described in them.

With the exception of Ibn Saʿd, the majority of extant *dalāʾil al-nubūwa* works that date back to this early period were *ḥadīth* compilations in the narrower sense. In the following, I examine the earliest extant works based on the disciplinary backgrounds of the compilers rather than their chronological order. I first study the works of the *ḥadīth* scholars, that is, Maʿmar b. Rāshid, al-Bukhārī, al-Tirmidhī, and al-Jūzajānī and their methodological approaches. I examine Ibn Saʿd's compilation of "signs of prophecy" separately and more extensively, not only because his two chapters constitute the earliest comprehensive collection of such accounts, but also because these accounts were part of a *sīra* section in his biographical dictionary the *Ṭabaqāt*, rather than a *ḥadīth*

 | DOI:10.1163/9789004687349_005

collection. Given that *sīra/maghāzī* literature followed its own distinct disciplinary approach, Ibn Saʿd's methodology must be studied thoroughly in order to compare it with contemporaneous works of *ḥadīth*.

1 Methodologies of Authentication in Early *Dalāʾil al-Nubūwa* Works

Maʿmar b. Rāshid's (d. 153/770) *al-Jāmiʿ* contains a short chapter of six accounts entitled "Bāb al-nubūwa";[1] this most likely constituted the first systematic compilation of what developed into the *dalāʾil al-nubūwa* literature. A dedicated student of al-Zuhrī, Maʿmar b. Rāshid sought to uphold his teacher's strict methodological standards and, therefore, enjoyed a reputation as a reliable transmitter and scholar. Accordingly, all six accounts in his "Bāb al-nubūwa" are introduced with their full *isnād*s. *Ḥadīth* authentication was still in its infancy during Maʿmar's lifetime and *isnād*s were not yet evaluated by the parameters of later *isnād* criticism. Nevertheless Maʿmar was aware of the importance of introducing each *ḥadīth* with an individual chain of transmission and clearly sought to authenticate his traditions with the means accessible at the time. The perceived authenticity of these accounts appears to be further validated by the fact that all six of them are included in the later canonical *ḥadīth* compilations of al-Bukhārī and, to a lesser degree, Muslim, as I show in the next chapter.

In addition, we know of chapters dedicated to the signs of prophecy in two collections that later gained recognition as canonical collections for Sunnī Islam. The chapters "ʿAlāmāt al-nubūwa fī l-Islām" in al-Bukhārī's *Ṣaḥīḥ* and "Bāb mā jāʾ fī ayāt Nubūwa al-Nabī wa-mā qad khaṣṣa Allāh bihi" in al-Tirmidhī's *Ṣaḥīḥ Sunan* are, of course, shaped by the compilers' intentions to single out only those *ḥadīth* that were deemed sound in transmission. Among the compilers of canonical *ḥadīth* collections al-Tirmidhī is particularly interesting because he was the only scholar to provide his evaluation of the *isnād* for each account. He categorizes eight of the accounts he selected as "signs of prophecy" as sound (*ṣaḥīḥ*) and one as acceptable (*ḥasan ṣaḥīḥ*), even though we must keep in mind that at that time these were not yet universal standards.

It may seem intuitive to automatically designate these accounts in Maʿmar, al-Bukhārī, and al-Tirmidhī as authentic based on their inclusion in later canonical works, but such an a priori assumption is problematic. It involves projecting parameters of authentication that were applied by later legal theorists onto earlier scholars of *ḥadīth* rather than examining them in their own specific intellectual environment and with their own methodological

---

1 ʿAbd al-Razzāq, *al-Muṣannaf*, 11:276–280.

approach. In order to evaluate the compilations in the framework of their authors' intellectual environments, we must bear in mind that their works did not gain prestige and rank immediately. All canonical works acquire that status over time and were not necessarily held in such regard at the time of their composition. "Canonization involves a community's act of authorizing specific books in order to meet certain needs. It entails the transformation of texts, through use, study, and appreciation, from nondescript tomes into powerful symbols of divine, legal or artistic authority for a particular audience."[2] In the case of the *ṣaḥīḥ* movement, which started with al-Bukhārī and Muslim, this act that transformed generally acclaimed works took many decades and was not as inevitable as one might assume today.[3] At the time of al-Bukhārī and Muslim, the culture of *ḥadīth* transmission had been undergoing significant change. Initially, the collection and transmission of *ḥadīth*, like all fields of Muslim scholarship, emerged in the circles of pious individuals rather than in established institutions. For these individuals, the impetus to collect and transmit *ḥadīth* was not so much a legal necessity, rather it "carried pietistic significance as a means for everyday Muslims to bind themselves to the inspirational authority of the Prophet and incorporate his charisma into their lives."[4] A self-aware class of religious scholars that distinguished itself from the pious masses only emerged in the late Umayyad and early ʿAbbāsid periods and caused a bifurcation between, on one side, those with knowledge of Islamic law and ritual and, on the other side, laymen and professional scholars.[5] The influential legal scholar al-Shāfiʿī (d. 204/820) divided knowledge of Islamic law and ritual into what is required of the masses (*ʿāmm*) and what is the purview of scholars or specialists (*khāṣṣ*).[6] Jonathan A. C. Brown points to the introduction of Muslim's *Ṣaḥīḥ* collection and to a letter written by Abū Dāwūd al-Sijistānī to scholars in Mecca in which Abū Dāwūd explains the content and structure of his *Sunan* collection; this shows that *ḥadīth* scholarship began to adopt a paternalistic view.[7] Thus, the *ṣaḥīḥ* movement furthered and deepened the gulf between laymen and specialists. Compiling *ḥadīth* collections that were vetted and deemed authentic was supposed to offer the Muslim masses access to the Sunna without expecting them to acquire an understanding of the increasingly more complicated intricacies of *ḥadīth* criticism. This position

2 Brown, *The Canonization of al-Bukhārī and Muslim*, 5.
3 Brown, *The Canonization of al-Bukhārī and Muslim*, 6.
4 Brown, *The Canonization of al-Bukhārī and Muslim*, 57.
5 Brown, *The Canonization of al-Bukhārī and Muslim*, 57.
6 Brown, *The Canonization of al-Bukhārī and Muslim*, 57.
7 Brown, *The Canonization of al-Bukhārī and Muslim*, 57.

marked a departure from existing practice, as it undermined "amateur" *ḥadīth* collection as a means of spiritually connecting to their Prophet.

Furthermore, the *ṣaḥīḥ* movement also led to divergent views among the scholarly class of *muḥaddithūn*. The concept of selective *ḥadīth* collections that excluded vast parts of the body of the *ḥadīth* based on considerations of authenticity was a strident break from the common practices at the time and was met with significant disapproval.[8] "Professional" *ḥadīth* collectors strove to collect as many *ḥadīth*s as possible regardless of their quality, based on the commonly held view that any tradition traced back to Muḥammad and containing his name carried prophetic authority and was *prima facie* compelling in a way. For the majority of scholars in this early period, a problematic *isnād* did not necessarily undermine the Prophet's authority nor did it necessarily preclude a *ḥadīth* from being used. Such *ḥadīth*s were "indispensable in fields like the history of the Prophet's campaigns, contextualizing Qurʾānic verses or recounting the virtues of the Prophet's Companions."[9] Even in legal issues, scholars like Ibn Ḥanbal and Abū Dāwūd depended on weak (*ḍaʿīf*) *ḥadīth*s.[10]

Another point to bear in mind is that the parameters for authenticity and reliability of *ḥadīth* criticism were still in flux during this time. There is no reason to doubt the stated commitment of early scholars like Maʿmar, al-Bukhārī, and al-Tirmidhī to safeguard the authenticity of the *ḥadīth* corpus, but the means by which they achieved this should not be conflated with the epistemological framework employed by later Sunnī legal theorists. During the late second/eighth and early third/ninth centuries, the prevalence of forged and fabricated *ḥadīth*s led to the emergence of a shared three-tiered process of authentication that included requiring individual *isnād*s for each account, evaluating transmitters listed in the *isnād*s, and demanding corroboration of the *ḥadīth*. We have to keep in mind, however, that the theoretical framework for the evaluation of *isnād*s, including the paradigm of *ṣaḥīḥ* (sound), *ḥasan* (good), and *ḍaʿīf* (weak) divisions had not been fully established nor was it generally agreed upon.

The historical reliability of the *ḥadīth* was also not viewed through the same epistemological lens that required numerous chains of transmission as a measure of reliability.[11] Later legal theorists considered the most reliable of reports to be those that were *mutawātir* (i.e., transmitted so frequently that they were very unlikely to have been forged). Reports that were transmitted from the Prophet by a less substantial number of *isnād*s, or *āḥād ḥadīth*s (those *ḥadīth*s

---

8 Brown, *The Canonization of al-Bukhārī and Muslim*, 6.

9 Brown, *The Canonization of al-Bukhārī and Muslim*, 59.

10 Brown, *The Canonization of al-Bukhārī and Muslim*, 59.

11 Brown, "Did the Prophet Say It or Not?," 259.

transmitted from a single person), only yielded "legally compelling probability (*ẓann*)" in the eyes of later legal theorists and were mostly excluded in regard to legal and ritual matters. This epistemological category of *mutawātir*, however, was not universally held in the discourse of *ḥadīth* critics in the third/ninth century; Brown states that *ḥadīth* scholars of this time period described *ḥadīth* as "widely transmitted" (*tawātara*) or "having become manifest" (*taẓāhara*), which simply meant that a *ḥadīth* "appeared widely."[12] By the same token, *ḥadīth* with less substantial numbers of people in the *isnād* constituted the bulk of the *ḥadīth* corpus dealt with by Ibn Ḥanbal and his cohort.

These gradually evolving notions of authenticity and reliability mostly came to fruition after the generation of al-Bukhārī and Muslim. As a consequence, the fact that chapters dedicated to signs of Muḥammad's prophetic mission occur in the *ṣaḥīḥ* works that became the yardstick for authenticity by later Sunnī scholars is not relevant for tracing the history of *dalāʾil al-nubūwa* literature or gaining an understanding of how the accounts they contained were evaluated at the time of their compilation. It is more significant that these early chapters of *dalāʾil al-nubūwa* emerged in the context of a scholarly discourse. These scholars may not have agreed among themselves regarding the epistemological categories of *ḥadīth* collection and transmission, as we see in chapter 4; however, they are unified in the sense that they constituted a distinct class and they participated in these discourses that excluded the Muslim masses. This stands in stark contrast to the views of Orientalists, who sought the origins of *dalāʾil al-nubūwa* literature in circles of people that intentionally fabricated narratives to entertain the masses, that is, beyond Muslim scholars. One of the most prominent members of the *ṣaḥīḥ* movement, Muslim b. Ḥajjāj, perceived his colleagues' approach to strive for exhaustive rather than critical *ḥadīth* collections as a laxity in criticism. Muslim went so far as to accuse scholars who aimed at compiling all prophetic traditions, irrespective of their degree of authenticity, of trying to win the acclaim of the masses.[13] It is highly likely, then, that the early chapters on the signs of prophecy compiled by al-Bukhārī and al-Tirmidhī, and by extension the pre-*ṣaḥīḥ* scholar Maʿmar whose six accounts were incorporated by al-Bukhārī, were compiled with the highest standards of authentication available at the time.

1.1 *Al-Jūzajānī's "Amārāt al-Nubūwa"*

Al-Jūzajānī's "Amārāt al-nubūwa" appears to be the earliest textual evidence of a self-contained *ḥadīth*-based *dalāʾil al-nubūwa* work that has been preserved,

12 Brown, *The Canonization of al-Bukhārī and Muslim*, 53–54.

13 Brown, *The Canonization of al-Bukhārī and Muslim*, 58.

partially, in a unique manuscript.[14] The title page of the manuscript indicates that it contains selected *ḥadīth*s from the sixth chapter of al-Jūzajānī's work rather than representing the entirety of the chapter.[15] This selection was presumably recorded by ʿAbd al-Raḥīm b. al-Ḥaytam [?] b. ʿAbd al-Raḥīm, who copied it from a manuscript in the hand of Abū l-Khayr al-Salāma b. Ibrāhīm b. al-Salāma al-Ḥaddād, without providing any information about when the selection was made or what the motivation behind it was. The selective nature of the manuscript poses some challenges for the evaluation of al-Jūzajānī's methodological approach and the contents of his work overall, and this makes it difficult to establish a continuous and systematic notion of the way this literature developed. But this particular manuscript allows us some insights into al-Jūzajānī's mode of authentication as well as the reception of the work.

This selection from the sixth chapter appears to be preserved in its entirety, and contains thirteen individual accounts. Similar to previous chapters on *dalāʾil al-nubūwa*, this text presents the accounts without any exegesis or explanation of the selection parameters. The first *ḥadīth* is introduced with an *isnād* that traces the transmission from the Prophet Muḥammad through the Companion Jābir ʿAbdallāh to the last transmitter, al-Ḥaddād. The *isnād*, thus, links the record of the transmission of the specific selection, even though it is unclear when it occurred, to the work's author (al-Jūzajānī) with the individual *isnād* that al-Jūzajānī presumably provided for this particular *ḥadīth*. All subsequent *ḥadīth*s are also introduced with individual *isnād*s, starting with Abū l-Daḥdāḥ, who transmitted it from the book's author al-Jūzajānī, back to Muḥammad's Companions.

The manuscript closes with a reproduction of an audience certificate; this provides further details about its mode of transmission. Al-Ḥaddād had read the text back to his own teacher, Abū l-Majad Fatayān b. Ḥaydra b. ʿAlī l-Bajalī, in the latter's house in the eastern precincts of Damascus during the middle ten days of Ramaḍān 567/1172. According to the audience certificate, several other students of the same cohort also read the text to al-Bajalī and all were given permission (*ʾijāza*) to transmit this material. Al-Bajalī himself had heard the book while sitting in the audience of Abū Muḥammad al-Ḥasan b. ʿAlī b. al-Ḥusayn b. Aḥmad b. Ṣafr while it was being read to the teacher in the year 480/1087. Abū Muḥammad, in turn, had heard the book when another student read it to their teacher Abū l-Ḥasan ʿAlī b. Aḥmad b. Mūsā b. al-Samsār, who had read it directly back to his teacher, Abū l-Qāsim ʿAlī b. al-Ḥasan b. Ṭaʿān, in

14 Damascus Asad Library, MS Majmūʿ 104, fols. 162–165; cf. al-Albānī, *Fihris*, 250 / Riyadh, 2001, p. 339; cf. Sezgin, *GAS*, 1:135.

15 The manuscript is entitled *Juzʾ fīhi aḥādīth muntakhaba min al-juzʾ al-sādis min kitāb amārāt al-nubūwa*, cf. fol. 162a.

Shaʿbān 367/987. The latter had heard the book when it was being read back to Abū l-Daḥdāḥ, who was in the audience while another student was reading it back to the book's author, al-Jūzajānī.

As the audience certificate at the end of the manuscript indicates, it had become common to record details of public lectures in Damascus, such as this lecture, which was read with the teacher present and the students read the text back to the teacher during the later stages of this work's transmission. However, there seem to be no extant records of this particular gathering.[16] Furthermore, there are no records of the individuals named in the manuscript other than Abū l-Ḥasan ʿAlī b. Aḥmad b. Mūsā b. al-Samsār, who was a *ḥadīth* transmitter in Damascus and transmitted *Ṣaḥīḥ al-Bukhārī* on the authority of Abū Zayd al-Marūzī, and was said to have attracted large audiences. Abū l-Walīd al-Bājī accused al-Samsār of being weak in his *ʿuṣūl* and of harboring Shīʿī leanings and writing about them excessively.[17]

1.2 *Ibn Saʿd's "ʿAlamāt al-nubūwa"*

Ibn Saʿd's "ʿAlamāt al-nubūwa" is the only compilation dedicated to signs of prophecy during this early time period that is not contained in a *ḥadīth* collection but rather appears as part of the author's extensive *Kitāb al-Ṭabaqāt al-kubrā*. This biographical dictionary aims at providing information on the lives and reliability of *ḥadīth* transmitters and, thus serves as an important device to facilitate the assessment of *ḥadīth* transmitters. Given his commitment to critically assessing *ḥadīth* transmitters, it appears plausible that Ibn Saʿd himself also upheld standards that safeguarded the integrity and authenticity of *ḥadīth* to the extent possible at this early time. The fact that these chapters are not part of *ḥadīth* collections in the narrower sense may have consequences for Ibn Saʿd's methodological considerations, as he would not have been held to the same methodological standards. In the following, I examine the general methodological approach Ibn Saʿd employed in his biography of Muḥammad. I then focus more specifically on the two chapters dedicated to signs of prophecy, in order to see if Ibn Saʿd's methodological approach there differed from his approach to the remaining *sīra* section. Rare examples of *ḥadīth* that display obvious shortcomings in their *isnād* function as case studies by which we can explore whether or not Ibn Saʿd utilized unauthenticated materials.

---

16 There are no entries for these individuals in the register of the Damascene audience certificates compiled by Stefan Leder and Yāsīn Muḥammad al-Sawwās covering the period from 550/1155 to 750/1349; cf. Leder and al-Sawwās, *Muʿjam al-samāʿat*, passim.

17 Ibn Ḥajar al-ʿAsqalānī, *Lisān al-mizān*, 5:259.

The *Ṭabaqāt* opens with the *sīra*, which constitutes the earliest biography of Muḥammad that has been preserved in its entirety, other than Ibn Hishām's edition of the *sīra* by Ibn Isḥāq. There was some question about whether Ibn Saʿd's *sīra* was originally an independent work entitled *Kitāb Akhbār al-nabī*.[18] Regardless of whether the *sīra* sections were originally intended to be part of the *Ṭabaqāt* or not, it is important to consider the methodological parameters Ibn Saʿd employed in its compilation, because, from it we can understand the mechanisms by which he sought to authenticate its contents. Ibn Saʿd's biography of the Prophet has two parts, which correspond to the first two volumes of the *Ṭabaqāt*'s printed editions. The first part covers the Prophet's biography in general, like other works of *sīra*, while the second part is dedicated to his campaigns, and thus constitutes a *maghāzī* work in the narrower sense of the term. Ibn Saʿd appears to have applied two distinct methodologies to the *sīra* and the *maghāzī* sections respectively. The *maghāzī* section is prefaced with a comprehensive list of his most important transmitters. For each of the campaigns, Ibn Saʿd provides a principle account, which is collectively based on the authority of the transmitters identified in the preface but does not identify other elements of its origin. There are no individual *isnād* for the general accounts of these campaigns. He then amplifies this general narrative with individual accounts, which each include a specific *isnād*.[19] By contrast, the *sīra* section consists mostly of individual accounts that are grouped in chapters following a mostly chronological order. Each account is introduced by its individual *isnād*, though Ibn Saʿd occasionally employs collective *isnād*s. As such, the *sīra* section displays a stricter degree of authentication than the *maghāzī* section.

The overall chronological arrangement of the *sīra* section is sporadically interrupted by thematic chapters. Ibn Saʿd seems to have given the question of signs of Muḥammad's prophecy special attention because his *sīra* section includes two extensive chapters dedicated to the subject of *ʿalamāt al-nubūwa*. The first describes the alleged "signs of prophecy" that occurred before the beginning of revelation, while the latter addresses those that took place after Muḥammad's call to prophecy. Ibn Saʿd took a particular interest in this subject, as is evidenced by these two chapters that are the longest (containing forty-seven and forty-two accounts, respectively) in the entire *sīra* section. In the chronological biography, the thematic chapters of "signs of prophecy" are

18 Otto Loth argued that Ibn Saʿd only edited the biography of the Prophet in its current form and communicated it to his students for further transmission, while the *Ṭabaqāt* work was preserved in its current form by al-Ḥusayn b. Fahm (d. 289/902). Both works were then allegedly combined by Ibn Maʿrūf around the year 300/913; Loth, *Classenbuch*, 25–34. For a succint summary of the entire debate including the references to Arabic biographical dictionaries, see Mūsā, *Ibn Saʿd wa-ṭabqātuhu*, 23f.

19 Horovitz, *Earliest Biographers*, 121.

distinctive because they do not establish a continuous narrative, but rather highlight individual events or occurrences without reference to their historical context. Furthermore, each account in these chapters is introduced with its own full *isnād*. Many of these *isnād*s go back to Companions (*ṣaḥāba*), and include some of the most prominent *ḥadīth* transmitters, such as ʿĀʾisha, Ibn ʿAbbās, Ibn Masʿūd, Anas b. Mālik, ʿAlī, and other members of the Prophet's family, or to Followers (*tābiʿūn*), including such prominent figures as ʿUrwa b. al-Zubayr, al-Zuhrī, ʿĀṣim b. ʿUmar b. Qatāda, and Thābit b. Bunānī. Only five accounts have obvious shortcomings in their *isnād*, such as an unidentified transmitter. By contrast, there are even fewer *isnād*s that go back to the Prophet; most of the accounts in these two chapters appear to have unbroken chains of transmission going back to a Companion or Follower. The overall picture is further complicated by the fact that the chapter dedicated to the "signs of prophecy" prior to the call to prophecy includes several accounts that do not mention the Prophet in the *isnād* or in the *matn*. Narratives announcing or predicting the prophecy of Muḥammad, in particular, occur in the framework of conversations about the Prophet without him being present. These accounts, therefore, are not *ḥadīth*s in the technical sense of the term, but rather reports (*akhbār*). These are much more limited in their application than *ḥadīth*s as they may not be used to support legal and ritual rulings but, consequently, do not fall under the same demands of authentication.

It appears as if Ibn Saʿd employed varying degrees of authentication throughout the parts of the *Ṭabaqāt* that relate to Muḥammad's life. As we have seen previously, the *sīra* section is more strictly authenticated than the *maghāzī* section, as the *sīra* relies much more consistently on individual *isnād*s for each account, while the *maghāzī* sections rely on collective *isnād*s that provide the general narrative. In the *sīra*, the chapters on the signs of prophecy are held to an even higher standard. There are no collective *isnād*s and only five of the ninety-nine accounts are introduced by *isnād*s with obvious shortcomings. While these *isnād*s do not meet the criteria of later legal theorists, we should keep in mind that they comply, for the most part, with the standards of *ḥadīth* scholarship as it was practiced during Ibn Saʿd's lifetime.

1.2.1 The Question of Unauthenticated Materials in Ibn Saʿd's *Ṭabaqāt*

Contemporary scholars frequently suggest that authors of *sīra* works incorporated unidentified sources.[20] This assumption raises particularly interesting questions for Ibn Saʿd's chapters on the signs of prophecy because these

20 Schoeler and Görke, for instance, suggested that many *qiṣāṣ* narratives entered the *sīra* literature through the unauthenticated reports of Mūsā b. ʿUqba (d. 140/758) and Ibn Isḥāq (d. 150/767); Schoeler and Görke, *Die ältesten Berichte*, 275f.

chapters were compiled using the methodological framework of a *sīra*, yet are part of *dalāʾil al-nubūwa* literature, which has commonly been viewed as a popular sub-genre of *sīra*. In order to examine whether Ibn Saʿd indeed incorporated unauthenticated materials in his *sīra*, in general, and in the specific chapters on the signs of prophecy, in particular, I identify narratives found in both in the prophetic biographies of Ibn Saʿd and Wahb b. Munabbih, and juxtapose them, whenever possible, with authenticated traditions. Identifying unauthenticated materials and ascribing them accurately to their alleged sources is methodologically challenging given that there are no chains of transmission to trace back and evaluate. Therefore, my analysis is limited to comparing narrative elements and highlighting textual parallels.

Ibn Saʿd's *sīra* section includes three episodes that overlap with the biography of the Prophet by Wahb b. Munabbih. Wahb's narrative of the *hijra*, for instance, includes Muḥammad's encounter with Umm Maʿbad and her lambs, which Muḥammad milked, even though they had not yet conceived; an encounter with a Qurayshī pursuer named Surāqa; and the well-known narrative of a cobweb and a pigeon settling at the entrance of a cave to conceal Muḥammad and Abū Bakr during their escape.

1.2.1.1 *Muḥammad's Encounter with Umm Maʿbad*

The papyri of Wahb b. Munabbih's *sīra* include the following episode that allegedly took place during Muḥammad's *hijra*: The Prophet passed the camp of Umm Maʿbad al-Khuzāʿīya, who was praised by a third-person narrator for her generosity and kindness. Muḥammad and his Companions asked for food but she could not provide them with any due to a winter drought. The Prophet saw a sheep and asked whether it had milk. Umm Maʿbad denied that it had milk. The Prophet then asked permission to milk it and asked for the sheep's name, which is ʿAqīṣ. The Prophet said: "Its name is Baraka." He then called it by its (new) name, and milked it. The milk satiated him and his men. He milked it a second time and gave the milk to Umm Maʿbad. After a while Abū Maʿbad returned home and questioned his wife about the milk, indicating that all the sheep are out in the pastures grazing. Umm Maʿbad told him about "a blessed man" who came by, and she described his appearance at length. Abū Maʿbad realized that it was the fugitive that the Quraysh were looking for and he regretted not having met him.[21] The next morning, the inhabitants of Mecca heard an unidentified voice relating that the Prophet had stopped at Umm Maʿbad's camp. The Prophet and his Companions are praised and the

21 Khoury, *Wahb b. Munabbih*, 1:150f.

voice related how the Prophet drew milk from a barren sheep. This is followed by a poem.[22]

The narrative of Muḥammad milking Umm Maʿbad's animals occurs twice in Ibn Saʿd's work; one account is in the chronological biography as part of the narrative of the *hijra*; the second account is listed among the signs of Muḥammad's prophecy after the revelation. As such, the methodological paradigms of these two accounts differ. Ibn Saʿd's account of the *hijra* is a continuous narrative with a collective *isnād* combining five different chains of transmission. This main narrative is frequently interrupted by additional accounts that provide more detailed information and are usually not transmitted on the authority of al-Wāqidī. The main narrative on the authority of al-Wāqidī relies heavily on Ibn Isḥāq's work, though not as much in order than in content.[23] It is noteworthy that the works of al-Wāqidī and Ibn Isḥāq include the poem recited by a *jinn* and vaguely refer to Muḥammad's encounter with Umm Maʿbad, but the encounter itself is missing in Ibn Isḥāq's *sīra*.[24] Ibn Saʿd, however, inserts a detailed account of the encounter, which has striking parallels to Wahb's version and includes all the details, such as Muḥammad drawing milk from a barren sheep and the physical description of Muḥammad's features that Umm Maʿbad relates to her husband.[25] Given that neither al-Wāqidī nor Ibn Isḥāq included this narrative in their biographies, it seems at least probable that this account was taken from Wahb b. Munabbih.

In the chapter on the signs of prophecy after the beginning of revelation, the narrative of Umm Maʿbad is related in another account. While all accounts in this chapter have individual *isnād*s, this particular account is transmitted on the basis of one of the few *isnād*s with an obvious shortcoming because the account's original narrator is only identified as "a shaykh of the Banū Jumah." The account reads as follows.

> When the Prophet came to Umm Maʿbad, he said, "Is there something to offer a guest?" She said, "no." He and Abū Bakr withdrew. Her son came

22 Khoury, *Wahb b. Munabbih*, 1:152f.

23 Earlier scholarship debated whether al-Wāqidī in fact used Ibn Isḥāq's work, given that al-Wāqidī does not mention him in any of his *isnāds*; this was probably due to Ibn Isḥāq's questionable reputation among *ḥadīth* scholars. Wellhausen suggested this in his partial edition of the *Kitāb al-Maghāzī*, see Wellhausen, *Muhammed in Medina*, 12–15. This view was rejected by Marsden Jones in the Arabic introduction to his edition (Jones, "The Maghāzī Literature," 29f.) and in Lecker, "Wāqidī's Account," 15–32. Schoeler finally provided conclusive evidence for al-Wāqidī's usage of Ibn Isḥāq; Schoeler, *Charakter und Authentie*, 134–142; cf. Horovitz, *Earliest Biographers*, 114.

24 Ibn Isḥāq, *The Life of Muhammad*, 222f.

25 Ibn Saʿd, *Ṭabaqāt*, 1:196f.; Khoury, *Wahb b. Munabbih*, 1:150f.

> with the sheep and said to his mother, "Who is that figure who I saw leaving?" She said, "A people looking for provisions. I said we do not have any water." He came to them and apologized, saying, "She is a weak woman; we have what you need." The Prophet said, "Go bring me a sheep from your flock." He went and took a young lamb [younger than one year old]. His mother said, "Where are you going?" He said, "they asked for a sheep." She said, "What are they doing with it?" He said, "Whatever they want." The Prophet touched its udder and its teats and they were full with milk and he milked it until a cup was filled and he left it filled with milk. He said, "Bring this to your mother and bring me another sheep from your flock." He brought his mother the cup. She said, "From where did you get it?" He said, "The milk of such-and-such a sheep." She said, "How is it [possible]? She has not yet conceived! I think—by al-Lāt—this is the one who departed from his religion to another religion in Mecca!" She drank from it. Then he came with another lamb and he [i.e., the Prophet] milked it until a cup was filled; then he left it filled with milk. Then he said, "drink!" He drank. Then the Prophet said, "bring me another!" and he brought him another and he milked it and poured [the milk] for Abū Bakr. Then the Prophet said, "Bring me another!" and he brought it and the Prophet milked it and left it.[26]

While both accounts relate the same encounter between Muḥammad and Umm Maʿbad, there are significant narrative differences between the account in the chronological section about the *hijra* and that in the thematic chapter on signs of prophecy. In the *hijra* account, the male relative is identified as Umm Maʿbad's husband, but in the thematic chapter of "signs of prophecy," he is identified as her son. The age of the animal and the reason for its inability to produce milk also differ. The account in the *hijra* also includes a theme of blessing, as expressed in the Prophet's renaming of the sheep. The general episode of Muḥammad milking an animal that is deemed incapable of producing milk is common in the account of Wahb b. Munabbih's biography and in Ibn Saʿd's two accounts. But while both of Ibn Saʿd's accounts relate to the same episode, only the one in the chronological framework of the *hijra* closely parallels Wahb b. Munabbih's account. This should not, however, automatically lead to the conclusion that Ibn Saʿd introduced Wahb's material into the emerging *dalāʾil al-nubūwa* literature. Even though the provenance of the account in the chapter on the signs of prophecy is not sufficiently identified, it does appear that Ibn Saʿd deliberately chose a different source than Wahb b. Munabbih,

26 Ibn Saʿd, *Ṭabaqāt*, 1:156f.

who was discredited in scholarly circles. This could signify diverging standards of authentication between the chronological *sīra* overall and the particular thematic chapters in which Ibn Saʿd may have felt obliged to provide individual *isnād*s that he could not produce for the one from Wahb b. Munabbih.

1.2.1.2 *Muḥammad's Encounter with Surāqa*

Another case study is the narrative of Muḥammad's encounter with a Qurayshī man called Surāqa, who pursued the Prophet after his escape from Medina. One version of this account, found in the *Maghāzī* of Mūsā b. ʿUqba (d. 140/758), is partially preserved in a unique manuscript.[27] This manuscript includes twenty excerpts of the *maghāzī* work, each containing the *isnād* and actual text.[28] The *maghāzī* contains the following account: After Muḥammad left Mecca, the Quraysh offered a reward of one hundred camels for anyone who returned him to Mecca. A man came to a group of Quraysh and claimed that he had seen three men passing by, one of whom he thought was the Prophet. Eager to pursue Muḥammad himself, Surāqa diverted the group's attention by stating that those men were in search of their animals that had gone astray. Then Surāqa went home and took his divination arrows and rode into the deepest part of the valley. He drew an arrow, which read "He will not harm him." He followed Muḥammad's traces and drew another arrow. The result was the same as the first time. Surāqa was even more insistent on finding Muḥammad and continued his pursuit. Once Muḥammad and his men came into sight, the feet of Surāqa's horse sank into the ground and Surāqa fell off. A cloud of dust accompanied the Prophet and Surāqa realized that he could not harm the Prophet. He shouted that he did not intend to harm the Prophet and Abū Bakr wrote an agreement between the Prophet and Surāqa. When Mecca was conquered eight years later, Surāqa approached the Prophet to show him the letter of agreement. Muḥammad pardoned him and Surāqa converted to Islam.[29]

The episode of Surāqa and his horse also appears in Wahb b. Munabbih's account of the Prophet's life, as summarized in chapter 1.[30] The context is the

27 Sachau, "Der Berliner Fragment des Mūsā Ibn ʿUḳba," 445–470; a new edition of this text includes a detailed introduction and systematic listing of parallel accounts; cf. Ibn Qāḍī Shuhba, *Aḥādīth muntakhaba*.

28 The excerpts reflect the ten parts of the original work. It is not clear whether the structure of ten parts goes back to Mūsā himself or to a later compiler; cf. Sachau, "Der Berliner Fragment des Mūsā Ibn ʿUḳba," 448. At least twelve of these accounts are found in passages from Mūsā as al-Bayhaqī quotes them in his *Dalāʾil al-nubūwa*; Schoeler, "Mūsā b. ʿUqbas Maghāzī," 69.

29 Sachau, "Der Berliner Fragment des Mūsā Ibn ʿUḳba," 452f.

30 Khoury, *Wahb b. Munabbih*, 148f.; chapter 1, 17f.

same as in Mūsā's account, but in Wahb's account, Surāqa's encounter with the Prophet is presented in more detail. Abū Bakr noticed Surāqa and asked Muḥammad to make supplications (*duʿāʾ*) to keep Surāqa away from them. The horse's legs then sank into the ground in response to Muḥammad's supplication. Then Surāqa requested the Prophet to ask God to release the horse's legs and in return, he promised not to harm them. The horse was set free and Surāqa accompanied the Prophet and his Companions until he spotted men from his family. He left the Prophet in order to divert the men and thus protect the Prophet.

The two versions display a common context and a number of the same details, but there are also some divergences. Thus, it seems initially that the two accounts of Surāqa's encounter with the Prophet relate to one another the way the accounts of the *hijra* by ʿUrwa b. al-Zubayr and Wahb b. Munabbih do. However, the overarching message conveyed in the accounts of Mūsā and Wahb are significantly different. The most prominent difference being that Mūsā b. ʿUqba does not directly connect the stumbling of Surāqa's horse to any action of the Prophet, as the dialog between Abū Bakr and Muḥammad and the supplication (*duʿāʾ*) are absent in Mūsā's version. Wahb, by contrast, does not mention the letter or the second half of Mūsā's account that is situated at the conquest of Mecca. The reference to men searching for their straying animals appears in both versions, albeit in different contexts. Mūsā's account mentions it as a means for Surāqa to divert his companions' interest in pursuing the Prophet, in order to secure the opportunity for himself. In Wahb's account, Surāqa uses the same statement to divert the attention of his tribesmen, but this time his intention is to protect the Prophet from his Surāqa's family members. Surāqa's encounter with the Prophet is also mentioned in the letter that Abū Bakr sent the Quraysh after the Prophet's arrival at Medina. This letter presents the sunken horse of Surāqa as a sign, which was acknowledged by Surāqa, whereas the other Quraysh still required proof for the Prophet's cause.[31] Following the arrival of the letter, the Banū Mudlij are reproached for their member's support of the Prophet, but Surāqa himself refutes the criticism in the letter, stating that they, too, would have acknowledged the Prophet if the same thing had happened to them.[32] As such, the two accounts may have many elements in common, but generally convey very different messages. Mūsā's version evokes the sense that Surāqa realized his inability to capture Muḥammad following the accidental stumbling of his horse, and this leads to a truce between the two protagonists, while Wahb portrays the encounter as

31 Khoury, *Wahb b. Munabbih*, 1:154f.

32 Khoury, *Wahb b. Munabbih*, 1:158f.

an act of divine protection of the Prophet which causes Surāqa to acknowledge the Prophet and even defend his actions against his fellow tribesmen.

Mūsā b. ʿUqba's account was transmitted on the authority of al-Zuhrī and is also found—with very similar wording—in ʿAbd al-Razzāq,[33] al-Ṭabarānī,[34] al-Bukhārī,[35] Aḥmad b. Ḥanbal,[36] Ibn Isḥāq,[37] al-Wāqidī,[38] and al-Bayhaqī.[39] These accounts are linked to various *isnād*s but they all go back to al-Zuhrī.[40] Therefore, this account should be regarded as part of the "scholarly" tradition. The account of Wahb, however, only resurfaced in Ibn Saʿd's account of the *hijra*. Ibn Saʿd's work includes this episode in three accounts: two appear in the context of the *hijra* in his chronological *sīra* section[41] and a third is part of the chapter on the signs of prophecy.[42] In the thematic chapter, the episode with Surāqa is supported by an obviously deficient *isnād* based on the authority of "a shaykh from the Quraysh."[43] Ibn Saʿd's general biography, however, includes shorter versions of Surāqa's encounter with the Prophet, which are closer to the account of Wahb than they are to that of al-Zuhrī.

1.2.1.3 *The Cobweb and the Pigeon*

A third example of unauthenticated materials in Ibn Saʿd's biography is the narrative about a pigeon and a cobweb at the entrance of the cave in which Muḥammad and Abū Bakr hide from their Qurayshī pursuers. The narrative is part of Wahb b. Munabbih's prophetic biography[44] and might have been the source for Ibn Saʿd, as it is not found in this form in other biographies of the time. The narrative is notably absent in Ibn Isḥāq and al-Wāqidī only briefly mentions the cobweb over the cave's entrance without providing further

33 Al-Zuhrī's *maghāzī* includes two versions; cf. ʿAbd al-Razzāq, *al-Muṣannaf*, 5:392f.
34 Al-Ṭabarānī, *al-Muʿjam al-kabīr*, 7:133 (no. 6602).
35 Al-Bukhārī, *Ṣaḥīḥ*, 5:149–152.
36 Aḥmad, *Musnad*, 4:175f.
37 Ibn Isḥāq, *The Life of Muhammad*, 225f.
38 Wellhausen, *Muhammad in Medina*, 374.
39 Al-Bayhaqī, *Dalāʾil al-nubūwa*, 2:485f.
40 Schacht claimed that of some of Mūsā's *isnād*s going back to al-Zuhrī, including the one in question, were not authentic; cf. Schacht, "On Mūsā b. ʿUqba's Kitāb al-Maghāzī"; however, Schoeler rejected this view and demonstrated the authenticity of these *isnād*s based on parallel accounts from independent traditions going back to al-Zuhrī; cf. Schoeler, "Mūsā b. ʿUqbas Maghāzī," 83f.
41 Ibn Saʿd, *Ṭabaqāt*, 1:199.
42 Ibn Saʿd, *Ṭabaqāt*, 1:159.
43 Ibn Saʿd, *Ṭabaqāt*, 1:159.
44 Khoury, *Wahb ibn Munabbih*, 1:144f.

details.[45] Ibn Saʿd diverges from al-Wāqidī's brevity and inserts a tradition that provides more detail:

> The Prophet passed the night in the cave. God commanded a tree to grow in front of the Prophet, which concealed him. God [also] commanded a spider to weave its cobweb and thus conceal him. God [furthermore] commanded two wild pigeons, and they began to live at the mouth of the cave. The youth of the Quraysh—one from each tribe—with their swords, clubs, and rods approached, and they were at a distance of just 40 cubits from the Prophet. The first among them noticed the two pigeons, and so he withdrew. His companion said to him: "Why did you not look into the cave?" He replied: "I saw two wild pigeons at the mouth of the cave from which I concluded that there was no one inside." [Ibn Saʿd] said: The Prophet heard his voice and realized that God had kept them away. Then the Prophet wished them [i.e., the pigeons] well and in reward they were shifted to the sanctuary of God.[46]

This passage displays some parallels with the account of Wahb b. Munabbih, as well as additional details, such as a tree that grew in front of the cave and the destiny of the pigeons. Based on the extant textual evidence, it appears that Ibn Saʿd might have used Wahb b. Munabbih's account here, at least partially. It is noteworthy, however, that both versions of Ibn Saʿd's narrative are found in the general section on the *hijra* in the *sīra*, but do not appear in the chapter on the "signs of prophecy." The absence of this account from the *dalāʾil al-nubūwa* chapters is not necessarily related to its apparently unauthenticated source, but could indicate that Ibn Saʿd did not ascribe evidentiary relevance to this particular episode.

These three cases show that Ibn Saʿd most likely included some unauthenticated materials in his general *sīra* of the Prophet. His chronological chapters include three narratives that closely resemble accounts in Wahb's biography, but the thematic chapter on the "signs of prophecy" provides a more nuanced situation. Two accounts designated as signs of prophecy relate general episodes that are also found in Wahb's *sīra*, namely the Prophet's encounters with Umm Maʿbad and Surāqa, and both accounts display significant shortcomings in the chain of transmission. However, only the account of Surāqa shows strong narrative parallels to Wahb's account in contrast to the numerous authenticated reports that are transmitted on the authority of al-Zuhrī. Muḥammad's

45 Khoury, *Wahb ibn Munabbih*, 1:195.

46 Ibn Saʿd, *Ṭabaqāt*, 1:197.

encounter with Umm Maʿbad appears twice in Ibn Saʿd's work, once in the chronological part, and a second time in the thematic chapter. But only the version included in his chronological biography exhibits parallels with Wahb's account, while the one in the "signs of prophecy" chapter shares the encounter as a theme but differs decisively in content. Finally, the narrative of the spider and pigeon also shares some details with Wahb b. Munabbih's account but is completely left out of the chapters of the "signs of prophecy." The episodes of Umm Maʿbad and Surāqa may suggest that Ibn Saʿd was more critical in selecting *ḥadīth* for these thematic chapters. In conjunction with Ibn Saʿd's generally thorough employment of *isnād*s to support these thematic accounts, these results suggest that, contrary to the claims of earlier scholars, "unauthenticated" materials constituted a marginal number in Ibn Saʿd's accounts. The vast majority of accounts found in Ibn Saʿd's chapter on the "signs of prophecy" therefore seem to originate in scholarly circles and follow their standards of authentication.

1.2.2 "Popular" Materials in Ibn Saʿd's Chapters on the Signs of Prophecy

I have shown in the introduction to this book that earlier Orientalists have largely dismissed *dalāʾil al-nubūwa* literature based on the assumption that many narratives found in these compilations were "popular tales" in the sense that they originated among circles of storytellers who were assumed to be untrained in the Islamic sciences and therefore often fabricated narratives to entertain Muslim masses. Part of the Orientalists' argument relate to narrative styles; these were deemed too detailed and embellished compared to the supposedly more factual style of *ḥadīth*. Ibn Saʿd's chapters on the proofs of prophecy include three accounts (a speaking wolf, Miqdād's encounter with the devil, and *jinn* being chased by meteors) that display such narrative styles. In the following, I trace the inclusion of these narratives in early *ḥadīth* compilations. I argue that while some later Sunnī scholars and Orientalists may have questioned the authenticity of these accounts, many scholars contemporaneous with Ibn Saʿd had no such doubts and included them in their own collections.

I describe the first of these narratives in the introduction of this book: Tor Andrae classified as folklore an account of a speaking wolf that directs a shepherd to drive his flock to Medina and follow Muḥammad and his community. Andrae asserted that this particular account allegedly incited the suspicion of *ḥadīth* scholars because of its folkloristic nature.[47] Andrae's reference is to an account that he had found, not in *ḥadīth* collections or the early *dalāʾil*

47 Andrae, *Die Person Muhammed*, 27.

al-nubūwa compilations, but in *al-Shifāʾ* by Qāḍī ʿIyāḍ (d. 543/1149).[48] Thus, Andrae's point of departure was one relatively late text and his judgment was primarily based on a comment Qāḍī ʿIyāḍ made in reference to this *ḥadīth* in which he stated (*al-ḥadīth fī-hi qiṣṣa*). Andrae read this statement as an indication that Qāḍī ʿIyāḍ suspected a folkloristic origin that went back to the *quṣṣāṣ* rather than being the work of *ḥadīth* scholars.[49] For Western scholars of Andrae's time, these storytellers were synonymous with charlatans who freely invented stories to please their mostly uneducated audiences. As I laid out in chapter 1, Jonathan Berkey and Lyall Armstrong have more recently shown that, until well into the fourth/tenth century, these storytellers were for the most part scholars who were properly trained in various fields, and that the profession was only later haunted by dubious characters who entertained the masses with imaginary tales or Isrāʾīliyyāt.[50] Andrae's reliance on one late text combined with his generalized notion of *qiṣās* as untrustworthy led him to dismiss the entire *dalāʾil al-nubūwa* literature without investigating whether or how this account appeared in other texts. In fact, the narrative of the shepherd and the speaking wolf appears in a number of early and often prominent *ḥadīth* collections, such as the *Ṭabaqāt* of Ibn Saʿd, the *Musnad* of Ibn Ḥanbal (d. 241/855),[51] the two canonical *ḥadīth* collections of al-Bukhārī (d. 256/870)[52] and Muslim (d. 261/875),[53] as well as in later compilations, such as the *dalāʾil al-nubūwa* works of al-Bayhaqī,[54] Abū Nuʿaym,[55] and *al-Sīra al-nabawiyya* of

48 Qāḍī ʿIyād, *al-Shifāʾ bi-taʿrīf ḥuqūq al-Muṣṭafā*, 1:432.

49 Andrae, *Die Person Muhammeds*, 27.

50 Berkey, *Popular Preaching*.

51 Ibn Ḥanbal, *Musnad*, 3:203f. (no. 8049; this is a shorter account only relating the shepherd's encounter with the wolf, without many descriptive details), 4:210f. (no. 11814); 4:222 (no. 11863).

52 This *ḥadīth* was only partially related to the one in Ibn Saʿd's "signs of prophecy." The book of cultivation and agriculture states, "While a man was riding a cow, it turned toward him and said, 'I have not been created for this purpose, I have been created for ploughing.' The Prophet added, 'I, Abū Bakr, and ʿUmar believe in this story.' The Prophet said further, 'A wolf caught a sheep, and when the shepherd chased it, the wolf said, 'Who will be its guard on the day of wild beasts, when there will be no shepherd for it except I?' After narrating it, the Prophet said, 'I, Abū Bakr, and ʿUmar, too, believe it.'" Abū Salama said, "Abū Bakr and ʿUmar were not present"; cf. al-Bukhārī, *Ṣaḥīḥ*, 3:295 (no. 2324).

53 Muslim, *Ṣaḥīḥ*, 15:103 (no. 2388).

54 The *Dalāʾil al-nubūwa* encompasses a chapter containing various versions of this narrative. Their *isnād*s vary in strength. Two of these accounts are very close to the one in Ibn Saʿd; cf. al-Bayhaqī, *Dalāʾil al-nubūwa*, 6:41–44.

55 Abū Nuʿaym's work also includes two versions of this account; cf. al-Iṣfahānī, *Dalāʾil al-nubūwa*, 222f.

Ibn Kathīr[56] (d. 774/1373). It is noteworthy that the same *ḥadīth* appears, at the same time and sometimes even in the same collections, in shorter and longer versions. The core of the story (a wolf speaking to a shepherd to inform him about Muḥammad's prophetic mission in Medina) is central in all versions; the differences relate to descriptive details, such as what kind of leaves the sheep were feeding on. Therefore, the story of the speaking wolf clearly was part of the scholarly discourse from the early third/ninth century onward. Given that the word *qiṣṣa*, more generally, is associated with the notion of relating a piece of information, Qāḍī ʿIyāḍ probably meant that this particular version of the *ḥadīth* is unusually detailed in its descriptions, as compared to other versions; that is, he was not indicating that its provenance was unreliable storytellers. Andrae, however, failed to trace this account to other texts and thus considered these texts part of popular veneration of the Prophet.

The version of this episode also appears in Ibn Saʿd's chapter on the signs of prophecy after the beginning of the revelation. Even though Ibn Saʿd's version appears to be one of the longer accounts containing even more descriptive details than the one in *al-Shifāʾ*, Qāḍī ʿIyād's remark should not be taken as a dismissal of this account by scholars. We have seen that many other respected scholars included it in their *ḥadīth* compilations. Thus, this account may have stirred the suspicion of later Muslim scholars and Western Orientalists with regard to its "scholarly" provenance, but the frequent references to it in *ḥadīth* works that are closer in time to Ibn Saʿd seem to attest to its acceptance among earlier scholars.

The same can be said about two other lengthy accounts in Ibn Saʿd's chapter. The first describes Miqdād being tempted by Satan to drink Muḥammad's share of milk. In this account, Miqdād relates the following:

> I and two of my companions—our hearing and sight had gone due to hardship—approached [Medina]. We set out to submit ourselves to the Companions of the Prophet but not a single one received us. We rushed to the Prophet and he rushed with us to his family. There were three goats. The Prophet said: "Draw that milk and [distribute it] among us." We drew the milk and everyone drank his share and we kept the Prophet's share. He [i.e., the Prophet] came at night and greeted us [in such a way that] he did not wake the sleeping [people] but those awake heard [his greetings]. He went to the mosque and prayed; then he came for his drink and drank it. Satan came to me that night and said: "Muḥammad goes to the Anṣār [i.e., Helpers in Medina] and they offered him presents, he

56 Ibn Kathīr, *al-Sīra al-nabawiyya*, 4:183.

> takes meals with them, and he has no need of this mouthful [of milk], so drink it!" He did not cease to persuade me until I drank it. When it [the milk] penetrated my stomach and he knew there was no way for me to regurgitate it, he made me regret it: "Woe to you for what you did! You drank Muḥammad's drink! [When] he comes and he does not see it, he will curse you and you will perish, you lose this life and the afterlife!"
>
> I had a cloak of wool and whenever it was raised to my head, my feet came out, and when it was extended over my feet, my head would come out. Sleep would not come to me, but as for my two companions, they were fast asleep. The Prophet came and greeted us like he had greeted us before, went to the mosque to pray, and [then] came for his drink and uncovered it but he did not find anything there. He raised his head toward the sky and I said: "Now he is praying that I will die." He said: "oh God, feed whoever fed me, and give [something] to drink [to] whoever gave me [something] to drink." I approached with my cloak tightened around me and I took the knife. Then I rushed to the goats, touching them [to see] which [one of them] was the fattest to slaughter it for the Prophet, and they were all filled [with milk]. I approached the vessel of the Prophet's family that was [used to] draw the milk and I drew the milk into it until there was foam on it. Then I went with the vessel to the Prophet and he asked: "Have you not drunk your drink tonight, oh Miqdād?" I said: "Drink, Messenger of God!" He drank and then he passed it to me. I said: "Messenger of God, drink!" He drank and then he passed it to me; I took what was left and drank it. When I knew that the Prophet was satiated and his beneficial supplication had reached me, I laughed until I fell on the ground. The Prophet said: "[Tell me] one of your shameful acts, Miqdād." I said: "Messenger of God, I have done such and such." The Prophet said: "This was only out of God's mercy. Had you not been close to me you would have woken those two Companions and they would have had their share of it [i.e., the milk]." I said: "By Him who sent you with truth, I do not mind sharing with anyone of the people if you and I have partaken of it."[57]

This account stands out from the larger body of *ḥadīth* in terms of its content and style. While Miqdād's encounter with and temptation by the devil may be thematically reminiscent of folktales, it is the style of the narrative that sets it apart from most *ḥadīth*s, which tend to be characterized by a succinct, matter-of-fact tone, conveying few circumstantial descriptions or statements

57 Ibn Saʿd, *Ṭabaqāt*, 1:154f.

of emotion.[58] Yet, the account is found in copious *ḥadīth* compilations that are contemporary with Ibn Saʿd's work, such as the *Musnad* compilations of al-Ṭayālisī[59] (d. 204/820), Ibn Abī Shayba[60] (d. 235/850), and Aḥmad b. Ḥanbal,[61] the *Ṣaḥīḥ* of Muslim,[62] *al-Jāmiʿ al-ṣaḥīḥ* of al-Tirmidhī,[63] and the *Musnad* of al-Bazzār[64] (d. 292/905). Thus, there can be no doubt that this account was also firmly established in the scholarly circles of the time.

In addition to the narratives of the speaking wolf and Miqdād's encounter with Satan, Ibn Saʿd's chapter on the proofs of prophecy includes another narrative that appears to display "popular" elements that Ibn Saʿd might have taken from *ḥadīth* and *sīra* collections in general, but may also be drawn from material that usually pertains to the interpretation of the Qurʾān. The account reads as follows.

> When the Prophet was sent, the *jinn* were chased away and stars were cast upon them. Before that they had listened—to every tribe there was a place [for the *jinn*] to sit and they listened—the first who were afraid of [the presence of the *jinn*] were the people of Taif; they started slaughtering whatever camel and sheep they had every day [as sacrifice] for their deities until their means ran out. Then they stopped and some of them said to others, "Have you not seen the sign of the heavens, as if a thing had come from it?" Iblīs said, "That thing happened on earth. Bring me soil from every land!" Soil was brought and he sniffed it and drew near it until soil was brought from Tihama. He sniffed it and said, "It is happening here."[65]

This narrative draws on the Qurʾānic notion of *jinn* listening to celestial discourses. According to several verses in the Qurʾān, certain *jinn* were said to have played a role in facilitating the work of fortune-tellers and sorcerers in pre-Islamic Arabia by listening to conversations among the angels and conveying this information to human beings.[66] The Qurʾānic commentary (*tafsīr*)

58 Cf. Leder, "Conventions of Fictional Narration in Learned Literature," 37; Leder, "The Literary Use of Khabar," 307f.

59 Al-Tayālisī, *Musnad*, 2:476f. (no. 1256).

60 Ibn Abī Shayba, *Musnad*, 1:330f. (no. 487).

61 Ibn Ḥanbal, *Musnad*, 7:889f. (no. 24810 and no. 24813; the latter is the most extensive and closest to the one in Ibn Saʿd).

62 Muslim, *Ṣaḥīḥ*, 14:13f.

63 Al-Tirmidhī, *Sunan*, 5:66 (no. 2719).

64 Al-Bazzār, *al-Baḥr al-zakhār*, 6:41f.

65 Ibn Saʿd, *Ṭabaqāt*, 1:140f.

66 Q. 15:16–18, 37:6–10, 67:5, 72:8f.

tradition holds that God cut off all such access to angelic discussions after Muḥammad began receiving revelation; at that point He established angels as sentries and repelled the *jinn* with meteors. This particular episode in which Iblīs tried to establish what caused the disruption and where these meteors took place, however, is not commonly found in exegetical and *ḥadīth* literature. The *Muṣannaf* of Ibn Abī Shayba[67] appears to be the only *ḥadīth* work containing this account. It is also found in the *tafsīr* of al-Ṭabarī (d. 310/923).[68] This account is seldom attested in other scholarly works, and only rarely surfaces in *tafsīr* literature about a generation after Ibn Saʿd. While this does not allow us to trace the origins of this particular tradition, it does suggest that Ibn Saʿd might have occasionally looked to other fields of scholarship when compiling the materials for his chapters on the "signs of prophecy."

In conclusion, it seems that the earliest works of *dalāʾil al-nubūwa* were authored by *ḥadīth* scholars who compiled thematic chapters in accordance with the standards of their field and employed the appropriate level of authentication available in their respective times. Even Ibn Saʿd, whose expertise was not *ḥadīth* compilation in the narrower sense, proves to have worked according to the scholarly methodological framework of his time. His work displays several standards of authentication, depending on the context of the *maghāzī* or *sīra*, and we could even argue that he attempted to apply stricter standards to his thematic chapters on the "signs of prophecy." Even in the few cases in which Ibn Saʿd included less authentic materials, the accounts themselves mostly appear in other *ḥadīth* collections of his times or in later ones. This is true for methodological and stylistic aspects. While modern scholars have rejected the notion that literature was part of the scholarly discourse, my analyses of the authors' networks and the extant early texts show that the origins of *ḥadīth*-based *dalāʾil al-nubūwa* works are squarely situated in scholarly circles.

2 Methodologies of Authentication in Later *Dalāʾil al-Nubūwa* Works

The examination of *dalāʾil al-nubūwa* authors in chapter 2 shows a clear distinction between the early authors of the late third/ninth century and later scholars of the fourth/tenth and fifth/eleventh centuries in terms of their intellectual backgrounds and their interconnectedness with other authors of this literature. As such, authors of the third and fourth generations had little personal interaction with previous *dalāʾil al-nubūwa* authors. In this section I analyze three later extant works, those of al-Khargūshī, Abū Nuʿaym al-Iṣfahānī,

67 Ibn Abī Shayba, *al-Muṣannaf*, 8:436.

68 Al-Ṭabarī, *Tafsīr*, 23:38.

and al-Bayhaqī, with the primary goal of establishing whether the lack of personal student-teacher relations between the earlier and later generations of authors also manifests itself in the methodological approaches and structure of the works. A couple of methodological considerations should be noted: The body of sources dating from this transitional period is limited because there are no works preserved from the third generation. This creates a considerable gap between the last compilation of the second generation, the chapter in the *Sunan* of al-Tirmidhī, and the first of the fourth generation, the *Sharaf al-nabī* by al-Khargūshī. Therefore, the analysis of the later works only allows us to juxtapose their approaches; it does not allow an extensive outline of the continuously evolving methodology in the third and fourth generations, and this appears to be when this literature was systematized. I focus on the question of the authors' methodological approaches, particularly the presence of *isnād*s and the ways in which they were employed, and, to a lesser degree, the extent to which these compilations included narratives that did not have authenticated sources.

2.1 *Al-Khargūshī's* Sharaf al-Nabī

Al-Khargūshī studied with some scholars of *ḥadīth* but was mostly known as an ascetic. His *Sharaf al-nabī* differs significantly from previous works in terms of its methodological approach, scope, and arrangement. While his antecedents followed the scholarly methodology of *ḥadīth* by authenticating their accounts, al-Khargūshī's compilation provides minimal support by including authenticated *isnād* chains. He frequently presents what seems like a complete *isnād* at the beginning of a chapter. However, this appears to be a stylistic feature rather than evidence of his methodological integrity, as the vast majority of the subsequent accounts allude to a single Companion or Follower who transmitted a *ḥadīth*, but omit the subsequent chain of transmission. Therefore, his methodology partially resembles the approaches of *sīra* works that provide collective *isnād*s for the overall framework, and then supplement them with individual reports. Contrary to those individual *sīra* accounts, however, the chain of transmission in al-Khargūshī's subsequent accounts includes just the alleged narrator; this does not allow a proper authentication according to the standards of Sunnī *ḥadīth* scholars of his time. In many other instances accounts are simply introduced with an impersonal construction, such as "it has been said that …" without any identification of the transmitter. Thus, al-Khargūshī's methodology differs sharply from that of his predecessors, as he fails to meet their scholarly standards of authenticating individual accounts.

Al-Khargūshī's work also contains a number of narratives that are well-known from "unauthenticated" traditions, such as the account of the cobweb concealing the entrance of the cave where the Prophet and Abū Bakr hid during the *hijra*,[69] or the Prophet sprinkling dust on the heads of the Quraysh while lying in ambush outside of his house.[70] These accounts are found in the biographical reports of Wahb b. Munabbih[71] and Ibn Saʿd.[72] By including these episodes, al-Khargūshī diverges from previous *dalāʾil al-nubūwa* authors who selected only materials accepted by *muḥaddithūn*. As we have seen, Ibn Saʿd also utilized these sources throughout the *sīra* section of his *Ṭabaqāt*, but did not include them in his chapters on the "signs of prophecy" and generally upheld higher methodological standards in these chapters than throughout the *sīra*. Thus, al-Khargūshī is more lax in relation to these sources than any of the previous authors we have studied here. He is the first *dalāʾil al-nubūwa* author we can identify who abandoned the methodological parameters of *ḥadīth* scholarship and more closely approximates those of *sīra*/*maghāzī* literature, as we also see in our analysis of the organizational structure of his work.

2.2 *Abū Nuʿaym al-Iṣfahānī's* Dalāʾil al-Nubūwa

Abū Nuʿaym al-Iṣfahānī's *Dalāʾil al-nubūwa* is one of the most well-known works of this kind and is printed in various editions. The author was a prominent and respected scholar of *ḥadīth*, and, contrary to al-Khargūshī, he studied with several earlier authors of *dalāʾil al-nubūwa*, such as al-Ṭabarānī (d. 360/971) and Ibn Mandah (d. 395/1005). Al-Sakhawī attributes a work entitled *Dalāʾil al-nubūwa* to another teacher of Abū Nuʿaym, namely Abū l-Shaykh al-Iṣfahānī.[73] Like the earlier *dalāʾil al-nubūwa* compilers, Abū Nuʿaym presents a full *isnād* for every account. His sources, however, also include transmitters that are more commonly found in *sīra* works and related literary genres. In addition to many well-known *ḥadīth* transmitters, such as ʿUrwa b. al-Zubayr, al-Zuhrī, Maʿmar b. Rāshid, or ʿAbd al-Razzāq, Abū Nuʿaym's *isnād*s frequently include figures such as Wahb b. Munabbih and Kaʿb al-Aḥbār, who were mostly known for transmitting Isrāʾīliyyāt,[74] as well as Ibn Isḥāq and al-Wāqidī, who

69 Al-Khargūshī, *Sharaf al-nabī*, 154.

70 Al-Khargūshī, *Sharaf al-nabī*, 175f. The theme of the Prophet throwing dust or soil also occurs in an account of the battle of Badr in which the Muslim army was vastly outnumbered. The Prophet threw soil at the opposing army, which incapacitated them and led to the Muslims' victory; Al-Khargūshī, *Sharaf al-nabī*, 159f. In Qurʾānic exegesis, this episode from the battle of Badr is commonly associated with verse 8:17.

71 Khoury, *Wahb b. Munabbih*, 1:140f.

72 Ibn Saʿd, *Ṭabaqāt*, 1:195.

73 Al-Sakhawī, *al-Iʿlān*, 91. Abū l-Shaykh's extant work *Akhlāq al-nabī wa-adabuhu* is not a *Dalāʾil al-nubūwa* work but a compendium on the Prophet similar to al-Khargūshī's work or the *Shamāʾil* work of al-Tirmidhī. It describes the Prophet's physical appearance, mannerisms, character traits, and numerous objects he possessed.

74 Armstrong, *The Quṣṣāṣ of Early Islam*, 93.

were prominent in the fields of *sīra*, *maghāzī*, and early Muslim history, but were often criticized by scholars of *ḥadīth*. This broader pool of sources is also reflected in Abū Nuʿaym's accounts. Like al-Khargūshī before him, Abū Nuʿaym includes several narratives that are well-known from the "unauthenticated" tradition, such as the incident in which the Prophet sprinkled soil on the heads of the Quraysh who lay in ambush for him on the night of the *hijra*.[75] Furthermore, he mentions the incident of wild pigeons sitting at the mouth of the cave and God ordering a tree to grow in front of it to prevent the Quraysh from finding the Prophet and Abū Bakr who were hiding there.[76] These latter elements (the tree and pigeons) are less common in earlier traditions of the *hijra*. Wahb b. Munabbih mentions a cobweb that was spun across the entrance of the cave and an angel in the shape of a pigeon.[77] Al-Wāqidī also mentions the cobweb but no pigeons,[78] and Ibn Isḥāq's account does not mention the incident. Ibn Saʿd presents an account similar to Abū Nuʿaym's description of the pigeons and the tree in his chronological biography of the Prophet, but this episode is absent from his chapters on the "signs of prophecy." Like al-Khargūshī before him, Abū Nuʿaym breaks with the trend of previous *dalāʾil al-nubūwa* authors who selected only those materials that were accepted by *muḥaddithūn*. But unlike al-Khargūshī, Abū Nuʿaym makes the case that his approach still follows the methodological parameters of Islamic scholarship. He provides a preface to his work in which he (indirectly) defends this inclusion of "unauthenticated" materials. Notably, he specifically points to prophetic miracles as the aspect of Muḥammad's biography that requires him to include less authenticated materials, because "the miracles of the Prophet are too many to enumerate and more famous than just those that can be supported by proper *isnāds*."[79] As such, he briefly touches on questions of methodology but the main subjects in his preface are theological expositions on prophecy, which are discussed in a later section.

2.3 *Al-Bayhaqī's* Dalāʾil al-nubūwa

In the preface to his work, al-Bayhaqī sought to legitimize the sources he used, to include them in the methodological framework of *ḥadīth* scholarship and legal theory. Like Abū Nuʿaym, al-Bayhaqī drew on an extensive and

75 Abū Nuʿaym al-Iṣfahānī relates this account on the authority of Ibn Isḥāq and the narrative is also found in Wahb b. Munabbih, as I have previously shown; al-Iṣfahānī, *Dalāʾil al-nubūwa*, 115f.

76 Al-Iṣfahānī, *Dalāʾil al-nubūwa*, 191.

77 Khoury, *Wahb b. Munabbih*, 1:144f.

78 Ibn Saʿd, *Ṭabaqāt*, 1:195.

79 Al-Iṣfahānī, *Dalāʾil al-nubūwa*, 15.

varied pool of material, ranging from accounts transmitted by participants of the *ṣaḥīḥ* movement, such as Abū Dāwūd, al-Tirmidhī, Aḥmad b. Ḥanbal, Ibn Mājah, al-Nisāʾī, al-Darāmī, or Mālik b. Anas to less rigorously authenticated ones. Al-Bayhaqī states in the preface of the *Dalāʾil al-nubūwa* that he intended to differentiate "sound" narratives from less authoritative ones.[80] He considers the two *Ṣaḥīḥ* works of al-Bukhārī and Muslim the foundation of his own work and identifies the *ḥadīth*s that are included in these two collections. However, he also accepts accounts from the *maghāzī* works of Mūsā b. ʿUqba and al-Wāqidī and frequently relies on material from Ibn Isḥāq's *Sīra*. As these sources lack the authority of proper *ḥadīth*s, al-Bayhaqī offers an extensive discussion in his preface, in which he argues that employing less authenticated materials for this kind of literature is, in fact, in line with the methodological requirements of *ḥadīth* scholarship. Al-Bayhaqī relies on al-Shāfiʿī's *Risāla* as his authority for scholarly methodology, as we see in the following.

Al-Bayhaqī begins his systematic approach to these methodological questions by reproducing al-Shāfiʿī's argument that the Qurʾān's command to the Prophet to be obedient legitimizes the Sunna as a guideline for Muslim conduct.[81] He continues to reiterate the notion that it is expected that ordinary Muslims and *ḥadīth* experts will possess different levels of knowledge of the Sunna; this reinforces the bifurcation of laymen and specialists' engagement with *ḥadīth* that emerged around the time of the *ṣaḥīḥ* movement. Drawing on al-Shāfiʿī's *Risāla*, he categorizes the accounts into general reports (*akhbār*), such as those that prescribe the basic practices of the faith, which must be known by laymen and scholars alike; and specific *akhbār* that pertain to details of legal rulings and opinions, which only scholars are required to know.[82] Al-Bayhaqī goes on to list al-Shāfiʿī's criteria for specific *akhbār*, in terms of the requirements for their transmitters and levels of authenticity in order for them to be accepted.[83] He classifies these specific *akhbār* as (1) those on whose soundness scholars agree, (2) those on whose weakness scholars agree, (3) and those on which scholars disagree.[84] Of particular interest for this study is the first category, which he further subdivides into accounts transmitted through numerous initial transmitters (*mutawātir*), and those that can be traced back

80 Al-Iṣfahānī, *Dalāʾil al-nubūwa*, 47.

81 Al-Bayhaqī, *Dalāʾil al-nubūwa*, 20–27.

82 Al-Bayhaqī, *Dalāʾil al-nubūwa*, 22.

83 The transmitter must be trustworthy in his religion, truthful in his knowledge of *ḥadīth*, of sound mind, and knowledgeable in the meanings derived from *ḥadīths*; he must know the account verbatim exactly like he heard it or studied it from a book, and must be free of any accusations of deceit in *ḥadīth* transmission; cf. al-Bayhaqī, *Dalāʾil al-nubūwa*, 29–31.

84 Al-Bayhaqī, *Dalāʾil al-nubūwa*, 32–38.

to only one transmitter (*āḥād*). Based on its less rigorously established reliability, the latter category may not serve for legal rulings (*aḥkām*) but remains acceptable for works on edification and admonishment.[85]

Like Abū Nuʿaym before him, al-Bayhaqī specifically addressed the question of miracles that are often transmitted by only one Companion, as they were frequently said to have occurred in the presence of one person only, who then spread the account among the people. If such an account were corroborated by other widespread accounts of a miracle or sign, it could even be considered *tawātur*.[86] By the same token, al-Bayhaqī asserts that relying on weak transmitters may also be permissible, depending on the context in which the accounts are used, and stresses that those transmitters who have been accused of lying may not be relied on for legal rulings but their accounts may be used for edifying purposes. He quotes Aḥmad b. Ḥanbal regarding the scholarly value of these transmitters in historical contexts but not for legal or ritual purposes.[87] Al-Bayhaqī also elucidated conditions that permit the use of *ḥadīth*s with a *mursal isnād*, that is, a sound chain of transmission that is traced back to Followers (*tābiʿūn*) as transmitters, but that do not mention the Companion (*ṣaḥāba*); he also discussed diverging or contradictory *ḥadīth*s and questions of abrogation. Al-Bayhaqī's elaborate discussion of the permissibility of *āḥād ḥadīth* and weak transmitters in certain contexts is clearly meant to justify his own incorporation of *maghāzī* and historical materials.

With this extensive preface al-Bayhaqī comprehensively builds the case that his *Dalāʾil al-nubūwa* upholds the required scholarly standards. Since he does not argue for the foundation of religious practices or make legal rulings, the inclusion of *ḥadīth*s based on weak *isnād*s and on accounts taken from histories and *maghāzī* works is acceptable. Nevertheless, al-Bayhaqī privileges accounts from sound *ḥadīth* compilations whenever possible and identifies these as such. If he resorts to less authoritative sources, these are commonly identified as well. In some cases, he indicates the weak *isnād* in the heading of a sub-chapter.[88] The same applies to his inclusion of accounts from *maghāzī* literature.[89] However, for the most part, this information must be derived from the *isnād*. The way al-Bayhaqī uses these less authoritative materials differs from case to case. When the same event is related in both sound and weak accounts, he lists these in the same thematic chapter, first the most

85 Al-Bayhaqī, *Dalāʾil al-nubūwa*, 27f.

86 Al-Bayhaqī, *Dalāʾil al-nubūwa*, 33.

87 Al-Bayhaqī, *Dalāʾil al-nubūwa*, 37f.

88 For instance, al-Bayhaqī, *Dalāʾil al-nubūwa*, 5:421, 423.

89 For an account on the authority of Mūsā b. ʿUqba, see, al-Bayhaqī, *Dalāʾil al-nubūwa*, 3:101; for an account on the authority of Ibn Isḥāq, see al-Bayhaqī, *Dalāʾil al-nubūwa*, 3:164.

authoritative accounts and then the weaker ones at the end of the chapter. For instance, the water miracle at Ḥudaybiyya is related first in several accounts taken from al-Bukhārī and Muslim and then with accounts on the authority of Mūsā b. ʿUqba.[90] When weaker materials relate an incident for which there is no sound account, the weak accounts are interspersed between the authoritative ones chronologically, so the chapter as a whole provides a cohesive narrative. For instance, the chapter on the Prophet's emigration mainly relies on sound accounts based on the authority of al-Zuhrī, ʿUrwa b. al-Zubayr, and ʿĀʾisha, as they are recorded in al-Bukhārī and Muslim. Toward the end of the chapter, however, we find the account of the young Qurayshī men who discover the cave in which the Prophet and Abū Bakr were hiding, but do not enter it because God caused a tree to grow in front of its entrance, a spider to build a cobweb, and pigeons to nest.[91] As I have shown above, this account might be insufficiently authenticated, but it nevertheless appears in other works and is also found in general biography sections in the works of Ibn Saʿd, and in the *dalāʾil al-nubūwa* works of al-Khargūshī, and Abū Nuʿaym. While there is some less authenticated material found in his *Dalāʾil al-nubūwa*, overall, al-Bayhaqī maintains the scholarly standards required for non-legal prophetic traditions as he carefully laid out in his preface.

•••

This section has outlined the evolving methodological framework applied to *dalāʾil al-nubūwa* compilations. The earliest extant compilations of *dalāʾil al-nubūwa* literature emerged in the environment of highly critical *ḥadīth* scholarship. While the collections of Maʿmar b. Rāshid, al-Bukhārī, and al-Tirmidhī may not fully meet the criteria of authenticity and reliability articulated by later legal theorists, they all took part in the scholarly discourses that contributed to establishing these standards and, in so doing, furthered the bifurcation of professional scholarly engagement with *ḥadīth*, on the one hand, and endeavors by ordinary Muslims to fulfill spiritual devotions, on the other. It is abundantly clear, then, that *dalāʾil al-nubūwa* literature was squarely rooted in scholarly circles.

This fact is true even for the one extensive compilation authored by Ibn Saʿd, whose expertise lay in the auxiliary field of the science of narrators (*ʿilm al-rijāl*) rather than *ḥadīth* proper, and whose chapters were situated in the methodological context of *sīra* rather than *ḥadīth*. The analysis of Ibn Saʿd's

90 Al-Bayhaqī, *Dalāʾil al-nubūwa*, 4:115–128.

91 Al-Bayhaqī, *Dalāʾil al-nubūwa*, 2:481f.

methodological approach in the *sīra* section of his *Ṭabaqāt* shows that he tended to employ *isnād*s for *ḥadīth* but would occasionally insert collective chains of transmission. It has also become clear that he drew on a number of sources for his *sīra* sections; these sources ranged from well authenticated accounts, to material that was likely drawn from the discredited Wahb b. Munabbih, though he is not identified by name. There is also a possibility that Ibn Saʿd drew on materials from other emerging fields of scholarship, such as Qurʾān commentary (*tafsīr*). While Ibn Saʿd's approach in his chronological biography shows varying degrees of authentication and several instances in which he included unauthenticated material, there are reasons to think that he might have consciously applied stricter levels of criticism to those accounts he included in the chapters dedicated to the signs of prophecy. First, there are no collective *isnād*s in this section, though a few of the individual chains of transmission in these chapters display clear shortcomings, such as unidentified transmitters. In addition to the consistent use of individual *isnād*s, Ibn Saʿd's selective choices of *ḥadīth* for his thematic chapters might also suggest that he sought to use higher standards of authentication. At least the first two episodes, Muḥammad's encounter with Umm Maʿbad and Surāqa, are related in unauthenticated accounts in the *sīra* but were then, in the chapter on the signs of prophecy after the revelation, were replaced by accounts with more rigorously authenticated *isnād*s. Even those accounts whose content later led to questions about its provenance, such as the speaking wolf, were corroborated in *ḥadīth* works contemporaneous with Ibn Saʿd's *Ṭabaqāt*. Based on the parameters *ḥadīth* scholars used to measure historical reliability at this time, this widespread circulation would most likely have been considered sufficient support for the *ḥadīth* in question. Both formal aspects of *ḥadīth* criticism and circumstantial evidence of problematic accounts being corroborated by other contemporaneous scholarly works indicate a scholarly provenance of the "signs of prophecy" and the specific exclusion of laymen masses, even when these works did not yet meet the strictest standards prevalent among scholars of *ḥadīth* in the narrower sense.

We see significant shifts in the methodological approaches of later works of al-Khargūshī, Abū Nuʿaym, and al-Bayhaqī. All three include materials from a much broader pool of sources than earlier generations of *dalāʾil al-nubūwa* authors utilized; these included authenticated accounts from well-respected scholars of *ḥadīth* as well as less stringently authenticated materials from specialists in *maghāzī*, *sīra*, Isrāʾīliyyāt, and historical sources. The extent to which authentication was considered relevant for this type of literature differs among the three authors. Having the least rigorous scholarly credentials, al-Khargūshī provides only minimal support for his accounts, and often reduces the means of authentication to stylistic features by simply providing the name of an individual narrator without any chain of transmission or even providing entirely anonymous accounts. Therefore, his methodology represents the sharpest departure from his predecessors' dedication to authenticating their contents. Abū Nuʿaym and al-Bayhaqī both remained committed to providing chains of transmission but also broadened the pool of sources for the material they included. Abū Nuʿaym dedicated the preface of his work to address questions of theological import and only mentions, in passing, that Muḥammad's miracles were too numerous and famous to be related exclusively in properly authenticated accounts. Thus, methodological considerations play a much less important role for him than they do for his contemporary al-Bayhaqī. The latter extensively elaborated on why his inclusion of less rigorously authenticated materials fully aligns with the methodological requirements of *ḥadīth* scholarship, given that his work does not relate to matters of legal or ritual norms; therefore, this remains acceptable even with lower levels of reliability and authenticity. It becomes clear that all extant works of *dalāʾil al-nubūwa*, perhaps with the exception of al-Khargūshī's, actively operated in the existing framework of authentication and the scholarly acceptance of their work, and did not seek to gain the attention of Muslim masses.

3 Structure and Arrangement of *Dalāʾil al-Nubūwa* Works

In addition to methodological changes, *dalāʾil al-nubūwa* literature has undergone considerable development in the ways authors structured and arranged their materials. The majority of extant *dalāʾil al-nubūwa* works from the earliest period are organized into thematic chapters dedicated to the signs of prophecy, and appear in larger multi-thematic *ḥadīth* compilations. By contrast, al-Jūzajānī's work is a monograph dedicated entirely to the topic of the signs of prophecy. Unfortunately only fractions of one of its chapters have been preserved in a manuscript. This selective process, which was most likely undertaken by someone other than the author himself, causes significant challenges for this study because it makes it impossible to gauge the entire work's extent, content, or structure. Therefore, al-Juzajānī's work is excluded from the discussion of the structure and arrangement these works.

The chapters in Maʿmar, al-Bukhārī, and al-Tirmidhī share common features; they display very little internal ordering and they record numerous *ḥadīth*s without thematic or chronological sub-categories. Consistent with many approaches to thematically organized *muṣannaf* compilations, these chapters are not arranged to provide a continuous narrative and are not contextualized with commentary explaining the choice of accounts or related considerations, such as theological or methodological approaches that may have led to their selection. Later works differ in structure, in that they are crafted to portray Muḥammad in a more systematic way and often, directly or indirectly, address questions of theological import regarding the nature of his prophecy. Given the brevity of the earliest extant works and the analytical challenges posed by the selective excerpt of al-Jūzajānī, this section focuses on Ibn Saʿd and the later authors, al-Khargūshī, Abū Nuʿaym, and al-Bayhaqī.

3.1 *Ibn Saʿd's "ʿAlamāt al-Nubūwa"*

Given that Ibn Saʿd's chapters appear in the framework of the *sīra*, his arrangement of materials clearly differs from that of *ḥadīth* scholars. I briefly outline the arrangement of the *sīra* part of his *Ṭabaqāt*, then more closely examine those chapters dedicated to the signs of prophecy.

In the *sīra* section, Ibn Saʿd presents the major events of the Prophet's life in 199 chapters, roughly in a chronological order. He begins with the genealogy of previous prophets (chapters 1–9); the genealogy of Muḥammad's tribe (chapters 10–18); Muḥammad's childhood and youth, including his father's marriage, Muḥammad's conception, and his mother's pregnancy; the death of both parents and his paternal grandfather; his "adoption" by his uncle and going to Syria; and then some stories from Mecca (chapters 19–33). Ibn Saʿd then moves on to Muḥammad's immediate family, including Khadīja and his children (chapters 34–37). While Ibn Saʿd arranged this material largely according to chronological order, he also inserted chapters based on themes. The next set of chapters are dedicated to his call to prophecy and the first revelations, their description, the physical impact revelations had on Muḥammad, and the early stages of the dissemination of the message (chapters 38–47). This part of the book includes the two chapters I study here: chapter 39 on the signs of prophecy prior to the call to prophecy, and chapter 41 on the signs of prophecy after the call to prophecy. These two chapters are part of a cluster of four chapters that address issues of prophecy: chapter 38 is entitled "Dhikr nubūwa rasūl Allāh" (Reports of the prophecy of the Messenger of God), which introduces the topic of prophecy and places the beginning of Muḥammad's prophecy in the age of Adam's creation. Chapter 39 is the first chapter on the signs of prophecy; it focuses on narratives that are historically placed before the first revelation. The very short chapter 40 is interspersed between the two chapters on the signs of prophecy; it contains three accounts of Arabs who, having heard from the People of the Book (*ahl al-kitāb*) or Soothsayers that a prophet named Muḥammad would emerge among the Arabs, named their sons Muḥammad in order to attain prophecy. Finally, chapter 41 is dedicated to signs of Muḥammad's prophecy following the onset of revelations. Chapters 42–47 cover narratives from the early days of Muḥammad's revelation, then cover the persecution of Muslims in Mecca, emigration to Abyssinia and Taif; the *isrāʾ*, *ḥijra* to Medina (chapters 48–62), and life in Medina, including many aspects of worship and practice (chapters 63–72). The last thematic group of chapters includes accounts of Arabs dying during raids (chapters 73–144); the description of Muḥammad's appearance, including his description in the Torah and Gospel; the mole between his shoulder blades commonly known as the "seal of prophecy"; and his character, habits, and possessions (chapters 145–199).

In contrast to the chronologically arranged historical chapters of Ibn Saʿd's prophetic biography, the chapters dedicated to the "signs of prophecy" are largely thematic in their arrangement. While in general, these chapters interrupt the chronology of the Prophet's biography, the ordering principle in these chapters is roughly chronological, though they do not include direct references to historical events of the nascent Muslim community. In some instances, the contexts of the narratives allow for a historical approximation; however, in general, the historical context is of little relevance to an event's designation as a "sign of prophecy." The additional ordering principles in these two specific chapters seem to be thematic as well as based on the accounts' transmitters. Notably, the accounts compiled in chapters 39 and 41 exceed Maʿmar b. Rāshid's accounts dedicated to this topic. Their significance in Ibn Saʿd's biography of the Prophet is attested to by the fact that these two chapters are the most voluminous of his entire *sīra*, containing forty-seven and forty-two accounts, respectively. The following provides a brief description of the chapters 38, 39, and 41 based on the arrangement and content of these chapters. A detailed thematic analysis of the accounts compiled in chapters 39 and 41 and the author's methodological approach follows in chapter 4 of this book.

In Ibn Saʿd's *sīra* section, chapter 38 is entitled "Dhikr nubūwa rasūl Allāh" (Reports of the prophecy of the Messenger of God) This chapter encompasses nine *ḥadīth*s that introduce the topic of prophecy in a general manner. Rather than relating events from Muḥammad's life, the accounts in this chapter present brief utterances of the Prophet, either a response to a question or an individual statement about the time or nature of his prophecy. The first four accounts portray Muḥammad being asked about when he became a prophet. Answering the question, Muḥammad states that he was a prophet when "Adam was between the spirit and body"[92] or when "Adam was between the spirit and his clay."[93] In the last of these four accounts, Muḥammad adds that this was the

92 Ibn Saʿd, *Ṭabaqāt*, 1:123.

93 Ibn Saʿd, *Ṭabaqāt*, 1:123.

time when the *mīthāq*[94] was taken.[95] In the next three accounts, Muḥammad describes himself as "the [answer to] Abraham's prayers" and "Jesus' good tidings."[96] The fifth account mentions an episode from the Prophet's birth, relating that his mother "had a vision" during the delivery "like the mothers of all prophets" do.[97] Following this first-person narration of the Prophet, an anonymous third-person narrator explains that Āmina (the Prophet's mother) saw a light illuminating the palaces of Busra; this account is found in Ibn Saʿd's chronological *sīra* and the "signs of prophecy" preceding the call to prophecy.[98] The sixth account only mentions "Abraham's prayer" (omitting the reference to Jesus), but adds a Qurʾānic verse.[99] Accounts seven and eight include both references to "the prayer of Abraham" and "Jesus' good tidings," but differ from accounts five and six in that the Prophet refers to Abraham as "my father."[100] The final account of this chapter is in the Prophet's direct speech: "I was the first of man in creation and the last of them in being sent [as a prophet]."[101]

In contrast to most chapters in the *sīra* section, chapter 38 does not recount specific events in the Prophet's life but rather creates the notion of a continuous sacred history by situating Muḥammad's prophecy in the chain of previous prophets. As such, he is depicted as a prophet even before the first prophet was sent. This unique position amidst creation is indicated through the statement that his prophecy preceded the corporal creation of Adam. His prophetic mission is the conclusion of the chain of prophets. This stress on Islam as an integral part of a continuing sacred history is also reflected in the extensive chapters dedicated to prophets preceding the Prophet at the beginning of the book.[102] Thus, this chapter functions as an introduction to the topic of prophecy and prepares the reader for the upcoming section of Muḥammad's call to prophecy.

The opening of chapter 39, "Dhikr ʿalāmāt fī rasūl Allāh qabl an yuwḥa ilayhī" (Reports about the signs of prophecy prior to the call to prophecy), is closely linked to the preceding chapter. The first account addresses various topics and serves an introductory function. Being asked to share some personal

94 The covenant God enjoined on Muḥammad and other prophets, such as Noah, Abraham, Moses, and Jesus, is mentioned in the Qurʾān 33:7 and 3:81; cf. Böwering, "Covenant," 1:464.

95 Ibn Saʿd, *Ṭabaqāt*, 1:123.

96 Ibn Saʿd, *Ṭabaqāt*, 1:124.

97 Ibn Saʿd, *Ṭabaqāt*, 1:124.

98 Ibn Saʿd, *Ṭabaqāt*, 1:124.

99 "Oh Lord, send a prophet from among them to them"; cf. Q. 2:129.

100 Ibn Saʿd, *Ṭabaqāt*, 1:124.

101 Ibn Saʿd, *Ṭabaqāt*, 1:124.

102 Individual chapters are dedicated to Eve, Idrīs, Noah, Abraham, and Ismāʿīl; cf. Ibn Saʿd, *Ṭabaqāt*, 1:23–33.

information, Muḥammad's first statement reflects back to the preceding chapter, noting that he is the prayer of Abraham, that Jesus announced him, and that his mother saw a light illuminating the palaces of Busra emanating from her while she delivered the Prophet. After this introductory account, Ibn Saʿd returns to the chronological order of the Prophet's life by describing various events of Muḥammad's infancy and childhood, including his birth, his stay with his foster mother Ḥalīma, and various instances in which he is recognized as a future prophet.[103] Most of these accounts, such as the Prophet's birth, one of his journeys to Syria, or the advent of his prophecy, only allude to the broader historical context. The remaining accounts can be historically approximated through the presence of the Prophet's respective caregivers: Āmina (his mother), Ḥalīma, ʿAbd al-Muṭṭalib, and Abū Ṭālib. Thus, the chapter is organized in accordance with the chronology of the Prophet's childhood. Only the fourth account breaks this chronology, as Ḥalīma's quest for a foster child is placed after the opening of Muḥammad's heart, which occurred while he was in Ḥalīma's care. The account further interrupts the chronology, as the Prophet's mother provides a retrospective description of her pregnancy and delivery. The following 37 accounts all constitute predictions or announcements that foreshadow Muḥammad's prophecy in one form or another. These predictions or announcements are presented from a monotheistic perspective, expressed by Jews and Christians based on descriptions found in their scriptures, and also by a *ḥanīf* (non-denominational monotheist), and from a pagan perspective, expressed by soothsayers (*kuhān*), astronomers, idols, sacrificial animals, *jinn*, and even Iblīs himself.[104] The last account in this chapter describes a food "miracle."[105]

Chapter 41 is entitled "Dhikr ʿalāmāt al-nubūwa baʿd nuzūl al-waḥī ʿala rasūl Allāh" (Reports about the signs of prophecy subsequent to the call to prophecy). It consists of 42 accounts that mainly encompass narratives of food and/or water "miracles," natural phenomena, and to a lesser degree, aspects pertaining to the Prophet's states, his interaction with the divine, and his hidden knowledge. A thematic arrangement is less obvious, albeit not completely absent. The overarching arrangement in this chapter is ordered based on the narrator who transmitted the account to Ibn Saʿd.

Overall, Ibn Saʿd clearly and deliberately crafted a section of multiple chapters dedicated to the topic of Muḥammad's prophetic mission. His selection of topics may indicate certain implicit theological notions and epistemological

103 Ibn Saʿd, *Ṭabaqāt*, 1:125–127.
104 Ibn Saʿd, *Ṭabaqāt*, 1:127–141.
105 Ibn Saʿd, *Ṭabaqāt*, 1:142.

approaches to verify his prophetic mission. The presence of chapters dedicated to previous prophets in the beginning of the *sīra* section, as well as the introductory chapter 38 suggest that Ibn Saʿd emphasized integrating Muḥammad's prophetic mission into a continuous sacred history. However, like other *dalāʾil al-nubūwa* authors of his time, he did not provide explanations or commentaries in this regard.

3.2 *Al-Khargūshī's* Sharaf al-Nabī

Al-Khargūshī's *Sharaf al-nabī* is an extensive and self-contained work that covers more than 700 pages in its printed edition, and thus considerably exceeds earlier works in size. It is divided into fifty-seven thematic chapters but does not constitute a comprehensive biography of the Prophet, rather it is a compendium on select aspects of the Prophet's genealogy, household, and physical environment, similar to Abū l-Shaykh al-Iṣfahānī's *Akhlāq al-nabī*. The arrangement is roughly grouped as follows: (1) the person of the Prophet, (2) his relationships, and (3) historical events. The first 14 chapters describe the light coming forth from the Prophet, his virtues, manners, and qualities, his names as they appear in the Qurʾān and *ḥadīth*, the oath God made by the Prophet,[106] his physique as described in the Qurʾān, Muḥammad's relationship to or interaction with other prophets, the way his nobility is mentioned in the Qurʾān, the miracles of the Prophet, and his distinguishing characteristics mentioned in poetry.[107] Chapters 15 through 23 describe his lineage, family, and other household members,[108] and the subsequent three chapters address topics of Muḥammad's faith preceding his corporal existence, noting that he was distinguished by his virtues and recognized by soothsayers.[109] Following a chapter on the virtues of the members of his household (*ahl al-bayt*),[110] al-Khargūshī dedicates several chapters to individual historical events, such as the Prophet's stay in the cave, reports of the ascension (*miʿrāj*), the battles of Badr and Uḥud, the Prophet's arrival at Qubāʾ, and the changing of the *qibla* from Jerusalem to Mecca; descriptions of various objects the Prophet possessed, such as his horses, his mules, and his swords; and historical reports or physical descriptions of the Prophet's environment, such as descriptions of Mecca and Medina, the Kaʿba, the Prophet's mosque, the chambers of the Prophet's wives, the house of his daughter Fāṭima, and the history of the well Zamzam.[111] This last group

106 Possibly a reference to Q. 81:15–29.
107 Al-Khargūshī, *Sharaf al-nabī*, 9–185.
108 Al-Khargūshī, *Sharaf al-nabī*, 186–211.
109 Al-Khargūshī, *Sharaf al-nabī*, 212–246.
110 Al-Khargūshī, *Sharaf al-nabī*, 247–280.
111 Al-Khargūshī, *Sharaf al-nabī*, 280–447.

of chapters is not arranged in chronological order, nor is it strictly thematic, as historical events are interspersed with descriptions of specific locations, and inventories of certain personal items. Descriptions of locations are frequently linked to accounts of their virtues and the spiritual significance of visiting them. As such, the last chapters of the work treat the Prophet's death, the virtues of visiting his tomb, the virtues of the martyrs and visiting their tombs, the virtues of praying for the Prophet, seeing the Prophet in one's dreams, and the banner of the Prophet; the book closes with a chapter on the Prophet's intercession.[112]

3.3 *Abū Nuʿāym al-Iṣfahānī's* Dalāʾil al-Nubūwa

Abū Nuʿaym's *Dalāʾil al-nubūwa* is arranged chronologically and covers the entire span of the Prophet's life, including his parents' marriage, his birth, various episodes from his childhood and adolescence, events that occurred during his adult life, and finally his death and signs that appeared after his death. While a comprehensive *sīra*, Abū Nuʿaym's work omits aspects that not related to his notion of the "proofs of prophecy." The raids (*maghāzī*), for instance, are only mentioned if events occurred in a context that the author viewed as proofs or signs of prophecy; they are not related as historical accounts of the military campaigns in their own right. Abū Nuʿaym's accounts, however, frequently include poetry like that found in early *sīra* works, and occasionally introduce chapters that provide theological contextualizations of accounts or—more commonly—historical contextualization or summaries of related events in the *sīra*.[113]

The two parts of Abū Nuʿaym's work are arranged differently from each other. In the first part, the biographical material of the Prophet's life up to his emigration to Medina is arranged chronologically, while in the second part, many of the episodes that were already part of earlier *dalāʾil al-nubūwa* works are systematically arranged into thematic chapters. Abū Nuʿaym's work differs significantly in its arrangement from previous extant works; it appears to be the result of a process of systematization that merges the form of a comprehensive *sīra* with the teleological presentation of narratives to provide evidence of Muḥammad's prophetic mission. Thus, Abū Nuʿaym's comprehensive biography is arranged systematically into thematic chapters and sub-chapters with individual titles.

112 Al-Khargūshī, *Sharaf al-nabī*, 448–533.

113 For instance, al-Iṣfahānī, *Dalāʾil al-nubūwa*, 134, 157, 241, 279, 321, 333.

3.4 *Al-Bayhaqī's* Dalāʾil al-Nubūwa

Comprising seven volumes in its printed edition, al-Bayhaqī's *Dalāʾil al-nubūwa* is the most extensive work of this kind; it is a comprehensive biography that is dedicated to the theme of the "proofs of prophecy." Following an extensive preface outlining the author's methodological approach and a brief introduction to the book itself, several thematic parts mostly follow the chronology of the Prophet's life. The first volume contains two thematic parts: The first is dedicated to the Prophet's birth and infancy, including the history of his immediate ancestry and genealogy, and the second part lists detailed descriptions of the Prophet's physical appearance followed by shorter descriptions of him found in pre-Islamic prophetic accounts. The second volume includes two sections: The first returns to the birth and infancy of the Prophet, but focuses on Muḥammad's spiritual preparation for his future prophetic mission. It covers the cleansing of Muḥammad's heart and the removal of "Satan's share"; his encounter with the monk Baḥīrā, who recognizes the signs of prophecy; and God's protection (*ʿiṣma*) of Muḥammad from pagan practices. The other part of the second volume covers Muḥammad's call to prophecy, his life in Mecca, the *hijra*, and the early years in Medina. In addition to major events in the Prophet's life, such as the first revelation, the passing of Abū Ṭālib and Khadīja, and his marriage with ʿĀʾisha, this section contains many conversion stories. Volumes 3, 4, and 5 treat the Muslim conquests and raids, combining historical information on dates and participants with detailed accounts of incidents and miraculous events. In volume 6 al-Bayhaqī departs from the chronological arrangement to address the miracles and signs, the cases in which the Prophet's prayers were answered, and conversations with Jews who were consulted about the Prophet's prophecy. The final volume covers the Prophet's final illness and his passing.

Al-Bayhaqī's *Dalāʾil al-nubūwa* shares some features with Abū Nuʿaym's work, as both emerged after a process of systematizing previous materials. They deliberately arranged the accounts of Muḥammad's early life to illustrate the spiritual foundation of his prophetic mission. At the same time, this teleological tale merges the well-established corpus of traditions with theological and doctrinal positions current at their times.

•••

This chapter focused on the methodological approach and organizational structure that were employed in the extant *dalāʾil al-nubūwa* works up to the fifth/eleventh century. With regard to methodology, it has been shown that all of the early *ḥadīth* scholars who contributed to this literature listed *ḥadīth* without commentary or contextualization. They employed the highest standard of authentication available at their time by introducing each individual account with a proper *isnād*. In the case of Ibn Saʿd's work, I have shown that he likely adopted certain accounts from Wahb b. Munabbih or other sources that lacked proper authentication. Yet, while many of these questionable accounts would have fit into the thematic compilations of "signs of prophecy," most are only found in the chronological biographies and have been replaced by better attested ones or have been omitted altogether in chapters on the "signs of prophecy." Therefore, it seems that the methodology applied in the two chapters of "signs of prophecy" is actually more rigorous than it is in the remainder of the biography, in which he occasionally used collective *isnād*s. Furthermore, I have demonstrated that even those accounts that formally or stylistically evoke doubt about their scholarly provenance are attested in other *ḥadīth* compilations contemporary to Ibn Saʿd, and thus were accepted in the scholarly discourse of the time.

Dalāʾil al-nubūwa works in the late fourth/tenth and early fifth/eleventh century expand the pool of sources from which they draw their accounts and include accounts from the *sīra* and *maghāzī* literature. In doing so, they maintain scholarly methodologies to varying degrees. Al-Khargūshī uses a relatively low standard of authentication; he only lists a complete *isnād* at the beginning of a chapter and confines himself to name the Companion or Follower who narrated it throughout the remainder of the chapter. Some accounts are even presented without any transmitter. By contrast, Abū Nuʿaym states in his introduction that he only included sound or well-known accounts; this may imply a similar approach to that of al-Bayhaqī, as both provide complete chains of transmissions for each account. Al-Bayhaqī outlines his methodological approach in an extensive preface and defends the incorporation of less authoritative materials in light of the nature of his own work. He quotes al-Shāfiʿī extensively in his ruling that states that less authoritative sources, such as Ibn Isḥāq, are permissible to include in accounts as long as legal rulings are not derived from them. He also addresses the question about accounts transmitted on the authority of a single transmitter; he deems these perfectly acceptable, particularly with regard to miracles and other accounts used for edifying purposes. Even though al-Bayhaqī never explicitly mentions his *Dalāʾil al-nubūwa* in the context of his methodological elaborations, we can infer that this discussion is intended to vindicate his inclusion of accounts from *sīra* and *maghāzī* literature. As such, the works of Abū Nuʿaym and al-Bayhaqī present a shift in the nature of *dalāʾil al-nubūwa* literature, but do not sacrifice their scholarly provenance. The *dalāʾil al-nubūwa* literature is not part of *ḥadīth* scholarship that must uphold the legal stipulations of authenticity and reliability; rather it is part of a body of literature of *sīra*, including *maghāzī*, and historiography. Therefore all of these compilations of the "signs of prophecy" are part of scholarly discourses upholding their respective methodological criteria.

In terms of arrangement, Maʿmar b. Rāshid, al-Bukhārī, and al-Tirmidhī listed a few select *ḥadīth* in designated chapters without any apparent thematic order and presented individual events without positioning them in the framework of his biography. Ibn Saʿd's main goal was to provide a chronological and comprehensive narrative of Muḥammad's life in which he included two thematic chapters on the signs of prophecy, but did not make them the focus of the work itself. None of these early authors provided any explanation as to why they chose the particular episodes, at the expense of others, in their chapters. The three later works share several features that set them apart from the previous generations of *dalāʾil al-nubūwa* compilations. The most notable difference is their wider scope; later compilations are expansive self-contained works. Their individual arrangements, however, differ. Al-Khargūshī's selective aspects of Muḥammad's life that are thought to prove his status as a prophet is more extensive than that of previous works, but is arranged thematically like a compendium rather than a *sīra*. The *Dalāʾil al-nubūwa* of Abū Nuʿaym is partial, and that of al-Bayhaqī is a comprehensive biography. The latter two resemble one another in that they combine the chronological narrative of the Prophet's life with a thematic part. Abū Nuʿaym's work recounts the Prophet's life up to his emigration to Medina, then shifts to a more selective thematic approach. Al-Bayhaqī's extensive *sīra* fills seven volumes, this includes his coverage of the raids and one volume that is thematically focused on the proofs of prophecy.

Overall, we see that the tradition-based *dalāʾil al-nubūwa* literature evolved structurally and methodologically over time. The literature moved away from the early thematic chapters in the *ḥadīth* collections of Maʿmar b. Rāshid, al-Bukhārī, and al-Tirmidhī with all of their required standards of authentication toward larger scale monographs that merge the stylistic and methodological framework of *sīra* literature with an explicitly teleological arrangement of materials in Abū Nuʿaym and al-Bayhaqī. This methodological shift in and systematization of *dalāʾil al-nubūwa* literature was foreshadowed by Ibn Saʿd, who was the first to explicitly place notions of the signs of prophecy in the context of a prophetic biography. Ibn Saʿd's chapters, as well as the more extensive later works of Abū Nuʿaym and al-Bayhaqī, contain specifically selected narratives that each author designated as evidentiary events for Muḥammad's legitimacy as a prophet. The individual selection process of narratives and the sense of religious purpose that predetermined their respective portrayal of the prophet is further explored by way of content analyses of the extant *dalāʾil al-nubūwa* works in chapter 4 of this book. It is noteworthy, however, that while the specific methodological requirements had shifted away from *ḥadīth* scholarship by the time of Abū Nuʿaym and al-Bayhaqī, the authors were dedicated to staying within the disciplinary boundaries and went to great lengths to argue their respective cases in their introductions. As such, it is clear that while the disciplinary context might have changed, the *dalāʾil al-nubūwa* authors still very much viewed their works as contributions to the religious sciences, not as writings of pietistic laymen.

CHAPTER 4

Content Analysis of Early Extant *Dalāʾil al-Nubūwa* Works

From the first brief chapter of only six accounts in Maʿmar's work, compilations of the signs of prophecy quickly grew in size. The study of the authors' methodological approaches shows that they applied rigorous standards of authentication. In the case of Ibn Saʿd, he may have applied these standards even more rigorously for his thematic chapters than he did in the remainder of his work. Overall, the exponential growth and careful authentication indicate the importance the authors ascribed to this topic. But what did they understand to be a proof of prophecy? Were there established notions of evidence of Muḥammad's prophetic mission? Since the majority of authors of the early *dalāʾil al-nubūwa* works were in direct contact with one another and were frequently linked through student-teacher relations, the question emerges, were the corpora of *dalāʾil al-nubūwa* compilations simply handed down from one scholarly generation to the next, or did the individual works differ in their content. In order to answer that question, I analyze the contents of the first two generations of *dalāʾil al-nubūwa* works to establish possible patterns across the compilations. As none of these authors provided explicit information regarding their selection processes, I subsumed the accounts of the "proofs of prophecy" compilations under thematic categories in order to evaluate whether various authors held similar views as to what constitutes such evidence. I am fully aware that this type of thematic categorization is, like all literary analyses, an external process based on my subjective interpretation of the accounts at hand, and that the authors themselves likely did not conceive of these "themes" in the same way while compiling their works. To an extent, these categories are subjectively chosen elements in each account and I have grouped narratives together based on my interpretations and formed new, second-order classifications. With these methodological caveats in mind, I nevertheless consider this approach very useful because it enables me to present the broad spectrum of elements that individual authors considered to have evidentiary value for the veracity of Muḥammad's prophetic mission and for the diversity of these authors' notions of the "proofs of prophecy."

 | DOI:10.1163/9789004687349_006

1 Maʿmar b. Rāshid's "Bāb al-Nubūwa"

Maʿmar b. Rāshid's short chapter "Bāb al-nubūwa" appears to have been the earliest compilation of this kind. While the chapter's title does not specifically refer to "proofs" or "signs" of prophecy, the *ḥadīth*s it contains clearly indicate that it was meant to cover aspects that signify Muḥammad's exceptional status rather than the specifics of his prophetic mission. The majority of accounts, four out of six, relate to the supernatural emergence or provision of water in a moment of need. The first two *ḥadīth*s present the same event, albeit with different *isnād*s: One of the Companions is unable to find water to make ablutions. The Prophet places his hand in a vessel that had only a little water in it. As he calls the people to make their ablutions, water gushes forth from between his fingers and suffices for approximately seventy people to make ablutions (*wuḍūʾ*).[1]

The third *ḥadīth* is also set in the context of water scarcity. The Prophet was traveling with his Companions; when they run out of water, the Prophet sent two of his Companions to a certain place where they are supposed to find a woman with a camel and two water bags. They find the woman and bring her to the Prophet, who pours some water from her water skins into a vessel. Then he returned the water to the water bags and ordered the people to fill their vessels and their water skins. After all the vessels were filled, the woman's water bags appeared to be even bulkier than before. The Prophet stated: "We have not taken a thing from your water but God has given us [water] to drink." The account concludes with a conversion narrative, as the woman relates her encounter to her kinsmen who then convert to Islam.[2]

The fourth *ḥadīth* is a water miracle similar to the first two accounts, but it is part of an elaborate narrative of a journey that takes place throughout a night and the next day. By midday the Prophet and his Companions were in dire need of water. The Prophet asked for his ablution bowl and passed it around for the men to drink and make ablutions from it. After seventy-two men had filled their water bags, Muḥammad returned it to the person who gave it to him and the bowl is filled with the same amount of water it had held before.[3]

The fifth account describes an act of material transformation. On the day of the battle of Uḥud, ʿAbdallāh b. Jaḥsh goes to the Prophet because he lost his

1 ʿAbd al-Razzāq, *al-Muṣannaf*, 11:276f. Very similar accounts are found in *Ṣaḥīḥ al-Bukhārī*, cf. al-Bukhārī, *Ṣaḥīḥ*, 1:151 (no. 169); 4:470f. (nos. 3576, 3577, 3579); 7:305f.

2 ʿAbd al-Razzāq, *al-Muṣannaf*, 11:276f. This account is also found in al-Bukhārī; cf. al-Bukhārī, *Ṣaḥīḥ*, 1:230f.

3 ʿAbd al-Razzāq, *al-Muṣannaf*, 11:278f. This account is also found in Muslim and Ibn Saʿd; cf. Muslim, *Ṣaḥīḥ*, 5:156f.; Ibn Saʿd, *Ṭabaqāt*, 1:152.

sword. The Prophet gave him a leafless branch from a palm tree and it turned into a sword in his hand.[4]

The last account in this chapter refers to an aspect of Muḥammad's physical appearance as a "sign of prophecy." A Companion described seeing the sign (*ʿalāma*) between the Prophet's shoulders toward the end of his right shoulder blade, it is in the shape of a fist with moles on it.[5] The inclusion of a physical feature in this chapter is interesting given that Maʿmar's work also includes a short chapter called "Bāb ṣifat al-nabī," which has two accounts describing the Prophet's appearance, similar to later *shamāʾil* works.[6] The presence of this description thus indicates that Maʿmar's view of the signifiers of Muḥammad's prophetic mission included events and deeds as well as external features.

While this short chapter is the earliest known thematic compilation, Maʿmar's authorship is questionable. The *Jāmiʿ* of Maʿmar b. Rāshid has not come down to us in its original form but was preserved by his foremost student, ʿAbd al-Razzāq b. Hammām al-Ḥimyarī, as an appendix to his *Muṣannaf*.[7] Mahar Jarrar argued that ʿAbd al-Razzāq did not include all of his teacher's materials but only preserved accounts of the most important events of the Prophet's life and campaigns in his chapter on the campaigns/raids (*maghāzī*). Other accounts were either entirely omitted or integrated into other chapters.[8] Therefore, we cannot be certain whether the chapter on prophecy was arranged in its present form by Maʿmar himself or by his student ʿAbd al-Razzāq. In either case, it precedes that of Ibn Saʿd, which has often been taken as a precedent for both the genres of *dalāʾil al-nubūwa* and *shamāʾil al-nabī*. Even though this compilation is still very limited in terms of the number of accounts it contains, its characteristics are similar to Ibn Saʿd's chapters dedicated to the "signs of prophecy." As we see in the following, Ibn Saʿd included all of these accounts in his compilations of the "signs of prophecy" and similarly focused on accounts pertaining to water miracles.

2 Ibn Saʿd's "ʿAlamāt al-Nubūwa"

Given that Ibn Saʿd's chapters are found in the framework of a *sīra*, it is not surprising that his arrangement of the material differs from that of the *ḥadīth*

4 ʿAbd al-Razzāq, *al-Muṣannaf*, 11:280.

5 ʿAbd al-Razzāq, *al-Muṣannaf*, 11:280. This account is also found in Muslim; cf. Muslim, *Ṣaḥīḥ*, 15:80f. (no. 2346).

6 ʿAbd al-Razzāq, *al-Muṣannaf*, 11:259f.

7 ʿAbd al-Razzāq, *al-Muṣannaf*, 10:379–468; vol. 11.

8 Jarrar, *Die Prophetenbiographie im Islamischen Spanien*, 29f.

scholars. Ibn Saʿd presents the major event of Muḥammad's life following a roughly chronological order. In contrast to the majority of his chapters, the two chapters dedicated to the "signs of prophecy" are almost exclusively thematic in nature. There are a few references to historical events of the nascent Muslim community, such as the treaty of Ḥudaybiyya or the battle of Badr. In other cases, such as the conversion narratives of particular Companions, the contexts of the narratives allow for a historical approximation. In general, however, the historical context seemed to be of little relevance to Ibn Saʿd when he designated an event as a "sign of prophecy."

In this section, I group the narratives thematically across both chapters. The majority of the ninety-nine accounts fall into the following thematic categories: (1) predictions or announcements, (2) food or water miracles, or (3) natural phenomena. Less frequently accounts pertain to historical events in the Prophet's life, to his states, to his interaction with the divine, to hidden knowledge, or to material transformation or healing. These themes are treated together in a fourth category. The categorization is at times equivocal, as several accounts potentially fall into more than one category. In these cases, I selected the strongest aspect to determine the category.

2.1 *Announcement or Prediction of Prophecy*

The largest thematic category is that of predictions or announcements of Muḥammad's prophecy. Prediction narratives refer to those accounts that are set in the past and foreshadow the coming of the Prophet in the future, while announcements refer to accounts contemporaneous with Muḥammad's prophetic mission. With a total of forty-one accounts, this category encompasses nearly half of all the "signs of prophecy" *ḥadīth*s. The vast majority of these accounts are listed in chapter 39 of Ibn Saʿd, as "signs of prophecy prior to the call to prophecy" and only two accounts are listed after the revelation. This category is subdivided based on the agent articulating the announcement.

2.1.1 Monotheistic Predictions

The most frequently occurring announcements are those related to Abrahamic or monotheist beliefs; that is, there are twelve accounts in which Jews announce and/or recognize the Prophet, and five accounts in which Christians do so. Some of these accounts overlap and refer to both groups. More than half of these accounts allude to the respective scriptures of these religious groups as containing Muḥammad's description, and most commonly these references are found in Jewish scriptures.

Christian accounts frequently constitute lengthy narratives of monks recognizing the Prophet, such as the well-known narrative of the monk Baḥīrā that is set during Muḥammad's childhood. In this account, Baḥīrā notices a cloud following Muḥammad to shade him until he settled under a tree, which then shifts its branches to provide shade for the boy. Upon his discovery, Baḥīrā invites all the men traveling with Muḥammad to a meal. Invoking the deities al-Lāt and al-ʿUzza, Baḥīrā asks the young Muḥammad to inform him about himself, but the Prophet refuses to speak because deities were invoked. Baḥīrā then repeats his question invoking God, and Muḥammad responds. Then Baḥīrā examines the boy's eyes and back, and begins questioning Abū Ṭālib with regard to his relation to the Prophet, the Prophet's family situation, and finally, Baḥīrā predicts "a great cause" for the boy, as his description is found in the scriptures. Baḥīrā warns Abū Ṭālib that the Jews would recognize and inflict hardship on Muḥammad and Jewish men intend to assassinate him. After Abū Ṭālib and Muḥammad'a departure, Jewish men confer with Baḥīrā, who questions them about whether they have read about the boy in their scripture. After confirming their discovery, the monk indicates that the Jewish men have no way to harm Muḥammad.[9]

The subsequent account relates the same incident including a monk warning Abū Ṭālib not to travel to Syria with his nephew because the young boy would arouse the envy of the Jewish people, who want the Prophet to be from among the Banū Isrāʾīl.[10] In another version, Abū Ṭālib encounters two monks, and both stress the same features in the young Muḥammad as signs of prophecy, namely, that he is an orphan, and has the face and the eyes of a prophet. The first monk also cautions Abū Ṭālib about the Jews.[11]

While most of these narratives are set in the context of the Prophet's first journey to Syria with his uncle Abū Ṭālib, another account describes an encounter with a monk in a different context. An introductory section describes an impoverished Abū Ṭālib sending his twenty-five-year-old nephew Muḥammad to work for Khadīja. Accompanied by Khadīja's servant Maysara, the Prophet traveled to Syria, and on the way they rested under a tree in close proximity to a monk's cell in the market (*sūq*) of Busra. This account gives the monk's name as Nesṭūr, who is acquainted with Maysara. The monk questions Maysara, and indicates that only prophets rest under that particular tree. The Prophet was supposed to finalize his trade by invoking al-Lāt and al-ʿUzza but he refused to make the invocation and canceled the deal. The monk tells Maysara that Muḥammad is a prophet. As they return home Maysara sees two angels flying over the Prophet in order to shade him. Upon entering Mecca, Khadīja also

9 Ibn Saʿd, *Ṭabaqāt*, 1:128f.

10 Ibn Saʿd, *Ṭabaqāt*, 1:130f.

11 Ibn Saʿd, *Ṭabaqāt*, 1:127f.

witnesses the angels and Maysara relates to her what the monk had said. The narrative closes by suggesting that Muḥammad brought blessings in the form of increased profits, because her transactions made twice the usual profits.[12]

Other accounts are set after Muḥammad's call to prophecy. One *ḥadīth* relates that a delegation from Najrān that included the city's bishop came to Medina. During the journey, the bishop's mule stumbled and his brother understood the mule's mishap as a bad omen indicating that the bishop intended to follow the Prophet. Confronted by his brother, the bishop cursed and admonished him for vilifying one of the prophets who was announced by Jesus and mentioned in the Torah. At the end of this account, Ibn Saʿd informs us that the bishop embraced Islam immediately after his arrival in Medina.[13]

While Christians acknowledge the Prophet in all five accounts, Jews announce or recognize him, yet display a more ambivalent attitude: seven accounts express Jews acknowledging the Prophet, albeit this acknowledgment does not preclude envy or enmity toward him by individual Jews; thus they contain both acknowledgments and dismissive attitudes. Five accounts relate a general sense of envy toward the Prophet. Two accounts express outright denial of the Prophet. In one of these, Abū ʿUmayr al-Hayyabān (a Jew from Syria who had come to Medina a few years before Islam) tells three young men from the Jewish tribe Banū Qurayẓa that he migrated to Medina because he had hoped to witness the appearance of a prophet. He cautions the young men that this appearance will cause bloodshed and that they should not hesitate to follow the new prophet. Years later, on the night before the Banū Qurayẓa were conquered by Muslim armies, the three young men remember their past encounter with Ibn al-Hayyabān and warn their fellow tribesmen. While the tribe rejected their warning, the three young men embrace Islam prior to the siege.[14] Very similar accounts describe Jewish people who were aware of the Prophet who was described in their scripture but they refused to depart from the Torah.[15]

The chapter on the signs prior to Muḥammad's call to prophecy contains one account that is set in the context of the king of Yemen threatening to destroy Medina because they are Jewish. The most learned of the Jews, Sāmūl, addresses the king and predicts that a prophet of the Banū Isrāʾīl, born in Mecca and named Aḥmad, will settle in this very town; he then provides various details about the struggle between the Meccans and the Muslims and a

12 Ibn Saʿd, *Ṭabaqāt*, 1:130f.

13 Ibn Saʿd, *Ṭabaqāt*, 1:138f.

14 Ibn Saʿd, *Ṭabaqāt*, 1:134f. and 1:138.

15 Ibn Saʿd, *Ṭabaqāt*, 1:138.

description of the appearance of the future prophet. The king accepts that he will not succeed in destroying Medina and departs for Yemen.[16]

All of these accounts invoke the impression that the Jewish community—or at least its learned stratum—was aware of the coming of a prophet. In the case of the first and the last accounts, this awareness is passed on to other individuals: the three young Jews remember Ibn al-Hayyabān's prediction of the Prophet and this causes them to embrace Islam; and the king of Yemen, whom the learned Jews convince that Yathrib (an early name for Medina) is the city of a future prophet, acknowledges that the city is therefore inaccessible to him. These two accounts stand out from most others because they allude to the historical context of the narrative. While the time of the young men's encounter with Ibn al-Hayyabān is not specified, their remembering it and acknowledgment of the Prophet is historically situated on the eve of the Muslim siege of the Banū Qurayẓa. The "king of Yemen" who seeks the destruction of Yathrib most likely refers to the Ḥimyārī king Abū Karib Asʿad (r. 390–420), who passed through Yathrib during a military campaign to curb Byzantine influence in northern Arabia. After his son was killed, Abū Karib pledged to destroy the city until two Jewish scholars dissuade him from this act of violence and engage his interest in Judaism. Both Jewish and Muslim sources view Abū Karib as the first of the Arab kings to convert to Judaism.[17] This historical contextualization is relevant for Ibn Saʿd's notions of the "proofs of prophecy" because it gives the impression that those anticipating the Prophet were not limited to the era immediately preceding his prophecy.

Two other accounts express the Jews' denial of the Prophet despite their alleged awareness that Muḥammad is mentioned in their scripture.[18] Seven other accounts express Jewish envy of the Prophet. None of these accounts is exclusively dedicated to the jealousy of the Jews, rather they overlap with the Prophet being referred to in their scripture, his acknowledgment by Christian monks or other Jews. These narratives are set at various stages of the Prophet's life. For instance, on the night of Muḥammad's birth, a Jewish merchant living in Mecca asked the Quraysh whether a boy has been born. The merchant specifies that the boy will be the last of the prophets, he will be called Aḥmad, and the merchant provides a description of the mole on the Prophet's shoulder. After the Jews confirm that a boy fitting this description was born to the family of ʿAbd al-Muṭṭalib, the Jew is brought to the child and expresses his envy, stating: "Prophecy has departed from the Banū Isrāʾīl and the scripture has

16 Ibn Saʿd, *Ṭabaqāt*, 1:133.

17 Graetz, Löwy, Bloch (eds.), *History of the Jews*, 3:64; Ibn Isḥāq, *The Life of Muhammad*, 7–9.

18 Ibn Saʿd, *Ṭabaqāt*, 1:133f.

left their hands. The Arabs gained prophecy. Are you glad, people of Quraysh? Indeed, God will provide you with great authority and its prophecy will spread from the East to the West."[19] In another *ḥadīth*, the Jewish tribes of Medina, Qurayẓa, al-Naḍīr, Fadak, and Khaybar, found the Prophet's description in their scripture as well as a reference to Medina being the destination of his emigration. When the Prophet was born shortly after this discovery, a learned Jewish man recognized the sign. "They knew that and acknowledged him and did not reflect on him except with envy and injustice."[20] Other accounts are set in the time after Muḥammad received the call to prophecy. In one, the Prophet walked by a Jew who was reading the Torah to his sick nephew, and Muḥammad asked whether his description is found in the scripture. The elder Jewish man shook his head in negation, but his nephew answered in the affirmative and converted to Islam. When the young man passed away, the Prophet himself held the funeral prayers.[21]

There are also a number of accounts in which learned Jewish men were consulted in order to establish Muḥammad's prophecy. In one instance, the Quraysh sent delegates to verify Muḥammad's claim to prophecy. A rabbi asks for a description of Muḥammad and his followers and affirms that he is the prophet whose description is found in Jewish scripture.[22] In another account the Prophet himself sought confirmation from the most learned of the Jews and is told that his description is found in the Torah. Being warned of the envy of the Jewish community, Muḥammad asks the rabbi what prevents him from acknowledging him. Weary of disagreement among his people, the learned man confesses that he would embrace Islam if his people did so first.[23] In another account, Jews question the Prophet about "customs, which are only known to a prophet." He answers all the questions to their satisfaction.

The chapter on the "signs of prophecy" after Muḥammad's call includes an account in which a Jewish woman attempts to verify Muḥammad's prophetic identity. The woman presents the Prophet with a roasted sheep, and Muḥammad starts eating it with his Companions, when the sheep announces to him that it was poisoned. The Prophet cautions his Companions, relating what the sheep had told him, and they also stop eating. The warning, however, comes too late and one of his Companions dies from the poisoned meat. The Prophet sent for the woman and questioned her about her reasons. She

---

19 Ibn Saʿd, *Ṭabaqāt*, 1:136f.
20 Ibn Saʿd, *Ṭabaqāt*, 1:134.
21 Ibn Saʿd, *Ṭabaqāt*, 1:156.
22 Ibn Saʿd, *Ṭabaqāt*, 1:139.
23 Ibn Saʿd, *Ṭabaqāt*, 1:138.

responded, "I desired to know. If you were a prophet, you would not be harmed, but if you were a king, I would have saved the people from you."[24]

Many of the elements of the awareness of Jews and Christians of the coming of the Prophet are reiterated by the *ḥanīf* Zayd b. ʿAmr b. Nufayl. Two separate accounts relate that his quest for a "true" religion had led him to Jews, Christians, and others. As all of these groups foretell the coming of a prophet in Mecca, he settles there to await the Prophet's appearance, but passes away before Muḥammad's call to prophecy.[25]

2.1.2 Previous Prophets

In addition to adherents of monotheistic faiths, Ibn Saʿd presents previous prophets as a group of individuals who predicted or were informed about the Muḥammad's prophecy. A number of accounts include indirect predictions from previous prophets, such as the accounts in chapter 38 that refer to Muḥammad as "the prayer of Abraham" and "the good tidings of Jesus,"[26] the first account of the "signs of prophecy prior to the call of prophecy,"[27] and the account of a Christian delegation traveling to Medina.[28] In addition, the chapter on the signs prior to the prophetic mission includes a number of accounts predicting Muḥammad's prophecy by or in the presence of one of the previous prophets. One account states that God revealed to Yaʿqūb: "I send from your offspring kings and prophets until I send the Prophet of the *ḥaram*, whose people built the temple in Jerusalem. He is the 'seal of prophets' and his name is Aḥmad."[29] In another account, God said to Abraham that his offspring will be a succession of people until He sends the illiterate prophet, who will be the 'seal of prophets'.[30] Two other accounts focus on Abraham as Muḥammad's forefather.[31] Another account relates that Hagar was told that her son will be "father to many peoples and from his people the illiterate prophet living in Mecca will come."[32] Finally, there is an account that states that God revealed to an unnamed prophet of the Banū Isrāʾīl: "I severed my anger of you because of what you destroyed from my order. I swear to you the holy spirit (*rūḥ al-qudus*)

---

24 Ibn Saʿd, *Ṭabaqāt*, 1:145.
25 Ibn Saʿd, *Ṭabaqāt*, 1:135f.
26 Ibn Saʿd, *Ṭabaqāt*, 1:124.
27 Ibn Saʿd, *Ṭabaqāt*, 1:125.
28 Ibn Saʿd, *Ṭabaqāt*, 1:138f.
29 Ibn Saʿd, *Ṭabaqāt*, 1:137.
30 Ibn Saʿd, *Ṭabaqāt*, 1:137.
31 Ibn Saʿd, *Ṭabaqāt*, 1:138.
32 Ibn Saʿd, *Ṭabaqāt*, 1:138.

will not come to you living. I send the illiterate prophet from the land of the Arabs to whom the *rūḥ al-qudus* will come."[33]

The majority of accounts pertaining to announcements or predictions of the Prophet occur through Jews or Christians. While their reaction toward the Prophet and his message varies significantly, in these accounts the overarching notion is that the learned men of these respective faiths were aware that a future prophecy would be revealed. Knowledge of the Prophet and the ability to recognize him is grounded in the respective scriptures, and to a lesser degree in statements of previous prophets. In some instances, monotheists announced the birth of a new prophet based on astronomical signs in conjunction with scriptural predictions of a future prophet. One narrative relates that the Jewish tribes Qurayẓa, al-Naḍīr, Fadak, and Khaybar found Muḥammad's description prior to his call to the prophecy and learned that the destination of his flight would be Medina. When the Prophet was born, the learned man of the Jews said: "Aḥmad was born tonight, this planet has risen." When the Prophet Muḥammad became a prophet, they said: "Aḥmad has become a prophet, the planet that had risen, rose." They knew that and acknowledged him and did not reflect on him except with envy and injustice.[34]

2.1.3 Predictions by Pagans

In addition to statements by monotheists regarding a future prophet, there are a number of accounts of announcements, and to a lesser degree, predictions by various pagan entities, such as soothsayers, idols, or sacrifice animals. Three accounts narrate instances in which soothsayers recognize the prophetic future of the child Muḥammad and ask their tribes to kill the boy.[35] Other accounts relate how idols or sacrifice animals announced the beginning of the prophecy. One account states that the Banū ʿIfār intended to sacrifice a calf to their idols, but the animal began crying out, announcing that Muḥammad was testifying in Mecca that there is no god but God.[36] A very similar account mentions a fatted cow being brought to the idol Suwāʿ. After they sacrificed the animals, the idol worshipers heard a voice from inside it. The voice announced that a prophet had come, who forbade adultery and sacrificing [animals] to idols, and said that heaven was guarded and shooting stars were thrown at intruders. The idol worshipers met Abū Bakr al-Ṣiddīq who confirmed the beginning of

33 Ibn Saʿd, *Ṭabaqāt*, 1:140.
34 Ibn Saʿd, *Ṭabaqāt*, 1:134.
35 Ibn Saʿd, *Ṭabaqāt*, 1:125f., 1:140.
36 Ibn Saʿd, *Ṭabaqāt*, 1:132.

the revelation.[37] Finally, there is an account that provides some insight into the Prophet's position toward idol worship prior to his call to prophecy. A group of pagans was worshiping an idol at Buwāna. Abū Ṭālib was attending with his people and he told the Prophet to attend the "festival," but the Prophet refused. Abū Ṭālib became angry and reprimanded him for not participating in the customs of their ancestors. Muḥammad withdrew from them but later returned, frightened and alarmed. He stated: "Every time I am near an idol, a man appears to me, tall and white, and he yells at me, 'Behind you, Muḥammad, do not touch it!'" The account concludes that Muḥammad was said not to have returned to their festival until he became a prophet,[38] implying that he never returned at all.

Ibn Saʿd also includes *jinn* as agents who announced Muḥammad's prophecy. There are five accounts that relate very similar narratives of women having a follower (or lover) among the *jinn*; the *jinn* visit them and inform them of the beginning of prophecy and the prohibition of wine and adultery.[39] Building on a Qurʾānic theme, two of these accounts mention that *jinn* are no longer allowed to listen to the conversations of the angels and are chased away by shooting stars.[40] This is based on the pre-Islamic notion that *jinn* have the capacity to enter the heavenly realm and listen to the discourse of angels, which they then pass on to pre-Islamic soothsayers. The idea that the *jinn*'s access to heaven was blocked at the beginning of the revelation is found in various passages of the Qurʾān, which describe how those *jinn*, who continued to attempt to enter the heavenly realm were driven out by shooting stars.[41] One account that is thematically linked to this Qurʾānic motif narrates that the shooting stars frightened the Arabs and confused the *jinn* themselves. The *jinn* consulted Iblīs (Satan), who sent them to retrieve samples of soil from their earth to establish what was happening. Iblīs identified the origin of the occurrence as something that happened in Tihāma, that is, the coastal region in Arabia that also includes Mecca and Medina.[42] Another account related to this Qurʾānic notion presents pagan Arabs, rather than *jinn*, as agents. Some Arabs were terrified by the shooting stars and consulted ʿAmr b. Umayya's opinion. He stated that a prophet was sent to the Arabs and was revealed through these

37 Ibn Saʿd, *Ṭabaqāt*, 1:141. Another account narrates a very similar event at the idol Suwāʿ but in this case the sacrifice animal was a sheep; cf. Ibn Saʿd, *Ṭabaqāt*, 1:149.

38 Ibn Saʿd, *Ṭabaqāt*, 1:132f.

39 Ibn Saʿd, *Ṭabaqāt*, 1:140f., 1:159.

40 Ibn Saʿd, *Ṭabaqāt*, 1:141.

41 See Q. 15:17–18, 37:6–10, 67:5, 72:8–9.

42 Ibn Saʿd, *Ṭabaqāt*, 1:140f.

shooting stars.[43] As such, this account almost functions like a human reiteration of the narrative.

In other instances, Meccans encountered the infant Muḥammad and his future leadership is foreshadowed in a worldly sense rather than a religious one. In one account, news of Muḥammad's birth reached the family of Lihb, who proclaim that "this newborn will overcome the people of the earth."[44] Another account narrates that the Prophet's grandfather, ʿAbd al-Muṭṭalib, spread a cushion out in the shade of the Kaʿba. Still a toddler, Muḥammad climbed on the cushion and his paternal uncles went to remove him; however, ʿAbd al-Muṭṭalib intervened and said that the boy was just getting accustomed to rule.[45] Two accounts describe a vision and a dream, respectively, that announce the coming of the Prophet.[46] Finally, there are two accounts in which people are informed of the Prophet's activities. The first account relates an encounter between a Syrian caravan and a horseman who announces that "Aḥmad has come! The *jinn* have been chased away." The caravan leaves immediately to hear news of the prophecy.[47] The second account narrates an encounter between a shepherd and a wolf; this became a central point of Tor Andrae's view on *dalāʾil al-nubūwa*. The wolf reprimanded the shepherd for withholding his ordained share and informed him about Muḥammad's prophetic mission. The account then became a conversion narrative as the shepherd drives his flock to Medina and embraces Islam.[48]

In sum, almost half of Ibn Saʿd's accounts of the "signs of prophecy" include various monotheistic and pagan entities that function as agents of predictions and announcements of Muḥammad's prophetic mission. In some instances, monotheistic and pagan elements are combined, for example, when Jews determine the night of the Prophet's birth through astronomy, or in the Qurʾānic motif of the *jinn*. Interestingly, narratives that have monotheistic agents are not centered on conversions to Islam, but rather on the ability of learned monotheists to predict and recognize Muḥammad's prophecy based on their scripture.

2.2 *Water- and/or Food-Related Incidents*

The second largest thematic category contains narratives in which water and/or food is obtained or increased through supernatural means. These incidents

43 Ibn Saʿd, *Ṭabaqāt*, 1:137.
44 Ibn Saʿd, *Ṭabaqāt*, 1:125.
45 Ibn Saʿd, *Ṭabaqāt*, 1:127 and 139.
46 Ibn Saʿd, *Ṭabaqāt*, 1:139.
47 Ibn Saʿd, *Ṭabaqāt*, 1:135.
48 Ibn Saʿd, *Ṭabaqāt*, 1:146f.

most commonly occur in situations of scarcity or dire need, both before and after Muḥammad's call to prophecy, and usually affect other people, not just Muḥammad himself. In some instances, these accounts fit into more than one category.

These narratives are commonly set in a context in which water (either for drinking or less often, for ablutions) is scarce. The first account occurs in the Prophet's childhood. During a journey with his uncle, Abū Ṭālib complained about thirst. The young Muḥammad dismounted from his riding animal and dropped his heel into the ground. Water came forth and he invited his uncle to drink.[49] Most accounts are set later, after Muḥammad has reached adulthood and received the call to prophecy. One account describes the severe scarcity of water as part of a lengthy narrative of the Prophet traveling with his Companions. Using a small water bowl, he poured each of the men some water and it sufficed everyone.[50] This account was noted in the chapter by Maʿmar b. Rāshid.[51] Two other accounts specifically name the treaty of Ḥudaybiyya as historical context. The Prophet arrived at Ḥudaybiyya with a large army that was in dire need of water. In the first account, the Prophet sat on their watering trough and either spat in it or prayed over it and it overflowed with water.[52] In other accounts describing similar circumstances, water gushed forth between the Prophet's fingers.[53] An additional statement at the end of both of these accounts notes that the men drank water and used it for ablutions. The same narrative is also found in relation to ablutions; the purpose of the water was not unanimously certain. In one of these accounts, the event is referred to as one of the "marvelous (*ʿajāʾib*) things".[54] This is the only incident that any of the "signs of prophecy" are explicitly described as being out of the ordinary, as Ibn Saʿd generally does not make theological assessments or provide any other context for the accounts. Two further accounts relate the same occurrence with minor variations.[55]

A number of accounts in the chapter dedicated to the "signs of prophecy" that follow Muḥammad's call to prophecy include narratives in which the milk of a single goat or sheep suffices numerous people. At other times milk is drawn from a specific sheep or goat that is known to have no milk at the time;

49 Ibn Saʿd, *Ṭabaqāt*, 1:127.
50 Ibn Saʿd, *Ṭabaqāt*, 1:152f.
51 ʿAbd al-Razzāq, *al-Muṣannaf*, 11:278f.
52 Ibn Saʿd, *Ṭabaqāt*, 1:151.
53 Ibn Saʿd, *Ṭabaqāt*, 1:150, 154.
54 Ibn Saʿd, *Ṭabaqāt*, 1:150f.
55 Ibn Saʿd, *Ṭabaqāt*, 1:150f.

these include the accounts of Ibn Masʿūd,[56] Umm Maʿbad,[57] and Miqdād,[58] which were discussed in chapter 3. Occasionally milk-related accounts feature various elements from other categories, such as hidden knowledge or a divine response to the Prophet's invocations. One of these accounts is set in a situation similar to many water miracles, but in this account Muḥammad's foreshadowing of a future occurrence is emphasized more than the milk sufficing a large number of people.

> Nāfiʿ said, "The Prophet was at Zuhāʾ with 1,400 men, and we were [severely] suffering from a lack of water. They saw that the Prophet had dismounted [his riding animal] when a goat approached him so closely that [its] sharp horns touched the Prophet. The Prophet milked it and gave the army [milk] to drink and he drank [himself]. Then he said, 'Oh Nāfiʿ, take it [but] I do not see you taking [possession of] it.' I took a stick and rammed it into the ground, and I took a rope and tied the goat [to it] and checked on it. The Prophet and the people and I slept. I woke up and the rope was untied and the goat was gone. I went to the Prophet and told him, 'The goat is gone.' The Prophet said to me, 'Oh Nāfiʿ, have I not told you that you would not take possession of her? The one who came with her, [should] leave with her.'"[59]

Food-related incidents go hand in hand with those related to water or milk. It is interesting to note that while scarcity of water and milk required Muḥammad to perform some specific action, increases in food occasionally occurred simply through his presence. The earliest "sign of prophecy" pertaining to food is the account of Ḥalīma taking in the orphaned Muḥammad as a foster child. The lengthy account describes the poverty of Ḥalīma and her family while they were traveling to Mecca as well as the blessings of abundant food and healthy livestock they experienced once they had taken in the infant Muḥammad.[60] Another account relates that the poverty that struck Abū Ṭālib for some time was not felt in Muḥammad's presence, as food would suffice everyone eating in his company. Thus Abū Ṭālib said to the Prophet, "you are a blessing."[61] In another account, the Prophet's presence provides a sufficient amount of food to feed a large group of guests after a woman from the Anṣār (lit., Helpers)

56 Ibn Saʿd, *Ṭabaqāt*, 1:155.
57 Ibn Saʿd, *Ṭabaqāt*, 1:156f.
58 Ibn Saʿd, *Ṭabaqāt*, 1:154f.
59 Ibn Saʿd, *Ṭabaqāt*, 1:150f.
60 Ibn Saʿd, *Ṭabaqāt*, 1:125f.
61 Ibn Saʿd, *Ṭabaqāt*, 1:142.

prepared only enough food to host the Prophet. Muḥammad extended the invitation to everyone sitting with him and the host feared the embarrassment of not having enough food to feed her guests. The people ate until they were satiated but the amount of food remained the same.[62] A similar account presents the family of ʿAlī and Fāṭima who were so impoverished that they skipped several meals. After obtaining a little food, Fāṭima told her husband to invite her father. Once the Prophet arrived at her house, he instructs her to fill a plate not only for the three of them, but also for each of his wives, and the food sufficed all of them.[63] In one account the Prophet, who had very little food, served it to forty members of the Banū ʿAbd al-Muṭṭalib, hoping to convince them to follow him.[64] This last account appears to be the only instance in which the increase of food is performed deliberately to convince his adversaries to convert.

Muḥammad's role in providing food differs in an account that describes the Prophet and his Companions running out of provisions during a raid. ʿUmar b. al-Khaṭṭāb suggested that the Prophet should collect the remaining provisions and invoke God's blessings over them. The Prophet followed the advice and made a supplication (*duʿāʾ*). Then he called the army to fill their containers and the provision sufficed everyone and left them plenty of excess.[65] This is the only case in which Muḥammad explicitly sought divine intervention to provide food. All the other accounts related to food show that Muḥammad could supply food either by interacting with it, such as pouring or serving it himself, or with his mere presence during a meal.

2.3 *Natural Phenomena*

Natural phenomena are the third most common thematic category in Ibn Saʿd's two chapters. These phenomena include Muḥammad's interaction with animals and plants (or an array of natural elements). Both notions are premised on nature's recognition of his prophetic status. The first account in this category reflects the effect the Prophet had on animals. After a visit by the Prophet, Saʿd lent him his donkey to ride home and the donkey returned to Saʿd smarter and swifter than before.[66] Thus, the act of serving the Prophet was rewarded with a blessing for the donkey's owner through his animal. This is reminiscent of the account of Ḥalīma's riding animals, which were old and

62 Ibn Saʿd, *Ṭabaqāt*, 1:152.
63 Ibn Saʿd, *Ṭabaqāt*, 1:157f.
64 Ibn Saʿd, *Ṭabaqāt*, 1:158.
65 Ibn Saʿd, *Ṭabaqāt*, 1:152.
66 Ibn Saʿd, *Ṭabaqāt*, 1:138.

lame on her way to Mecca, becoming swifter after she took in the orphaned Muḥammad.[67]

Animals also interacted with the Prophet by seeking his protection. In one account the Prophet was sitting with others in the mosque when a camel approached him and placed its head in his lap and brayed. The Prophet told his Companions that the camel claimed that it belonged to a man who wanted to slaughter it as a dish for his father and it was seeking his help and protection. A man sitting with the Prophet recognized the camel and confirmed that its owner had such intentions. The Prophet summoned the owner and asked him to spare the camel.[68] In this case, an animal was aware of the Prophet's moral reputation and social position; this allowed him to intervene with the owner. The Prophet not only showed mercy for the animal, but was also able to understand the message it conveyed through braying. Hence, there is also an element of the Prophet's hidden knowledge in this account. Overall, these two accounts that pertain explicitly to animals differ in that the first account describes a passive act in which qualities were given to an animal, while the second account relates an animal actively interacting with the Prophet.

As another element of nature, trees serve multiple purposes in Ibn Saʿd's "signs of prophecy" chapter. Prior to the revelation, trees and stones recognized the future prophet and greeted him.[69] A protective aspect of nature is mentioned in the lengthy account of the Prophet's childhood encounter with the monk Baḥīrā. The monk witnesses first a cloud and then a tree shading the Prophet. The tree itself reacted to Muḥammad's presence and moved its branches such that he was shaded.[70] Other accounts describe trees relocating on demand to serve several purposes. In one account the Prophet wanted to relieve himself but could not find anything that would shield him for privacy. He saw two trees far apart and asked Ibn Masʿūd to tell the trees to draw closer to one another so that they could cover him. One of the trees moved next to the other and Muḥammad relieved himself behind them.[71] Similar incidents are found as explicit "signs" of prophecy. Chapter 41 contains two accounts of trees that changed their locations, one serving as a sign for the Prophet himself,[72] and the other providing evidence of prophecy to another man.[73]

67 Ibn Saʿd, *Ṭabaqāt*, 1:125f.
68 Ibn Saʿd, *Ṭabaqāt*, 1:157.
69 Ibn Saʿd, *Ṭabaqāt*, 1:132.
70 Ibn Saʿd, *Ṭabaqāt*, 1:128f.
71 Ibn Saʿd, *Ṭabaqāt*, 1:143f.
72 Ibn Saʿd, *Ṭabaqāt*, 1:143f.
73 Ibn Saʿd, *Ṭabaqāt*, 1:154.

Finally, there is an account in which a palm tree expressed its desire to be close to the Prophet. The Prophet used to give sermons standing on the trunk of a palm tree that was in the mosque. When the *minbar* was built and the Prophet ascended it, the palm tree yearned audibly. The Prophet descended from the *minbar* and embraced the palm tree until it became quiet.[74]

Clouds also fulfill a protective function. In addition to the incident noted in the previously mentioned encounter with Baḥīrā,[75] there is an independent account of clouds shading the Prophet. This narrative is set during the Prophet's time with his foster mother, Ḥalīma, who came looking for the young boy and found him out in the heat. His foster sister assured Ḥalīma that Muḥammad was in no danger because a cloud had been moving around with him, shading him from the scorching midday heat.[76] In another account, Muḥammad mentions that he was shaded by clouds in response to a rabbi who asked him about favors God bestows on him.[77]

In two accounts, soil and rain, respectively, interact with Muḥammad as a result of his prophetic status. Soil concealed the Prophet's excrement, as we can see in a short account relating a dialogue with his wife ʿĀʾisha. ʿĀʾisha said, "I said, 'Oh Messenger of God, you relieve yourself and nothing offensive is visible of you.' He said, 'Do you not know, oh ʿĀʾisha, that the earth takes what comes out of prophets and nothing is seen of it?'"[78] The soil concealing the Prophet's waste granted him dignity and decency; in this he is distinguished from other humans and at the same time is grouped with previous prophets. In another account rain indicated that the Prophet's prayers were answered. Anas b. Mālik related that he was in the mosque during the Friday prayer when people informed the Prophet that a drought was threatening their livelihood and they asked him to pray for rain. Immediately after the Prophet's prayer a heavy rain set in and continued for seven days until the people turned to the Prophet during the next Friday prayer and informed him that the rain was now threatening them. The Prophet said: "O God, around us, not on us!" Anas b. Mālik reported that the clouds split asunder and separated until they were encircled by clouds but it did not rain on them.[79]

While Ibn Saʿd chose an array of natural phenomena as "signs of prophecy" only three of these accounts describe acts that were explicitly and deliberately performed to prove Muḥammad's claim to prophecy. The vast majority of

74 Ibn Saʿd, *Ṭabaqāt*, 1:159.
75 Ibn Saʿd, *Ṭabaqāt*, 1:128f.
76 Ibn Saʿd, *Ṭabaqāt*, 1:126f.
77 Ibn Saʿd, *Ṭabaqāt*, 1:138.
78 Ibn Saʿd, *Ṭabaqāt*, 1:144.
79 Ibn Saʿd, *Ṭabaqāt*, 1:149.

accounts of natural phenomena qualify as "signs of prophecy" simply because they are placed in chapters dedicated to "proofs of prophecy." The agents of these phenomena include animals, trees (and stones), clouds, soil, and rain. There is no clear pattern in these natural elements and how they react to or interact with the Prophet. Animals are seen to interact both actively and passively, while trees fulfill various functions. On the most basic level, they acknowledge and greet him; they actively protect the Prophet from the sun; they relocate in order to shield him from the public eye while he is relieving himself and thus protect his decency, or they provide evidence for his prophetic mission. Some of these functions are also fulfilled by other agents, such the soil that absorbed his excrement in order to protect his decency. By contrast, rain is a means of demonstrating God's responsiveness to the Prophet's supplications (*duʿāʾ*), rather than interacting with or reacting to the Prophet. But while specific reactions to the Prophet vary considerably, a common feature of almost all of these accounts is that an element of nature recognizes Muḥammad's status and is aware of his significance. Given that these incidents take place before as well as after the call to prophecy, natural phenomena corroborate the underlying idea of announcement and prediction accounts of the future or present prophet.

2.4 *Events in the Prophet's Childhood*

There are a number of less frequently recurring themes, such as events that took place in Muḥammad's early life prior to the beginning of the prophetic mission; these start with the first four *ḥadīth*s in the chapter on the "signs of prophecy."[80] The first *ḥadīth* echoes the preceding chapter's statements that Muḥammad is Abraham's prayer and Jesus' good tidings while linking them to the accounts of the Prophet's birth and the opening of his heart. The birth and opening of his heart are treated separately in the second and third report, respectively. The fourth account relates Ḥalīma's journey in search of a foster child and the blessings her family received after taking in the infant Muḥammad, and an encounter with a soothsayer predicting his future prophecy.

These childhood narratives provide an opportunity to contextualize some evidentiary narratives amidst the larger framework of Ibn Saʿd's prophetic biography and to study how the selection and presentation of otherwise biographical material shaped Ibn Saʿd's notion of the "signs of prophecy." Those biographical accounts found in the thematic chapters dedicated to the "signs of prophecy" are also found in the chronological biography of the Prophet. Their presentation, however, frequently differs from one another depending

80 Ibn Saʿd, *Ṭabaqāt*, 1:125f.

on their structural context. The chronological biography provides the broader historical context without emphasizing the exceptionality of individual events. By contrast, the thematically compiled chapters identify specific events and describe them in great detail to convey their exceptional significance. Ibn Saʿd's portrayal of the Prophet's conception, birth, and infancy showcases the various modes of presenting events in these frameworks as well as the selections Ibn Saʿd made to compile the thematic chapters. I have demonstrated elsewhere that these themes constituted an intricate part of the Prophet's life in al-Zuhrī's corpus.

Ibn Saʿd's chronological biography of the Prophet includes a chapter containing two accounts of the marriage of Muḥammad's parents, ʿAbdallāh and Āmina,[81] as well as a chapter with four accounts relating the narrative of another woman offering herself to ʿAbdallāh. The first account states that ʿAbdallāh displayed a "bright light in his face," but adds that some people say it was a "blaze like the white spot on a horse's face." The third account conveys an interpretative theological notion referring to the light as the "light of prophecy" and the fourth account mentions a "brightness between the eyes shining up to heaven." In the account about the light, ʿAbdallāh was just married to Āmina and was on his way to consummate his marriage when a woman offered herself to him, because of the light on his head. ʿAbdallāh rushed to his wife and they conceived Muḥammad. He returned to the other woman, who stated that she was no longer interested in him because the light had disappeared. Thus, the chronological *sīra* contains several accounts stating that, at the time immediately preceding the conception of the Prophet, a light had been visible on ʿAbdallāh's face. Even though this light is at least once explicitly referred to as a marker of prophecy, Ibn Saʿd does not list any of these accounts among the "signs of prophecy."

Āmina's pregnancy is also less emphasized among the "signs of prophecy" than in the general biography. The chronological *sīra* contains five accounts, the first of which states that she did not experience the burdens of pregnancy, only the cessation of her menstruation. Furthermore, it was said that a visitor came to her twice; the first time he related that she was pregnant and bearing "the lord of this community and its prophet"; and the second time he exclaimed that the child would receive divine protection.[82] The second account also mentions that she would not experience any discomfort and the third account

81 Ibn Saʿd, *Ṭabaqāt*, 1:75.

82 Ibn Saʿd, *Ṭabaqāt*, 1:75.

describes her pregnancies as being "as light as a lamb."[83] Finally, the fifth report recounts that Āmina was told to call the child Aḥmad.[84] By contrast, the chapter the "signs of prophecy before the call to prophecy" does not contain an individual account of the pregnancy, though Āmina briefly mentions (in the account of the blessings the wet nurse experienced after taking him) to Ḥalīma that she did not experience any discomfort during the pregnancy.[85]

The Prophet's birth is mentioned in Ibn Saʿd's chronological *sīra* in fifteen accounts. The first five accounts identify the day the Prophet was born;[86] the sixth account relates that his mother did not experience any discomfort during the pregnancy and that a light was emitted with him as emerged from her. This cast a bright light on everything between the East and the West; some narrators add that the Prophet himself fell on the ground resting on his hands, and raised his head.[87] The next account also mentions that the light that was emitted from the womb illuminated the palaces of Syria, and the newborn was described as being as clean as a lamb, without impurities, resting on his hands.[88] The eighth account recounts Āmina stating "I noticed the earth was lit, as if a meteor came out of me."[89] The narrative found in the ninth account is unique, as it states that following the delivery, Āmina placed the Prophet under a stone vessel, which then split in two.[90] And she saw him gazing toward heaven. The next two accounts recount, in the Prophet's first-person narration, the lights that illuminated Busra.[91] The twelfth and thirteenth accounts describe the Prophet's state during the delivery, and how he rested on his palms and knees, gazed toward the sky, was born circumcised, and his umbilical cord was cut, respectively. The last account includes ʿAbd al-Muṭṭalib stating "A child of mine will achieve greatness."[92] The next account reiterates many of the preceding details, as Āmina sent for ʿAbd al-Muṭṭalib and related to him everything she perceived during her pregnancy and childbirth.[93] The final

83 Ibn Saʿd, *Ṭabaqāt*, 1:79. The account immediately following this one quotes Muḥammad b. ʿUmar al-Aslamī, that is, al-Wāqidī (d. 207/823), who remarked that the preceding account was not known because it referred to the Prophet's children in the plural, while she only had one child, Muḥammad.

84 Ibn Saʿd, *Ṭabaqāt*, 1:79.

85 Ibn Saʿd, *Ṭabaqāt*, 1:125.

86 Ibn Saʿd, *Ṭabaqāt*, 1:81f.

87 Ibn Saʿd, *Ṭabaqāt*, 1:81f.

88 Ibn Saʿd, *Ṭabaqāt*, 1:82.

89 Ibn Saʿd, *Ṭabaqāt*, 1:82.

90 Ibn Saʿd, *Ṭabaqāt*, 1:82.

91 Ibn Saʿd, *Ṭabaqāt*, 1:83.

92 Ibn Saʿd, *Ṭabaqāt*, 1:83.

93 Ibn Saʿd, *Ṭabaqāt*, 1:83.

account reports the lines of poetry ʿAbd al-Muṭṭalib uttered on his grandson's birth.[94] These fifteen accounts of the Prophet's birth find only few counterparts in the chapter on the "signs of prophecy." Only three accounts mention these events; most accounts include the ease of his mother's pregnancy, the lights that were visible during the delivery, and the Prophet's position resting on his hands. Furthermore, they touch on a visitor announcing Āmina's pregnancy and the omen of the Banū Lihb, the last of which is not found in the chronological biography.[95]

Both in the general biography and in the chapter on the "signs of prophecy," Ibn Saʿd dedicates more attention to the time period the Prophet spent in the care of his wet nurse Ḥalīma than to the conception, pregnancy, and birth. The chronological *sīra* contains a total of twenty-six accounts related to "those who suckled the Prophet." The first twelve accounts note the names of foster mothers and siblings as well as stories about them.[96] The following account contains the narratives of Ḥalīma accepting the orphaned Muḥammad as her foster child, and Āmina recounting her experiences during her pregnancy.[97] The fourteenth account captures Āmina's reaction to her son's departure with Ḥalīma.[98] The subsequent account is a condensed narration about when his breast was opened and when Ḥalīma took him back to his mother, who urged her to take him back. Later Ḥalīma watched a cloud shading him and intended once again to return him to his mother. However, young Muḥammad was lost on the way, and his grandfather ʿAbd al-Muṭṭalib prayed at the Kaʿba for his safe return.[99] The sixteenth account in this chapter is closely related to the fifteenth and recounts ʿAbd al-Muṭṭalib praying at the Kaʿba for the return of his grandson. In this account, however, the reason for Muḥammad's disappearance differs: he went missing trying to find one of his grandfather's camels.[100] The Prophet's return to his grandfather is related in the subsequent account.[101] The eighteenth account simply constitutes a statement that the Prophet was nursed by a woman from the Banū Saʿd b. Bakr.[102] The nineteenth account describes Jews coming to Ḥalīma; in it, she relates details about the Prophet's conception and birth, and this incites the men to kill the infant. Ḥalīma then

94 Ibn Saʿd, *Ṭabaqāt*, 1:84.
95 Ibn Saʿd, *Ṭabaqāt*, 1:125.
96 Ibn Saʿd, *Ṭabaqāt*, 1:87–89.
97 Ibn Saʿd, *Ṭabaqāt*, 1:89f.
98 Ibn Saʿd, *Ṭabaqāt*, 1:91f.
99 Ibn Saʿd, *Ṭabaqāt*, 1:91f.
100 Ibn Saʿd, *Ṭabaqāt*, 1:92.
101 Ibn Saʿd, *Ṭabaqāt*, 1:92.
102 Ibn Saʿd, *Ṭabaqāt*, 1:92.

claims that Muḥammad is her own son, and the Jewish men lose interest in him, as they were seeking an orphan.[103] The next account contains a statement that the Prophet derived his eloquence from the Quraysh and from the tribe in which he was nursed.[104] The remaining accounts describe the interaction between the Prophet as an adult and his foster mother.[105]

The chapters on the "signs of prophecy" include several of these episodes, some of which occur in the framework of longer, multi-themed accounts, while others are presented in shorter, individual accounts, and some occur in both modes. The opening of the Prophet's breast and the cleansing of his heart are treated in greater detail as a "sign of prophecy," as they are mentioned both in the introductory first account as well as in one independent account.[106] In the chronological biography, the incident in which Ḥalīma witnessed a cloud shading her young foster child is merely one aspect of a multi-themed account, whereas the "signs of prophecy" include an independent account of the same event.[107] Finally, the general biography also mentions that Ḥalīma showed the infant boy to a soothsayer because his mother had instructed her to. The soothsayer ordered that the boy be killed and predicted his prophetic future. In the "signs of prophecy," this episode is presented in several individual accounts.[108] In addition to the variety of lengths in which events are related in the specific chapters, the accounts also exhibit different thematic *foci*. For instance, the "signs of prophecy" chapter includes a lengthy account of Ḥalīma's quest for a foster child and the numerous blessings her formerly impoverished family received after accepting the orphaned child.[109] As we have seen, the chronological biography also mentions this episode. However, it is noteworthy that the previous dire need of Ḥalīma's family and the blessings are only alluded to in the general biography, but described in great detail in the chapter on "signs of prophecy."

Finally, the chronological biography contains a chapter dedicated to the "First Journey to Syria"; this contains numerous incidents that are also part of the "signs of prophecy." Its first account describes the Prophet's closeness with his uncle Abū Ṭālib and relates a food-related incident[110] that is paralleled in

103 Ibn Saʿd, *Ṭabaqāt*, 1:92.
104 Ibn Saʿd, *Ṭabaqāt*, 1:93f.
105 Ibn Saʿd, *Ṭabaqāt*, 1:93f.
106 Ibn Saʿd, *Ṭabaqāt*, 1:125f.
107 Ibn Saʿd, *Ṭabaqāt*, 1:125f.
108 Ibn Saʿd, *Ṭabaqāt*, 1:125f.
109 Ibn Saʿd, *Ṭabaqāt*, 1:125f.
110 Ibn Saʿd, *Ṭabaqāt*, 1:98.

an account of the signs of prophecy preceding the call to prophecy.[111] The next two accounts refer to incidents with ʿAbd al-Muṭṭalib's cushion; these foreshadow Muḥammad's future leadership qualities. The next account refers to a monk in Syria who recognizes "a pious man" among Abū Ṭālib's group and warns that he should be protected from the Jews.[112] The fifth account in the "First Journey to Syria" contains only very short references to Baḥīrā in the description of virtues.[113] The remaining thirteen accounts all discuss Abū Ṭālib's children, his death, and subsequent revelations that pertain to matters for which Abū Ṭālib set a precedent, such as a funeral prayer for non-Muslims and their salvation.[114] Thus, while some of the accounts in this chapter have counterparts in the "signs of prophecy" chapter, the vast majority of them are unrelated. As noted, the presentation of those events that overlap differs in thematic focus. In the chronological biography, the encounter with a monk is only briefly referred to while it is covered extensively in the chapter dedicated to the "signs of prophecy prior to the call to prophecy."

The juxtaposition of accounts of the "signs of prophecy" narratives with their counterparts in the general biography demonstrates that accounts occurring in both sections generally corroborate one another; however, they frequently differ with regard to the extent of detail provided on a certain event and on their thematic foci. The most prominent examples of such divergent foci in the presentation of the same event are Ḥalīma's quest for a foster child and the lengthy accounts of the Prophet's encounter with Baḥīrā. The most prominent themes are emphasized by being included more than once, such as the water-related incident at Ḥudaybiyya, which is presented several times with a number of differing aspects. Therefore, it is obvious that Ibn Saʿd chose precisely which narratives to include in the chapters of the "signs of prophecy," and to what extent certain details would be elaborated. Such a selective approach corroborates Leder's observation that "the editing of *akhbār* implies operations similar to authorship."[115] This editorial process of selecting some accounts and omitting others presupposes that Ibn Saʿd held a notion of the "signs of prophecy" that functioned as a guiding principle in compiling these thematic chapters.

---

111 Ibn Saʿd, *Ṭabaqāt*, 1:142.

112 Ibn Saʿd, *Ṭabaqāt*, 1:99.

113 Ibn Saʿd, *Ṭabaqāt*, 1:99.

114 Ibn Saʿd, *Ṭabaqāt*, 1:100–103.

115 Leder, "The Literary Use of Khabar," 284. Leder concluded this based on a comparative study of parallel narratives found in the works of early compilers such as Ibn Isḥāq, al-Wāqidī, and Ibn Saʿd. The results of this chapter, however, allow us to extend this observation of the authorial processes of a single compiler.

2.5 *States of the Prophet*

In addition to narratives of Muḥammad's childhood, one of the less frequently employed themes in Ibn Saʿd's chapters are narratives that refer to the heightened sense of discretion and decency that distinguished Muḥammad from his contemporaries, and also connected him to other prophetic figures. In one account Ibn al-ʿAbbās states that he first became aware of Muḥammad's prophetic status when Muḥammad was told to "cover" (his private parts) as a young boy. Ibn al-ʿAbbās states that from that day onward he never saw the Prophet's private parts again.[116] In the account immediately following, ʿĀʾisha confirms this notion and states in a report that can only be understood in conjunction with the previous one: "I did not see that of the Prophet."[117] The Prophet's heightened sense of discretion and decency is also reiterated in the accounts relating the relocation of trees that shielded him from the public eye while he was relieving himself[118] and the dialogue with ʿĀʾisha stating that nothing offensive is ever seen if prophets relieve themselves because the soil absorbs it.[119] These two accounts have already been discussed in the section on natural phenomena, as Muḥammad's sense of propriety was facilitated by natural elements. In addition to this sense of discretion, the Prophet's sleep is described as a state affecting his eyes, not his heart.[120] Like the soil absorbing excrement, this particular state of sleep is explicitly described as only reaching prophets.

The accounts that I subsumed under this theme of prophetic states combines the notion of the external recognition of Muḥammad's prophetic mission, including instances that occurred long before the first revelations, with those of his exceptional personal characteristics. These characteristics single him out from his contemporaries while also linking him to previous prophets. The image that is crafted here implies a unique human being who is, at the same time, part of a continuous sacred history, equal in character to the other prophets.

2.6 *Interactions with the Divine*

Six accounts relate various aspects of the Prophet's interactions with the divine; these can be further subdivided into acts of revelation, divine protection, and divine responses to the Prophet's invocation. One of these two accounts is a

116 Ibn Saʿd, *Ṭabaqāt*, 1:131.
117 Ibn Saʿd, *Ṭabaqāt*, 1:131.
118 Ibn Saʿd, *Ṭabaqāt*, 1:143f.
119 Ibn Saʿd, *Ṭabaqāt*, 1:144.
120 Ibn Saʿd, *Ṭabaqāt*, 1:145.

first-person narration by the Prophet describing how he encountered Gabriel during the revelation.

> The Prophet said, "When I was standing during the day Gabriel entered, he struck me between my shoulder blades so that I went to a tree in which there was the like of two bird's nests. He sat in one of them and I sat in the other. They began to rise up until [they reached] the final point of the East and the West. If I wanted to touch the heaven I touched [it] and I turned my side and bent over to Gabriel and he was like a wrapped saddle-cloth. [Thereby] I came to know his knowledge of God. The door of heaven was opened for me and I saw a great light and there was before me a curtain with patches of pearls and rubies in it. Then God revealed to me what He willed."[121]

One account narrates the Prophet's dream, in which the angels Gabriel and Michael relate an allegory to him.

> The Prophet came to us and said, "I saw in my dream as if Gabriel was at my head and Mīkhāʾīl [Michael] at my legs. One of them said to his companion, 'Impart words of wisdom to him.' He said, 'Listen! Your ears must listen to it. Comprehend! Your heart must comprehend it. You and your Companions are like the king who erected a mansion then built in it a room, then prepared a table in it, then he sent a messenger to invite the people to [share] his food; among them [i.e., the people] there are those who respond to the invitation and [those who] decline it. As for God, He is the king and the mansion is Islam, the room is heaven, and those who accept the invitation, [are those who] embrace Islam and those who embrace Islam enter heaven and eat what is in it.'"[122]

Another account contains a lengthy narrative about the Prophet sitting with ʿUthmān b. Maẓʿūn in the courtyard of his house at the moment a revelation occurred. Engaged in conversation, the Prophet suddenly turned away from his guest and stood up gazing toward the sky. ʿUthmān noticed the Prophet's nodding as if he was indicating his comprehension of information that was conveyed to him. Then the Prophet returned to his previous position facing his guest, who expressed his surprise over the Prophet's behavior. The Prophet explained that he had just received a revelation from God and ʿUthmān inquired

121 Ibn Saʿd, *Ṭabaqāt*, 1:144.
122 Ibn Saʿd, *Ṭabaqāt*, 1:145.

about what was revealed. After the Prophet recited the newly revealed verses,[123] ʿUthmān b. Maẓʿūn immediately embraced Islam.[124] Given that receiving and conveying divine messages became the defining feature of prophecy in Islam, it is surprising that only two of ninety-nine accounts of the "signs of prophecy" explicitly refer to revelation, and a third relates a dream-based encounter with the angels Gabriel and Michael.

In addition to revelation, divine interaction is presented in one account that explicitly describes an act of divine protection. ʿĀʾisha relates that the Prophet used to have guards who protected him. When a verse was revealed that God protects him,[125] Muḥammad was at ease and dismissed his guards.[126]

A third form of divine interaction pertains to immediate responses to the Prophet's prayers. Three accounts refer to God's response to the Prophet's invocations. The first two were treated under previous thematic divisions. The first of these two relates the Prophet's *duʿāʾ*, in which he asked for rain on behalf of his suffering community, and was instantly answered with a rainfall so strong that the Prophet invoked God again, asking Him to stop the rain. The second *duʿāʾ* was also immediately answered.[127] God's response is part of a lengthy narrative of Miqdād seeking milk. Miqdād came to the Prophet and shared the milk of a goat with his companions and the Prophet. One night he was tempted by the devil to drink the Prophet's share. When the Prophet came to the mosque at night and did not find his share of milk, he made a *duʿāʾ* asking God to feed the one who had fed him. After the *duʿāʾ*, Miqdād found the goats' udders full of milk in spite of having been milked recently. He drew milk from them and shared it with the Prophet.[128] The third account is the Prophet's well-known encounter with Surāqa b. Mālik, who was following the Prophet and Abū Bakr. The Prophet prayed that the legs of Surāqa's horse would become firm, and they sank into the ground. Surāqa promised to prevent further persecution if the Prophet would set his horse free. The Prophet made another *duʿāʾ*, asking God to release the horse, and the legs of the horse came out.[129] The accounts of Miqdād and Surāqa have been discussed in other sections of this book.

---

123 "God enjoins justice and kindness, and giving to kinsfolk, and forbids lewdness and abomination and wickedness. He exhorts you in order that you may take heed" (Q. 16:90).

124 Ibn Saʿd, *Ṭabaqāt*, 1:146.

125 "O Messenger, proclaim what has been revealed to you from your Lord; but if you do not, you would not have delivered His message. God will protect you from mankind. God does not guide the unbelieving people" (Q. 5:67).

126 Ibn Saʿd, *Ṭabaqāt*, 1:144.

127 Ibn Saʿd, *Ṭabaqāt*, 1:149.

128 Ibn Saʿd, *Ṭabaqāt*, 1:154f.

129 Ibn Saʿd, *Ṭabaqāt*, 1:159.

2.7 *Hidden Knowledge*

Three accounts imply that the Prophet had access to hidden knowledge. I define hidden knowledge broadly as the Prophet's access to any information he could not have gained from his surroundings. In the first account, he is aware of the conversations of some hypocrites (*munāfiqūn*)—members of his community who converted outwardly but continued to resent the Prophet:

> The Prophet said, "If men among you gathered and said such-and-such, then get up and ask for forgiveness and I will ask forgiveness for you." They did not get up. He said, "What is the matter with you? Get up and ask for God's forgiveness and I will seek forgiveness for you." [He said this] three times and then he said, "Get up or I will call you by your names!" He said, "Get up such-and-such!" They got up, ashamed, covering their faces.[130]

The second account refers to a goat that appeared to a group of hungry Muslims during a raid. The animal walked up to the Prophet and he milked it. Then he commanded one of his Companions to secure it, but also announced that the Companion should not think of himself as having taking possession of the goat. The Companion secured the goat with a rope only to find it gone in the morning. The Prophet said that the animal had been taken by God, who provided it.[131]

The third account is set during the Quraysh's boycott of the Banū Hāshim. The boycott was put into writing in the form of a document that declared that none of the Quraysh was allowed to buy from, sell merchandise to, or associate with a member of the Banū Hāshim. Three years after the document was drafted, God informed the Prophet that a termite ate the part of the document that specified the terms of the boycott, but those parts mentioning God remained intact. The Prophet mentioned this to Abū Ṭālib, who in turn asked the elders of the Quraysh to look at the document. Abū Ṭālib negotiated with the elders to end the boycott if the document is indeed in the state Muḥammad described it. When they found that the Prophet had spoken the truth, they remained silent. Abū Ṭālib realized that they will not keep their word to lift the boycott and invoked God to help the Muslim community.[132]

---

130 Ibn Saʿd, *Ṭabaqāt*, 1:149.

131 Ibn Saʿd, *Ṭabaqāt*, 1:151.

132 Ibn Saʿd, *Ṭabaqāt*, 1:159f.

2.8 *Material Transformation and Healing*

Finally, Ibn Saʿd's chapters contain accounts that describe incidents of material transformation and the Prophet healing another person's ailment. The first material transformation occurs in the context of Salmān al-Fārisī being released from his owner through a contract. The price for Salmān's manumission was three hundred saplings of fruit-bearing date palms and forty ounces of gold. Since Salmān did not have the means to pay this price, the Prophet asked his community to provide for him. The people came and brought two or three saplings each until they collected three hundred. The Prophet instructed Salmān to dig pits and helped him plant the saplings. In the meantime, someone brought a piece of gold the size of a pigeon's egg, but Salmān realized that it would not suffice to buy his freedom. The Prophet touched it with his tongue and it increased in weight. Salmān took forty ounces of it to pay for his manumission and still had an equal amount left.[133]

The second account of material transformation states that ʿUkāsha b. Miḥṣan broke his sword on the day of Badr. The Prophet gave him the stem of a tree and in his hand it turned into a sharp sword of pure iron.[134]

Finally, the only healing narrative found among the "signs of prophecy" relates that the eye of Qatāda b. al-Nuʿmān was infected and the eyeball was dropping down his cheek. The Prophet brought the eye back with his hand, and it [became] the healthier of the two eyes and the better one.[135]

•••

The juxtaposition of narrative accounts of the "signs of prophecy" with their counterparts in the general biography demonstrates that accounts occurring in both sections generally corroborate one another, but frequently differ with regard to the extent of detail provided about an event and their thematic foci. As such, the chronological biography usually aims at providing the general historical framework of events, while accounts in the thematic chapters emphasize the exceptionality of individual events. It is, therefore, obvious that Ibn Saʿd selected specific narratives to include in the chapters of the "signs of prophecy." Such a selective approach corroborates Leder's observation that "the editing of *akhbār* implies operations similar to authorship."[136] This

133 Ibn Saʿd, *Ṭabaqāt*, 1:155.

134 Ibn Saʿd, *Ṭabaqāt*, 1:158.

135 Ibn Saʿd, *Ṭabaqāt*, 1:158.

136 Leder, "The Literary Use of Khabar," 284. Leder concluded this based on the comparative study of parallel narratives found in the works of early compilers such as Ibn Isḥāq, al-Wāqidī, and Ibn Saʿd. The results of this chapter, however, allow us to extend this observation to the authorial processes of a single compiler in his work.

editorial process of selecting some accounts and omitting others presupposes that Ibn Saʿd had a notion of the "signs of prophecy" that functioned as a guiding principle in compiling these thematic chapters.

The analysis of the "signs of prophecy" chapters in the *Ṭabaqāt* establishes that Ibn Saʿd designated certain incidents as "signs of prophecy" and deliberately selected them from the larger pool of *ḥadīth*. Only three of the ninety-nine accounts actually mention that Muḥammad's actions were intended as proofs of his prophetic mission or are an attempt to convince others to convert. In all other cases, there are no explicit indications of "signs of prophecy" in the accounts themselves and Ibn Saʿd established the supposed evidentiary nature of the particular incidents simply by including them in these designated chapters. Therefore, we can approximate Ibn Saʿd's epistemological notion of what exactly constitutes evidence of Muḥammad's prophetic mission by looking at the various themes he highlights in these chapters. The accounts fall into three large categories of (1) predictions and announcements, (2) food- and/or water-related signs, and (3) natural phenomena, and a number of themes that occur less frequently. The following chart illustrates the distribution of themes.

With forty-one accounts, predictions and announcements make up the largest thematic group by far, accounting for almost half of the ninety-nine accounts found in these two chapters. These predictions and announcements occur in both monotheistic and pagan contexts, and frequently imply that the monotheists not only anticipated the coming of a future prophet but were also able to accurately identify Muḥammad based on information found in their own scriptures. Many of these accounts are set in a time long before the first revelation and, therefore, suggest that Muḥammad embodied particular features indicating his prophetic status long before he actively began the prophetic mission.

A similar notion underlies many accounts involving natural phenomena. Here, too, various natural elements, such as animals, trees, or clouds, react to

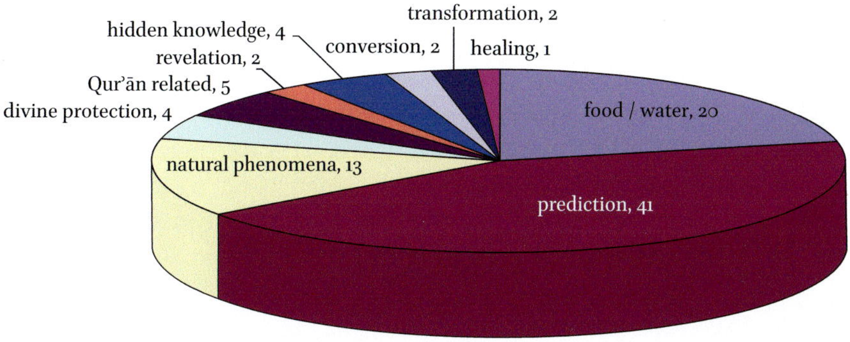

FIGURE 1 Thematic categories in Ibn Saʿd's *Ṭabaqāt*

or interact with Muḥammad based on their innate ability to recognize his status and significance. Another common motif in these accounts highlights his character traits as exceptionally empathetic, generous, and sincere.

Narratives related to an increase in food and water make up the second largest group and are, of all the thematic groups, the ones that correspond most closely to Ibn Saʿd's predecessor, Maʿmar b. Rāshid, whose main focus was on water-related narratives. All six of Maʿmar's accounts can be found in Ibn Saʿd's two chapters. The sudden emergence or increase in food or water always occurred in moments of dire need and mostly benefited individuals or groups other than just Muḥammad himself. These occurred through a deliberate action or simply because of Muḥammad's presence and, thus, occasionally carried the notion of "blessings."

Certainly, the most astonishing feature of Ibn Saʿd's selection is that the act of revelation itself is hardly found.[137] Given that Islam views receiving and conveying divine messages as the defining feature of prophecy, it is surprising that acts of revelation appear explicitly in only two accounts. Furthermore, these two describe marginal aspects when compared to the more well-known narratives of the beginning of the revelation, such as Muḥammad's retreats in the cave of Ḥirāʾ or the first revelation and the fear it invoked in him. These prominent narratives are all left to several other chapters in the chronological biography, but are not mentioned with regard to the "signs of prophecy." Dovetailing this paucity of revelation as a "sign of prophecy" is the absence of any references to challenges from pagans or adherents of other faiths to prove the revelation, or references to the literary qualities of the revelation. This seems to indicate that theologically charged questions, such as the inimitability of the Qurʾān, did not influence Ibn Saʿd's notion of the "signs of prophecy."

Scholars like Tor Andrae and Annemarie Schimmel have stated that the works of *dalāʾil al-nubūwa* are compilations of miracle narratives. However, this thematic analysis demonstrates that not every account included in the "signs of prophecy" of Ibn Saʿd involved miraculous elements. In fact, the majority of accounts of prediction and announcement are based on descriptions found in religious scriptures or information conveyed to previous prophets through revelation. Other announcements were based on dreams, visions, or the appearance of *jinn*. Neither one of these would be considered "miraculous" in nature by contemporary scholars. By the same token, not every incident that later came to have "miraculous" significance is included in the "signs of prophecy." An elucidation of various Qurʾān-inspired materials demonstrates this. In the two chapters dedicated to the "signs of prophecy," there are various accounts

137 Ibn Saʿd, *Ṭabaqāt*, 1:146.

that refer to *jinn* as agents announcing the beginning of the revelation. These accounts frequently mention a "fire in the sky" or shooting stars (*shihāb*, pl. *shuhūb*), which are thrown at demons or *jinn*.[138] In Ibn Saʿd's chapters on the "signs of prophecy," both the *jinn* and the shooting stars appear as agents announcing the advent of the revelation; thus, their placement in these chapters corroborates the thesis that Ibn Saʿd followed a specific notion of the "signs of prophecy." Notably, other Qurʾān-inspired narratives that play a prominent role in later *dalāʾil al-nubūwa* works and that are, arguably, more "miraculous" incidents, only find their way into Ibn Saʿd's general biography, but not into these specific chapters. Among these narratives are the Prophet's night journey to Jerusalem,[139] the Prophet's ascension to heaven where he encounters previous prophets,[140] and the splitting of the moon.[141] We can conclude that the "miraculous" quality of an incident or event was not a contributing factor in Ibn Saʿd's selection of the "signs of prophecy."

3 Al-Bukhārī's "ʿAlāmāt al-Nubūwa fī l-Islām"

The canonical *ḥadīth* compilation of *Ṣaḥīḥ al-Bukhārī* contains a chapter of sixty-four "signs of prophecy in Islam" in the book of virtues.[142] About fifteen of these accounts are parallel to Ibn Saʿd's "signs of prophecy," such as various water- or food-related incidents,[143] the Prophet's *duʿāʾ* for rain on behalf of his community,[144] the yearning of the palm tree after the Prophet started using the *minbar* for his sermons,[145] and the Prophet's encounter with Surāqa.[146] The remaining accounts in this chapter relate incidents that are not mentioned in Ibn Saʿd. Most of these accounts pertain to the Prophet's knowledge of things

138 Ibn Saʿd, *Ṭabaqāt*, 1:135 (explicit); 1:139f. (five subsequent accounts: implied; listening explicit; explicit; explicit; explicit).

139 "Glory be to Him Who caused His servant to travel by night from the Sacred Mosque to the Farthest Mosque, whose precincts We have blessed, in order to show him some of Our Signs. He is indeed the All-Hearing, the All-Seeing" (Q. 17:1).

140 "He has indeed seen him (Gabriel) a second time; By the Lotus Tree of the outermost limit. Close by it is the Garden of Refuge. His gaze did not shift nor did he exceed the bound. He saw some of the Great Signs of his Lord" (Q. 17:13–18)).

141 "The Hour is drawing near and the moon is split asunder. If they see a sign, they turn away and say: 'Continued sorcery'" (Q. 51:1–2).

142 Al-Bukhārī, *Ṣaḥīḥ*, 4:466–500.

143 Cf. al-Bukhārī, *Ṣaḥīḥ*, 4:467–470 (nos. 3571, 3572, 3573, 3574, 3575, 3576).

144 Cf. al-Bukhārī, *Ṣaḥīḥ*, 4:474f. (no. 3582).

145 Cf. al-Bukhārī, *Ṣaḥīḥ*, 4:475f. (nos. 3583, 3584, 3585).

146 Cf. al-Bukhārī, *Ṣaḥīḥ*, 4:490f (no. 3615).

unknown to man, such as references to "the Hour,"[147] and future trials and afflictions (*fitna*) of the Muslim community.[148] In one account, Muḥammad informs his daughter Fāṭima about his impending death and she begins to weep. He consoles her by saying that she will be the first of his family members to join him in paradise.[149] According to Muslim tradition, Fāṭima died less than six months after her father. In other accounts, the Prophet predicts the victory of the Muslim armies during the conquests, and is aware of the death of his Companion at the moment of their passing, even though he died far from Medina and news only reached the city hours or even days later.[150]

A comparison between the selections of Ibn Saʿd and al-Bukhārī clearly shows that they differ in their epistemological notions of the "proofs of prophecy." The most prominent difference between the two compilations is that al-Bukhārī only includes accounts of events after Muḥammad's call to prophecy while Ibn Saʿd dedicates an entire chapter to signs preceding the first revelation, including Muḥammad's childhood. It is quite likely that al-Bukhārī excluded this material on methodological grounds. The standards of authentication required in a *ṣaḥīḥ* collection mean that most accounts from Muḥammad's early life would not be included.

By contrast, there is a partial congruence between the notion of the "signs of prophecy" of Ibn Saʿd and that of al-Bukhārī, given that both include a number of common accounts, mostly including water-related incidents. Furthermore, Ibn Saʿd and al-Bukhārī overlap in their notion that the Prophet's hidden knowledge constitutes a "sign of prophecy," but this is only a thematic congruence given that the specific accounts do not correspond. Ibn Saʿd's other

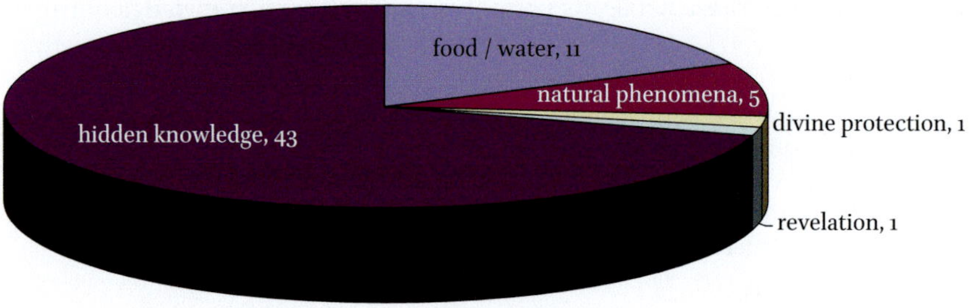

FIGURE 2 Thematic categories in the *Ṣaḥīḥ* of al-Bukhārī

147 Cf. al-Bukhārī, *Ṣaḥīḥ*, 4:477f. (nos. 3587; 3590; 3591; 3592).
148 Cf. al-Bukhārī, *Ṣaḥīḥ*, 4:481f. (nos. 3597; 3599; 3600; 3601).
149 Al-Bukhārī, *Ṣaḥīḥ*, 4:495f.
150 Al-Bukhārī, *Ṣaḥīḥ*, 4:497.

large categories, such as predictions and announcements or natural phenomena, and the less significant categories are almost completely absent from al-Bukhārī's chapter. All of this suggests that there was a shared understanding among *ḥadīth* scholars that certain aspects of Muḥammad's life are evidence of his prophetic mission, but there was no generally accepted notion of what constituted the signs of prophecy. While the scholars shared many accounts in their general repertoire, they constructed their own epistemological notions of the proofs of prophecy through their own selection processes and by grouping their choices of accounts under thematic headings.

4 Al-Jūzajānī's "Amārāt al-Nubūwa"

Unlike the collections that have been studied so far in this chapter, al-Jūzajānī's *Amārāt al-nubūwa* is not extant in its entirety; from it we have a selection of *ḥadīth*s from the sixth chapter. The excerpt of al-Jūzajānī's work contains thirteen *ḥadīth*s that I group into four thematic categories, including two that were not part of the *dalāʾil al-nubūwa* compilations discussed earlier.

4.1 *Food-Related Incidents as "Proofs of Prophecy"*

Food-related events appear frequently in this selective compilation; they makeup five of the thirteen accounts. The fourth *ḥadīth* of this excerpt sees a group traveling with the Prophet setting up camp, when the Prophet asks Saʿd to milk a particular goat. Saʿd states that he is familiar with the territory and that there are not many "milk-giving" goats in the area. Then he successfully milks the goat countless times and assigns someone to milk them but the goat disappears. The Prophet said: "As for the goat, the one requesting it left with it."[151]

The next *ḥadīth* presents a significantly more elaborate version of the same incident. The *ḥadīth* describes the Prophet's habit of retreating to the mountains with Abū Bakr to reflect on the Qurʾān. One day Muḥammad asked Abū Bakr's slave, Saʿd, for something to eat. Saʿd gave them raisins and asked the Prophet to request that Abū Bakr manumit him. Abū Bakr did so after initial concerns and Saʿd reiterated his loyalty to both of them. His loyalty was further stressed in a tangent that mentions that Saʿd had saddled their riding animals on the day of the *hijra*. At a later point, the Prophet set out on a raid without bringing provisions and turned to Saʿd who brought some dates for the Prophet and Abū Bakr. Muḥammad invoked a blessing over the dates and they

151 Al-Jūzajānī, *Amārāt al-nubūwa*, fol. 162b, line 21 to fol. 163a, line 3.

were spread out over leather mats. He then pointed to a goat behind a tree and instructed Saʿd to milk it. Using his drinking cup, Saʿd milked the goat and called the army to come and have food with them. The men ate and drank until they were all satisfied, and the remaining dates still filled a vessel. Saʿd asked permission to leave and assigned another person to guard the goat, but this person soon reported to Saʿd that the goat had disappeared even though he was holding its neck. The Prophet was informed but told the two men to forget about it.[152] Ibn Saʿd's chapter on the "proofs of prophecy" after the call to prophecy includes a very similar account in which Nafiʿ is instructed to milk a goat, which then fed an army of 1,400 men before disappearing. In this version, the Prophet foretold the goat's disappearance.[153] The narrative in al-Juzajānī's work is interesting because it merges the tropes of increasing a small amount of food to sustain a large crowd and milking an animal that is otherwise incapable of providing milk.

The next *ḥadīth*, written in the third person, states that the Prophet fed Khadīja with grapes from paradise.[154] The twelfth *ḥadīth* of the excerpt describes how Abū Hurayra brought dates to the Prophet, who then invoked blessings over them. Abū Hurayra put them into his bag of provisions and continued eating from them until the day ʿUthmān was killed.[155]

The last *ḥadīth* mentions the Prophet going to the Bāhila tribe. He arrived while they were having a meal and was invited to join them but declined saying that he had come to forbid the kind of food they were indulging in. He identified himself as a prophet but the Bāhila rejected him and drove him away. Muḥammad, overcome by severe hunger and exhaustion, slept and was provided with food and milk to such an extent that his stomach became extended. One of the Bāhila men admonished the others for rejecting the Prophet and sent men after him to offer him whatever food was permissible to him. When the men find Muḥammad, he declined their offer saying that God had provided for him and pointed to his extended belly. The men convert to Islam.[156]

While the theme of abundant food is common in both previous compilations, the specific accounts differ. Maʿmar focused on water-related incidents that are not found in this excerpt of al-Juzajānī's work. There is more thematic overlap with Ibn Saʿd's compilation, including the tropes of milking a single goat to feed a large crowd, the goat's disappearance, and Muḥammad being

152 Al-Jūzajānī, *Amārāt al-nubūwa*, fol. 163a, line 3 to fol. 163b, line 18.
153 Ibn Saʿd, *Ṭabaqāt*, 1:151.
154 Al-Jūzajānī, *Amārāt al-nubūwa*, fol. 163b, line 18 to fol. 164a, line 1.
155 Al-Jūzajānī, *Amārāt al-nubūwa*, fol. 164b, lines 15–22.
156 Al-Jūzajānī, *Amārāt al-nubūwa*, fol. 164b, line 22 to fol. 165a, line 10.

provided for by God, but the specific accounts differ. In other places, al-Juzajānī includes tropes that are absent in previous compilations of *dalāʾil al-nubūwa*, such as the increase in dates after Muḥammad invoked blessings over them or his feeding Khadīja in paradise. The subtext also differs as al-Juzajānī presents narratives in which the abundant food is directly linked to Muḥammad's actions or directions to his Companions, while Ibn Saʿd also included many accounts in which Muḥammad's presence automatically led to the abundance in food. This notion of a "blessed presence," both before and after the call to prophecy, is absent in the excerpt we have of al-Juzajānī.

4.2 *The Prophet's Character as "Proof of Prophecy"*

The first two *ḥadīth*s of the excerpt both relate an incident in which the Prophet asked Jābir to sell him his camel. In the first account, Jābir named a price for the camel but the Prophet paid more than Jābir asked for and later returned the camel. The second account describes Muḥammad and Jābir traveling together. Muḥammad rides Jābir's camel and asks him to sell it to him. No further details of the transaction are mentioned, but on their return the Prophet told Jābir that his request was not serious and he should keep both the animal and the money.[157]

The third *ḥadīth* relates, on the authority of Jābir b. ʿAbdallāh, that the Prophet never said no when he was asked a favor.[158] Another *ḥadīth*, the seventh of the excerpt, describes how Abū Hurayra and others were praying with the Prophet when his two young grandsons, Ḥasan and Ḥusayn, leaped onto the Prophet's back. The Prophet gently put them down. Once he had finished praying, the boys climbed into his lap, one sitting on each of the Prophet's thighs. Abū Hurayra asked the Prophet whether he wanted the children removed but the Prophet insisted that he let them be. Then a light appeared and immersed the boys until his mother came to take them.[159]

The predominant motif in these four *ḥadīth*s appears to be the Prophet's exceptional character, as seen in his generosity, kindness, and patience. Ibn Saʿd included narratives that highlighted Muḥammad's character as evidence for his prophetic mission. In these cases, it is the sense of discretion and decency that is emphasized and presented as a feature of all prophets. This demonstrates that Ibn Saʿd and al-Juzajānī only shared the general notion that the quality of Muḥammad's character can serve as evidence for his prophetic

---

157 Al-Jūzajānī, *Amārāt al-nubūwa*, fol. 162b, lines 13–19.
158 Al-Jūzajānī, *Amārāt al-nubūwa*, fol. 162b, lines 19–21.
159 Al-Jūzajānī, *Amārāt al-nubūwa*, fol. 164a, lines 1–8.

mission but each one highlighted different traits and selected different narratives for their respective compilations.

4.3 *Light as "Proof of Prophecy"*

A thematic category that appears for the first time in al-Jūzajānī's work relates to light. In the eighth *ḥadīth*, Qatāda takes advantage of a dark and rainy night to watch the Prophet pray *ʿishāʾ*. When the Prophet noticed him, he asked Qatāda why he was in the mosque while Satan is hiding in his house with his family. The Prophet offered him his walking stick and told him "to seek light from it until you reach your house. You [will] find him in the corner of the house. Beat him with the branch."[160] The moment Qatāda left the mosque the walking stick lit up like a candle and illuminated the way home. Qatāda found Satan in the corner of his house and beat him until he disappeared.[161]

Illuminated walking sticks are also the topic of the next *ḥadīth* which describes two men leaving the Prophet. When they leave, the walking stick of one of the men lit up and illuminated their way home until they reached a fork where they had to separate and the other man's walking stick also lit up. Both walked home in the light of their sticks.[162] It is noteworthy that al-Bukhārī's *Ṣaḥīḥ* includes a very similar account, though it is listed in the "Bāb al-Manāqib" (Book of virtues).[163] This chapter also includes the "signs of prophecy in Islam," but unlike al-Jūzajānī, al-Bukhārī includes this light-themed account in a later *ḥadīth* without a heading. The following *ḥadīth* in al-Jūzajānī relates that camels scattered during the night and that the Prophet's fingers provided light until the people had collected their possessions.[164]

The degree to which the Prophet actively engaged with the light source differs in these three accounts. In the first account, the Prophet's walking stick is given to Qatāda to illuminate his way home. In the next *ḥadīth*, the walking sticks of the two companions light up and illuminate the way and the only connection to the Prophet is a reference to the fact that the two men were leaving the Prophet. In the last *ḥadīth* of this category, the Prophet, actively and without the agency of another object, provides light with his fingers.

Light also plays a role in another *ḥadīth* listed in this excerpt; this one relates to the Prophet's kindness toward his grandsons who are immersed in light when they sit in their grandfather's lap. Notably, the compiler of the excerpt

160 Al-Jūzajānī, *Amārāt al-nubūwa*, fol. 164a, lines 16–17.

161 Al-Jūzajānī, *Amārāt al-nubūwa*, fol. 164a, lines 8–20.

162 Al-Jūzajānī, *Amārāt al-nubūwa*, fol. 164a, line 20 to fol. 164b, line 4.

163 Al-Bukhārī, *Ṣaḥīḥ*, 4:502 (no. 3639).

164 Al-Jūzajānī, *Amārāt al-nubūwa*, fol. 164b, lines 4–9.

placed this *ḥadīth* immediately before the three *ḥadīths* with light themes. In this *ḥadīth*, however, the light symbolism appears to be of secondary importance and therefore I have subsumed this *ḥadīth* under another category.

In general, evidentiary incidents revolving around light were not part of *dalāʾil al-nubūwa* compilations, though light symbolism was a part of other accounts. The birth narrative of the Prophet, for instance, describes a light coming forth from the Prophet's mother; this light was so bright that it illuminated the fortresses of Syria. This narrative was among some of the earliest *ḥadīth* compilations and *sīra* works predating al-Jūzajānī but it does not figure prominently in the early *dalāʾil al-nubūwa* works as the analysis of Ibn Saʿd's chapters shows.

4.4 *Interactions with the Divine*

A single *ḥadīth* mentions the Prophet's encounter with Gabriel in the cave Ḥirāʾ. The angel announced that the Prophet's wife Khadīja bring a certain dish and then conveyed God's greetings to her. When Khadīja arrived the Prophet asked about the dish and told her about Gabriel's presence and the greetings he sent to her.

The analysis of the content of al-Jūzajānī's *Amārāt al-nubūwa* shows that the thematic categories are much more evenly distributed; in particular it is more even than in the compilations of Ibn Saʿd and al-Bukhārī, with food- or water-related incidents, the Prophet's character, and light providing five, four, and three "proofs," respectively. It should be borne in mind, however, that the present analysis is based on a selective fragment al-Jūzajānī's *Amārāt al-nubūwa* rather than the entire work.

Furthermore, al-Jūzajānī's *Amārāt al-nubūwa* displays thematic arrangements to a greater degree than previous works. In two instances, two accounts of the same incidents are placed one after the other, possibly to provide the context.

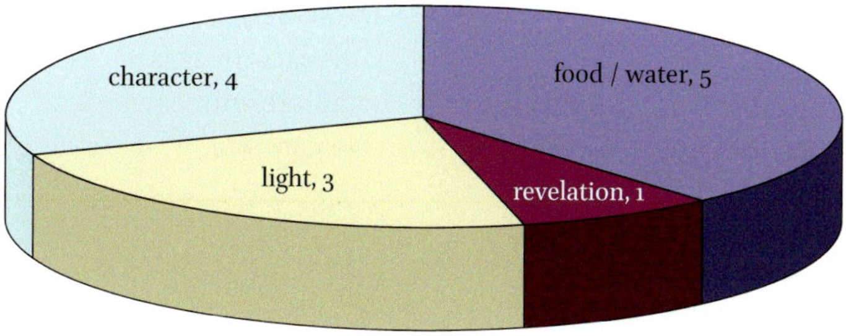

FIGURE 3 Thematic categories in an extract from al-Jūzajānī's *Amārāt al-nubūwa*

5 Al-Tirmidhī's "Bāb mā jāʾ fī ayāt Nubūwa al-Nabī wa-mā qad khaṣṣa Allāh bihi"

Al-Tirmidhī's canonical collection of *ḥadīth* contains a small chapter with nine accounts dedicated to "the signs of the Prophet's prophecy and how God distinguished him." The *ḥadīth* in al-Tirmidhī's chapter on the "signs of prophecy" fall into four thematic categories: food- or water-related incidents, natural phenomena, blessings (*baraka*) through the Prophet's touch, and revelation. Both the food- or water-related incidents and natural phenomena overlap at least partially with accounts found in Ibn Saʿd's and Bukhārī's compilations.

5.1 *Food/Water Related Incidents*

The most frequently occurring theme in al-Tirmidhī's chapter is food- and water-related incidents, which overlap considerably with the compilations of Ibn Saʿd and al-Bukhārī. Al-Tirmidhī's second *ḥadīth* relates that the Prophet was passing a large bowl—presumably filled with water—among a large group of people from daybreak until night fell. The people wondered how there remained water in it and the Prophet pointed toward heaven in response.[165] The sixth *ḥadīth* in this chapter provides an elaborate account of a conversation between Abū Ṭalḥa and Umm Sulaym. On hearing the Prophet's weakened voice, Abū Ṭalḥa concluded that he was very hungry and approaches Umm Sulaym to ask for food for Muḥammad. Abū Ṭalḥa found the Prophet sitting among the people in the mosque. The Prophet inquired about whether Umm Sulaym had sent him with food, and after Abū Ṭalḥa answered in the affirmative, Muḥammad invited the people to join him. Abū Ṭalḥa raised the concern that the amount of food would not suffice, but Umm Sulaym reassured him that "God and His messenger know best." The people lined up and were fed in groups of ten.[166] The same account is also contained in al-Bukhārī's chapter.[167] The seventh and ninth *ḥadīth*s relate the well-known narrative of water coming forth from the Prophet's fingers and providing enough water for a large group to make the ablution;[168] this is also found in the chapters of Ibn Saʿd[169] and al-Bukhārī.[170]

165 Al-Tirmidhī, *Sunan*, 3:192.
166 Al-Tirmidhī, *Sunan*, 3:193f.
167 Al-Bukhārī, *Ṣaḥīḥ*, 4:470f. (no. 3578).
168 Al-Tirmidhī, *Sunan*, 3:193f.
169 Ibn Saʿd, *Ṭabaqāt*, 1:150, 1:154.
170 Al-Bukhārī, *Ṣaḥīḥ*, 4:468f. (nos. 3572, 3573, 3574).

5.2 *Natural Phenomena*

The second largest thematic category generally overlaps with Ibn Saʿd's category of natural phenomena, albeit at a much smaller scale. In the first account, the Prophet relates that a rock greeted him in Mecca when he received the call to prophecy.[171] The third *ḥadīth* describes the yearning of a palm tree that the Prophet had used to deliver his Friday sermon. Once a *minbar* was built and the Prophet delivered his first sermon there, the palm tree wailed in sadness until the Prophet consoled it.[172] Another natural phenomenon is recounted in the fourth *ḥadīth*, in which Muḥammad was approached by Arabs asking for a sign of his prophecy. The Prophet asked a palm tree to testify to the veracity of his prophetic mission. The Bedouins accepted Islam after the palm tree bowed down and the Prophet told it to return to its original position.[173] All of these accounts also occurred in Ibn Saʿd's *Ṭabaqāt*.

The two remaining accounts in al-Tirmidhī's chapter do not fall into any of these categories. One short account relates that the Prophet ran his hand over a man's face and prayed for him, and the man lived for one hundred twenty years and had only little white hair.[174] This implies a blessing (*baraka*) through the Prophet's touch. The other account relates, on the authority of ʿĀʾisha, that when God initiated the beginning of the prophetic mission, Muḥammad would see the break of dawn in a dream. This situation remained as long as God wanted it to last and He caused Muḥammad to seek solitude and seclusion above all else.[175] This account, which al-Tirmidhī evaluated as *ḥasan ṣaḥīḥ* (a good sound *ḥadīth*), is situated in the context of the first revelation, though it does not explicitly refer to revelation itself.

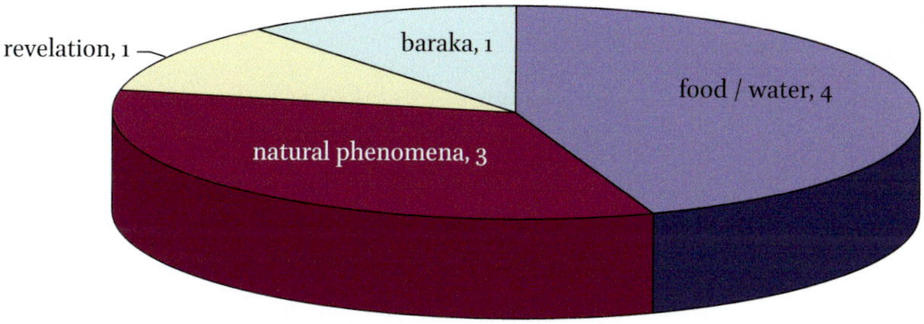

FIGURE 4 Thematic categories in al-Tirmidhī's chapter

171 Al-Tirmidhī, *Sunan*, 3:192.
172 Al-Tirmidhī, *Sunan*, 3:192.
173 Al-Tirmidhī, *Sunan*, 3:193.
174 Al-Tirmidhī, *Sunan*, 3:193.
175 Al-Tirmidhī, *Sunan*, 3:193.

Overall, al-Tirmidhī's selection of accounts overlaps considerably with his predecessors, though there are a significantly smaller number of accounts dedicated to the "signs of prophecy" and unprecedented accounts that indicate that each author held their own notion of what the "signs of prophecy" encompassed; this was reflected in their individual selections of accounts.

• • •

In this early time period, these extant compilations demonstrate a considerable diversity in terms of size, scope, and content. Very few of the accounts in all these compilations explicitly refer to any intention of providing evidence of Muḥammad's prophetic mission, rather their intended epistemological meaning rests almost entirely on their inclusion in specifically dedicated thematic chapters. The analyses of the chapters in Ibn Saʿd and al-Bukhārī, in particular, show that the authors undertook a deliberate editorial process of selecting certain accounts from their vast repertoires and including them in their thematic chapter. As I have shown in the previous chapter, Ibn Saʿd deliberately chose narratives and specific accounts for his thematic chapters rather than including them in his overall chronological biography of Muḥammad. A similar observation can be made for al-Bukhārī's chapter, which includes many accounts that are also found in other chapters. Bülow shows that there are more "miraculous" *ḥadīth*s in al-Bukhārī's *Ṣaḥīḥ* than can be found in his chapter on the signs of prophecy, and thus she concluded that al-Bukhārī only used a selection of these narratives to provide legitimacy for Muḥammad's prophetic mission.[176] Therefore, the question guiding this analysis is whether or not these authors held a common notion of the "signs of prophecy" that guided their deliberate selections.

The analytical comparison of these five early *dalāʾil al-nubūwa* compilations shows that there was considerable variance in the size, scope, and contents of the various chapters. Maʿmar's first contribution to this literature included only six accounts; this stands in stark contrast to the voluminous compilations of Ibn Saʿd and al-Bukhārī, who present ninety-nine and sixty-four accounts, respectively. By contrast, Ibn Saʿd stands out in this group as the only one whose scholarly background was in fields other than *ḥadīth*, a fact that is reflected in the scope of his compilations. While all the other authors I examine limit their compilations to accounts after the first revelations, Ibn Saʿd dedicates an entire chapter to "signs of prophecy" preceding Muḥammad's call to prophecy, and starts with Muḥammad's conception and birth. As *ḥadīth* scholars,

176 Bülow, "Ḥadīthe über Wunder des Propheten Muḥammad," 109.

authors like al-Bukhārī and al-Tirmidhī were bound by strictly defined requirements of authentication that precluded most biographical information on Muḥammad's early life. Ibn Saʿd, however, explored a greater pool of sources in his scholarly field, and this clearly shaped his notion of "signs of prophecy" as compared to other contributors to this literature.

The starkest differences are found in the thematic distribution of these compilations. A number of themes, and even specific accounts, occur in all the compilations, such as water- or food-related incidents. Other themes are unique to particular authors. Ibn Saʿd's overwhelming emphasis on predictions and announcements of Muḥammad's mission are absent from all the other compilations, given that the vast majority of these accounts concern Muḥammad's early life. But even among the *ḥadīth* scholars proper, there are significant differences in their themes.

In other instances, authors agreed on the thematic motifs they emphasized in their accounts, but project them through very different narratives.

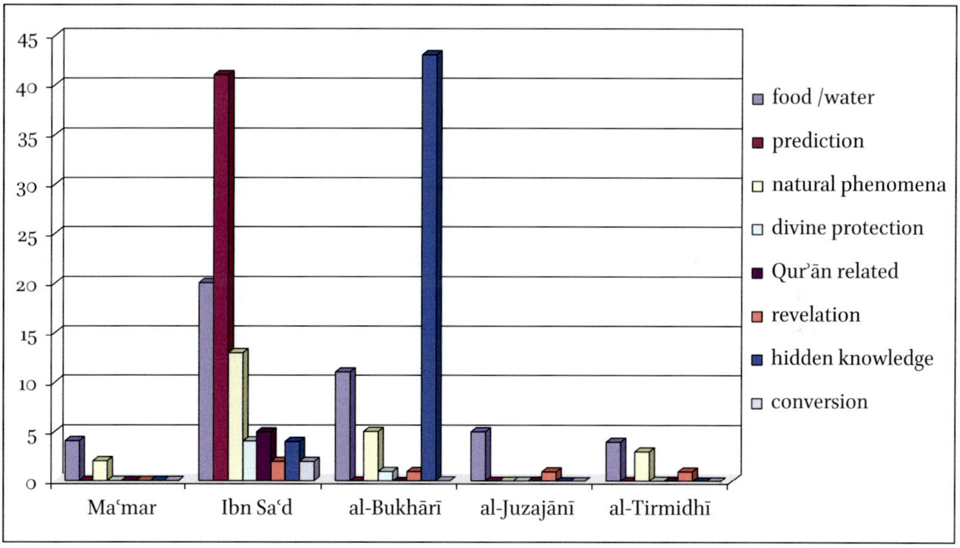

FIGURE 5 Distribution of themes

CHAPTER 5

Ibn Saʿd's "Proofs of Prophecy" and Its Intellectual Landscape

Since early authors of *dalāʾil al-nubūwa* works did not display a consistently agreed-upon notion about which kinds of events provide evidence of Muḥammad's prophetic mission, I understand each author's selective designation of accounts as "proofs of prophecy" and the epistemological notions on which they operate as a creative act of theologizing Muḥammad's biography. In doing so, I borrow Sean Anthony's concept of "narrativized theology" in *sīra-maghāzī* works.[1] This use of "theology" is not meant in the narrower sense of *kalām*, but more generally as a sense of a religious purpose that predetermines the portrayal of the Prophet. While it is common to view authors of *sīra-maghāzī* works as simply scholars transmitting existing traditions, we must keep in mind that each author's individual selection of accounts consciously or unconsciously led to the construction of a theological notion of prophecy and shaped particular images of Muḥammad and his prophetic mission. Being part of a hagiographical discourse of constructing distinct personae of the Prophet, the texts bear witness to the diverse political, social, and intellectual stimuli their authors experienced. Rather than reproducing an objective past, these texts enact a past that informs and gives meaning to the authors' present context by providing a foundation for their ideological and doctrinal views. Therefore, when we study them in relation to the political, social, and intellectual environments in which they emerged, we gain significant insight into the larger discourse on prophecy and the purposes these texts may have served.

Ibn Saʿd's chapters on the proofs of prophecy provide an interesting case for such an analysis. First, his chapters appear to be the only extant texts from the first wave of *ḥadīth* scholars' extensive engagement with the notion of the proofs of prophethood. While he is not the first known author to compile accounts thematically, there is a considerable increase in the number of accounts compared to his predecessor. Maʿmar's chapter included only six accounts while Ibn Saʿd's chapters contain ninety-nine accounts. At the same time, it seems as if Ibn Saʿd was not the only author of his period to be interested in the proofs of prophecy. Biographical dictionaries indicate that autonomous

1 Anthony, *Muḥammad and the Empires of Faith*, 11.

 | DOI:10.1163/9789004687349_007

works dedicated to the topic were written by al-Ḥumaydī (d. 219/834) and al-Madāʾinī (d. 224/839), respectively. Even though none of their works seem to have been preserved, the fact that they emerged concomitantly with Ibn Saʿd's chapters indicates that interest in this topic was not limited to an individual author but may have been part of a larger scholarly discourse during this period. This raises the question of what was happening at the time to trigger numerous authors to provide "proof" of Muḥammad's prophetic mission and, by extension, contribute to the epistemological boundaries of "legitimate" prophecy. Did methodological developments in various Islamic sciences play a role? Were broader social circumstances of an ʿAbbāsid era multi-confessional milieu central to these processes?

Ibn Saʿd's compilation of proofs of prophecy is also particularly interesting because of its methodological context. As part of a prophetic biography which is itself situated in the framework of a work on the transmitters (*rijāl*, lit. men), Ibn Saʿd's selection of narratives was not confined by the methodological restrictions of *ḥadīth* works, which focused on the question of reliability and authority. Ibn Saʿd's broader potential pool of sources allowed him greater freedom to craft an epistemological notion of the "proof" of Muḥammad's prophetic mission. Did the closer proximity to other faith communities and scholarly debates among scholars of various religious communities shape his selection? This is certainly a plausible assumption given Ibn Saʿd's notable focus on the notion that Muḥammad's prophetic mission was recognized based on predetermined signs prior to the advent of his prophecy by members of other religious groups, both pagans and monotheists. The narratives centered on monotheists are notable for the way they imply that both Christian and Jewish individuals were aware of the coming of another prophet based on their own scriptures. While the notion of an ongoing sacred history in which Muḥammad is the last link in a chain of prophets is a common element in Islamic doctrine, Ibn Saʿd is the only early *dalāʾil al-nubūwa* author to distinctly anchor his notion of the "proofs of prophecy" in the awareness and recognition by other monotheistic communities of Muḥammad's prophetic mission. Investigating the intellectual landscape in which Ibn Saʿd worked sheds some light on his thematic choices.

1 Political and Religious Impulses on the Notion of Prophecy

Born in Basra around 168/785, Ibn Saʿd settled in Baghdad sometime after 189/805 and remained there until his death in 230/845. Not much is known about his life, but given the time period in which he lived, we can assume that he witnessed a period of immense intellectual flourishing as well as deep-rooted strife. The time and locale of his life place him in the midst of the burgeoning developments in *ʿilm al-kalām* (theology) and the concurrent struggle among scholars over the legitimacy of the sources of religious knowledge. It is attested that Ibn Saʿd was personally affected by some of these debates.[2] As an avid proponent of the Sunna, he was tried during the trials (*miḥna*) imposed by al-Maʾmūn, where he proclaimed, and later revoked, the doctrine of the createdness of the Qurʾān.[3] This was probably the most immediate way in which Ibn Saʿd was impacted by the attempts of the political elite to dictate matters of theology. But it was not the first nor the last time that political rulers tried to intervene in questions of faith and Ibn Saʿd's conceptualization of prophecy was shaped by the ongoing processes of negotiation and interpretation of prophetic authority that occurred at the intersection of religious knowledge and political power.

The locus of doctrinal authority was contested after Muḥammad's death, particularly after the generation of Companions, who had intimate knowledge of the Prophet and his practices, perished. Scholars, political rulers, and some of Muḥammad's kinsmen all vied for religious authority long before Ibn Saʿd's lifetime. Some of the Umayyad caliphs, particularly those most skilled in administrative affairs, became central in shaping the way religious thought unfolded by imposing "orthodoxy" and persecuting "heresy" as they defined it.

> ʿAbd al-Malik's reign was crucial both for the survival of the Umayyad dynasty and for the development of the Islamic faith. His extensive efforts to centralize authority, consolidate military command, standardize coinage and articulate a uniform vision of Islam have been subject to extensive scholarly attention. In addition to his better known reforms, ʿAbd al-Malik also initiated the systematic interrogation and persecution of suspected heretics. He holds the distinction of being the first Umayyad caliph to execute heretics for what appears to be purely doctrinal offenses.[4]

Almost all of the Umayyad persecutions focused on the question of human free will, and frequently targeted its proponents, the Qadarīs, as the Umayyad rulers advocated for predestinarian views in order to legitimize the caliph

2 Mūsā, *Ibn Saʿd wa-ṭabaqātuhu*, 17.
3 Mūsā, *Ibn Saʿd wa-ṭabaqātuhu*, 17.
4 Judd, "Muslim Persecution of Heretics during the Marwānid Period," 3.

as God's chosen and absolute ruler.[5] The first victim of ʿAbd al-Malik's persecution, al-Ḥārith b. Saʿīd al-Kadhdhāb, was executed around 80/699 on the grounds of heresy after he had declared himself a prophet. It is clear that claims to prophecy served as a potent ideological vehicle for some of the challengers to the Umayyads; this required the political elite to restrict the notion of prophecy to Muḥammad.

Before, during, and after Muḥammad's lifetime, there was a continuous stream of self-proclaimed prophets. The concept of prophecy permeated the Near Eastern world and Late Antiquity, from the prophets of ancient Israel, early Christian groups like the second-century Montanist sect, or the third-century Mesopotamian prophet Mani, who established Manichaeism as a major religion.[6] With the concept of prophecy being so widely known in the pre-Islamic Near East, it is not surprising that claims to prophecy continued during Muḥammad's lifetime. Among the contemporaneous prophets, Khālid b. Sinān allegedly performed miracles, while Musaylima b. Ḥabīb from Yamāma tried to establish relations with Muḥammad but was eventually killed in battle. The prophetess Sajāḥ, who hailed from northeastern Arabia was reportedly married to Musaylima for some time; in addition, Aswad b. Kaʿb al-ʿAnsī from Yemen and Ṭulayḥa of the Banū Asad emerged as self-proclaimed prophets. All of them held political and military aspirations in addition to religious ambitions and some indeed rose to prominence as political leaders.[7] As claims to prophecy were (at times successfully) tied to political control, it is also not surprising to find that self-proclaimed prophets after Muḥammad's death occurred geographically closer to new centers of power in Syria and Mesopotamia. The most famous of these claimants was Mukhtār al-Thaqafī, who rebelled against the Umayyads in Kufa in 66/685 and remained in control there for two years until his rebellion was quelled by Umayyad forces.[8] Mukhtār's main ideological rallying points were his pro-Hashimite leanings; he rebelled in the name of ʿAlī b. Abī Ṭālib's son Muḥammad b. al-Ḥanafiyya (d. 81/700). Rebellions by self-proclaimed prophets persisted until the end of the Umayyad dynasty. A Jewish rebel by the name Abū ʿĪsā l-ʿIṣfahānī and his movement rose against the caliphate during the reign of ʿAbd al-Malik (r. 65–86/685–705); he mixed Jewish and Muslim elements in his teachings.[9] Between the 110s/730s and 130s/750s, several individuals claimed prophecy,

5 Judd, "Muslim Persecution of Heretics during the Marwānid Period," 3.

6 Asatryan, "Prophecy after Muhammad" (forthcoming).

7 Asatryan, "Prophecy after Muhammad," 15f.

8 Asatryan, "Prophecy after Muhammad," 16.

9 Asatryan, "Prophecy after Muhammad," 16.

including three different rebellions in the town of Kufa.[10] The self-proclaimed prophets Bayān b. Samʿān al-Nahdī and Mughīra b. Saʿīd al-ʿIjlī organized the first of these rebellions in 119/737. While their aspirations for the rebellion are not clear, their threat was considered great enough to merit a public execution, which was presided over by Kufa's governor, Khālid b. ʿAbdallāh al-Qasrī.[11]

The fact that claims to prophecy remained common in the decades after Muḥammad's death shows that the concept of prophecy was well enough established to provide a potentially powerful ideological conduit for the political ambitions of numerous individuals who sought to wrestle power from the Umayyads. Furthermore, it highlights the reality that the doctrine of Muḥammad's prophetic mission held neither the theological sophistication nor the exclusivity of later generations. As we noted, the continuous challenges to political power through claims to prophecy contributed to the Umayyad's growing interest in defining and implementing notions of orthodoxy with the full coercive power of the state apparatus in an effort to consolidate their own power.

There are several other indications that legal and religious authority was not exclusively associated with Muḥammad in the first/seventh century, nor was it as central to Islamic law, theology, and piety as later scholars held. Recent studies show, for instance, that Muḥammad's name and title as prophet of Islam did not begin to appear in inscriptions on coins, monuments, and tombstones until the second half of the first/seventh century. In 72/691, the first major use of an inscription appeared on the newly erected Dome of the Rock and brought Muḥammad's prophetic mission into full public display. From this time onward, Muḥammad's name and other religious formulae appeared regularly on coins, inscriptions, and epitaphs, though at the time, these references were not anchored in a well-established theology of prophecy and could still have gone unnoticed by broad parts of the population, particularly as Arabic continued to be the minority language and literacy was still limited.[12] These formulae were, however, part of a broader process by which the Umayyads sought to elaborate the theological and textual content of Islam. During the last decades of Umayyad rule, the same process eventually led scholars, under court patronage, to write Muḥammad's biography as part of an Islamic salvation narrative in an effort to bolster their political legitimacy. This text, as we see later in this chapter, had a significant impact on Ibn Saʿd's work in the early ʿAbbāsid period.

---

10 Asatryan, "Prophecy after Muhammad," 4.

11 Asatryan, "Prophecy after Muhammad," 16f.

12 Asatryan, "Prophecy after Muhammad," 17f.

Another shift in the notion of Muḥammad's prophetic authority was still underway during Ibn Saʿd's lifetime; this was the consolidation of the legal concept of the Sunna. As the normative precedence of human behavior, the term Sunna existed in pre-Islamic Arabia; the concept simply signified any behavior by individuals or groups that formed a normative precedent that was to be followed. While Muḥammad's behavior was almost immediately understood to be exemplary, the scope of the Sunna remained broader during the first/seventh century and a half and included, in addition to Muḥammad, the precedent of certain Companions and the *khulafāʾ al-rāshidūn* (rightly-guided caliphs). The narrowing of the term to exclusively designate a generally-approved practice of the Prophet is commonly associated with the legal scholar al-Shāfiʿī (d. 204/820), although it took significantly longer to establish this notion universally in Islamic legal thinking. Thus, Ibn Saʿd lived and worked in an environment in which the religious and legal authority of Muḥammad's prophetic mission was continuously evolving along with, and in part in service of, the consolidation of political power. His ideas of what constituted a proof of prophecy were, therefore, part of extensive discourses on prophecy in the context of an emerging Muslim empire and various nascent religious sciences.

His intellectual milieu was, of course, also defined by rapid demographic changes, particularly in the urban centers of the Muslim empire. These changes took place as a result of increased conversion to Islam, the social proximity in which Muslims and Christians lived, the languages they shared, and the intellectual exchanges that occurred directly and indirectly among scholars. While demographic changes occurred among the wider population, we should keep in mind that the competing theological positions of various Muslim and Christian groups as well as the exchanges between them, likely only represented the discourses of intellectual elites rather than the religious conceptions of the general population. The vast majority of Christians and Muslims were mostly unfamiliar with the minutiae of theological teachings that dominated the writings of their religious leaders.[13] The "simple" believers, Muslims and Christians alike, seem to have frequently practiced and believed beyond the confines of what the religious elite defined as orthodoxy and may well have seen the boundaries between religions, let alone theological or sectarian factions within them, as fluid and permeable. The religious and intellectual elites, on the other hand, were deeply engaged in fleshing out the demarcations of acceptable religious teachings in relation to, and often in dialogue with, each other. The Greco-Arabic translation movement added to the intellectual wealth of this period by introducing Greek texts from various fields of knowledge to

---

13 Tannous, *The Making of the Medieval Middle East*.

an Arabic-speaking audience. Christian scholars and ecclesiastics actively participated in this rich exchange and challenge of notions and ideas. Ibn Saʿd's time in Baghdad saw a new height in direct and indirect Muslim-Christian intellectual interaction.[14] The Christian theologians Abū Qurra, ʿAmmār al-Baṣrī, and Ḥabīb Abū Rā'iṭa were all active during Ibn Saʿd's lifetime writing apologetic works and engaging in public debates at the caliphal court in the capital. The Jewish theologian Dāwūd b. al-Marwān al-Raqqī l-Muqammiṣ (d. after 248/862), who addressed the question of the "signs of prophecy" in one of his treatises and specifically appears to have aimed at countering the challenge of Islam, was also active during this time. Of all the factors that fueled discourses on prophecy among Muslim scholars, this inter-religious aspect appears to have had the potential to shed some light on Ibn Saʿd's selection of "proofs" of prophecy. Could his strong emphasis on Jewish and Christian religious figures foretelling or confirming Muḥammad's prophetic mission reflect arguments from a number of Christian-Muslim exchanges that are attributed to this period?

2 Christian-Muslim Encounters in the Early ʿAbbāsid Period

A number of political, social, and religious factors converged over the decades prior to Ibn Saʿd's arrival in the capital; these factors brought forth a wealth of apologetic and polemic texts among the Christian and Muslim communities, and contributed to the exchanges and debates between them. When Arab Muslim armies initially conquered the Christian territories in the early first/seventh century, they frequently made contracts that allowed Jewish and Christian communities, the so-called People of the Book (*ahl al-kitāb*), to continue their religious practices in exchange for a special tax (*jizya*). These contracts frequently included certain conditions and stipulations for Christian practices and were designed to lower the social profile of subject religious groups living under Islamic rule.[15] Based on the earliest Syriac, Armenian, Greek, and Coptic texts written after the Islamic conquests, Christian authors living in newly conquered territories seem to have been preoccupied with these restrictions and hardships, and frequently viewed the conquests as a

---

14 Muslims seem to have been preoccupied with refuting Christianity; by contrast, there seem to be no polemical works from the first four centuries of the Islamic era specifically directed against Judaism. See Adang, "Medieval Muslim Polemics," 16.

15 Griffith, "Answering the Call of the Minaret," 92.

consequence of Christian sinfulness.[16] Yet during this time, few Christian writers took an interest in Islam's doctrines or religious objections to Christianity.

Serious inter-religious controversies between Christians and Muslims emerged in the context of the attempts by Muslim political rulers to impose social hegemony in the public sphere under the caliph ʿAbd al-Malik (r. 65–86/685–705) and his sons. From a religious perspective, this campaign was mostly concerned with symbolic dominance, as it sought to remove the ubiquitous cross from the public sphere and replace it with symbolic manifestations of Islam. The realm of Islam was expressed through large monuments such as the Dome of the Rock in Jerusalem and the Umayyad Mosque in Damascus, which both proudly broadcast the call to prayer to the cities' diverse populations.[17] At the same time, however, these monuments displayed a remarkable merging of stylistic continuity to Byzantine architectural and decorative features; this was largely because many of the Byzantine artisans were hired to build these edifices, and to shape the symbolism of the newly established religion. Coins signaled this shift in cultural hegemony as well. Following the conquests and for many decades, the Umayyads initially continued to use the Byzantine and Sassanid coinage with their respective religious symbolism. Distributing the newly minted Muslim coinage that displayed the testimony of faith (*shahada*) across the burgeoning empire conveyed a similar notion of symbolic cultural dominance over non-Muslim populations.[18] The program of ʿUmar b. ʿAbd al-ʿAzīz (r. 99–101/717–720) to financially equalize, at least in theory, the status of all Muslims, Arab conquerors, and new converts alike was the most relevant socially. This incentivized conversion to Islam, particularly among Christians who sought upward social mobility. On the one hand, this intensified the perception of Islam as a religious challenge but, on the other hand, it also triggered a process of inculturation among Christian communities into the cultural realm of Islam around them, and included the churches' adoption of the Arabic language. The early second/eighth century was the beginning of a codependent, but at times inimical, intellectual relationship between Muslim and Christian thinkers that maintained them in tension with one another throughout the first ʿAbbāsid century. Christian scholars were central to the state-sponsored Greco-Arabic translation movement, and Christian theology developed parallel to and often in dialogue with Islamic *kalām*.

16 Griffith, "Answering the Call of the Minaret," 92.
17 Griffith, "Answering the Call of the Minaret," 93.
18 Griffith, "Answering the Call of the Minaret," 93. For more on early Muslim coinage, see Heidemann, "The Evolving Representation of the Early Islamic Empire."

While this period is marked by the ʿAbbāsid elite's political and military rule over non-Muslim communities and by their attempts to establish cultural hegemony through newly disseminated Islamic symbols, the Muslim political and intellectual elites also experienced momentous frictions. The most prominent political conflict was the fourth civil war over the succession of Hārūn al-Rāshid (d. 193/809) between his sons, al-Amīn (r. 193–198/809–813) and al-Maʾmūn (r. 198–218/813–833). At the same time, the Muslim intellectual landscape was deeply conflicted over questions of the legitimacy of sources for the dissemination of religious knowledge. Muslim scholars, broadly speaking, fell into two camps: first, those who held firmly and exclusively to the scriptural sources of the Qurʾān and Sunna as the foundation for all religious questions, and second, those who allowed human reasoning and public debates in the form of *kalām*. *Kalām* brought forth the particular theological notion of the createdness of the Qurʾān, which was briefly favored among the ruling class and enforced through the trials (*miḥna*), which in turn led to unrest among the disfavored partisans of *ḥadīth* (*ahl al-ḥadīth*).

Various Christian churches were equally divided over Christological doctrines, but they faced the religious challenge of Islam collectively. Various genres of Christian apologetics emerged in response to both internal and external challenges.[19] Many texts emerged during a period when large numbers of Christians converted to Islam.[20] Medieval conversion rates to Islam suggest that the late second/eighth and early third/ninth centuries marked the beginning of the first great wave of conversions in Iraq, Syria, and even Egypt. The years 175–274/791–888 comprise the period of the "early majority" when up to thirty-four percent of the population may be estimated to have converted to Islam.[21] These demographic shifts triggered responses in Christian churches, and are reflected in some apologetic texts. Christian church leaders viewed converts to Islam with contempt, and some Christian texts portrayed their conversions to be merely for the sake of gaining personal power and social advancement. The author of a fictitious Christian-Muslim correspondence, for instance, puts this view in the mouth of al-Maʾmūn, with the caliph allegedly acknowledging the Christian charge that Muslim converts at his court were spiritually insincere.[22] Conversely, Muslims argued that particularly learned Christians had recognized the veracity of Muḥammad's prophetic mission but refused to embrace his message in order to maintain their personal power. For

19 Griffith, "Excursus I: Christian Theological Thought," 91.
20 Griffith, "The Prophet Muḥammad," 109.
21 Bulliet, *Conversion to Islam in the Medieval Period*, 1979.
22 Griffith, "The Prophet Muḥammad," 110.

instance, this sentiment is articulated in the voice of a bishop, Abū Ḥāritha of Najrān, in Ibn Isḥāq's *Sīra*[23] and is found in a number of accounts presented by Ibn Saʿd.[24] However, even though the resentments of conversion certainly provide a significant social context, we should not discard the religious aspect of these apologetic texts altogether. The sheer number of such texts that emphasize the credibility of Christian doctrines, provide responses to Islamic religious challenges to Christian doctrines, and refute Islamic teachings and practices confirm the genuine presence of spiritual challenges that church leaders and theologians sought to counter. The confluence of religious and social aspects in Muslim and Christian texts then, is simply a manifestation of the social proximity in which the two communities lived and the intellectual exchange that resulted from it.

This social proximity and intellectual exchange of Muslim and Christian scholars is evident in Arabic Christian apologies. First, unlike Greek Christian authors, Arab Christian apologists were not writing in isolation from Islam.[25] While they were adversaries in religious controversies, the personal isolation that must have contributed to the hostile fantasies we find in Greek or Latin works were absent; Near Eastern Christians were in personal contact with Muslims in their daily lives, shared a common language, and had at least a basic knowledge of Islamic practices, the Qurʾān, and other Muslim traditions.[26] Therefore, the majority of Near Eastern Christian apologetics are far less hostile in tone than their Latin and Greek counterparts. The intellectual exchange between Muslim and Christian scholars is also reflected in the fact that all the apologetic literature that has survived from the under ʿAbbāsid rule in the second/eighth century, across religious communities and languages of composition, is dialectical in form. Disputation narratives, epistolary exchanges, and even formal treatises were designed to counter the questions or views of an alleged inquirer from a rival religious community.[27] This shared methodology for discussing religious questions is not surprising given that Christian apologetic theology was methodologically and idiomatically deeply connected to Islamic *kalām* and Christian apologists frequently participated in formal scholarly conversations with Muslim intellectuals at the courts of high administrative officials.[28]

---

23 Ibn Isḥāq, *The Life of Muhammad*, 271.
24 Ibn Saʿd, *Ṭabaqāt*.
25 Griffith, "The Prophet Muḥammad," 117.
26 Griffith, "The Prophet Muḥammad," 131.
27 Griffith, "The Prophet Muḥammad," 116.
28 Griffith, "The Prophet Muḥammad," 117.

A correspondence, allegedly between the Umayyad caliph ʿUmar b. ʿAbd al-ʿAzīz (r. 99–101/717–720) and the Byzantine emperor Leo III (r. 717–741) is mentioned in several Eastern Christian and Muslim sources from the third/ninth and fourth/tenth centuries onward. The correspondence appears to consist of ʿUmar's epistle to Leo and the latter's response.[29] ʿUmar's letter raises critical questions about Christian doctrines and practices, and furthermore adduces biblical passages to argue for the corruption of the Hebrew Bible and the New Testament and provides evidence for biblical predictions of the coming of Muḥammad as a future prophet. Leo responds to the caliph's questions and rejects his invitation to convert based on his own refutation of Islam.

An entry in the section "On heresies" in John of Damascus's *The Fount of Knowledge* is generally viewed as one of the earliest Greek texts denouncing Islam. As the section title suggests, John of Damascus (d. 750) viewed Islam as a heretical branch of Christianity rather than a religion in its own right. The earliest Syriac apology is the brief report of a letter exchanged between the Jacobite Patriarch John I (d. 648) and a Muslim official named ʿAmr.[30] The Syriac treatise that presents the first detailed argument for Christianity against the standard Muslim objections, such as the trinity and incarnation, can be found in a chapter by Theodore bār Kōnē (fl. ca. 792). This chapter is composed as a dialogue between a Christian master and his Muslim disciple, in which the master provides a defense of Christian doctrines and religious practices that Muslims find objectionable. Theodore completed this work in the last decade of the second/eighth century; thus, he was a contemporary of the most well-known Syriac anti-Muslim apologist, the Nestorian Patriarch Timothy I.

Timothy I (r. 780–823) was a Patriarch of the Church of the East (i.e., Nestorian), first in Seleucia-Ctesiphon and then in Baghdad. He certainly spoke Arabic, but composed his writings in Syriac. In a half dozen of his letters, the patriarch describes in some detail the responses he gave to questions put to him by Muslims or inspired by Muslim concerns.[31] By far the best known of these are the patriarch's account of his debate with the caliph al-Mahdī (r. 158–169/775–785) on the beliefs and practices of the Christians. The letter

29 The original documents of the "correspondence" between ʿUmar b. ʿAbd al-ʿAzīz and Leo III are lost, but it is recorded or mentioned in numerous Christian and Muslim sources, including manuscripts in Greek, Latin, Armenian, Aljamiado, and Arabic. The dating, authorship, original language, and function of the text(s) are still open to debate. Cecilia Palombo recently suggested that all the extant versions of the "correspondence" derive from an original Arabic Christian apologetic work, composed in the monastic circles of Syria-Palestine in the mid-eighth century CE. For a summary of the main theories, see Palombo, "The 'Correspondence' of Leo III and ʿUmar II."

30 Griffith, "The Prophet Muḥammad," 99.

31 Griffith, "The Prophet Muḥammad," 103.

became so popular that it circulated in the Christian community in a longer Syriac recension, in an abridged version, as well as in several Arabic copies.[32]

The Jacobite writer Nonnus of Nisibis (d. ca. 870?) composed a treatise in Syriac that was structured as a guide for someone searching for the true religion among the several options available in third-/ninth-century Iraq. Yet in spite of its purported intent it is quite clear that it was primarily addressing Islam as a spiritual contender.[33] In addition, there is an incomplete Christian Arabic document from the early third/ninth century that records a debate that was allegedly held in Jerusalem in the year 199/815 between a monk named Abraham of Tiberias and a Muslim official named ʿAbd al-Raḥmān b. al-Mālik b. Ṣāliḥ.[34]

The three most important Christian apologists writing in Arabic during the first ʿAbbāsid century were the Melkite Theodore Abū Qurra (d. ca. 820), his Jacobite rival Ḥabīb b. Khidma Abū Raʾiṭa (d. ca. 851), and the Nestorian ʿAmmār al-Baṣrī (fl. ca. 236/850). Abū Qurra was the most prolific of these apologists to author a long defensive treatise of Christianity as well as a dozen shorter ones on specific Christian doctrines. The popularity of his apologetic works among Arabic-speaking Christians is attested to by the considerable number of manuscripts that have survived, including one with a transcript of an alleged conference between Abū Qurra and a Muslim official, usually designated as the caliph al-Maʾmūn.[35]

Perhaps the most well-known of the early Christian apologies circulated under the pseudonym of ʿAbd al-Maṣīḥ b. Isḥāq al-Kindī. This fictitious epistolary text written in Arabic consists of a letter allegedly written by a Muslim named ʿAbdallāh b. Ismāʿīl al-Hāshimī, who invites his Christian interlocutor to convert to Islam and provides the principal features of Islam. The Christian ʿAbd al-Maṣīḥ b. Isḥāq al-Kindī's response letter is a lengthy defense of the standard Christian doctrines and practices along with a vigorous polemic against the Qurʾān, the Prophet, and the teachings and practices that characterize Islam. The two letters circulated as halves of a single work, and the correspondents are presented as members of the court of the caliph al-Maʾmūn. Both letters can be traced back to the same Christian author, hence it is noteworthy that the author's knowledge of Islam and scripture is very extensive. The text had a long-lasting impact on Christian polemic thinking against Islam. It circulated widely among Melkite, Jacobite, and Nestorian Christians in the Middle East. Later, it was adopted by Mozarabs, Iberian Christians living

32 Griffith, "The Prophet Muḥammad," 100.
33 Griffith, "The Prophet Muḥammad," 101.
34 Griffith, "The Prophet Muḥammad," 104.
35 Griffith, "The Prophet Muḥammad," 105.

under Muslim rule in al-Andalūs, and in the twelfth century even translated into Latin on the commission of Peter the Venerable (d. 1156). French and English missionaries even used it in the nineteenth and twentieth centuries.[36] The text's prominence was not limited to Christian audiences; some later Muslim scholars, such as Abū Ḥayyān al-Tawḥīdī (d. 414/1023) and al-Bīrūnī (d. 440/1048) mention ʿAbd al-Masīḥ b. Isḥāq al-Kindī as if he had been a real Christian author. While they do not refer to the text itself, the fact that it is the only known work attributed to this fictitious author suggests that it must have been well-known among Muslim scholars.[37]

A Christian legend of Baḥīrā is closely related to apologetic works. From about the eighth century onward, Muslims and Christians told the story of Muḥammad's encounter with the Christian monk named Baḥīrā. We have seen in previous chapters that Muslim accounts depict Baḥīrā as recognizing the signs of true prophecy in his encounter with the young Muḥammad. Christian versions of the same encounter, as we see below, insist that the monk recognized Muḥammad as a future heretic and pretender to prophecy. Although the communities offered vastly different views about the specific events that allegedly took place, both agreed that the encounter was central to understanding the origins of Islam, its message, and the issue of whether it was truly a divine revelation. These questions were ultimately tied to the self-images of the various authors writing about it, since each religious community claimed to possess divine truths and automatically excluded the truths of others.[38]

Taken together, apologetic texts from the first ʿAbbāsid century create a mosaic of competing self-images grounded in cultural elements common to Near Eastern peoples; these include literary genres, prophetic history, contact between humans and the divine, and types of philosophical argumentation. Through complex strategies of adaptation and rejection of these shared elements, each community came away with their own coherent exclusive and exclusivist self-image.[39] The creation, recreation, and reinforcement of the self-image of various Christian churches occur simultaneously in response to competing Christian doctrines and the emergence of Islam, which each posed threats to their communities' disintegration and the dilution of their religious identities.

Taken together, the aspects outlined above paint a picture of an intellectual landscape marked simultaneously by social proximity and spiritual

36 Griffith, "Answering the Call of the Minaret," 107.

37 Griffith, "Excursis I: Christian Theological Thought," 98.

38 Roggema, *The Legend of Sergius Baḥīrā*, 1.

39 Roggema, *The Legend of Sergius Baḥīrā*, 2.

competition among Muslim and Christian elites. This social context led to the emergence of various literary genres aimed at reassuring their own community of the veracity of their beliefs, addressing doubts or critiques from both within and outside their group, while also discrediting the views of rival religious communities. Muslim and Christian religious scholars were, to some extent, aware of their competitors' discourses and engaged with one another in direct and indirect exchanges. They frequently employed their knowledge of each other's scriptures and traditions to craft counter-historical narratives and discredit the other's doctrines.

3 Analysis: Approaches to Christian Apologetic Literature

The works presented above typically fall into three categories: disputation narratives, epistolary exchanges, and formal treatises. Disputation narratives were the most popular genre of Christian apologetic writing. These works typically feature accounts of monks or other ecclesiastics summoned to the presence of Muslim authorities in order to defend their faith in an open debate with a caliph, official, or scholar. The most commonly known disputation narratives detail the previously mentioned encounters of Patriarch John I (r. 631–648) and the Muslim amir ʿUmayr b. Saʿd al-Ansārī, the encounter of a Christian monk of Bēt Ḥālē and a Muslim notable, the debate of Patriarch Timothy I (r. 780–823) and a Muslim scholar that is said to have occurred at the court of the caliph al-Mahdī (r. 158–169/775–785), as well as the debate between Theodore Abū Qurra and the caliph al-Maʾmūn. Closely related to this genre were epistolary exchanges, that is, Christian apologetics written in the style of letters that were allegedly exchanged between Muslims and Christians. The most well-known text dating to the period prior to or contemporary with Ibn Saʿd's lifetime was the aforementioned fictitious exchange between ʿAbdallāh b. Ismāʿīl al-Hāshimī and ʿAbd al-Maṣīḥ b. Isḥāq al-Kindī.

We can question the historicity of these texts. In some cases it appears that disputation narratives and epistolary exchanges refer to real historical encounters, though the texts themselves might not have been written at the exact time of the event. The narrative structure of the disputation between Patriarch Timothy I and caliph al-Mahdī, for instance, suggests that the text is the recording of an actual encounter rather than a carefully but predictably crafted literary piece.[40] In other cases, the accounts appear to be entirely fictional. The dispute between the monk of Bēt Ḥālē and a Muslim notable does

40 Heimgartner, *Die Disputatio des ostsyrischen Patriarchen Timotheos*, 54.

not provide any details of the participants' identities and solely focuses on the contents of their debate; this suggests that these are literary personae rather than historical figures. The fictionalization is most obvious in the alleged exchange of letters between the Muslim ʿAbdallāh b. Ismāʿīl al-Hāshimī and the Christian ʿAbd al-Masīḥ b. Isḥāq al-Kindī. The three elements of each of the authors' names neatly represent the confessional statement of each creed; this makes their historicity highly unlikely. Furthermore, the narrative model suggests that both letters can be traced back to the same Christian author.[41] But the actual historicity of the encounters overall is a secondary issue, because all of these texts clearly had their own literary and social functions, independent of their historical roots. As apologetic texts they were intended for circulation among the Syriac- and Arabic-speaking Christian communities. The contexts of the exchanges mirrored the circumstances of the milieu of religious competition in which the audience lived. The Christian responses to religious challenges were likely intended to defend the credibility of Christian doctrines, perhaps to prevent Christian conversions to Islam, and also to provide the reader with potential responses for their own challenging encounters with their Muslim neighbors.

While Christian apologists often display extensive knowledge of the Qurʾān and Islamic traditions, it is noteworthy that the details of Muslim narratives in these apologetic texts are clearly limited to and shaped by the Christian authors' intention to discredit Muslim religious claims. This was part of a Christian strategy to defend their own faith by creating what the intellectual historian Amos Funkenstein described as the phenomenon of counter-history. Working mostly on Jewish-Christian polemics, Funkenstein identified one community's tendency to rewrite the history of the rival community by appropriating and exploiting their most trusted sources in order to deconstruct their memory and distort their self-image.[42] The most obvious examples of this approach are the various ways the Islamic tradition of Baḥīrā was used in Christian texts. In the Muslim context, this narrative is a standard component of the prophetic biography that describes an adolescent Muḥammad traveling to Syria with his uncle Abū Ṭālib. They passed a monk in his cell who questioned Muḥammad and examined his body for signs of prophecy and then identified him as a future prophet who will be envied by the Jewish community. The narrative serves to anchor Islam in the continuous sacred history of the Abrahamic traditions, with Baḥīrā as a representative of the most important scriptural tradition at

41 Bottini, "al-Kindī," 587.

42 Funkenstein, "History, Counterhistory, and Narrative," 69; cf. Roggema, *The Legend of Sergius Baḥīrā*, 31.

the time and as a witness to the authenticity of Muḥammad's prophetic mission. In the Christian context, this legend is retold in a way that bears little or no resemblance to the Islamic accounts. It is extant in two Syriac versions, and one in Arabic, and referenced in numerous apologetic texts. While the major outlines of these versions of the legend itself are the same, there are considerable differences in the details. In all versions, the story is told by a traveling monk who is said to have met Baḥīrā on his deathbed. Baḥīrā recounts his apocalyptic vision of Muslim history to his visitor, including a story about his own encounter with the young Muḥammad, who is said to have accepted Baḥīrā's teachings. Muḥammad appears in princely style in Baḥīrā's cell. Described as the leader of his band of Arabs, he returns many times to learn the monk's doctrines. The monk ultimately takes responsibility for the very wording of the Qurʾān and explains at each step the real Christian meanings, which were distorted by Arabs and Muḥammad himself, a result of their moral and intellectual shortcomings.[43] The Christian account is built on the Islamic tradition but completely reframes the narrative to convey two distinct messages. First, the broader apocalyptic vision interprets Muslim rule as a phase in human history that will end at a future time when God will bring victory and peace to his people. Such an apocalyptic interpretation of the events in the second/eighth century was also current in the Jewish community.[44] Second, aspects of the legend that specifically reinterpret Baḥīrā's encounter with Muḥammad serve the purpose of designating the Christian monk, rather than God, as the source of Muḥammad's teachings and as the real author of the Qurʾān.

The fictional correspondence between al-Kindī and al-Hāshimī also includes a reworking of the Baḥīrā narreme. Here the author argues in the voice of the Christian al-Kindī that Nestorians were the sort of Christians whose monks evangelized Muḥammad, and who, once revelations began to come to the Prophet, even protected him from the Jews and the polytheists of the Quraysh. For this reason, Muḥammad offered Christians the covenant of protection.[45] Like the aforementioned Christian reworking of the Baḥīrā legend, al-Kindī's version of the narreme shares little with the known Muslim accounts of Muḥammad's encounter with the monk. This narrative in the voice of al-Kindī serves a double-purpose, of discrediting Islam's message and elevating Nestorians over rival Christian doctrines.

---

43 Griffith, "The Prophet Muḥammad," 138.
44 Griffith, "The Prophet Muḥammad," 108.
45 Griffith, "The Prophet Muḥammad," 129.

Another prominent example of narratives that discredited both Islamic scripture and Muḥammad's biography is the account of Muḥammad's marriage to Zaynab bt. Jaḥsh. According to Muslim tradition, Zaynab was married to Muḥammad's adopted son Zayd, who divorced her so that Muḥammad could marry her. The Qur'ān itself addresses this situation and declares that there were no obstacles to Muḥammad's marriage to Zaynab, once she was divorced.[46] While in the Muslim tradition this episode constituted a relatively marginal aspect of Muḥammad's biography, it became a standard component in Christian polemical writing to discredit Muḥammad as an immoral opportunist. While these counter histories clearly run counter to the narratives as they are told in respected Islamic sources, they do so in an implicit or subtle way, presenting themselves as factual eyewitness accounts rather than as subversive retellings of existing narratives. This obvious selection and adaptation of Muslim sources clearly indicates that these texts were tailored toward Christian rather than Muslim readers. Yet it is precisely the inclusion of key elements of Muslim narratives that are vaguely recognizable to a Christian audience living in close proximity to Muslims that makes a convincing argument for Christians. The faint familiarity with the story and objective mode of presentation were deliberately chosen to create a sense of historical evidence for the Christian audience, who then need little convincing to conclude the impermissibility of Muḥammad's prophetic mission, based on their own intrinsic understanding of prophethood.

While their own community was the intended audience, the intellectual endeavors of church leaders and Christian *mutakallimūn* certainly did not go unnoticed by Muslims. Letters and narratives written in Syriac were quickly translated into Arabic, while Christian works of *kalām* were frequently composed in the new lingua franca, Arabic. Thus, the common language enabled Arabic-speaking Muslim audiences to access these texts and there are numerous indicators that Muslims were aware of many Christian apologetic texts. As we have seen, the fictional al-Kindī was well known among later Muslim authors. The Christian apologetic efforts, furthermore, drew the counter-fire of contemporary Muslim intellectuals; there is clear textual evidence that Muslim and Christian thinkers' theological discourses were intertwined. The Nestorian ʿAmmār al-Baṣrī was deeply influenced in his topical outlines and mode of discourse by the intellectual milieu of his native Basra. He rejected the specific reasoning of the Muʿtazilī Abū Hudhayl al-ʿAllāf (d. ca. 226/840), which apparently elicited Abū Hudhayl's refutation in a treatise called "Against

46 Q. 33:37.

ʿAmmār the Christian, in Refutation of the Christians."[47] There are a number of similar rebuttals, such as that of ʿĪsā b. Ṣubayḥ al-Murdār (d. 226/840), who wrote an attack against Abū Qurra, the early Muʿtazilī Ḍirār b. ʿAmr (fl. 169–193/786–809) wrote a refutation of Christians in general, as did Abū ʿĪsā Muḥammad b. Hārūn al-Warrāq (d. 247/861). The Zaydī imam al-Qāsim b. Ibrāhīm (d. 240/860) wrote a refutation of Christians based on his stay in Egypt during the years 199–211/815–826, where he frequented the discussions of *mutakallimūn* in the company of a Copt named Salmūn. And there is, of course, the well-known work of ʿAlī b. Rabbān al-Ṭabarī, a Nestorian who converted to Islam at some point between 223/838 and 233/848. His rebuttal of the Christian claim to be the only true religion includes a treatise against the doctrines of the trinity and the incarnation.[48] Furthermore, Christians actively participated in debates at the caliphal court; these brought more public attention to their intellectual work. Religious debates at court were especially fruitful in the reigns of al-Mahdī, al-Mutawakkil (r. 232–247/847–861), and al-Maʾmūn. The public aspect of these debates provided a high social profile to non-Muslims and eventually aroused the opposition of al-Mutawwakil, who finally put an end to them and demanded the rigorous application of strictures against the high profiles of the non-Muslim population (*dhimmī*).[49]

Ibn Saʿd worked in the same environment in which these developments took place. He most likely arrived in Baghdad just a few years after al-Mahdī's reign ended, though the account of that caliph's debate with Patriarch Timothy I, which allegedly took place in 165/782 or 166/783, was soon translated into Arabic and might have been accessible to Ibn Saʿd. Theodore Abū Qurra's disputation allegedly took place at the court of al-Maʾmūn,[50] a period when Ibn Saʿd was a resident of the capital. Furthermore, it seems to be established that Abū Qurra's *Maymar fī wujūd al-khāliq wa-l-dīn al-qawīm* (Treatise on the Existence of the Creator and True Religion) was written at the outset of his monastic life in Mar Saba monastery in Judea, perhaps between the years 163/780 and 168/785.[51] At least the latter text might have been available in Baghdad during Ibn Saʿd's time. A majority of scholars also attributed the fictional exchange

47 Griffith, "Excursis I: Christian Theological Thought," 97.

48 Griffith, "The Prophet Muḥammad," 112.

49 Griffith, "Faith and Reason," 2.

50 Following the judgment of Georg Graf, most modern scholars doubt the authenticity of these widely differing reports, and conclude that later Christians in the Muslim milieu produced them, elaborating on Abū Qurra's well-known retorts to particular Muslim allegations about Christian beliefs or practices, Griffith, "The Prophet Muḥammad," 103.

51 Griffith, "Faith and Reason," 10.

between al-Hāshimī and al-Kindī to this era.[52] With many of these developments taking place shortly prior to or during Ibn Saʿd's residency in Baghdad, it is useful to explore whether Ibn Saʿd's potential awareness of Christian perspectives toward Muḥammad might have influenced his selection of the proofs of prophecy. This is not to suggest that Ibn Saʿd intended to address a Christian audience, but rather that he might have attempted to counter existing polemical arguments in an effort to reassure his co-religionists in their faith. The following section examines the kinds of tropes Christian thinkers employed in their rejection of Islam. Christian arguments against Islam roughly fall into three, often inter-related themes, which I examine in the following.

3.1 *Christians Addressing Muḥammad's Prophetic Status and Islam's Role in Sacred History*

Islam perceives itself as the last iteration of divine messages sent to mankind through a chain of prophets; the Qurʾān declares "what We have revealed to you from the Book is the truth, confirming what was before it."[53] Muḥammad is represented in the Qurʾān as following in the footsteps of earlier prophets and the ancient prophets themselves promised God that they would have faith in and support a prophet who would come in the future and confirm their message.[54] But the Qurʾān also judges the communities to whom the earlier prophets were sent because these communities altered or forgot their messages, and this was one of the principal reasons for Muḥammad's mission.[55] Christian scholars, however, rejected both of these notions. They argued that the Hebrew Bible and New Testament, and their respective messengers, constituted a continuum of sacred history that culminated in and ended with Christianity, while refuting Islamic claims that it was the final iteration of divine revelation. Christian apologists had to explain their own views of Islam's position within, or outside sacred history and thus they presented a number of

52 Bottini, "al-Kindī," 587f. In the course of the twentieth century, scholars formulated different hypotheses that were affected by the lack of critical editions of Arabic texts and the fact that the Latin translations were made in the twelfth century. Some believe it originated in the fourth/tenth century because of its supposed borrowings from Ibn al-Rāwindī (d. 297/910), al-Ṭabarī (d. 310/923), and Yaḥyā b. ʿAdī (d. 363/974). Others propose a date as late as the ninth/fifteenth century. On the basis of internal historical references, a majority of scholars, however, situate the text in the era of the caliph al-Maʾmūn. The epilogue of the text refers to the fact that al-Maʾmūn, while in Marw or Baghdad, became aware of the letters and ordered them to be read to him. Also see Griffith, "The Prophet Muḥammad," 106–107.

53 Q. 3:3; cf. Q. 2:4, 2:41, 2:91, 2:97, 3:3, 4:47, 6:92, 5:46–48, 10:94, 35:31.

54 Q. 3:81.

55 Roggema, *The Legend of Sergius Baḥīrā*, 11.

strategies to reject Muḥammad's prophetic mission and the legitimacy of the religious tradition he founded.

One of the earliest Christian thinkers to address the religious challenge of Islam, John of Damascus, in the final entry in the section titled "On heresies" of his work *The Fount of Knowledge*, outright rejected Islam's claim to be part of sacred history. He argued that Arabs were pagans until Muḥammad falsely claimed to be a prophet and composed his own scripture after accessing the Hebrew Bible and the New Testament and speaking to an old Arian monk. While John acknowledged that Muḥammad taught Arabs the existence of one God and that Jesus was understood as the word of God, born "without a seed" from Mary, he viewed Islam as a falsification of Christian teachings, and, thus, a Christian heresy rather than a religion in its own right.

In his disputation with al-Mahdī, Patriarch Timothy I presented an integrative notion of Islam as a marginal development of Judaism on its way toward Christianity. This notion denies Islam the status of a revelatory tradition but grants Muḥammad a relatively favorable position as a teacher who spread aspects of the Hebrew Bible and New Testament in line with teachings of Arab Christian communities.[56] Muḥammad was said to essentially have imitated previous prophets without being one himself. Even if not a prophet, Timothy portrays Muḥammad as a figure of sacred history, sent to punish the Persians for their sins. By the same token, Timothy does not fully reject the Qurʾān but views it as a text that—while not scripture itself—functions to bring Arabs to Christianity.[57] Heimgartner argues that Timothy presented more benevolent views to win over the caliph and his Muslim entourage to Christianity.[58] In a different letter addressed to his friend Sergius, which dates roughly to the same time period, Timothy's tone is more dismissive; he calls Muslims "the new Jew[s]," who cause "the same struggle and the same contest to distinguish falsehood and truth" as "in the days of Herod, Pilate, and the old Jews."[59] This echoes the opinion of Timothy's contemporary, the theologian Theodore bār Kōnē, whose literary dialogue between a Christian master and a Muslim disciple includes the master's assessment of his student who says, "as I see it, you are believing as a Jew."[60]

Nonnus of Nisibis compares Muslim views about Christ with Jewish ones and declares that Muslims are "more right minded than others."[61] A similarly

56 Heimgartner, *Die Disputation des ostsryrischen Patriarchen Timothy*, 48.
57 Heimgartner, *Die Disputation des ostsryrischen Patriarchen Timothy*, 48.
58 Heimgartner, *Die Disputation des ostsryrischen Patriarchen Timothy*, 45.
59 Griffith, "The Syriac Letters," 106.
60 Griffith, "The Syriac Letters," 106; cf. Griffith, "The Prophet Muḥammad," 121.
61 Griffith, "The Prophet Muḥammad," 121.

favorable view is portrayed in the debate between a monk of Bēt Ḥālē and a Muslim notable. The monk states that Muḥammad was a wise and God-fearing man who freed the Arabs from pagan beliefs and introduced them to monotheism. The Muslim interlocutor asks why Muḥammad did not engage in proper Christian doctrines and teach Arabs about the trinity. The Christian monk then provides two inter-related strands of reasoning. First, Arabs were religiously immature and would have seen the trinity as a pretext for idolatry. Second, he alleges that Muḥammad only taught Arabs what Baḥīrā taught him, and, thus, he blames the monk for any shortcomings in the allegedly Christian teachings of Muḥammad.[62]

Abū Qurra takes a different approach to the continuity of sacred history. In his *Treatise on the existence of the creator and true religion*, he attempts to devise a rational scheme to compare the truth claims made by nine contemporary religious communities on the basis of the Neoplatonic theory of knowledge that was current in Basra and Baghdad at the time. Unsurprisingly, the treatise concludes in favor of Christianity's claim to be the only religion whose history and doctrine warrants acceptance, as it fulfills all conditions set out in the Neoplatonic tract for discerning the true religion.[63] He argues that the Gospel is the scripture that reasonable individuals would recognize as truth.[64] Abū Qurra anchors Christianity's truth solely in Christ and the Gospel and acknowledges that this might raise a question concerning the Christian acceptance of Moses and the other prophets. He argues that Christ legitimizes previous scriptures, and that Christians consequently have to accept the Old Testament and its prophetic figures because Jesus understood them as such. This line of arguing, consequently, excludes both Muḥammad and the Qurʾān.[65] Abū Qurra's approach is particularly original because it accepts the Islamic scenario of successive messengers, including Muḥammad, but argues against the notion that being chronologically last in the series offers Muslims any advantage in the effort to convince those searching to find the true religion. God's true messenger and the message he delivers must be discerned not by chronology, rather they rely on rational stratagems to recognize God's true message.[66]

All of these early texts are marked by the tension of acknowledging Muḥammad's commitment to monotheism and also rejecting Islam's claim

62 Griffith, "Disputing with Islam in Syriac," 46.
63 Griffith, "Faith and Reason," 8.
64 Griffith, "Faith and Reason," 23.
65 Griffith, "Faith and Reason," 24.
66 Griffith, "Faith and Reason," 31f.

to being the final corrective iteration of divine revelation. Interestingly, many authors even grant Muḥammad some role in sacred history, albeit not as a prophet, but as an intermediary bringing an imperfect version of monotheism to Arabs. The reasons offered for Muḥammad's limited mission vary. Timothy I and Theodore bār Kōnē compare his teachings with those of the Jewish community and fault Muḥammad himself for any shortcomings. John of Damascus sought the origins of Muḥammad's teachings with an unnamed heretic monk. The monk in the debate of Bēt Ḥālē finds fault in Muḥammad's audience, the pagan Arabs who are presented as incapable of grasping the complex doctrine of the trinity, or his alleged teacher, Baḥīrā. This demonstrates that the debate of Bēt Ḥālē was probably conversant with the Christian legend of Baḥīrā, which was established in Christian lore explicitly linking Muḥammad's teachings with the Christian legend of Baḥīrā. In doing so, the blame for his "inadequate" monotheistic teachings lies with his teacher Baḥīrā. Abū Qurra then takes into account a model of successive prophets but excludes Muḥammad due the absence of Jesus' affirmation.

3.2 *Islam as a Vehicle for Muḥammad's Personal Gain or Immoral Behavior*

A number of Christian apologists referred to biographical details in Muḥammad's life in order to argue that he could not have been a prophet in the biblical sense.[67] A common approach included presenting incidents that allegedly occurred during Muḥammad's early career to argue that his alleged religious vocation was actually part of a broader attempt to gain political power and preeminence among the Arabs or to justify otherwise illicit and immoral behavior. This approach was often linked to Muḥammad's encounter with a Christian monk, which was presented as an attempt to craft a narrative that his religious message was not original to him nor did it come from God.[68]

John of Damascus foreshadowed many arguments that later Christian apologists presented to refute the new religion. These arguments were based on the notion that Islamic teachings provided an immoral and materialistic scenario that was incompatible with spiritual advancement and divine communication with mankind. John argued that Muḥammad had crafted his scripture to justify his lustful behavior and sexual promiscuity. He pointed to several passages in the Qurʾān that permit men to engage in polygamy, take concubines, and divorce. Furthermore, he mentions the narrative of Muḥammad's adopted son Zayd, who chose to divorce his wife Zaynab in order for Muḥammad to

67 Griffith, "The Prophet Muḥammad," 132.
68 Griffith, "The Prophet Muḥammad," 132.

marry her. As we have seen, this narrative became a prominent argument in Christian literature refuting Islam in the third/ninth and fourth/tenth centuries.[69] The fictionalized treatise of ʿAbd al-Masīḥ b. Isḥāq al-Kindī likewise seeks to demonstrate that Muḥammad, as opposed to previous prophets, had to be a false prophet because his violent and morally reprehensible behavior ran counter to ideas of divine dignity and he lacked the qualities of prophethood.[70] He dedicates many pages to describing the physical delights in paradise along with the permissible worldly joys for Muslims.[71] In addition, al-Kindī portrays Muḥammad as a violent brigand and describes him as "a man who had no care or concern except for beautiful women with whom he might be paired, or for a people whose blood he was zealous to shed, to take their wealth, and to marry their women."[72] Al-Kindī extended his critique of Islam to show that the Qurʾān was a false scripture that provides a law inspired by the devil, unlike the valid commandments of Christian scriptures. He further asserted that people's conversion to Islam should be explained as a result of their attraction for its laws regarding marriage, polygamy, the possession of concubines, and divorce.[73]

In his treatise on true religion Abū Qurra made similar observations regarding violence. Based on his premise that humans can discern true religions from false ones based on their ability to recognize reflections of God's attributes in their teachings, Abū Qurra's examination of the doctrines of nine communities included their respective teachings about permissible and forbidden human conduct (*ḥalāl* and *ḥarām*), as well as the kinds of reward or punishment that each group proposes as the appropriate recompense for human behavior. He claimed that non-Christian religions condone violence against other humans, including capital punishment and plunder. Therefore, these religions cannot be true, since this kind of behavior is antithetical to acceptable ethical values and morality.[74] By the same token, Abū Qurra pointed out that other religions' notions of reward for a good life stand in stark contrast to the Gospel's commands to curtail worldly pleasures.[75] Although Abū Qurra made these observations about all nine religious communities, in general, they reflect the charges of Christian polemicists that were consistently brought against Islam.

69 Bottini, "al-Kindī," 587.
70 Bottini, "al-Kindī," 588–589.
71 Griffith, "The Prophet Muḥammad," 129.
72 Griffith, "The Prophet Muḥammad," 134.
73 Bottini, "al-Kindī," 589.
74 Griffith, "Faith and Reason," 21–22.
75 Griffith, "Faith and Reason," 22.

While the alleged materialistic gains, sexual licentiousness, and violent inclinations formed the core of many Christian apologetic works, a number of less common strategies were used to delegitimize Muḥammad's prophetic status; these also drew on their authors' knowledge of Islamic teachings. One of John of Damascus's central arguments to reject Muḥammad's claim to prophecy was twofold. On one hand, John of Damascus argued that there were no witnesses to Muḥammad receiving revelation, while Moses received the Law of God on Mount Sinai in the clear sight of his people. According to John, Muslims hold that Muḥammad received his scripture in his sleep; hence he ridiculed Muslims' inconsistency in accepting Muḥammad's claim to prophecy without a witness to revelation while their tradition requires them to take witnesses for any transactions, such as the purchase of a donkey or entering marriages. He presented this reasoning in conjunction with the claim that all prophets, from Moses onward, foretold the coming of Christ, the Son of God who would be crucified, but no such verification exists for Muḥammad's claim. Overall, John of Damascus appears to be more concerned with the lack of witnesses to Muḥammad's revelation than the idea that it was not foretold in earlier scripture. In Timothy's report of their alleged encounter, the notion of Muḥammad having been announced was presented in the voice of caliph al-Mahdī, but this seems to reflect the discourses among Muslim scholars rather than Christian ones, as we see below.

Abraham of Tiberias presented Muḥammad's family history as an argument against the Muslim claim that Muḥammad is the paraclete whose coming Jesus foretold in the Gospel of John.[76] Specifically naming Muḥammad's father, mother, and both grandfathers, Abraham contends that his genealogy precludes the possibility that he could be the heavenly paraclete described in the Gospel as the spirit of God.[77] This reasoning was specifically aimed to counter Muslim interpretations of the Gospel of John, as discussed at greater length below.

3.3 *Miracles*

The contention that miraculous signs worked by prophets in the name of God are the only sufficient reason to accept a religion's genuine divine origin runs like a refrain through the Christian apologies of the late second/eighth and early third/ninth centuries.[78] At the center of this debate lies the Qurʾān's rejection of evidentiary miracles as a criterion for religious credibility. ʿAmmār

76 John, 14:16.
77 Griffith, "The Prophet Muḥammad," 132.
78 Griffith, "The Prophet Muḥammad," 141.

al-Baṣrī, for example, cites specific verses from the Qurʾān[79] and claims that the rejection of miraculous signs recorded in this verse came down to Muḥammad on the occasion of an oath sworn by Christians, Jews, and polytheists, in which they swore that if they should see such a sign at the hands of Muḥammad they would put their faith in him. ʿAmmār reasoned that since Muḥammad rejected the very notion of miraculous signs, even in an instance like this, neither Islam nor Muḥammad would have any reasonable claim to credibility. A couple of elements should be noted here. Christians and Jews are not explicitly mentioned in the passage he quotes and, while ʿAmmār claimed to be following the interpretation of ʿAbdallāh b. ʿAbbās, this interpretation of the verse attributed to Ibn al-ʿAbbās has not been located in a Muslim source.[80] Therefore, it is quite likely that ʿAmmār was crafting a counter-history in this particular statement. Nevertheless, this case clearly indicates that ʿAmmār was aware of the Qurʾān's negative view of personal evidentiary miracles in Muḥammad's instance and used this for his own doctrinal purposes.[81]

The author of al-Kindī's letter also referred to the Qurʾān's rejection of personal miracles, as found in another Qurʾānic verse.[82] He emphasized the tension between this Qurʾānic claim with a number of miracles, such as water-related miracles, and claimed that later Muslim traditions attributed them to Muḥammad against his wishes in order to provide evidence of his prophetic status. The author concludes that Muḥammad's claims to prophecy were initially only accepted by force of arms.[83] Based on this absence of evidentiary miracles, most Christian apologists of the first ʿAbbāsid century held similar views and believed that people accepted Islam and Muḥammad's status as a prophet, or in fact any non-Christian religious tradition, for unworthy motives. Christianity, by contrast, was viewed as the only religion that is accepted because of the divine testimony of the miracle of Christ. It is in this vein that Abū Qurra, Ḥabīb b. Khidma Abū Rāʾiṭa, ʿAmmār al-Baṣrī, and Ḥunayn b. Isḥāq all provide lists of various, though mostly similar, motives to explain why individuals follow other traditions, particularly Islam. In his *Kitāb*

79 "They swear by God with their most solemn oaths that were a sign to come unto them, they would surely believe in it. Say, 'Signs are with God alone.' What will make you realize that, even if they were to come, they would still not believe." (Q. 6:109).

80 Griffith, "The Prophet Muḥammad," 142.

81 Griffith, "The Prophet Muḥammad," 142.

82 "Naught hinders Us from sending signs, save for those of old denied them. And We gave Thamūd the she-camel as a clear portent, but they wronged her. And We do not send down Our signs, save to inspire fear."(Q. 17:59). ʿAmmār al-Baṣrī also refers to this verse in a passage of his *Kitāb al-Burhān*, see Griffith, "The Prophet Muḥammad," 142.

83 Griffith, "The Prophet Muḥammad," 142.

al-Burhān, ʿAmmār, for example, lists "tribal collusion," "the sword," "wealth, dominion, and power," "ethic bigotry," "personal preference," "licentious laws," and "sorcery" as predominant reasons.[84]

4 Ibn Saʿd and Christian Apologetics

The analysis of themes in Christian apologetic literature shows that the attempts by Christian authors to exclude Islam from their notion of continuous sacred history relied predominantly on arguments (1) denying the divine origin of Islam's message because of the absence of evidentiary miracles, or (2) attributing the origin of Islam to Muḥammad in conjunction with a heretic Christian monk, and (3) emphasizing the moral unworthiness of Muḥammad's character, actions, and teachings. If we juxtapose these arguments with the accounts Ibn Saʿd designated as "proofs of prophecy," it seems unlikely that Ibn Saʿd compiled these chapters in immediate response to Christian attempts to discredit Muḥammad's prophetic mission. First, Ibn Saʿd did not engage in the main polemical themes in which Christians portray Muḥammad's moral or ethical behavior. He addressed some moral questions of Muḥammad's character, such as his honesty in financial affairs, but none of the major Christian accusations of materialism, sexual licentiousness, or violent strife for political power are addressed in any significant way in Ibn Saʿd's conceptions of the proofs of prophecy. The same is true for the Christian emphasis on miracles as necessary proof for prophecy. In chapter 4 I have shown that Ibn Saʿd did not employ the theological category of miracles nor did he provide any differentiation between ordinary and miraculous events, though his chapters include narratives that were classified in such a way by other (mostly later) scholars. The Christian theologians' emphasis on the necessary requirement of evidentiary miracles may be reflected in the work of *mutakallimūn*, but Ibn Saʿd did not engage in that debate about the epistemological notion of prophecy at all.

By contrast, the question of previous prophets announcing the coming of a future prophet, which was central to Ibn Saʿd's proof for Muḥammad's prophetic mission, was not featured prominently among Christian apologists of this period. Only John of Damascus raised the issue as a secondary concern; he placed far greater emphasis on the absence of contemporary witnesses to the actual occurrence of revelation. A few authors argued against Muḥammad being the paraclete of the Gospel of John. These are counter-arguments to Muslim claims rather than original Christian notions and are limited to the

84 Griffith, "The Prophet Muḥammad," 143.

particular context of the Muslim approach to biblical exegesis rather than the question of the biblical prophets' collective awareness of a future prophet. Thus Ibn Saʿd's focus on external affirmation of Muḥammad's prophetic mission, particularly through learned Jewish or Christian individuals or prophets from the biblical tradition, cannot be seen as an immediate response to Christian discourses. Furthermore, his notion of prophecy does not function as a corrective to the ubiquitous Christian claim of Islam's message originating in the teachings of a heretical Christian monk. The Christian apologists' intention in this claim was to negate Muslim claims to divine revelation by attributing the message's origin to a single flawed member of their own communities. If Ibn Saʿd sought to invalidate these Christian claims and argue for the divine origin of Muḥammad's message, we would expect to find an emphasis on Muḥammad experiencing the act of revelation. Instead, revelation itself does not play a significant role in Ibn Saʿd's epistemological concept of the proofs of prophecy. Therefore it seems unlikely that he intended to counter specific Christian claims that sought to discredit Muḥammad's prophetic status but operated in the intellectual framework of Muslim discourses on prophecy. In order to explore more likely influences on Ibn Saʿd's decisions about which narratives to include in his chapters on signs of prophecy, we must examine Muslim approaches to the discourse of Muḥammad's prophetic mission as a source for his selection process.

5 Muslim Discourse on Pre-Qurʾānic Annunciations of Muḥammad

While Ibn Saʿd's epistemological concept of prophecy may not have been crafted to counter Christian apologetic literature, the focus on situating Muḥammad's prophetic mission in relation to preceding Abrahamic messengers and their scriptures was not uncommon among Muslim scholars. The prominence of this subject was, at least partially, a result of the Qurʾān's inherently ambiguous position toward biblical scriptures. On one hand, Islam's self-perception as the last iteration of a chain of revelations is based on the Qurʾān's declarations that Muḥammad's message not only confirms previous revelations[85] but was also announced by previous prophets. As such, Jesus addressed the Children of Israel as a messenger of God whose message confirms "that which was (revealed) before me in the Torah, and bringing good tidings of a messenger who comes after me, whose name is Aḥmad."[86] In another verse, the Qurʾān

85 For instance, Q. 2:89, 3:3, 4:47, 46:12, 46:30.
86 Q. 61:6.

assures God's mercy to those Jews and Christians who follow Muḥammad as the prophet described in the Torah and the Gospel.[87] Finally the ancient prophets themselves are said to have promised God that they would have faith in and support a prophet who would come in the future and confirm their message.[88]

On the other hand, the Qurʾān claims to abrogate the earlier scriptures, denies that Muḥammad was informed by nearby Jews and Christians,[89] and, maybe most importantly, accuses both Jews and Christians of tampering with their scriptures,[90] a practice that contributed to the widespread doctrine of scriptural corruption (*taḥrīf*). It is precisely this accusation that the messages of previous prophets were altered or forgotten that served as one of the principal justifications for Muḥammad's own mission.[91] Yet, despite common allegations of altered and, consequently, untrustworthy texts, pre-Qurʾānic scriptures played a prominent role in providing evidence for Muḥammad's prophetic status as Qurʾānic verses that refer to biblical annunciations or descriptions of Muḥammad encouraged a trend among a few select Muslim scholars (some of whom are discussed in the following) to adduce non-Muslim scripture to buttress their own positions. Even though most Muslims lacked the language skills to directly consult biblical texts in Hebrew, Syriac, or Greek, and Arabic translations were probably not available prior to the third/ninth century,[92] a number of texts indicate that Muslims drew on biblical passages.

The earliest text in which a Muslim voice adduces biblical passages to support the claim of Muḥammad's annunciation in pre-Qurʾānic scripture is found in a written exchange attributed to the caliph ʿUmar b. ʿAbd al-ʿAzīz and the Byzantine emperor Leo III. The exchange is preserved in four versions (Arabic, Armenian, Aljamiado,[93] and Latin), with considerable variations found in the texts. In the Armenian manuscript, a summary of ʿUmar's letter includes the coming of God's paraclete as predicted in the Gospel of John and the question of why Christians do not believe that Muḥammad is the "equal and the like of Jesus" since both prophets were allegedly foretold in Isaiah.[94] The

87 Q. 7:157.
88 Q. 3:81.
89 Q. 16:103, 29:48.
90 Q. 2:75–79, 4:46, 5:13.
91 Roggema, *The Legend of Sergius Baḥīrā*, 11.
92 Adang, "Torah," 8.
93 Aljamiado manuscripts use Arabic script to transcribe mostly Romance languages, such as Mozarabic, Aragonese, Portuguese, or Spanish; they were mostly produced in al-Andalus during the ninth/fifteenth and tenth/sixteenth centuries.
94 Palombo, "The 'Correspondence' of Leo III and ʿUmar II," 238.

Aljamiado version of ʿUmar's letter also references Christian scripture for the annunciation of the paraclete and interprets this biblical passage as a reference to Q. 61:6, which claims that the coming of "Aḥmad" was foretold in the Bible. The letter also applies Isaiah 21:7 to Muḥammad.[95] It is not clear whether the reference to the paraclete was part of the original text from which all versions derive or whether it was only selectively mentioned in some later versions, given that these passages are neither included in the Latin version that only records Leo's response, nor in the incomplete Arabic version. But at least two versions of these letters hint at Muslim attempts to interpret specific passages of the Bible for their own doctrinal purposes. Furthermore, Leo's response in the Armenian version appears to confirm that such approaches were common as the emperor highlights ʿUmar's ignorance regarding the scripture and aims to delegitimize any Muslim attempts to examine biblical texts exegetically. He accuses,

> It is this way, that you are accustomed to elude and mutilate the evidence of Holy Scriptures which you have not read and you still do not read. You are but merchants of the things of God and faith, who catch hold of some word in the Scriptures which appears favourable to your opinions.[96]

The complex textual history of this exchange complicates an accurate dating, or identification of its original language, authorship, target audience, and intended function. It has been convincingly argued, however, that all versions likely derive from an Arabic Christian apologetic work authored in the mid-eighth century in the monastic circles of greater Syria (Syria and Palestine).[97] But despite the Christian apologetic origin of the text, the various versions of the letter still give us insight into the Muslim discourses used to challenge Christian doctrines and defend Muḥammad's prophetic mission, because the positions presented in the voice of ʿUmar b. ʿAbd al-Azīz are in line with the positions presented in other texts from this period.

Another epistle between high-ranking ʿAbbāsid and Byzantine officials is the *Risāla* of Abū l-Rabīʿ Muḥammad b. al-Layth (d. ca. 203/819), which was written on behalf of Hārūn al-Rashīd (r. 170–193/786–809) to the Byzantine emperor Constantine VI. The young emperor ruled Byzantium between 790 and 797, and this is the period to which the epistle has commonly been dated. It has been preserved in a work by Ibn Abī Ṭāhir Ṭayfūr (d. 280/893); its authenticity

95 Palombo, "The 'Correspondence' of Leo III and ʿUmar II," 246.
96 Palombo, "The 'Correspondence' of Leo III and ʿUmar II," 238.
97 Palombo, "The 'Correspondence' of Leo III and ʿUmar II," 231.

and dating have not been seriously questioned by modern scholars.[98] Ibn al-Layth's defense of Muḥammad's prophetic mission is also based on the claim that Muḥammad fulfills the biblical predictions about him, as well as the Qurʾānic predictions about the victories of Islam. The author also argues that the Qurʾān was already proven to be inimitable during Muḥammad's lifetime, and that Muḥammad worked evidentiary miracles.[99] At the same time, many common Christian arguments, most prominently the claim that Muḥammad had been instructed by a monk, are refuted. Ibn al-Layth's letter states that the teachings of Christianity and Islam differ too much to share a common source and that Muḥammad's community would have been aware of frequent visits to a monk and, thus, would have realized his deception. Furthermore, being illiterate and unschooled, he could not have known about phenomena such as the shooting stars described in the Qurʾān. These, he argues, must be proofs of Muḥammad's miraculous foreknowledge of events.[100]

In addition to giving us insight into Ibn al-Layth's reasoning, the letter ascribed to him also furthers our understanding about the contexts in which questions of Muḥammad's prophetic legitimacy might have occurred, as the epistle's religious discourse is part of a deeply political agenda. Hārūn al-Rashīd reminds the emperor that Byzantium used to pay a certain amount to the ʿAbbāsids during the early 780s CE in exchange for a cessation of hostilities. Constantine VI, who halted these payments, is told that hostilities would resume if he neither converts to Islam nor reinstates the payment of tribute. This political context provides the framework for a refutation of Christianity and a detailed defense of Muḥammad's prophetic mission, both of which incorporate common themes of Muslim-Christian controversy and conflict during the early ʿAbbāsid period.[101] The discourse regarding Muḥammad's prophetic mission was, therefore, not limited to socio-religious contexts but extended to political interactions between Christian and Muslim communities as well.

In addition to Muslim texts, the disputation report of Patriarch Timothy I also provides glimpses into the line of argumentation employed by Muslim scholars and dignitaries. The report portrays the caliph al-Mahdī adducing some biblical passages and interpreting them in support of Muḥammad's prophetic mission. In this dispute, the caliph initially accused Christians of falsifying scripture to conceal the biblical announcement of Muḥammad's coming that is recorded in the Qurʾān. Like ʿUmar and Ibn al-Layth, al-Mahdī

98 Roggema, "Risālat Abī l-Rabīʿ Muḥammad ibn al-Layth," 349.
99 Roggema, "Risālat Abī l-Rabīʿ Muḥammad ibn al-Layth," 350.
100 Roggema, "Risālat Abī l-Rabīʿ Muḥammad ibn al-Layth," 350.
101 Roggema, "Risālat Abī l-Rabīʿ Muḥammad ibn al-Layth," 350.

quotes Qur'ān 61:6 but Timothy rejects the accusation altogether, stating that there is no textual evidence for alterations.[102] The caliph then shifted strategy and presented biblical passages that allegedly refer to Muḥammad, such as Deuteronomy 18:18 and Isaiah 21:6–9.[103] Here the persona of al-Mahdī is mainly a literary figure of Timothy's creation, but it represents an approach of adducing biblical passages as employed among Muslim scholars at the time. More specifically, these references by Ibn al-Layth and al-Mahdī clearly indicate that the approach was practiced in Baghdad prior to Ibn Saʿd's arrival in the capital and continued well beyond his lifetime.

From Ibn al-Layth's letter onward, fairly consistent lists of biblical passages were available to Muslim scholars. By the second half of the third/ninth century, there were at least two monographs dedicated to the proofs of Muḥammad's prophetic mission that mainly adduced biblical passages. ʿAlī b. Rabban al-Ṭabarī (d. 251/865) was a Christian-born physician who converted to Islam under the rule of al-Mutawakkil and authored two apologetic tracts in defense of his new religion.[104] The longest chapter of his *Kitāb al-Dīn wa-l-dawla fī ithbāt nubuwwat al-nabī Muḥammad*, which takes up almost half of the book, deals with the alleged references to Muḥammad in earlier scripture. Ibn Rabban searched the Bible for passages that he suggested refer to Muḥammad and events related to the advent of Islam. As far as we know, he was the first Muslim author to use this method on this scale. Apart from a few quotations from the New Testament, the testimonies in Ibn Rabban's work were all taken from the books of the Hebrew Bible, such as Genesis, Exodus, Numbers, Deuteronomy, Psalms, Isaiah, Hosea, Micah, Habakkuk, Zephaniah, Zechariah, Jeremiah, Ezekiel, and Daniel.[105] Interestingly, Ibn Rabban's work was aimed at a predominantly Christian audience, in the hopes of removing their doubts about Muḥammad's prophecy and the divine origin of his message. He provides the grounds on which Muḥammad should be accepted, including his preaching of monotheism, his pious and sincere character, his miracles, his prophesies about future events, his military victories, and the fact that earlier prophets annunciated his coming and described his mission.[106] These arguments clearly countered the immediate concerns Christian authors had laid out in their works. Furthermore, these or very similar criteria had been adduced by Jewish and Christian theologians as proof of the veracity

102 Roggema, "Risālat Abī l-Rabīʿ Muḥammad ibn al-Layth," 50.
103 Roggema, "Risālat Abī l-Rabīʿ Muḥammad ibn al-Layth," 52.
104 Adang, "Medieval Muslim Polemics," 17.
105 Adang, *Muslim Writers on Judaism*, 264–266.
106 Adang, "Medieval Muslim Polemics," 17.

of Moses and Jesus, respectively.[107] An examination of Isaiah proves particularly interesting because specific passages had to a large extent already been claimed by Christians as references to Jesus, which the former Christian Ibn Rabban must have known very well. In many cases, to suit his new pro-Muslim apologetic purpose all he had to do was explain why it was more plausible that they referred to Muḥammad rather than Jesus.[108] Ibn Rabban sought to demonstrate that Muslim acceptance of Muḥammad's mission was based on the same criteria as those that led Jews and Christians to lend credence to their prophets. Consequently, he argued that there was no reason for the People of the Book (*ahl al-kitāb*) to reject Muḥammad. Initially, Ibn Rabban's *Kitāb al-Dīn wa-l-dawla* circulated exclusively among Christian circles and apparently was unknown to Muslim scholars until the fifth/eleventh century.[109] The earliest Muslim author known to have consulted the work was the Muʿtazilī Abū l-Ḥusayn al-Baṣrī (d. 436/1045).[110] Later, Abū l-Ḥasan al-Māwardī (d. 450/1058) and Fakhr al-Dīn al-Rāzī (d. 606/1210) quoted some materials from this work using Abū l-Ḥusayn's work as an intermediary source.[111]

Another important work that circulated among Muslim scholars was the *Aʿlām* (or *dalāʾil*) *al-Nubūwa* by Ibn Rabban's contemporary Ibn Qutayba (d. 276/889). Most of the scriptural material included in Ibn Qutayba's work is also found in Ibn Rabban's otherwise much richer book.[112] The *Aʿlām* was used over the following centuries by various authors as a reference text for the biblical material it contained.[113] Camilla Adang suggests that Abū Naṣr Muṭahhar b. Ṭāhir al-Maqdisī (d. before 355/966) was apparently the earliest author to use Ibn Qutayba's work.[114] It was also cited by the Muʿtazilī ʿAbd al-Jabbār al-Hamadhānī (d. 415/1025) in his *Tathbīt dalāʾil al-nubūwa* and extensive segments cited in Ibn Ḥazm's (d. 446/1064) *Kitāb al-Uṣūl wa-l-furūʿ* attests that it reached al-Andalus.[115] In eastern territories, the work appears

107 The Jewish theologian al-Muqammiṣ (first half of the third/ninth century) had a similar list of prerequisites for the veracity of a prophet. As Sarah Stroumsa has shown, this Jewish author also took his argument from a yet unidentified Christian source. Even though the aim of this source was no doubt to prove the truth of Jesus' mission, al-Muqammiṣ sought to demonstrate the applicability of the same criteria to Moses and Judaism. See Stroumsa, *Dāwūd ibn Marwan al-Muqammiṣ's Twenty Chapters*, 31f.

108 Adang, "Medieval Muslim Polemics," 18.

109 Schmidtke, "The Muslim Reception of Biblical Materials," 52.

110 Schmidtke, "The Muslim Reception of Biblical Materials," 52.

111 Schmidtke, "The Muslim Reception of Biblical Materials," 52.

112 Schmidtke, "The Muslim Reception of Biblical Materials," 51.

113 Schmidtke, "The Muslim Reception of Biblical Materials," 53.

114 Adang, *Muslim Writers on Judaism*, 156.

115 Schmidtke, "The Muslim Reception of Biblical Materials," 54.

to have circulated mostly among *ahl al-ḥadīth* circles, including Ibn al-Jawzī's (d. 597/1200) *al-Wafāʾ bi-aḥwāl al-Muṣṭafā*[116] and some later Ḥanbalī scholars, such as Abū l-Qāsim al-Taymī l-Iṣfahānī (d. 535/1140–1141) and Ibn Taymiyya (d. 728/1328), who appear to have had access to the original work.[117]

These glimpses into the Muslim approach of adducing biblical materials demonstrates that Ibn Saʿd's extensive chapters on the proofs of prophecy, with their distinct focus on various monotheistic predictions of Muḥammad's prophetic mission, emerged during the relatively early stages of an ongoing Muslim discourse on biblical passages that allegedly referred to Muḥammad. While we may not be able to affirm with certainty that the original text of the correspondence between ʿUmar b. ʿAbd al-ʿAzīz and Leo III, dating from the mid-second/eighth century, contained references to biblical passages as a means to verify the Qurʾānic claims of Muḥammad's annunciation, we can safely assume that such a discourse was well underway during Ibn Saʿd's time in Baghdad. When he arrived in the new capital sometime after 189/805, the caliphal court had witnessed the disputation between Patriarch Timothy I and al-Mahdī and had commissioned Ibn al-Layth's letter to Constantine VI. From the time of Ibn al-Layth's letter onward, the discourse not only continued in both Muslim and Christian circles, but also gained momentum in the monographs of Ibn Rabban (who converted to Islam during the reign of al-Mutawakkil, at least two decades after Ibn Saʿd's death), and his contemporary Ibn Qutayba. The existence of these works and their prominence among later authors demonstrates that the discourse of anchoring Muḥammad's prophetic legitimacy in pre-Qurʾānic scripture was taking place during and continued for a considerable time after Ibn Saʿd's lifetime.

Emerging from Qurʾānic references, this discourse was decidedly Muslim in origin and was mostly concerned with legitimizing Islam in the framework of monotheistic continuity while simultaneously reflecting interactive dynamics with Christian scholarly audiences. First, Muslim scholars who were able to provide biblical exegesis in order to fit the Qurʾānic claims of Muḥammad's annunciation inevitably generated Christian refutations. At the same time, many of the verses adduced by Muslim scholars stood in the traditions of Jewish and Christian scholars who referred to the same verses as evidence of the prophetic status of Moses and Jesus, respectively. The parallel arguments are particularly clear in Ibn Rabban's *Kitāb al-Dīn wa-l-dawla*, as he could capitalize on his extensive familiarity with Christian doctrine. The thematic

116 Schmidtke, "The Muslim Reception of Biblical Materials," 55.

117 Schmidtke, "The Muslim Reception of Biblical Materials," 56.

structure of this discourse is very much in line with Ibn Saʿd's focus on narratives in which monotheistic practitioners or even prophetic figures confirm Muḥammad's prophetic mission. But Ibn Saʿd clearly relied on a very different set of texts as evidence. With the exception of the Qur'ānic-inspired narrative of the shooting stars preventing *jinn* from overhearing heavenly discourses, which are mentioned both in Ibn Saʿd and the epistle of Ibn al-Layth, the narratives Ibn Saʿd presents are entirely different than the ones used by scholars who adduced biblical passages. Ibn Saʿd's sources might be found elsewhere as heavily Islamicized canonical and extra-canonical biblical materials took a prominent position in various forms of early Muslim literature, such as exegesis (*tafsīr*), historiography, and *ḥadīth*. These materials usually serve one of two purposes: they substantiate the Qur'ānic claim that Muḥammad was predicted and described in the Bible, or they serve as raw material for accounts of universal history, of which the lives of the earlier prophets often constitute a substantial part.[118]

5.1 *The* Kitāb al-Maghāzī *of Ibn Isḥāq (d. 150/767)*

Ibn Isḥāq's *Kitāb al-Maghāzī* is the earliest narrative biography of the Prophet and the only extant biography that predates Ibn Saʿd's work. Its textual history is notoriously difficult to establish, as Ibn Isḥāq revised it continuously throughout his career and at least four different partially extant recensions have been transmitted by his numerous students. The most prominent recension is that of Ibn Hishām, which contains many of the narratives that we find in Ibn Saʿd's first chapter on the proofs of prophecy. In the context of Muḥammad's birth, for instance, Ḥassān b. Thābit (d. 54/674) relates a childhood encounter with a Jewish man who alerts his community that "the star has risen under which Aḥmad is to be born."[119] The same narrative is found in Ibn Saʿd.[120] Ibn Isḥāq's work also contains the account in which Muḥammad himself states that "I am what my father Abraham prayed for and the good tidings of Jesus"; this is followed by accounts of Muḥammad's birth and the opening of his chest.[121] Ibn Saʿd included three versions of the first account in the brief chapter immediately preceding the first chapter on "proofs of prophecy,"[122] while accounts of his birth and the opening of his chest and purification of his heart are found in the chapter on the proofs of prophecy prior to the onset of Muḥammad's

118 Schmidtke, "The Muslim Reception of Biblical Materials," 50.
119 Ibn Isḥāq, *The Life of Muhammad*, 70.
120 Ibn Saʿd, *Ṭabaqāt*, 1:134.
121 Ibn Isḥāq, *The Life of Muhammad*, 72f.
122 Ibn Saʿd, *Ṭabaqāt*, 1:124.

mission.[123] The narratives of ʿAbd al-Muṭṭalib predicting his grandson's future role as a leader[124] is included, as well as the story of the seer Liḥb who predicted Muḥammad's great future to his uncle, Abū Ṭālib.[125] Both of these are also found in Ibn Saʿd's chapter.[126] Prominent narratives of Muḥammad's encounters with the monks Baḥīrā and Maysara (whom he met later in life) are featured in both works.[127] Maysara's recognition of Muḥammad's future prophecy is taken up again in the context of Khadīja's marriage proposal to Muḥammad. Ibn Isḥāq portrays Khadīja seeking her Christian uncle Warāqa's advice prior to proposing marriage to Muḥammad. She relates Muḥammad's previous encounter with Maysara while working for her. Warāqa responded: "If this is true, Khadīja, verily Muhammad is the prophet of this people. I knew that a prophet of this people was to be expected. His time has come."[128] Ibn Isḥāq then includes an entire chapter titled "Akhbār al-Kuhān min al-ʿarab wa-l-aḥbār min al-yuhūd wa-l-rihbān min al-naṣāra bi-baʿthatihi" (i.e., Reports of Arab soothsayers, Jewish rabbis, and Christian monks about his prophecy), which starts with a summary of the events and then lists many narratives later found in Ibn Saʿd's chapters, such as the reference to *jinn* being stopped from listening to heavenly discourses after the beginning of Muḥammad's prophetic mission. Ibn Saʿd's chapters also include related references to the Qurʾān,[129] and an account of a voice coming from inside a sacrificed calf proclaiming the coming of a monotheistic prophet to the pagan worshipers present.[130] There are, furthermore, various accounts of Jews warning their co-religionists of a coming prophet who will be hostile to them. This account includes reference to three young Jewish men who encounter an older Jew from Syria who predicted the coming of an Arab prophet. After the older man's death, Muḥammad arrived in Medina and the three Jewish men recognized him as the foretold prophet and they converted to Islam.[131] Ibn Isḥāq also includes a lengthy account of Salmān al-Fārisī's conversion to Islam. In this narrative, Salmān left his devoted Zoroastrian father after being introduced to Abrahamic monotheism in a church. He traveled to various Christian officials in Syria and Iraq, and planned to convert to Christianity until he observed various moral inadequacies

123 Ibn Saʿd, *Ṭabaqāt*, 1:125–127.
124 Ibn Isḥāq, *The Life of Muhammad*, 73.
125 Ibn Isḥāq, *The Life of Muhammad*, 79.
126 Ibn Saʿd, *Ṭabaqāt*, 1:125, 127, 139.
127 Ibn Isḥāq, *The Life of Muhammad*, 79–82; Ibn Saʿd, *Ṭabaqāt*, 1:127f., 130f.
128 Ibn Isḥāq, *The Life of Muhammad*, 83.
129 Ibn Isḥāq, *The Life of Muhammad*, 90, cf. Q. 72:1, 46:28; Ibn Saʿd, *Ṭabaqāt*, 1:141.
130 Ibn Isḥāq, *The Life of Muhammad*, 93, Ibn Saʿd, *Ṭabaqāt*, 1:132.
131 Ibn Isḥāq, *The Life of Muhammad*, 93–95; Ibn Saʿd, *Ṭabaqāt*, 1:134f., 138.

among Christians. He then set out to Arabia after being told by a bishop about the coming of a prophet. He reached Medina and was purchased as a slave by a member of the Banū Qurayẓa; then he finally encountered Muḥammad. The narrative ends with Salmān's manumission after Muḥammad calls on his Companions to help provide the necessary number of palm tree seedlings, he himself contributed a piece of gold.[132] Similar versions of the last part of this narrative are found in Ibn Saʿd's chapter, including a narrative twist in which gold is transformed after Muḥammad licks it or puts it in his mouth.[133]

The striking parallels between this chapter in Ibn Isḥāq and Ibn Saʿd's selection of narratives in his first chapter on the "proofs of prophecy" suggest that Ibn Saʿd adopted Ibn Isḥāq's approach of presenting a host of witnesses to emphasize the legitimacy of Muḥammad's prophetic mission. While the specific accounts are not always the same, the overall narratives and their mostly chronological arrangement align in very similar clusters. At the same time, each chapter also contains narratives that are absent in the other collection, which is to be expected given their different thematic orientations. There are also a few non-annunciation narratives in Ibn Saʿd's chapters; these also occurred elsewhere in Ibn Isḥāq's prophetic biography. For instance, these include the incidents in which trees and stones greet Muḥammad,[134] and an account in which Muḥammad calls on a tree to relocate as evidence of his prophetic mission.[135] Ibn Isḥāq mentions these episodes only in passing, in the framework of longer narratives, rather than emphasizing their significance in the way Ibn Saʿd did by presenting them explicitly in the context of his thematic chapter. But overall, Ibn Saʿd's notion of proofs of prophecy prior to Muḥammad's call clearly reflect Ibn Isḥāq's attempt to present a comprehensive group of testimonies for the authenticity of his mission. These testimonies range from monotheist and pagan practitioners to prophetic figures, soothsayers, animals, and inanimate elements of nature. The parallels between Ibn Saʿd's selection and long stretches of Ibn Isḥāq's *Kitāb al-Maghāzī* raise interesting questions regarding Ibn Isḥāq's potential participation in the larger Muslim discourse on the proofs of prophecy.

The *Kitāb al-Maghāzī* was without a doubt formative for the *sīra*/*maghāzī* tradition as a whole, both in form and content. First, Ibn Isḥāq expanded the *maghāzī* tradition beyond the existing corpus of accounts by incorporating "a bricolage of prose and poetry of sundry origins," including *ḥadīth*, *akhbār*, tribal

132 Ibn Isḥāq, *The Life of Muhammad*, 95–98.
133 Ibn Saʿd, *Ṭābaqāt*, 1:155.
134 Ibn Isḥāq, *The Life of Muhammad*, 105; cf. Ibn Saʿd, *Ṭabaqāt*, 1:132.
135 Ibn Isḥāq, *The Life of Muhammad*, 178, cf. Ibn Saʿd, *Ṭabaqāt*, 1:154.

and ethnic genealogies, registers of battle participants, treaties, pacts, letters, and Christian and Jewish scriptural proof texts.[136] Along with these methodological and organizational innovations that triggered ample critique from his peers, Ibn Isḥāq's work provides the creative impetus to anchor Muḥammad's prophetic mission in a broader notion of the past. Ibn Isḥāq

> emplotted Muḥammad's prophethood and his community within a thick description of the Arabian past that entangled them in a historical tapestry of fateful interactions with a cast of imperial players and a host of spiritual seekers—be they Arabs, Romans, Egyptians, Abyssinians, Syrians, and Persians or pagans, Jews, and Christians.[137]

Ibn Isḥāq's incorporation of annunciation narratives clearly exemplifies a form of what Sean Anthony called narrativized theology, in which a particular sense of religious purpose predetermined the portrayal of the prophet. Many of these narratives of Muḥammad's early life were, individually, already part of earlier collections, as I have shown in chapter 2, and later became a common feature in *dalāʾil al-nubūwa* works. But it is Ibn Isḥāq's consolidated arrangement of materials in the section titled "Reports of Arab soothsayers, Jewish rabbis, and Christian monks" that crafts and accentuates the notion that existing spiritual communities anticipated and acknowledged Muḥammad's prophetic mission as a pivotal moment in their shared sacred history.

Ibn Isḥāq advanced this notion even further by linking these narratives with pre-Qurʾānic scriptures. The chapter containing annunciation narratives is followed by a chapter on the "Ṣifa rasūl Allāh min al-injīl" (Description of the messenger of God from the Gospel), which provides a lengthy, albeit Islamicized, quotation from the Gospel of John (15:26–16:1) referring to the paraclete. Here Ibn Isḥāq claimed that the Syriac word he found in this passage is a translation for Muḥammad, which is "paraclete" in Greek.[138] This reference to the Gospel immediately precedes Ibn Isḥāq's account of the first revelation and his claim that earlier prophets entered a covenant with God to accept Muḥammad's prophetic mission and help him against his adversaries, an obligation that was then transferred to the adherents of Judaism and Christianity.[139] Thus, Ibn Isḥāq skillfully embeds the biblical passage into a wider narrative of Muḥammad's prophecy having been predestined and anticipated by historical individuals

136 Anthony, *Muḥammad and the Empires of Faith*, 169.
137 Anthony, *Muḥammad and the Empires of Faith*, 170f.
138 Ibn Isḥāq, *The Life of Muhammad*, 103–104.
139 Ibn Isḥāq, *The Life of Muhammad*, 104–105.

from the past and by figures of sacred history. It is worthwhile, then, to explore what role Ibn Isḥāq might have played overall in the discourse about prophecy.

Ibn Isḥāq's biblical quotations appear to be the earliest recorded Muslim attempt to connect the Qurʾānic claim of Jesus announcing the Prophet (Q. 61:6) to the paraclete mentioned in the Gospel of John. This connection became ubiquitous in later Muslim literature as Muslim scholars frequently turned to this passage when looking to corroborate the Qurʾānic trope of Muḥammad's annunciation voiced by Jesus in Q. 61:6 and 7:157. After scanning the Gospel, they concluded that if Jesus only foretold the paraclete, then the paraclete must be Muḥammad. This interpretation, albeit not the precise textual *Vorlage* of Ibn Isḥāq's work, is found in almost all the texts previously examined in this chapter, including the Armenian and Aljamiado manuscripts of the correspondence between ʿUmar b. ʿAbd al-ʿAzīz and Leo III, the disputation between Timothy I and al-Mahdī, the epistle of Ibn al-Layth on behalf of Hārūn al-Rashīd, and Ibn Rabban's *Kitāb al-Dīn wa-l-dawla*. Naturally, the Christian apologists of the first ʿAbbāsid century simply denied this interpretation of the paraclete or any claim that other biblical passages refer to Muḥammad.[140] Muslim scholars, in turn, frequently explained the lack of references to Muḥammad by pointing to the doctrine of scriptural corruption (*taḥrīf*). Timothy I, for instance, emphasized the absence of any references to Muḥammad by stating that he himself would have converted to Islam had he found any evidence in the Gospel. He goes on to explain that the paraclete is actually the spirit of God and, therefore, cannot be identified with Muḥammad. The caliph counters by accusing Christians of having altered the scriptures, not only the Gospel, but also passages in the Hebrew Bible, such as Isaiah 21:7; Timothy, in turn, refutes this.[141] In his debate with Abraham of Tiberias, another Muslim scholar employs the doctrine of scriptural corruption (*taḥrīf*) and claims that John and his associates revised the Gospel after Christ's ascension to heaven.[142] The former Christian ʿAlī b. Rabbān al-Ṭabarī went a step further and employed his intimate familiarity with Christian scripture and doctrine to argue at some length in favor of the Muslim interpretation of the passages in question. He refuted the usual Christian objections to Muslims identifying the paraclete with Muḥammad, and in particular Timothy's claim that the paraclete is God's consubstantial spirit.[143] Thus, it is clear that Ibn Isḥāq's representation of Muḥammad's prophecy with his

140 Griffith, "The Prophet Muḥammad," 140.
141 Griffith, "The Prophet Muḥammad," 140.
142 Griffith, "The Prophet Muḥammad," 140.
143 Griffith, "The Prophet Muḥammad," 141.

innovative reproduction of a particular biblical passage became part of a broader discourse about Muḥammad's prophetic mission among numerous Muslim scholars interacting with Christian refutations of Islam. It is less clear to what extent this discourse was already underway when Ibn Isḥāq worked on his *Kitāb al-Maghāzī*.

In this context, Ibn Isḥāq's proximity to and, indeed, dependence on the ʿAbbāsid court are an intriguing aspect given the centrality of the court in Christian-Muslim oral and written exchanges. It raises the question of whether Ibn Isḥāq himself was influenced by these discourses. It is well-established that Ibn Isḥāq started compiling accounts in his native Medina before he sought patronage at several ʿAbbāsid courts during the reign of the caliph al-Manṣūr (r. 136–158/754–775). After being ostracized from Medinan scholarly circles, he initially joined al-Manṣūr's court in al-Ḥira, then in Harran, before traveling to Rayy, where he stayed at the court of the caliph's son and future successor, al-Mahdī. Eventually, around 146/763 during the construction of Baghdad as a new capital, he returned to al-Manṣūr.[144] The role of the ʿAbbāsid court in influencing the *Kitāb al-Maghāzī* has been debated. Al-Khaṭīb al-Baghdādī provides the most direct account of the court's influence over the text as it reports that al-Mahdī commissioned Ibn Isḥāq to compose for his son a comprehensive universal history, from God's creation to the present day. Once the work was complete, al-Mahdī deemed it too long and ordered Ibn Isḥāq to abridge it before it was stored in the caliphal library.[145] Thus, the account suggests that al-Mahdī's court in Rayy had an immediate impact on the work's content and scope. This possibility should, however, be taken cautiously. First, al-Khaṭīb al-Baghdādī himself points out that his source, al-Ḥasan al-Mu'addib, may not have been reliable. He further suggests that the caliph in question is more likely to have been al-Mahdī's father, al-Manṣūr, given that he is addressed with his full regal title and al-Mahdī did not succeed his father until after Ibn Isḥāq's death, making it implausible that al-Mahdī would have been addressed as the "commander of the faithful" during Ibn Isḥāq's sojourn in Rayy.[146]

---

144 Anthony, *Muḥammad and the Empires of Faith*, 157.

145 Al-Khaṭīb al-Baghdādī, *Tārīkh Baghdād*, 2:17.

146 Al-Khaṭīb al-Baghdādī, *Tārīkh Baghdād*, 2:17. Sean Anthony points to further problems and suggested that al-Ḥasan al-Muʿaddib actually merged two separate accounts which, if credible, might be better understood as referring to two separate events: the initial composition of the work for al-Manṣūr, who is erroneously referred to as al-Mahdī in an account narrated by ʿAmmār b. Muḥammad b. Makhlad (d. 387/997), and the fate of a copy of the Rayy recension of the *Maghāzī* narrated by Abū l-Haytham; Anthony, *Muḥammad and the Empires of Faith*, 166f.

Furthermore, an examination of the linguistic and geographical background of Ibn Isḥāq's particular rendition of the paraclete suggests that Ibn Isḥāq had already written this prior to leaving Medina and obtaining ʿAbbāsid patronage in Iraq. It has been convincingly argued that Ibn Isḥāq's translation of the Gospel of John was derived from a Syrian Umayyad-era tradition of ad hoc translations of the Bible into Arabic that is otherwise no longer extant.[147] What distinguishes Ibn Isḥāq's translation from all subsequent renderings of the paraclete discourse is that his version draws on neither a Greek nor a Syriac version of the Gospel text, but rather on a Christian Palestinian Aramaic (CPA) version.[148] As far as we know, Ibn Isḥāq himself possessed no knowledge of CPA.[149] This sheds considerable light on the translation's provenance, both in terms of geography and chronology, as CPA gradually emerged as a key language for the monastic communities of eastern Palestine and Transjordan from the sixth to the eighth centuries CE.[150] It was, however, foreign to the western cities in which Ibn Isḥāq sought exile and patronage. Consequently, Ibn Isḥāq probably acquired his translation of the Johannine paraclete before leaving Medina. Furthermore, the version of the *Kitāb al-Maghāzī* that Ibn Isḥāq taught Ibrāhīm b. Saʿd al-Zuhrī dates from the period prior to his departure from Medina, and likely offers us a glimpse into the work at its earliest stage.[151] This shows that Ibn Isḥāq had begun compiling the first part of the work, the *Mubtadāʾ*, in Medina and relied heavily on the works and knowledge of Jews and Christians. This is corroborated by the fact that it was this particular practice that stirred the rebuke of Mālik,[152] even though citing non-Muslim materials was not Ibn Isḥāq's innovation. He appears to have emulated his teacher Ibn Shihāb al-Zuhrī (d. 124/742). In his narrative of Muḥammad's letter to the Byzantine emperor Heraclius, al-Zuhrī refers back to a Christian cleric from Jerusalem, whom he claimed to have met during the reign of ʿAbd al-Malik.[153] A philological examination of this account suggests that he indeed drew, at least partially, on a source in CPA.[154] Ibn Isḥāq and al-Zuhrī are, in fact, the only Muslim scholars documented to have utilized CPA versions of the Gospel; this

147 Anthony, "Muḥammad, Menaḥem, and the Paraclete," 264.
148 Anthony, "Muḥammad, Menaḥem, and the Paraclete," 263.
149 Anthony, "Muḥammad, Menaḥem, and the Paraclete," 264.
150 Anthony, "Muḥammad, Menaḥem, and the Paraclete," 258–259.
151 Anthony, "Muḥammad and the Empires of Faith," 165.
152 Anthony, "Muḥammad and the Empires of Faith," 167.
153 Anthony, "Muḥammad, Menaḥem, and the Paraclete," 265.
154 Anthony, "Muḥammad, Menaḥem, and the Paraclete," 265.

suggests that Ibn Isḥāq either directly derived his translation from his teacher or relied on the same Christian networks as a source.[155]

All of this indicates that Ibn Isḥāq's interest in linking Muḥammad's prophetic mission with pre-Qurʾānic scripture did not emerge under ʿAbbāsid patronage and the intellectual exchanges taking place at the court but in fact dates back to the early days of his career. Yet after Ibn Isḥāq had established his residency at the caliphal courts, the discourse on the paraclete appears to have resonated with other Muslim scholars in the vicinity who were already engaged in Christian-Muslim debates over Muḥammad's prophecy. While Ibn Isḥāq's particular rendition based on a CPA text is scarcely cited outside Ibn Hishām's recension of the *Sīra*,[156] the passage that it reproduces became well-established as a central component in the subsequent Muslim-Christian discourse on prophecy, albeit on the basis of more easily accessible translations from Greek, Syriac, or a combination of the two. A similar process seems to have occurred with Ibn Isḥāq's distinct portrayal of Muḥammad's prophetic mission as an integral part of Arabia's greater sacred history in that Ibn Saʿd's focus on the annunciation narratives in his chapter on the "proofs of prophecy" frequently reproduces the narremes found in Ibn Isḥāq without relying on the same sources but replacing them with more reliable ones. The court's role in the formation and dissemination of this discourse is not based on an immediate influence of its contents since the corpus of traditions that served as the raw materials was already in circulation. It is, rather, the considerable resources and the prestige its patronage generated that amplified these sources and eventually facilitated their dissemination.

•••

Ibn Saʿd increased the scope of the "proofs of prophecy" as a topic and his particular integration of Muḥammad's prophetic mission into the tapestry of Arabia's sacred history occurred in and was shaped by a set of political, social, and intellectual circumstances of the early ʿAbbāsid period. The Muslim minority's political and cultural dominance that extended over a majority Christian and, to a lesser extent, existing Jewish population, in combination with their social proximity, a new common language of Arabic, shifting demographics, and the relative familiarity of their respective sacred histories and texts gave rise to unprecedented intellectual exchanges across the three Abrahamic faith traditions. Muslim and Christian religious discourses ran mostly parallel and

155 Anthony, "Muḥammad, Menaḥem, and the Paraclete," 265–266.
156 Anthony, "Muḥammad, Menaḥem, and the Paraclete," 265–266.

were focused on the epistemological needs of their own communities. Their encounters and exchanges were at once competitive and symbiotic, antagonistic and invigorating for their respective fields. The attempts by religious scholars to maintain, establish, or protect their respective community's political, social, and religious legitimacy brought forth discourses regarding the epistemological evidence of the veracity of various prophetic missions and the means by which they could be distinguished from fraudulent imposters. These discourses eventually found their expression in *dalāʾil al-nubūwa* literature and, in the Muslim context, could be addressed theologically or by using Muslim or non-Muslim scripture.

The broader discourses about prophecy that occurred in Muslim and Christian communities also left their mark on works of *sīra*, albeit indirectly. While Muslim theologians often interacted and engaged directly with their non-Muslim counterparts, frequently facilitated through the patronage of the courts, scholars like Ibn Saʿd contributed to the same discourses about the proofs of prophecy in the contours of their own fields and, presumably, with a Muslim audience in mind not a focus on Christian polemics against Muslims. Ibn Saʿd crafted his evidence of Muḥammad's prophetic mission in his thematic chapter on the proofs for prophecy not so much in direct response to Christian refutations as by drawing on the outlines of Muḥammad's life as it had been presented by Ibn Isḥāq. Ibn Isḥāq, in turn, was an innovator in the field of *maghāzī* and *sīra*; he anchored Muḥammad's prophetic mission in the broader historical and religious contexts of Arabia. Thus, neither Ibn Isḥāq nor Ibn Saʿd directly participated in Christian-Muslim exchanges but their works each display forms of narrativized theology that were shaped by the discourses of their times. This theologically predetermined portrayal of Muḥammad's early life became formative for later tradition-based *dalāʾil al-nubūwa* literature. Ibn Isḥāq's inclusion of annunciation narratives and the discussion of the paraclete in his portrayal of Muḥammad's early life was a prescient presentation of two approaches to Muslim discourses on the proofs of Muḥammad's prophetic mission and the wider body of *dalāʾil al-nubūwa* literature. On one hand, Ibn Saʿd used the accounts of annunciations from broader biographical traditions in a central way to craft epistemological evidence of Muḥammad's prophetic mission, as is reflected in his first chapter on "proofs of prophecy," and which eventually became an integral part of later tradition-based *dalāʾil al-nubūwa* works, as I show in the next chapter. On the other hand, there is an approach that adduces biblical passages in support of the prophetic character of Muḥammad's mission and as a rejection of Christian refutations of Muḥammad. This process constitutes a form of counter-history in the same way Christians have retold the account of Baḥīrā for their own purposes.

Furthermore, the early attempts by Ibn Isḥāq were foundational for later works, such as Ibn Qutayba's *Aʿlām al-nubūwa*, and some Christian-Muslim exchanges.

Ibn Saʿd's two chapters on the proofs of prophecy appear to be the earliest extant example of an emergent trend among scholars of *ḥadīth* at the time to address questions of theological significance through the lens of their own fields. Ibn Saʿd's contemporaries al-Ḥumaydī and al-Madāʾinī authored the first independent *dalāʾil al-nubūwa* works around the same time; interest in this subject increased thereafter, as numerous scholars of *ḥadīth* compiled their own independent works or chapters in large *ḥadīth* collections, including those of al-Bukhārī and al-Tirmidhī, which became part of the *ḥadīth* canon in later centuries. These examples of narrativized theology contributed to shaping the Muslim imagination of prophethood and to exploring its theological and historical boundaries even among audiences that were not closely familiar with concurrent theological debates. *Dalāʾil al-nubūwa,* then, are not so much a genre in one particular field of Muslim religious sciences, but more a discourse that took its impetus from the social and intellectual environment of the early ʿAbbāsid period and its form and specific content from the individual field or discipline of the scholar at hand.

CHAPTER 6

Recurring Themes in Later *Dalāʾil al-Nubūwa* Literature

With the exception of the partially preserved self-contained work of al-Jūzajānī, the compilations that I studied in chapter 3 were thematic chapters in larger multi-themed *ḥadīth* compilations. These chapters displayed very little internal ordering and recorded numerous *ḥadīth*s without sub-categorizing them by theme or chronology. Written in the late fourth/tenth and early fifth/eleventh centuries, the independent works of al-Khargūshī, Abū Nuʿaym al-Iṣfahānī, and al-Bayhaqī are marked by a much larger scope, more coherent structural organization, greater methodological leniency, and a mostly consistent systematization of materials that previously circulated in earlier *dalāʾil al-nubūwa* chapters and *sīra/maghāzī* literature. Unlike earlier contributors to this literature, all three authors were Shāfiʿī in law and Ashʿarī in theology, which their works reflect to varying degrees.

1 Al-Khargūshī's *Sharaf al-nabī*

Al-Khargūshī's *Sharaf al-nabī* is an extensive and self-contained work that covers more than 700 pages in its printed edition, and thus considerably exceeds earlier works in size. It is structured as a compendium of select aspects of Muḥammad's genealogy, biography, physical appearance, relationships, virtues, and characteristics, interspersed with inventories of his possessions and descriptions of his environment. As such it differs considerably in structure and content from the thematic chapters in *ḥadīth* compilations, as well as from Ibn Saʿd's thematic chapters in his comprehensive biography. Furthermore, there are questions concerning whether this work actually constitutes a collection of the signs of prophecy in the narrower sense. Al-Khargūshī is listed as an author of a work entitled *dalāʾil al-nubūwa*, but there is some uncertainty regarding the specific content of this work. Kātib Çelebī[1] and al-Dhahabī[2] mention a *dalāʾil al-nubūwa* by al-Khargūshī, which might be an extract of al-Khargūshī's

1 Kātib Çelebī/Ḥājjī Khalīfa, *Kashf al-ẓunūn*, 1045, 1047, 1569.
2 Al-Dhahabī, *Siyār aʿlām al-nubulāʾ*, 17:256.

 | DOI:10.1163/9789004687349_008

extant prophetic biography, *Sharaf al-Muṣṭafā*.[3] Brockelmann identified *Sharaf al-Muṣṭafā* with *dalāʾil al-nubūwa* literature and Storey also mentions an extant Persian translation with the alternative title of *Dalāʾil al-nubūwa*. Melchert suggested that Storey could be referring to a Persian abridgment. Finally, Kātib Çelebī listed a work under *Sharaf al-nubūwa*, and Melchert suggested that it might be an Arabic abridgment of *Sharaf al-Muṣṭafā*.[4] An existing Persian translation of the book has been published with yet another title, *Sharaf al-nabī*,[5] which is used throughout this study. It remains unclear how many versions, translations, or abridgments can be traced back to the author himself, how they relate to one another, and which, if any of them, were originally entitled *Dalāʾil al-nubūwa*. Nevertheless, *Sharaf al-nabī* is included in this study because it contains a number of narratives found in previous *dalāʾil al-nubūwa* compilations clustered together in one chapter; this provides valuable insight into the integration of the theme into theological discourses.

The chapter that overlaps most with the narratives found in previous "signs of prophecy" compilations is dedicated to miracles.[6] It is noteworthy that al-Khargūshī specifically employs the term "miracle" (*muʿjiza*) in the title of this chapter, which demonstrates that he deliberately distinguished the accounts gathered here from "ordinary" events in Muḥammad's life, though he does not provide a detailed definition of what constitutes a miracle in his view. The only exception to his silence on the theological discourses regarding miracles is one account that calls the Qurʾān the most glorious of all signs (*ʿalāmāt*).[7] This statement is in line with the contemporary theological position of the Qurʾān as a miracle of the Prophet Muḥammad but al-Khargūshī does not enter further into the theological arguments. His notion of prophetic miracles must be drawn from his selection of narratives subsumed under this chapter.

The chapter contains seventy-four accounts of varying lengths; these are only very roughly organized by theme. Like most of the earlier *dalāʾil al-nubūwa* authors, al-Khargūshī only includes narratives that are set in Muḥammad's adult life following his call to prophecy.[8] The miracles may be broadly sub-divided

---

3 *Sharaf al-Muṣṭafā* has recently been published as al-Khargūshī, *Manāḥil al-shifāʾ*. A 1967 Egyptian edition of the *Dalāʾil al-nubūwa* is mentioned by ʿIrāqī and Pūrjavādī, "Abū Saʿd-i Khargūshī-yi Nīshābūrī," 19f.

4 Cf. Kātib Çelebī/Ḥājjī Khalīfa, *Kashf al-ẓunūn*, 1045, 1047, 1569; al-Dhahabī, *Siyār aʿlām al-nubulāʾ*, 17:256; Storey, *Persian Literature*, 1:175f.; Brockelmann, *GAL*, Suppl. 1:361, no. 3; Melchert, "Khargūshī," 31.

5 Al-Khargūshī, *Sharaf al-nabī*.

6 Al-Khargūshī, *Sharaf al-nabī*, 150–181.

7 Al-Khargūshī, *Sharaf al-nabī*, 162.

8 Given the author's incoherent ordering system, miracles of the Prophet's birth and childhood may be compiled in a different chapter.

into food- and water-related miracles, divine protection of the Prophet against enemies, natural phenomena, speaking animals testifying to his prophecy, and conversion miracles. Many accounts are already found in previous compilations; these include Muḥammad's encounter with Umm Maʿbad and her barren sheep that provide milk for the Prophet,[9] trees and stones extending their greetings to Muḥammad,[10] trees relocating at his order,[11] various food- and water-related miracles,[12] a roasted goat that warns the Prophet that its meat has been poisoned,[13] a speaking wolf attesting to his prophecy,[14] voices announcing him from inside a sacrifice animal,[15] the account of Surāqa and his horse,[16] and a cloud shading the Prophet.[17]

While these narratives were already part of an established scholarly discourse on the signs of prophecy, al-Khargūshī's chapter also contains a number of narratives that are well-known from "unauthenticated" traditions, such as the account of the cobweb concealing the entrance of the cave where the Prophet and Abū Bakr hid during the *hijra*,[18] or the Prophet sprinkling dust on the heads of the Quraysh while lying in ambush outside his house.[19] These accounts were already included in the biographical reports of Wahb b. Munabbih,[20] Ibn Isḥāq[21] and Ibn Saʿd.[22] By including these accounts, al-Khargūshī treats his sources with much greater leniency than his predecessors, who only selected materials that were accepted by *ḥadīth* specialists (*muḥaddithūn*). This was not just true for authors whose main field of engagement was *ḥadīth* in the narrower sense. As I have shown in chapter 3, Ibn Saʿd utilized unauthenticated sources in the *sīra* section of his *Ṭabaqāt*, he upheld

9 Al-Khargūshī, *Sharaf al-nabī*, 151–153.
10 Al-Khargūshī, *Sharaf al-nabī*, 153.
11 Al-Khargūshī, *Sharaf al-nabī*, 155f.
12 Al-Khargūshī, *Sharaf al-nabī*, 157f.
13 Al-Khargūshī, *Sharaf al-nabī*, 156f.
14 Al-Khargūshī, *Sharaf al-nabī*, 157.
15 Al-Khargūshī, *Sharaf al-nabī*, 165.
16 Al-Khargūshī, *Sharaf al-nabī*, 153f.
17 Al-Khargūshī, *Sharaf al-nabī*, 165.
18 Al-Khargūshī, *Sharaf al-nabī*, 154.
19 Al-Khargūshī, *Sharaf al-nabī*, 175f. The theme of the Prophet throwing dust or soil also occurs in an account of the battle of Badr in which the Muslim army was vastly outnumbered. The Prophet threw soil at the opposing army; this incapacitated them and led to the Muslims' victory; al-Khargūshī, *Sharaf al-nabī*, 159f. In Qurʾānic exegesis, this episode from the battle of Badr is commonly associated with the verse 8:17.
20 Khoury, *Wahb b. Munabbih*, 1:140f.
21 Ibn Isḥāq, *The Life of Muhammad*, 222f.
22 Ibn Saʿd, *Ṭabaqāt*, 1:195.

stricter requirements in his thematic chapters, and did not include these kinds of sources in his chapters on the "signs of prophecy."

In addition to well-known narratives from the *dalāʾil al-nubūwa* compilations and unauthenticated sources, al-Khargūshī's chapter also contains a number of completely "new" accounts. For example, when a Bedouin asked for proof of the veracity of Muḥammad's prophetic mission, we encounter a lizard who testifies to it.[23] There are also narratives of speaking camels, one testifying to Muḥammad's prophethood in a context similar to that of the lizard, the other seeking refuge with the Prophet from its owners who want to slaughter it and the Prophet asking the owners to spare it.[24] In another account, a lion takes it upon himself to fulfill the Prophet's curse of Abū Lahab's son, ʿUtba, who was Muḥammad's son-in-law. The Prophet cursed him, saying: "O God, send after him a dog among your dogs!" after Abū Lahab ordered his son to divorce Muḥammad's daughter. One night, when ʿUtba was traveling with a trade caravan in Syria, they heard a lion. ʿUtba's companions reassured him that he would be safe in the crowd but he countered that the Prophet had cursed him and that his predictions always come true. At night the lion found ʿUtba in the midst of the men and camels and dragged him away by his head, without anyone hearing his screams.[25]

A number of accounts in al-Khargūshī's chapter focus on the physical transformation of humans and animals. In one account, ʿUmar sent some men to get water on behalf of the Prophet. They came across a black slave with full water skins and asked him to come to the Prophet. The slave does not believe in his mission until Muḥammad rubbed the slave's face with his hand and it became white. The slave returned to his people, told them the story, and they accepted Islam.[26] In another account, a woman took her child to the Prophet and asked him to touch his child's bald head so that hair may grow. The Prophet ran his hands across the child's head and hair appeared immediately. A remark is interpolated that this kind of hair became characteristic of the people of Yamāma ever since. Al-Khargūshī then presents the notion that this miracle is evidence of Muḥammad's genuine prophetic mission. He then juxtaposes it to a similar request that was asked of Musaylima, a man known in Muslim tradition as a false prophet. According to al-Khargūshī's account, Musaylima ran his hand across a child's head and it lost the little hair it had. The child's progeny is

23 Ibn Saʿd, *Ṭabaqāt*, 1:162–164.

24 Ibn Saʿd, *Ṭabaqāt*, 1:164f.; the latter account is similar to one found in Ibn Saʿd; cf., Ibn Saʿd, *Ṭabaqāt*, 1:157.

25 Ibn Saʿd, *Ṭabaqāt*, 1:170f.

26 Ibn Saʿd, *Ṭabaqāt*, 1:167.

said to have been bald ever since.[27] Another account relates that the people of ʿAbd al-Qays brought a sheep to Muḥammad and asked him to produce some form of sign that would prove his prophetic mission. The Prophet inserted his finger into the sheep's ears and they turned white. The account concludes, stating that, until today, white ears distinguish the sheep of this group.[28]

The narratives that largely shaped al-Khargūshī's notion of prophetic miracles concur with those found in previous *dalāʾil al-nubūwa* compilations. This appears to be a paradigm shift from most previous compilations, in which these narratives served as evidence of Muḥammad's prophetic mission more generally, but were not yet specifically defined or framed as miracles. Al-Khargūshī adopted rudimentary theological notions and subsumed many of these narratives under the chapter's title of miracles. However, his selection of narratives and, by extension, his notion of miracles does not entirely overlap with the narratives of previous compilations because al-Khargūshī added new material. At the same time, the framework of *dalāʾil al-nubūwa* literature was also drastically expanded to include biographical and historical information, the virtues and traits of his character, genealogy and relationships, as well as the inventories of his possessions and descriptions of his environment. This new structural framework was mostly crafted from accounts and narratives that were well-established in the prophetic biographical tradition and in unauthenticated materials. The arrangement as a compendium, however, is original in nature.

2 Abū Nuʿaym al-Iṣfahānī's *Dalāʾil al-nubūwa*

Abū Nuʿaym al-Iṣfahānī's *Dalāʾil al-nubūwa* is one of the most well-known works of this kind and has been printed in various editions. In contrast to al-Khargūshī, Abū Nuʿaym al-Iṣfahānī was a prominent and respected scholar of *ḥadīth* who had studied with several earlier authors of *dalāʾil al-nubūwa* works, such as al-Ṭabarānī (d. 360/971), Ibn Mandah (d. 395/1005), and possibly Abū l-Shaykh al-Iṣfahānī (d. 368/979). The extant text of Abū Nuʿaym's *Dalāʾil al-nubūwa* is most likely an abridgment of a longer original work.[29]

27 Ibn Saʿd, *Ṭabaqāt*, 1:159.

28 Ibn Saʿd, *Ṭabaqāt*, 1:159.

29 Three manuscripts have been preserved. Two of these contain abridgments of the original works, cf. no. 2246, Khan Bahadur Khuda Library in Patna, India; no. 510 of the Staatsbibliothek in Berlin. The third contains the first part of the original work, cf. no. 613 of the Dār al-Kutub al-Miṣriyya, Cairo; cf. al-Iṣfahānī, *Dalāʾil al-nubūwa*, ed. ʿAbbās and Qalʿajī, 20f. The manuscript encompasses the first thirteen of a total of thirty-five

Abū Nuʿaym's *Dalāʾil al-nubūwa* differs considerably from previous works with regard to its arrangement, content, and sources. The work covers the entire span of the Prophet's life, but it does not constitute a comprehensive *sīra*, as those aspects irrelevant to his notion of the "proofs of prophecy" are omitted. The raids, for instance, are not covered independently, but only mentioned with regard to proofs or signs of prophecy that manifested themselves in their historical context. I have shown in chapter 3 that Abū Nuʿaym intentionally broadened his pool of sources to include both well-known *ḥadīth* transmitters and less authenticated sources. Furthermore, Abū Nuʿaym's accounts frequently contain poetry like that included in early *sīra* works.

In contrast to previous *dalāʾil al-nubūwa* compilations, which listed *ḥadīth* without any apparent thematic order, Abū Nuʿaym arranged his accounts systematically into thematic chapters and sub-chapters with individual titles, and occasionally introduced chapters with a theological contextualization of the subsequent accounts or—more commonly—historical contextualization or summaries of related events.[30] His work is arranged in a mostly chronological form and is divided into two parts, which each display distinct presentational arrangements. In the first part, the biographical material of Muḥammad's life up to his emigration to Medina is arranged chronologically, the materials are presented teleologically to emphasize that Muḥammad was prepared early in life for his future prophetic mission. Events begin before the Prophet's birth, with one chapter containing numerous accounts of Jewish and Christian learned men aware of the coming of the Prophet based on their own scriptures,[31] another containing the reaction of soothsayers and "kings of the earth,"[32] what was heard from the *jinn*, and from within idols and from soothsayers;[33] it then proceeds to the marriage of the Prophet's parents,[34] and his mother's pregnancy.[35] A lengthy chapter covers key moments of the Prophet's youth, and as the chapter's title already indicates, one of Abū Nuʿaym's main intentions in his portrayal of Muḥammad's early life was to argue that these early years constituted the foundation for and prediction of his prophetic

chapters that are recorded on 203 folia. All references to al-Iṣfahānī's *Dalāʾil al-nubūwa* in this book refer to the work edited by al-Mājdī.

30 For instance, al-Iṣfahānī, *Dalāʾil al-nubūwa*, 134, 157, 241, 279, 321, 333.

31 Al-Iṣfahānī, *Dalāʾil al-nubūwa*, 35–50.

32 Al-Iṣfahānī, *Dalāʾil al-nubūwa*, 51–58.

33 Al-Iṣfahānī, *Dalāʾil al-nubūwa*, 59–72.

34 Al-Iṣfahānī, *Dalāʾil al-nubūwa*, 73–75.

35 Al-Iṣfahānī, *Dalāʾil al-nubūwa*, 76–80.

mission.[36] As such, we find the well-known account of his impoverished wet nurse Ḥalīma, who took in the orphaned Muḥammad as a foster child despite little prospect of compensation for her services, only to receive rich blessings during the Prophet's stay with her family.[37] In a new account Ḥalīma and the toddler Muḥammad encounter an Ethiopian man who studied the child's mole between his shoulder blades and identified him as a future prophet.[38] This new element is woven seamlessly into the common childhood narrative of Ḥalīma taking the young Muḥammad to a soothsayer, who also recognized the signs of a future prophet and called on his people to kill the child. Other well-known aspects of Muḥammad's childhood, such as the cleansing of his heart, are also interspersed with accounts of encounters in which the prophetic mission is anticipated. For example, an account that was already part of Ibn Saʿd's chapter relates that the young Muḥammad sat on his grandfather's cushion and his uncles attempted to remove him; however, ʿAbd al-Muṭṭalib ordered them to let him sit there so he can become accustomed to rule.[39] Two new accounts follow in which ʿAbd al-Muṭṭalib's interlocutors, a bishop he had befriended and a Jewish travel companion, respectively, see the prophetic future of his grandson.[40]

Following a brief chapter on the characteristics and physical appearance of the Prophet, Abū Nuʿaym portrays Muḥammad as having been "protected from venerating pagan deities, and protected from the ruses of *jinn* and men."[41] This chapter sets out with the famous account from Ibn Isḥāq in which the Prophet was tending sheep at night with a friend when they heard music from a wedding celebration. The young Muḥammad asked his companion to watch the sheep for him as he wanted to attend the festivities. But as soon as he came close, deep sleep overcame him even before he reached the premises and he woke only after the celebrations had ended. The following night he attempted to attend another wedding, but he fell asleep again and the account ends with Muḥammad stating that from that night onward he was never interested or engaged in any pre-Islamic practices or customs ever again.[42] Subsequent

36 The chapter's title is "About his development, behavior, and states until God bestowed upon him the revelation and established for him the foundation for prophecy and paved the path to messengership, and what became apparent to his people from his perfecting of excellent characteristics, and their recognition of him through what was made a proof for those who refrained from subjugation to him …"; al-Iṣfahānī, *Dalāʾil al-nubūwa*, 87.

37 Al-Iṣfahānī, *Dalāʾil al-nubūwa*, 89f.

38 Al-Iṣfahānī, *Dalāʾil al-nubūwa*, 91.

39 Al-Iṣfahānī, *Dalāʾil al-nubūwa*, 94; cf. Ibn Saʿd, *Ṭabaqāt*, 127.

40 Al-Iṣfahānī, *Dalāʾil al-nubūwa*, 94.

41 Al-Iṣfahānī, *Dalāʾil al-nubūwa*, 107–123.

42 Al-Iṣfahānī, *Dalāʾil al-nubūwa*, 107f.

accounts relate Muḥammad's failed attempts to attend gatherings around the idols, and how God protected him from several assaults Iblīs had plotted against him,[43] and that he was informed by a dead goat that a Jewish woman had attempted to poison him with its meat.[44]

Finally, Abū Nuʿaym's intention of presenting Muḥammad's early life as preparation for his prophecy continues in his chapter on the beginning of the revelation, in which accounts about the events of the first revelation are followed by others about the cleansing of the Prophet's heart.[45] These latter accounts are clearly set in Muḥammad's childhood and thus break the chronology. Furthermore, the narratives of the cleansing of his heart are emphasized here in connection with the revelation more than in their earlier chronological appearance. The chronological occurrence only includes one brief account of this incident, while the chapter on the revelation contains one longer account that presents the general outline of the Prophet's encounter with the angels who purify his heart, another one in which the two angels weigh him against his community to find that he outweighs them, and finally a third account that returns to the heart's cleansing and specifies that the angels removed "Satan's share" from the Prophet's heart. The chapter continues with the revelation itself and closes with the reactions of Satan and the *jinn*. The latter theme is elaborated in several accounts that echo some of Ibn Saʿd's accounts of the devil identifying the location of the new revelation by sniffing soil that the *jinn* bring to him, or accounts in which the *jinn* were chased away by shooting stars from overhearing the divine discourses.[46] I have previously identified this last theme as a Qurʾānic narrative. It is particularly interesting that Abū Nuʿaym, who links numerous accounts to relevant Qurʾānic verses, does not quote the related verses with this account.

Abū Nuʿaym dedicates the two final chapters of the first part of his work to the Qurʾān, the inimitable quality of its language, and how just listening to it compelled several individuals, such as Abū Dharr al-Ghifārī, ʿUmar b. ʿAbasa al-Sulamī, and Salmān al-Fārisī, to convert.[47] Other accounts tell of encounters between the Prophet and the *mushrikūn* who demanded signs, including the splitting of the moon;[48] this was not mentioned in any previous compilation, despite the fact that it appears in the Qurʾān. The first part of Abū Nuʿaym's *Dalāʾil al-nubūwa*, therefore, positions key elements of the prophetic biography

43 Al-Iṣfahānī, *Dalāʾil al-nubūwa*, 108–111.
44 Al-Iṣfahānī, *Dalāʾil al-nubūwa*, 114.
45 Al-Iṣfahānī, *Dalāʾil al-nubūwa*, 128f.
46 Al-Iṣfahānī, *Dalāʾil al-nubūwa*, 132f.
47 Al-Iṣfahānī, *Dalāʾil al-nubūwa*, 134–156.
48 Al-Iṣfahānī, *Dalāʾil al-nubūwa*, 157–187.

in such a way to make the theological or doctrinal points that Muḥammad's future prophetic mission was not only destined and known but that he had been prepared for that role.

The ordering principle of the second part of Abū Nuʿaym's work is very different from the first chronologically arranged part, as it mostly systematizes many of the narratives that were already part of earlier *dalāʾil al-nubūwa* works. He begins this part with a chapter on the signs of prophecy that became apparent during the *hijra*; it contains accounts of Muḥammad and Abū Bakr hiding in a cave while God places pigeons in the entrance of the cave; the Prophet's encounter with the young Ibn Masʿūd, who tends barren sheep that the Prophet nevertheless milks successfully; the account of Muḥammad's encounter with Surāqa; and accounts of his correspondence to the Byzantine emperor and the Persian ruler, and the reactions of several foreign delegations to Muḥammad's message.[49] The remainder of the second part of Abū Nuʿaym's *Dalāʾil al-nubūwa* systematically reworks well-known themes, such as interactions with animals,[50] the prostration and relocation of trees,[51] the wailing of the palm tree trunk during the Prophet's sermon (*khuṭba*),[52] water coming forth from his fingers,[53] or the increase of food in his presence.[54] While most of these chapters include the same or similar accounts as preceding works, the chapter dedicated to animals only shares the broader theme of animals showcasing Muḥammad's prophetic mission, but does not share specific accounts with previous works. This chapter includes the account of a wolf that approaches a shepherd and informs him about the Muḥammad's prophetic mission;[55] other accounts, such as a camel seeking the Prophet's protection because its owner intends to slaughter it,[56] are missing. However, a similar theme is found in an account in which the Prophet passes the hiding place of hunters and the gazelle they are ambushing. The gazelle tells the Prophet that she has two young fawns that depend on her milk for their lives. The Prophet asks her if she would return to the hunters if they let her feed her young first and the gazelle agrees. When the gazelle finally returns to them, the hunters, touched by her obedience to the Prophet, leave her to him. Muḥammad then

49 Al-Iṣfahānī, *Dalāʾil al-nubūwa*, 188–221.
50 Al-Iṣfahānī, *Dalāʾil al-nubūwa*, 222–230.
51 Al-Iṣfahānī, *Dalāʾil al-nubūwa*, 231–236.
52 Al-Iṣfahānī, *Dalāʾil al-nubūwa*, 237–240.
53 Al-Iṣfahānī, *Dalāʾil al-nubūwa*, 241–246.
54 Al-Iṣfahānī, *Dalāʾil al-nubūwa*, 247–256.
55 al-Iṣfahānī, *Dalāʾil al-nubūwa*, 222f.; cf. Ibn Saʿd, *Ṭabaqāt*, 157.
56 Ibn Saʿd, *Ṭabaqāt*, 146.

sets her free.[57] One account that is found in al-Khargūshī but not in previous works involves a lizard that testifies to Muḥammad's prophecy. In this account a man who was carrying a lizard in his bag of provisions meets the Prophet and states that he does not believe in his message. When the Prophet asks what would convince him of the veracity of his message, he says that only his lizard's testimony could convince him. Upon the Prophet's request, the lizard then testifies to his belief in the Prophet's message, and the man converts to Islam.[58] In other accounts, camels and sheep prostrate themselves in front of the Prophet.[59]

On one hand, Abū Nuʿaym's *Dalāʾil al-nubūwa* is predominantly marked by the systematization of materials that were already well established in the literary themes of *dalāʾil al-nubūwa*. This is particularly the case in the second part of his work, in which he systematically rearranges earlier materials into a coherent thematic structure. On the other hand, he significantly expands the teleological portrayal of Muḥammad's life to include the period prior to the first revelations. Thus, Abū Nuʿaym aims at presenting manifestations of Muḥammad's prophecy throughout his life. The incorporation of accounts from Muḥammad's life prior to his call to prophecy is not entirely new, as Ibn Saʿd had dedicated an entire chapter to this subject. But Abū Nuʿaym's incorporation and systematization of this material enabled him to present the notion that Muḥammad was destined to become a prophet.

3 Al-Bayhaqī's *Dalāʾil al-nubūwa*

In many ways, Abū Bakr Aḥmad al-Bayhaqī's work follows a similar trajectory of systematizing previously used narratives, though he extends the scope even further. Comprising seven volumes in its printed edition, al-Bayhaqī's *Dalāʾil al-nubūwa* is the most extensive work of this kind so far, and the first comprehensive biography that is dedicated to the theme of the "proofs of prophecy." As such, we find a combination of biographical information in line with *sīra* literature and specific teleological portrayals of Muḥammad's life. The first volume, for instance, provides mostly chronologically arranged accounts dedicated to the Prophet's birth and infancy, lineage, and physical appearance. The first part of the second volume returns to the birth and infancy narratives, but focuses on Muḥammad's spiritual preparation for his future prophetic mission. It

57 Al-Iṣfahānī, *Dalāʾil al-nubūwa*, 223f.
58 Al-Iṣfahānī, *Dalāʾil al-nubūwa*, 225f.
59 Al-Iṣfahānī, *Dalāʾil al-nubūwa*, 226f.

covers the cleansing of Muḥammad's heart and the removal of "Satan's share"; his encounter with the monk Baḥīrā, who recognizes the signs of prophecy; and God's protection (*ʿiṣma*) of Muḥammad from pagan practices. The second part of the second volume continues the chronological biography and covers Muḥammad's call to prophecy, his life in Mecca, the *hijra*, and the early years in Medina, as well as many conversion stories. Volumes three, four, and five treat the Muslim conquests and raids, combining historical information on dates and participants with detailed accounts of incidents and miraculous events. In volume six, al-Bayhaqī departs from the chronological arrangement to study miracles and signs that have occurred thus far, and the seventh volume covers Muḥammad's final illness and his passing.

Examining the material al-Bayhaqī included in his *Dalāʾil al-nubūwa*, we find material cited in previous *dalāʾil al-nubūwa* compilations. Like most of the earlier authors, al-Bayhaqī includes the several accounts of water miracles in Ḥudaybiyya.[60] Furthermore, al-Bayhaqī incorporated accounts of several natural phenomena, such as trees and stones greeting the Prophet or relocating upon his request[61] and the yearning of the palm tree trunk that the Prophet had used as an interim *minbar*,[62] that were also commonly included in other *dalāʾil al-nubūwa* compilations. We also find the account of Qatāda b. al-Nuʿmān's eye in the context of the battle of Uḥud,[63] which was incorporated in the earliest thematic chapter on the "proofs of prophecy" by Maʿmar b. Rāshid and Ibn Saʿd.[64] The account relates that Qatāda's eye was severely injured during the battle and he came to the Prophet with his eyeball outside its socket. The Prophet placed the eye back in its natural position and he was able to see even better with it than with his uninjured eye. A *ḥadīth* about a sheep that mysteriously disappeared after being milked to feed several hundred men[65] is also found in Ibn Saʿd[66] and al-Jūzajānī.[67] Finally, al-Bayhaqī also includes the accounts of Miqdād and his encounter with the devil who tempted him

---

60 Al-Bayhaqī, *Dalāʾil al-nubūwa*, 4:115–128; cf. ʿAbd al-Razzāq, *al-Muṣannaf*, 11:276–280; Ibn Saʿd, *Ṭabaqāt*, 1:150f.; al-Bukhārī, *Ṣaḥīḥ*, 4:466–472; al-Tirmidhī, *Sunan*, 193f.

61 Al-Bayhaqī, *Dalāʾil al-nubūwa*, 6:7–27; cf. Ibn Saʿd, *Ṭabaqāt*, 1:132, 1:143f., al-Tirmidhī, *Sunan*, 193f.; al-Khargūshī, *Sharaf al-nabī*, 155f.; al-Iṣfahānī, *Dalāʾil al-nubūwa*, 231–236.

62 Al-Bayhaqī, *Dalāʾil al-nubūwa*, 6:66; cf. Ibn Saʿd, *Ṭabaqāt*, 1:159; al-Bukhārī, *Ṣaḥīḥ*, 4:475f.; al-Tirmidhī, *Sunan*, 192; al-Iṣfahānī, *Dalāʾil al-nubūwa*, 237–240.

63 Al-Bayhaqī, *Dalāʾil al-nubūwa*, 3:251f. In one of these accounts, al-Bayhaqī points out that it has also been transmitted in the context of the battle of Badr.

64 Ibn Saʿd, *Ṭabaqāt*, 1:157.

65 Al-Bayhaqī, *Dalāʾil al-nubūwa*, 137f.

66 Ibn Saʿd, *Ṭabaqāt*, 1:151.

67 Al-Jūzajānī, *Amārāt al-nubūwa*, fol. 163a, line 3 to fol. 163b, line 18.

to drink the Prophet's milk[68] and the wolf who informed a shepherd about Muḥammad's prophetic mission.[69]

In addition to material that was long established as part of *dalāʾil al-nubūwa* collections, al-Bayhaqī also includes material that only appears in his own generation of *dalāʾil* authors; this includes the account of a lizard testifying that Muḥammad is the Messenger of God in order to convince a Bedouin,[70] which is shared with al-Khargūshī[71] and Abū Nuʿaym,[72] but absent from the previous compilations. Finally, al-Bayhaqī also includes some material that was not part of the earlier collections. He records several accounts of a man who is stranded on an island with a lion. The lion approaches to attack him, but instead becomes his trusted companion when the man tells him that he is on a mission for the Prophet.[73] Another account relates that a newborn child uttered the testimony of faith (*shahāda*) in order to convince a pagan of the veracity of Muḥammad's prophetic mission.[74]

Al-Bayhaqī's intellectual background as a scholar of *ḥadīth* and Shāfiʿī law, and follower of Ashʿarī theology[75] are apparent in his voluminous work. Like Abū Nuʿaym, he built on an established corpus of *ḥadīth* and biographical materials, which he then systematically rearranged. He justified his broader pool of sources in an extensive review of al-Shāfiʿī's thoughts on the permissibility of various sources based on their respective application and purpose, then argues for the legitimacy of including less authenticated sources. The originality of this extensive work lies in its structural rearrangement of mostly known materials into an extensive *sīra*. The heuristic framework of establishing proofs for Muḥammad's prophetic mission is, at times, diluted in the process.

4 Theology in Later *Dalāʾil al-Nubūwa* Works

Theological concepts were gradually integrated into *dalāʾil al-nubūwa* literature starting around the fourth/tenth century. Most of the earliest authors were scholars who frequently rejected the very notion of theology as a means

68 Al-Bayhaqī, *Dalāʾil al-nubūwa*, 6:85f.; cf. Ibn Saʿd, *Ṭabaqāt*, 1:154f.

69 Al-Bayhaqī, *Dalāʾil al-nubūwa*, 6:39; cf. Ibn Saʿd, *Ṭabaqāt*, 1:146f.; al-Khargūshī, *Sharaf al-nabī*, 157f., al-Iṣfahānī, *Dalāʾil al-nubūwa*, 222f.

70 Al-Bayhaqī, *Dalāʾil al-nubūwa*, 6:36f.

71 Al-Khargūshī, *Sharaf al-nabī*, 162–164.

72 Al-Iṣfahānī, *Dalāʾil al-nubūwa*, 225f.

73 Al-Bayhaqī, *Dalāʾil al-nubūwa*, 6:45f.

74 Al-Bayhaqī, *Dalāʾil al-nubūwa*, 6:59f.

75 Al-Subkī, *Ṭabaqāt al-Shāfiʿiyya al-kubrā*, 3:9.

to derive religious knowledge. Their collections of proofs of prophecy reflected this, in that they simply placed several *ḥadīth* together without providing any theological or doctrinal framework. Al-Khargūshī, Abū Nuʿaym, and al-Bayhaqī, by contrast, followed Ashʿarī theology and its influence can be seen throughout their works. Al-Khargūshī's incorporation of theological concepts is mainly restricted to the deliberate use of the term "miracles" in a chapter heading; that is, he indicates a categorical distinction between "miraculous" and "ordinary" events in Muḥammad's life. In addition, he refers to the Qurʾān as the most important miracle in Islam. Abū Nuʿaym and al-Bayhaqī, by contrast, extensively incorporate theological concepts in crafting a narrative of Muḥammad's life that serves, in its entirety, as evidence of his prophetic mission.

4.1 *Theology in Abū Nuʿaym al-Iṣfahānī's* Dalāʾil al-Nubūwa

Abū Nuʿaym displays his familiarity with Ashaʿrī theology throughout his work. In the preface, he addresses a potentially fictive interlocutor who allegedly asked the author to gather "all circulating traditions, proofs (*dalāʾil*), miracles (*muʿjizāt*), truths (*ḥaqāʾiq*), and particularities (*khaṣāʾiṣ*) of prophecy."[76] Thus, Abū Nuʿaym categorizes the accounts contained in his work according to specific theological notions, including that of miracles. He does not define miracles, but the categorization in itself is significant. First, it sets his work apart from the works of his predecessors who placed all the accounts together, without distinguishing between "miraculous" and ordinary or natural events. At the same time, his listing of "miracles" and "proofs of prophecy" as separate categories indicates that these were not to be considered synonymous, as some twentieth-century Western scholars hold. Rather, the miracles constitute a subtype of proofs of prophecy.

Beyond acknowledging miracles as a theological concept, Abū Nuʿaym establishes a hierarchy, ranking Muḥammad's miracles in relation to one another and in relation to those of other prophets. In the introduction, Abū Nuʿaym states that the Qurʾān is the greatest of all prophetic miracles, the "mother of miracles, which denial and ignorance cannot refute."[77] Introducing a later chapter, he extends this hierarchy of miracles beyond the ones Muḥammad received.

> God Almighty supported Muḥammad with what he had not supported any one of the two worlds, and He distinguished him with what surpassed the boundaries of the miracles (*karamāt*) of the prophets and the

76 Al-Iṣfahānī, *Dalāʾil al-nubūwa*, 11.

77 Al-Iṣfahānī, *Dalāʾil al-nubūwa*, 15.

> stations of the *awliyāʾ* [saints] for the signs of prophecy are in accordance with his [i.e., the Prophet's] station and position with God. There is no sign (*āyā*) and no indicator (*ʿalāma*) more exceptional and more marvelous than the signs of Muḥammad, and that is the eloquent Qurʾān[78]

Abū Nuʿaym corroborates this point with the incident in which the Meccans challenged the divine origin of the Qurʾān by claiming that they could match it. Abū Nuʿaym continues to state that they fell short in soundness (*faṣāḥa*) and expression (*lisān*), in eloquence (*balāgha*), and explanation (*bayān*).[79] Abū Nuʿaym then quotes one of the famous "challenge" (*taḥaddī*) verses in which God challenges those denying Muḥammad's prophetic mission: "Say: 'Were men and *jinn* to band together in order to come up with the like of this Qurʾān, they will never come up with the like of it, even if they back up one another.'"[80] Thus, Abū Nuʿaym adopts the theological position held by both Muʿtazilī and Ashaʿrī theologians, which identifies the Qurʾān as Muḥammad's primary miracle. More specifically, he shows that he was familiar with the literary approach to the doctrine of the inimitability of the Qurʾān (*iʿjāz al-Qurʾān*), which Muʿtazilī scholars like al-Jāḥiẓ (d. 255/868–869), ʿAlī b. ʿĪsā l-Rummānī (d. 384/994), or Ḥamd b. Muḥammad al-Khaṭṭābī (d. ca. 386/996) and Ashaʿrī theologians like Abū Bakr Muḥammad al-Bāqillānī (d. 403/1013), or ʿAbd al-Qāhir al-Jurjānī (d. 470/1078) had set forth.[81]

In addition to ranking Muḥammad's miracles, Abū Nuʿaym also juxtaposes those miracles ascribed to Muḥammad in extra-Qurʾānic sources with those of preceding prophets. In the introduction to the chapter on accounts of water gushing forth from the Prophet's hands, Abū Nuʿaym notes the similarity of this miracle to that of Moses, in which he caused water to come forth from a stone,

---

78 Al-Iṣfahānī, *Dalāʾil al-nubūwa*, 134.

79 Al-Iṣfahānī, *Dalāʾil al-nubūwa*, 134.

80 Q. 17:88.

81 While these scholars differed on the specific aspects of the Qurʾānic language that rendered it inimitable, they collectively rejected the notion of some Muʿtazilī scholars, like al-Naẓẓām (d. ca. 230/845), who held that the Qurʾān per se was not inimitable. Rather, al-Naẓẓām understood that the inimitability of the Qurʾān was because it was a divine intervention, and thus humans were incapable of producing any literary work of equal eloquence. This theory of *ṣarfa* found some acceptance in the fourth/tenth century among some of the *mutakallimūn* of the Baghdad branch of the Muʿtazila, and among some Imāmī Shīʿa. Al-Naẓẓām's doctrine of the Qurʾānic inimitability based on divine intervention (*ṣarfa*) was refuted most prominently by his one-time student in Basra, ʿAmr b. Baḥr al-Jāḥiẓ (d. 255/868 or 869); as well as Abū Hāshim (d. 321/933), his contemporary and founder of the Ashʿarī school of *kalām*; and Abū l-Ḥasan al-Ashʿarī; and eventually by the majority of Sunnī Muslims in the centuries to come.

but at the same time, Abū Nuʿaym argues for the superiority of Muḥammad's miracle.

> This sign is among the most wondrous of [Muḥammad's] signs, the most splendid miracle and the most effectual proof (*dalāʾil*), similar to the proof of Moses in his bringing forth water from a rock by tapping it with his cane. However, this is a more effectual wondrous act, since bringing forth water from flesh and bones is more wondrous and greater than its coming forth from a rock, because the rock is the root of the water's root [as is] well-known and commonly mentioned. But in the past, it has never been related nor heard of for water to come forth from a human being.[82]

Abū Nuʿaym's intention in writing his *Dalāʾil al-nubūwa*, therefore, appears to go beyond establishing the veracity of Muḥammad's prophetic mission; he also sought to prove Muḥammad's superiority over previous prophets based on their miracles.

Abū Nuʿaym invoked another theological concept, namely, that of the divine protection of the Prophet. One sub-chapter is entitled "ʿIṣma Allāhi rasūlahi ḥayna taʿāqad al-mushrikūn ʿala qatlihi" (God's protection (*ʿiṣma*) of His messenger when the *mushrikūn* agreed to kill him). The term used for protection here is *ʿiṣma*, which was further developed by the fourteen Shīʿī imāms to denote the theological concept of infallibility, but which also applies (in various degrees) to the Prophet in Sunnī theology. Abū Nuʿaym's selection of accounts in this sub-section indicates that he considered *ʿiṣma* to be only a form of divine protection from physical harm. He lists two accounts of a poisoned roasted goat presented to the Prophet by a Jewish woman. The Prophet gathered some of his Companions for the meal, but as he reached for the meat, the dead goat informed the Prophet that its meat was poisoned.[83] Other accounts include the Prophet being shielded from a stone that was flung at him during the prayer[84] and a lengthy account from Ibn Isḥāq's *sīra* in which the Quraysh plot Muḥammad's death in the night before the *hijra*. In the latter account, the Prophet was able to leave his house despite the Quraysh's ambush because God impaired their vision and enabled the Prophet to walk unnoticed through their midst.[85] In another chapter, Abū Nuʿaym presents accounts that show that the Prophet—prior to his call to prophecy—was protected from the

82 Al-Iṣfahānī, *Dalāʾil al-nubūwa*, 241.

83 Al-Iṣfahānī, *Dalāʾil al-nubūwa*, 113.

84 Al-Iṣfahānī, *Dalāʾil al-nubūwa*, 113f.

85 Al-Iṣfahānī, *Dalāʾil al-nubūwa*, 114–118.

pagan beliefs of the society he grew up in; this includes the famous account of the adolescent Muḥammad falling asleep on the way to a wedding as a form of divine protection that kept him away from the immoral conduct of the ignorant partying folk.[86]

4.2 *Theology in al-Bayhaqī's* Dalāʾil al-Nubūwa

Like Abū Nuʿaym, al-Bayhaqī employed his knowledge of Ashaʿrī theology in framing his work. He dedicated much attention to situating Muḥammad's miracles in the context of continuous sacred history. In his extensive preface, al-Bayhaqī introduces the topic of prophecy with a verse from the Qurʾān:

> We have revealed to you, as We have revealed to Noah and the prophets after him, and We revealed to Abraham, Ishmael, Isaac, Jacob and the tribes; and to Jesus, Job, Jonah, Aaron, and Solomon, and We gave David a book. [163] And We sent forth some messengers We have already told you about. And God spoke to Moses directly. [164] Messengers who were bearers of good news and warners, so that mankind will have no plea against God, after the Messenger's coming. God is Mighty and Wise.[87]

This verse places Muḥammad in the continuous history of revelation, as all prophets were sent to instruct mankind about the obligation to praise God, to teach them specific acts of worship, and to proclaim the heavenly reward they would receive for obedience and the threat of hellfire as a punishment for negligence.[88] In addition to their common task, all prophets were supported by God who granted them signs and miracles as evidence of the veracity of their missions. After establishing these commonalities, the author briefly discusses the miracles of Moses, David, and Jesus mentioned in the Qurʾān.[89] He concludes that the Prophet Muḥammad was granted more signs and miracles than previous prophets.[90]

Like Abū Nuʿaym before him, al-Bayhaqī's main focus is on the scripture itself. "The sign that has been linked to his mission extended [throughout] the days of his life and what remained in his community after his passing is the noble Qurʾān, the clear miracle."[91] Al-Bayhaqī then outlines some aspects of the miracle of the Qurʾān (*iʿjāz al-Qurʾān*) and uses the Qurʾān's arrangement

86 Al-Iṣfahānī, *Dalāʾil al-nubūwa*, 107–123.
87 Q. 4:163–165.
88 Al-Bayhaqī, *Dalāʾil al-nubūwa*, 1:7.
89 Q. 17:101 (Moses), 34:10 (David), 5:110 (Jesus); cf. al-Bayhaqī, *Dalāʾil al-nubūwa*, 1:7–10.
90 Al-Bayhaqī, *Dalāʾil al-nubūwa*, 1:10.
91 Al-Bayhaqī, *Dalāʾil al-nubūwa*, 1:10.

and the events surrounding the "challenge" (*taḥaddī*) verses as the main evidence of the inimitability of the Qurʾān.[92] In the process, he quotes two theologians: al-Ḥusayn b. al-Ḥasan b. Muḥammad b. Ḥalīm (d. 403/1013)[93] from Bukhara and Abū Manṣūr Muḥammad b. al-Ḥusayn b. Abī Ayyūb (d. 421/1030).[94] The former compares the revelation with the verses of the impostor Musaylima.[95] In addition to the Qurʾān's arrangement and inimitability, al-Bayhaqī finds in the Qurʾān knowledge of the unseen (*ghayb*) and stories of previous prophets as further evidence of its miraculous nature. According to al-Bayhaqī, tales of the previous prophets could not have been known to Muḥammad, who was illiterate and "did not sit with 'people of the book' to take [information] from them."[96] Having established the Qurʾān as the prime miracle of the Prophet Muḥammad, al-Bayhaqī lists additional miracles, and presents them with their full *isnād*s later in his book.

5 Conclusion

The first distinguishing feature that later *dalāʾil al-nubūwa* works share is their common shift in methodology and structure, as studied closely in chapter 3. The greater methodological leniency and the extended pool of permissible sources to draw from opened the possibility for al-Khargūshī, Abū Nuʿaym, and al-Bayhaqī to craft all-encompassing narratives of Muḥammad's life that teleologically steered their audiences to the inevitable conclusion that not only had Muḥammad been anticipated as a future prophet in the realm of a shared sacred history with the People of the Book, but that he had also been spiritually prepared to fulfill this function from the moment of his conception. These narratives about Muḥammad's life prior to the call to prophecy were likely absent from (most) earlier contributions to *dalāʾil al-nubūwa* literature, because, based on methodological grounds, they would not have met the authentication standards that applied to compilations of *ḥadīth*. But as the methodological and organizational structure of the *dalāʾil al-nubūwa* literature shifted to align more closely with *sīra* literature, the stylistic opportunities to craft a more wholesome epistemological proof for Muḥammad's prophetic mission expanded in tandem with the narratives that were at the authors' disposal.

92 Al-Bayhaqī, *Dalāʾil al-nubūwa*, 1:11; al-Bayhaqī also mentions the notion of *iʿjāz al-Qurʾān* in his brief introduction, cf. al-Bayhaqī, *Dalāʾil al-nubūwa*, 1:49.

93 Al-Bayhaqī, *Dalāʾil al-nubūwa*, 1:12.

94 Al-Bayhaqī, *Dalāʾil al-nubūwa*, 1:15.

95 Al-Bayhaqī, *Dalāʾil al-nubūwa*, 1:13.

96 Al-Bayhaqī, *Dalāʾil al-nubūwa*, 1:16.

The evolving incorporation of theological ideas is clearly visible when we consider the ways in which the authors of *dalāʾil al-nubūwa* literature approached the concept of miracles. In the earliest extant works, the designated chapters on proofs of prophecy do not classify particular events as miraculous and even throughout these works more generally, we seldom find references to miracles. Al-Bukhārī, for instance, relates *ḥadīth*s about the splitting of the moon in two chapters. The chapter of the splitting of the moon is listed in the same section as the signs of prophecy, it is in the "Bāb al-manāqib," (Book of virtues). But this event is not labeled as a miracle, but rather as a sign (*āyā*) that was requested by the polytheists (*mushrikūn*). While the content of the *ḥadīth* suggests that the splitting of the moon is evidence of the veracity of Muḥammad's prophetic mission, this event is surprisingly absent from the chapter specifically dedicated to the signs of prophecy. Other scholars do not raise the issue of miracles at all. Ibn Saʿd's chapters are devoid of theological commentary or the explicit use of theological terminology, though there appear to be implicit references to questions of theological import, such as the emphasis on Muḥammad's prophecy being part of a continuous sacred history that is expressed in a chain of prophets.

Al-Khargūshī's *Sharaf al-nabī* appears to be the first extant work that specifically employs the term "miracle" and dedicates a chapter to the subject. The chapter title, *Muʿjiza*, demonstrates that al-Khargūshī deliberately identified miraculous accounts gathered from "ordinary" events in the Prophet's life. He does not define what constitutes a miracle, but simply presents a number of accounts under this heading without further explanation. The only exception to his silence about the nature of miracles is one account in the chapter on miracles, which calls the Qurʾān the most glorious of all signs (*ʿalāmāt*).[97] This statement is in line with contemporary theological positions that the Qurʾān was a miracle of the Prophet Muḥammad but al-Khargūshī does not enter further into the theological arguments. The willingness and ability to incorporate these theological notions into *dalāʾil al-nubūwa* literature reached a new high point in the generation of Abū Nuʿaym and al-Bayhaqī.

While the extent to which specific theological concepts were employed in these works varies, the mere fact that all three works reflect their authors' acceptance of and commitment to Ashʿarī theology stands in stark contrast to earlier generations of *dalāʾil al-nubūwa* authors who frequently belonged to the *ahl al-ḥadīth* movement and rejected speculative theology as a whole. Ashʿarī theology is most prominently represented in the notion of the Qurʾān as Muḥammad's main miracle. While earlier authors seldom included the

---

97 Al-Bayhaqī, *Dalāʾil al-nubūwa*, 1:162.

Qurʾān in their notion of "proofs of prophecy," these later authors gave it prime importance among the prophetic miracles. Al-Khargūshī includes a single account in his chapter on the Prophet's miracles that simply states that the Qurʾān is superior to other prophetic miracles. Abū Nuʿaym mentions the same topic in his introduction and dedicates two chapters to the notion of the inimitability of the Qurʾān: one draws on literary considerations that are commonly associated with the concept of *iʿjāz al-Qurʾān* and the second chapter recounts a number of conversions caused by Qurʾānic recitation, most prominently the well-known account of ʿUmar b. al-Khaṭṭāb, who staunchly opposed Islam until he heard his sister's recitation. These chapters seem to lay the theoretical foundation for the miraculous nature of the Qurʾānic text, which is then bolstered by "case studies." Al-Bayhaqī discusses the superiority of the Qurʾān briefly in his introduction and lists, like Abū Nuʿaym before him, literary aspects of its inimitability but also adds content-related aspects, such as the fact that the Qurʾān contains knowledge of the unseen (*ghayb*) as well as knowledge of the previous prophets. Both Abū Nuʿaym and al-Bayhaqī stress the primacy of the Qurʾān's inimitability, not only in the context of Muḥammad's miracles, but also with regard to those of previous prophets.

Other commonalities between Abū Nuʿaym and al-Bayhaqī are their notion that Muḥammad was spiritually prepared for his prophetic mission and that he was granted divine protection (*ʿiṣma*). Abū Nuʿaym compiles one thematic chapter on signs that manifested the boy's significance, such as the blessings Ḥalīma received or several individuals' awareness of the child's prophetic future, and specific measures taken to prepare him for this mission, such as the cleansing of his heart. In a later chapter, Abū Nuʿaym cites God's protection of the Prophet from the beliefs of pagan society. Al-Bayhaqī combines these notions in a similar way in the second volume of his work. The notion of Muḥammad's spiritual preparation in childhood and adolescence were new additions. Only Ibn Saʿd listed events like the Prophet's birth or the cleansing of his heart. Yet, he does not seem to afford much significance to these accounts, given that his chapters on the "proofs of prophecy" only included four accounts on these topics, even though he lists many more accounts in the *sīra* section of his work.

Having completed the methodological and structural examination as well as the content analysis of several *dalāʾil al-nubūwa* works from the late second/eighth to the early fifth/eleventh centuries, it is clear that these works should be viewed as hagiographic texts. As part of a hagiographical discourse of constructing a distinct persona, each author sought to craft a particular theologically imbued image of Muḥammad and his prophetic mission by selecting materials from *ḥadīth*, and, in case of the later authors, from *sīra* and auxiliary literature. Their selection of these materials was determined both by the methodological restrictions of their respective field at the time and their own theological assumptions about how "genuine" prophecy might be proven through the materials at their disposal. These texts, then, are historiographic in the sense that each author's individual retelling of the past grants us glimpses into the social and intellectual circumstances that contributed to the construction of their own sense of historical identity. The texts bear witness to the diverse political, social, and intellectual stimuli and enact a past that informs and gives meaning to the authors' present by providing a foundation for their ideological and doctrinal views.

Epilogue: *Dalāʾil al-nubūwa* and the Promise of Comparative Hagiology

Captivating as their narratives may be, works of *dalaʾil al-nubūwa* were not authored for sheer entertainment, and diverse as their content may be, they were not the product of fabrications either. Rather, in recounting and reshaping narratives about his prophetic mission, the scholarly authors of these texts mapped their theories of truth onto the persona of the Prophet Muḥammad. These theories of truth are both reflective of and contribute to a complex web of distinct intellectual, social, cultural, and political contexts in which the texts' authors and their readers operate. These works of *dalāʾil al-nubūwa* were embedded in the wider discourses of their times. Yet, as I have laid out in the introduction, scholars of Islamic studies during the nineteenth and twentieth centuries commonly dismissed *ḥadīth*-based *dalāʾil al-nubūwa* literature based on a presumed juxtaposition between historiographic and hagiographic texts. In this presumed binary, historiographic texts were considered those that give accurate accounts of the past, while hagiographic texts were seen as those that intentionally misconstrued a person's life story and were generally written by authors who were stigmatized as unqualified or catering toward a "popular" audience. As a consequence, these works of *dalāʾil al-nubūwa* were deemed hagiographic, omitted from serious academic study, and were, for the most part, excluded from our understanding of Islamic intellectual history; this significantly limited our views of the discourses on prophecy that occurred across numerous fields of Islamic religious sciences.

In order to overcome many of these restrictive frameworks, in my examination of *dalāʾil al-nubūwa* literature I adopted theoretical and methodological advances from other disciplines, and by drawing on the works of LaCapra, Spiegel, Lifshitz, and Delooz. In doing so, I joined the emerging field of comparative hagiology. While these scholars refined their understanding of hagiography in the context of European intellectual history, with its focus on particular expressions of Christian texts, doctrines, and institutions, more recently, scholars of various fields and religious traditions have set out to reexamine and reimagine the study of hagiography in both comparative and collaborative ways. At a workshop at the annual meetings of the American Academy of Religion (AAR), conversations have led to a broader understanding of hagiography as well as "comparative hagiology" as a new methodological approach "by which scholars hailing from different disciplines and working in different fields might collaborate in threshing out commonalities and entanglements

 | DOI:10.1163/9789004687349_009

in their respective treatments of holy figures."[1] The first workshop, held at the AAR meeting in Boston in 2017, yielded a special issue of *Religions*, entitled "Comparative Hagiology: Issues in Theory and Methods." In one article, Aaron Hollander summarized three pillars of general consensus that grew out of these conversations:

> That hagiography (1) is constituted not only in verbal texts but in a wide array of media, both material and ephemeral; (2) is best interpreted by attending substantially to the "processes" of thought, life and society in which it is rendered; and (3) opens possibilities of cross-cultural and interdisciplinary comparison by way of the many family resemblances in how saints (or more broadly, religious and even para-religious exemplars) are rendered in transmittable media and mobilized for a particular group's benefit.[2]

All three aspects allow scholars working on various religious traditions and disciplines to apply the analytical methodologies and conceptualizations of studying hagiography, without being limited to the textual, social, and doctrinal particularities of the Christian context in which these approaches first emerged. It also necessitates a new and broader working definition of hagiography, which Massimo Rondolino offered as the "complex web of behaviors, practices, and productions (literary, visual, acoustic, etc.) in and by which a given community constructs the memory of individuals who are recognized as the embodied perfection of the religious ideal promoted by the community's tradition and socio-cultural context."[3] It is the emphasis of Rondolino and his colleagues on the social process of constructing an exemplary persona that allows scholars of various religious traditions to employ this heuristic tool to their respective fields of study and facilitate cross-cultural comparative analyses of the social functions of such hagiographic media. Rondolino, for example, employed the comparative study of sources on the lives of the Christian medieval saint Francis of Assisi (d. 1226) and the Tibetan Buddhist Milarepa (d. 1135) in his piece on hagiographic taxonomy.

The works of *dalāʾil al-nubūwa* that I have studied in this book suggest that applying hagiology as a methodological framework might offer more opportunities to deepen our understanding of Islamic intellectual history. In addition to demonstrating that these works were the product of established scholarly

1 Hollander, "Comparison as Collaboration," 1.
2 Hollander, "Comparison as Collaboration," 1.
3 Rondolino "Some Foundational Considerations on Taxonomy," 5.

circles, I argued that these works of *dalāʾil al-nubūwa* literature demonstrate the processes of constructing religious personae and their shifting imaginary frameworks that underlie Pierre Delooz's understanding of exemplary figures. As such, each *ḥadīth*-based *dalāʾil al-nubūwa* work is a selectively presented and discursively arranged narrative of Muḥammad's life taken from existing texts with the intended goal of constructing "evidence" of his prophetic mission, in dialogue with intellectual, social, and political discourses in the form of a kind of narrativized theology. During this process, sources and disciplinary methods, as well as theological and ideological agendas shifted over time. The initial thematic chapters that were part of larger *ḥadīth* collections adopted their methodological demands along with the evolving paradigms of *ḥadīth* criticism and were eventually transformed in scope, methodology, and structure to more closely resemble the framework of *sīra* literature. At the same time, *dalāʾil al-nubūwa* literature reflects disciplinary attitudes toward other religious sciences such as *kalām*. The earliest compilers of *ḥadīth* offered no interpretative or theological context for their selections while works in the late fourth/tenth and early fifth/eleventh centuries seamlessly integrated theological notions of miracles (*muʿjizāt*) and divine protection (*ʿiṣma*).

In this study, adopting core ideas of comparative hagiology as a methodological framework has proven helpful in various ways. First, the notion that the social and doctrinal construction of exemplary figures is not limited to one particular genre but rather occurs across numerous media has encouraged me to extend the scope of sources I used beyond the boundaries of genre or even fields in the Islamic sciences. The strong emphasis of hagiology on the numerous social, cultural, intellectual, and political contexts that shape the crafting of exemplary figures first provided me with an incentive to look into the wider social realities of Ibn Saʿd's time, as these realities marked the emergence of several works dedicated to the proofs of prophecy. Finally, the ambition of scholars employing comparative hagiology to compare the social processes by which religious exemplars are crafted and employed across traditions persuaded me to broaden my view of disciplinary fields. The academic study of Islam mostly locates discussions on the nature of prophecy in the realm of *kalām*. Works of *dalāʾil al-nubūwa* in the broader sense are no exception to this. As I outlined in the introduction to this book, works entitled *dalāʾil al-nubūwa* (or semantically related titles) were authored by scholars of various schools of thought and fields of religious sciences. They include Muʿtazilī works, Ismāʿīlī works, works by Ashʿarī theologians, as well as *ḥadīth* compilations, and studies adducing biblical or pseudo-biblical passages as "evidence" of Muḥammad's prophetic mission. Scholars of Islamic studies mostly examined these works individually and in the isolated context of their author's "discipline." That is, works whose author is commonly viewed as a theologian were examined in the context of theological discourses on prophecy, while works based on *ḥadīth* or biblical passages were examined under different parameters, such as linguistic provenance in the transmission and translations of the Bible or levels of authenticity or legitimacy with regard to *ḥadīth*-based works. This compartmentalized approach is certainly understandable in light of the distinct skill sets and kinds of expertise required of contemporary scholars by each of these forms of *dalāʾil al-nubūwa* literature. However, as a consequence, studying these expressions of *dalāʾil al-nubūwa* distinctly and in isolation from the others has impeded our recognition of the theological import that lies in biblical and *ḥadīth*-based approaches. Furthermore, the compartmentalization of these diverse forms of *dalāʾil al-nubūwa* leads scholars to overlook the fact that these were individual expressions of a larger discourse that transcended disciplinary and, at times, religious boundaries and potentially cross-pollinated notions of prophecy among these diverse scholars.

In the broader field of Islamic studies, theoretical and methodological reflections on hagiographic media are not new and are particularly useful in areas of study such as the lives of Sufi masters, Shīʿī imams, or the prophets, as well as the study of diverse sets of texts that make up virtues (*manaqib*), remembrance (*tadhkira*), or merits (*faḍāʾil*) literature. But the particular methodological framework of comparative hagiology appears to me to be a promising avenue to advance a more holistic understanding of Islamic discourses on prophecy. And I was heartened to see that these particular approaches seem to gain momentum among some scholars of Islam. When I participated in the AAR's now formalized Hagiology seminar in 2021, the largest group of participants was working in the field of Islam and I hope that this methodological approach will gain more traction in other fields of Islamic studies.

Appendix: A Detailed Comparison between ʿUrwa b. al-Zubayr and Wahb b. Munabbih

The following table lists elements that distinguish the account of ʿUrwa from that of Wahb and the divergences between strands of transmission of ʿUrwa b. al-Zubayr's account of the *hijra*. Furthermore, it indicates some divergences in the transmission of Hishām b. ʿUrwa: (a) designates the recension of the letter to ʿAbd al-Malik; (b) designates the shorter traditions that were transmitted by Abū Usāma via Hishām b. ʿUrwa; and (c) designates a short tradition on the authority of Ḥammād b. Salama via Hishām b. ʿUrwa.

TABLE 1 A comparison of *hijra* accounts of ʿUrwa and Wahb

ʿUrwa b. al-Zubayr via Hishām b. ʿUrwa	**ʿUrwa b. al-Zubayr via Ibn Shihāb al-Zuhrī**	**Wahb b. Munabbih**
	ʿUrwa inserts the following account from ʿĀʾisha: Abū Bakr decided to immigrate to Abyssinia, then he met Ibn Daghina who offered him protection. Ibn Daghina consulted with the Quraysh who imposed a condition on Abū Bakr's protection; i.e., he may pray and recite the Qurʾān in his house only. Abū Bakr established a prayer space outside his house; members of Quraysh insisted on their requirement, and Abū Bakr released Ibn Daghina from his vow of protection.	

 DOI:10.1163/9789004687349_010

TABLE 1 A comparison of *hijra* accounts of ʿUrwa and Wahb (*cont.*)

ʿUrwa b. al-Zubayr via Hishām b. ʿUrwa	**ʿUrwa b. al-Zubayr via Ibn Shihāb al-Zuhrī**	**Wahb b. Munabbih**
Seventy people from Medina met with the Prophet at al-ʿAqaba and guaranteed protection to the Muslims. The Prophet advised his people to immigrate to Medina. Here there is a reference to Q. 8:39. Abū Bakr wished to move to Medina but followed the Prophet's request to stay.	The Prophet had a dream about the destination of the immigration: it would be a landscape with date-bearing palm trees between two lava plains. Many Muslims immigrated to Medina.	Gabriel went to the Prophet and informed him of the Quraysh's intention to kill him. Here there is a reference to Q. 8:30. The Prophet went to Abū Bakr to tell him about the plot and the newly revealed verse. He informed Abū Bakr to prepare for their departure at night.
Abū Bakr took care of two camels and waited until the Prophet received permission to immigrate. The two rode together to the cave of Thawr.	Abū Bakr fed two of his camels with leaves from the Samur tree. He offered the Prophet one of the camels as a gift but Muḥammad insisted on buying the camel from Abū Bakr.	The Prophet left Mecca on foot, Abū Bakr followed him, on foot as well. ʿAlī joined them at the cave and was sent to hire three camels and a guide.

TABLE 1 A comparison of *hijra* accounts of ʿUrwa and Wahb (*cont.*)

ʿUrwa b. al-Zubayr via Hishām b. ʿUrwa	**ʿUrwa b. al-Zubayr via Ibn Shihāb al-Zuhrī**	**Wahb b. Munabbih**
(a) ʿAbdallāh b. Abī Bakr brought news from Mecca each night [they were in the cave]. ʿĀmir b. Fuhayra brought Abū Bakr's sheep (together with sheep from his own flocks) to the cave so that Abū Bakr and the Prophet could have the sheep's milk.	Food for the Prophet and Abū Bakr was prepared (possibly before they left). Asmāʾ tied the bag of food into her belt, from this she took the nickname Dhāt al-Niṭāqayn.	ʿAlī and Asmāʾ bt. Abū Bakr brought food to the cave.
(b) Very similar to (a) but there is no mention of a messenger from Mecca. (While Asmāʾ is not mentioned, there is an independent *ḥadīth* about the food preparations, Asmāʾs nickname, and ʿAbdallāh b. Abī Bakr taking the food to the cave.)	ʿAbdallāh b. Abī Bakr brought news from Medina.	
(c) ʿAbdallāh b. Abī Bakr brought news, ʿĀmir b. Fuhayra brought sheep, and Asmāʾ bt. Abū Bakr prepared food, which she tied up in her belt and for this reason she came to be called Dhāt al-Niṭāqayn.	ʿĀmir b. Fuhayra herded sheep to the cave for the Prophet to milk them.	

TABLE 1 A comparison of *hijra* accounts of ʿUrwa and Wahb (*cont.*)

ʿUrwa b. al-Zubayr via Hishām b. ʿUrwa	**ʿUrwa b. al-Zubayr via Ibn Shihāb al-Zuhrī**	**Wahb b. Munabbih**
(a) The *hijra* to Medina was undertaken by the Prophet, Abū Bakr, ʿĀmir b. Fuhayra, and a guide from the Banū ʿAbd al-ʿAdī. (b) A guide from the Banū ʿAbd al-ʿAdī is not mentioned. (c) The *hijra* was undertaken by the Prophet, Abū Bakr, and ʿĀmir b. Fuhayra; Abū Bakr and ʿĀmir took turns riding one of the camels.	A man from the Banū ʿAbd al-ʿAdī was trusted by Abū Bakr even though he was still a pagan; he took care of the camels. The *hijra* to Medina was undertaken by the Prophet, Abū Bakr, ʿĀmir b. Fuhayra, and the guide from the Banū ʿAbd al-ʿAdī.	The *hijra* to Medina was undertaken by the Prophet, Abū Bakr, and their guide; they rode three camels. The guide was ʿAbdallāh b. Urayqiṭ, a pagan who read books, presumably religious scriptures, and thus recognized the 'sign of prophecy' on the Prophet's shoulder. He embraced Islam.
(c) On their way to Medina, a gift from Ṭalḥa b. ʿUbaydallāh reached Abū Bakr. The gift consisted of white garments, which they wear when entering Medina.	The Prophet and Abū Bakr encountered al-Zubayr on their way to Medina. He was part of a caravan traveling from Syria to Mecca and presented them with white garments.	

Bibliography

Primary Sources

ʿAbd al-Razzāq b. Hammām al-Ḥimyarī. *al-Muṣannaf.* Edited by Ḥabīb al-Raḥmān al-Aʿẓamī. Beirut, 1970.

Abū Ḥātim al-Rāzī. *Aʿlām al-nubūwa*. Edited by Ṣalāḥ al-Ṣāwī. Tehran, 1977.

Abū Ḥātim al-Rāzī. *The Signs of Prophecy*. Edited and translated by Tarif Khalidi. Provo, UT, 2011.

al-Bāqillānī, Muḥammad b. al-Ṭayyib. *Kitāb al-Bayān ʿan al-farq bayna al-muʿjizāt wa-l-karāmāt wa-l-ḥiyal wa-l-kahāna wa-l-siḥr wa-l-nāranjāt*. Beirut, 1958.

al-Bayhaqī, Aḥmad b. Ḥusayn. *Dalāʾil al-nubūwa wa-maʿrifa aḥwāl ṣāḥib al-sharīʿa*. Edited by ʿAbd al-Muʿṭī Qalaʿjī. 7 vols. Beirut, 2008.

al-Bazzār, Abū Bakr Aḥmad. *al-Baḥr al-zakhār al-maʿrūf bi-Musnad al-Bazzār*. Edited by Maḥfūẓ al-Raḥmān Zaynallāh. Beirut, 1988.

al-Bukhārī, Abū ʿAbdallāh Muḥammad. *Kitāb al-Tārīkh al-kabīr*. Beirut, 2001.

al-Bukhārī, Abū ʿAbdallāh Muḥammad. *Ṣaḥīḥ al-Bukhārī*. Edited and translated by Muḥammad Muḥsin Khan. Riyadh, 1997.

al-Dhahabī, Muḥammad b. Aḥmad. *Siyar aʿlām al-nubulāʾ*. Beirut, 1996.

al-Dhahabī, Muḥammad b. Aḥmad. *Tadhkirat al-ḥuffāẓ*. Hyderabad, 1968–70.

al-Firyābī, Jaʿfar b. Muḥammad, and ʿĀmir Ḥasan Ṣabrī. *Kitāb Dalāʾil al-nubūwa*. N.p., 1986.

Kātib Çelebī/Ḥājjī Khalīfa. *Kashf al-ẓunūn ʿan asāmī l-kutub wa-l-funūn*. Edited by Şerefettin Yaltkaya and Rifat Bilge. 2 vols. Istanbul, 1941–43.

Ibn Abī Shayba, Abū Bakr. *al-Muṣannaf fī l-aḥādīth wa-l-athār*. Beirut, 1989.

Ibn Abī Shayba, Abū Bakr. *Musnad Ibn Abī Shayba*. Riyadh, 1998.

Ibn Ḥajar al-ʿAsqalānī, Shihāb al-Dīn. *Lisān al-mizān*. Cairo, 1996.

Ibn Ḥajar al-ʿAsqalānī, Shihāb al-Dīn. *Tahdhīb al-tahdhīb*. 12 vols. Hyderabad, 1325–27 AH.

Ibn Ḥanbal, Aḥmad, *Musnad al-Imām Aḥmad b. Ḥanbal*. Edited by Abū l-Maʿṭī l-Nūrī. Beirut, 1998.

Ibn Hibbān, Muḥammad. *al-Sīra al-nabawiyya wa-akhbār al-khulafāʾ*. Beirut, 1987.

Ibn Hishām, ʿAbd al-Malik. *al-Sīra al-nabawiyya*. Edited by Muṣṭafā l-Saqā. Cairo, 1955.

Ibn Isḥāq, Muḥammad. *The Life of Muhammad: Translation of Isḥāq's Sīrat Rasūl Allāh*. Translated by Alfred Guillaume. Karachi, 1967.

Ibn Jawzī, Abū l-Faraj. *Kitāb al-Quṣṣāṣ wa-l-mudhakkirīn*. Translation and critical edition by Merlin Swartz. Beirut, 1973.

Ibn Jawzī, Abū l-Faraj. *al-Muntaẓam*. 6 vols. Hyderabad, 1940.

Ibn Kathīr, Ismāʿīl b. ʿUmar. *al-Bidāya wa-l-nihāya fī l-tārīkh*. Cairo, 1932.

Ibn Kathīr, Ismāʿīl b. ʿUmar. *al-Sīra al-nabawiyya*. Edited by Muṣṭafā ʿAbd al-Wāḥid. Cairo, 1964–66.

Ibn Khallikān. *Wafayāt al-aʿyān wa-anbāʾ al-zamān*. Edited by F. Wüstenfeld. Göttingen, 1865.

Ibn al-Nadīm. *Fihrist*. Edited by Ayman Fūʾād Sayyid. London, 2009.

Ibn Qāḍī Shuhba, Yūsuf b. Muḥammad. *Aḥādīth muntakhaba min maghāzī Mūsā b. ʿUqba*. Beirut, 1991.

Ibn Rāshid, Maʿmar. *The Expeditions: An Early Biography of Muhammad*. Translated by Sean W. Anthony. New York, 2015.

Ibn Saʿd, Muḥammad. *al-Ṭabaqāt al-kubrā*. 8 vols. Beirut, 1957–68.

al-Iṣfahānī, Abū Nuʿaym. *Dalāʾil al-nubūwa*. Edited by Najīb al-Mājdī. Beirut, 2010.

al-Iṣfahānī, Abū l-Qāsim. *Nayl al-fadāʾil fī takhrīj Kitāb Dalāʾil: Dalāʾil al-nubūwa*. Edited by Rāshid al-Ḥumayd. Riyadh, 1991–92.

al-Juzājānī, Abū Isḥāq Ibrāhīm b. Yaʿqūb b. Isḥāq al-Saʿdī. *Juzʾ fīhi aḥādīth muntakhaba min al-juzʾ al-sādis min Kitāb āmārāt al-nubūwa*. Dār al-Kutub al-Ẓāhiriyya, Damascus Asad Library, MS Majmūʿ 104, fols. 162–165.

Kaḥḥāla, ʿUmar Riḍa. *Muʿjam al-muʾallifīn: Tarājim muṣannifī al-kutub al-ʿarabiyya*. Damascus, 1957–61.

al-Khargūshī, ʿAbd al-Malik. *Sharaf al-nabī*. Edited by Najm al-Dīn Maḥmūd Rāvandī. Tehran, 1361/1982.

al-Khaṭīb al-Baghdādī. *Tārīkh Baghdād*. 14 vols. Beirut, 1966.

Muslim b. Ḥajjāj. *Ṣaḥīḥ Muslim*. Edited by Muḥammad Fūʾād ʿAbd al-Bāqī. Beirut, 2003.

Qāḍī ʿIyād b. Mūsā. *al-Shifāʾ bi-taʿrīf ḥuqūq al-Muṣṭafāʾ*. Edited by ʿAlī Muḥammad al-Bajāwī. 2 vols. Cairo, 1977.

al-Sakhāwī, Shams al-Dīn Muḥammad. *al-Iʿlān bī-l-tawbīkh li-man dhamma ahl al-tārīkh*. Beirut, 1986.

al-Samʿānī, ʿAbd al-Karīm b. Muḥammad. *Ansāb*. Leiden, 1912.

al-Subkī, Tāj al-Dīn. *Ṭabaqāt al-Shāfiʿiyya al-kubrā*. Edited by Maḥmūd Muḥammad al-Ṭanāḥī and ʿAbd al-Fattāḥ Muḥammad al-Ḥilw. 10 vols. Cairo, [1964–76].

al-Ṭabarī, Ibn Jarīr. *Tafsīr al-Ṭabarī: Jāmiʿ al-bayān ʿan taʾwīl al-Qurʾān*. Edited by Maḥmūd Muḥammad Shākir and Aḥmad Muammad Shākir. 16 vols. [Cairo], [1961–69].

al-Ṭabarī, Ibn Jarīr. *Tārīkh al-Ṭabarī: Tārīkh al-rusul wa-l-mulūk*. Edited by Muḥammad Abū l-Faḍl Ibrāhīm. 11 vols. Cairo, [1990].

al-Tabarānī, Abū l-Qāsim Sulaymān b. Aḥmad. *al-Muʿjam al-kabīr*. Edited by Hamdī ʿAbd al-Majid. Baghdad, 1984.

al-Ṭayālisī, Abū Dāwūd Sulaymān b. Dāwūd. *Musnad Abī Dāwūd al-Ṭayālisī*. Edited by Muḥammad b. ʿAbd al- Muḥsin al-Turkī. Giza, 1999.

al-Thaʿlabī, Aḥmad b. Muḥammad. *ʿArāʾis al-majālis fī qiṣāṣ al-anbīyaʾ*. Edited and translated by William Brinner. Leiden, 2002.

al-Tirmidhī, Muḥammad b. ʿĪsā. *Ṣaḥīḥ Sunan al-Tirmidhī: bi-ikhtiṣār al-sanad*. Edited by Muḥammad Nāṣir al-Dīn al-Albānī and Zuhayr al-Shāwīsh. 3 vols. Riyadh, 1988.
al-Tirmidhī, Muḥammad b. ʿĪsā. *Shamāʾil al-nabī*. Edited by Māhir Yāsīn al-Faḥl. Beirut, 2000.
al-Wāqidī, Muḥammad b. ʿUmar. *Kitāb al-Maghāzī*. Edited by Marsden Jones. Beirut, 1966.
Yāqūt, Abū ʿAbdallāh al-Ḥamawī. *Kitāb Muʿjam al-buldān*. Tehran, 1965.
al-Zakkār, Suhayl (ed.). *al-Maghāzī l-nabawiyya*. Damascus, 1981.

Secondary Sources

Abbott, Nabia. *Studies in Arabic Literary Papyri*. Chicago, 1957–72.
Abdel-Malek, Kamal. "Popular Religious Prose," in Roger Allen and D. S. Richards (eds.), *Arabic Literature in the Post-Classical Period*. Cambridge, 2006, pp. 330–344.
Abdul Aleem. "The Miracle of the Qurʾān," in *Islamic Culture* 7 (1933): 64–82.
Abdul Rauf, Muhammad. "Hadīth Literature I: The Development of the Science of Hadīth," in A. F. Beeston et al. (eds.), *Arabic Literature to the End of the Umayyad Period*. Cambridge, 1983, pp. 271–277.
Adang, Camilla. "A Rare Case of Biblical 'Testimonies' to the Prophet Muḥammad in Muʿtazilī Literature: Quotations from Ibn Rabban al-Ṭabarī's *Kitāb al-Dīn wa-l-dawla* in Abū l-Ḥusayn al-Baṣrī's *Ghurar al-adilla*, as Preserved in a Work by Ḥimmaṣī l-Rāzī," in Camilla Adang, Sabine Schmidtke, and David Sklare (eds.), *A Common Rationality: Muʿtazilism in Islam and Judaism*. Würzburg, 2007, pp. 287–330.
Adang, Camilla. "Medieval Muslim Polemics Against the Jewish Scriptures," in Jacques Waardenburg (ed.), *Muslim Perceptions of Other Religions: A Historical Survey*. Oxford, 1999, pp. 143–159.
Adang, Camilla. *Muslim Writers on Judaism and the Hebrew Bible: From Ibn Rabban to Ibn Hazm*. Leiden, 1996.
Adang, Camilla. "Torah," in Camilla Adang and Sabine Schmidtke (eds.), *Muslim Perceptions of the Bible: Texts and Studies*. Atlanta, 2019, pp. 1–14.
Ahlwardt, Wilhelm. *Verzeichnis der arabsichen Handschriften der Königlichen Bibliothek zu Berlin*. Berlin, 1887–99.
al-Albānī, Muḥammad Nāṣir al-Dīn. *Fihris makhṭūṭāt Dār al-Kutub al-Ẓāhiriyya: al-Muntakhab min makhṭūṭāt al-ḥadīth*. Damascus, 1970.
Ali, Kecia. *The Lives of Muhammad*. Cambridge, 2014.
Aminrazavi, Mehdi and Everett K. Rowson. "Abū Ḥātim Rāzī," in Seyyed Hossein Nasr and Mehdi Aminrazavi (eds.), *Anthology of Philosophy in Persia:* Volume 2: *Ismāʿīlī Thought in the Classical Age*. New York, 1999, pp. 143–159.

Andrae, Tor. *Die Person Muhammeds in Lehre und Glauben seiner Gemeinde*. Stockholm, 1918.

Antes, Peter. *Prophetenwunder in der Ashʿarīya bis al-Ghazālī*. Freiburg, 1970.

Anthony, Sean. *Muḥammad and the Empires of Faith: The Making of the Prophet of Islam*. Oakland, 2020.

Anthony, Sean. "Muḥammad, Menaḥem, and the Paraclete: New Light on Ibn Isḥāq's (d. 150/767) Arabic Version of John 15:23–16:1," *BSOAS* 79, no. 2 (2016): 255–278.

Armstrong, Lyall Richard. *The Quṣṣāṣ of Early Islam*. Leiden, 2017.

Asatryan, Mushegh. "Prophecy after Muhammad: The View from Late Antiquity," in Sajjad Rizvi and Ahab Bdaiwi (eds.), *Oxford Handbook of Shiʿi Islam*. Oxford, forthcoming.

Atassi, Ahmad Nazir. "A History of Ibn Saʿd's Great Book of Strata or Kitāb al-Tabaqāt al-Kabīr," PhD dissertation, University of California–Santa Barbara, 2009.

ʿAthamina, Khalil. "Al-Qasas: Its Emergence, Religious Origin, and Its Socio-Political Impact on Early Muslim Society," *Studia Islamica* 76 (1992): 53–74.

Azami, Muhammad Mustafa. *On Schacht's Origins of Muhammadan Jurisprudence*. Cambridge, 1996.

Azami, Muhammad Mustafa. *Studies in Early Hadith Literature*. Indianapolis, IN, 1992.

al-Bastawī, ʿAbd al-ʿAlīm ʿAbd al-ʿAẓīm. *al-Imām al-Jūzajānī wa-manhajuhu fī l-jarḥ wa-l-taʿdīl*. Faisalabad, 1990.

Berg, Herbert. *The Development of Exegesis in Early Islam: The Authenticity of Muslim Literature from the Formative Period*. Richmond, Surrey, 2000.

Berkey, Jonathan P. *Popular Preaching and Religious Authority in the Medieval Islamic Near East*. Seattle, 2001.

Blochet, Edgar. *Catalogue des Manuscrits Persans de la Bibliothèque Nationale*. Paris, 1905–34.

Boekhoeff-van der Voort, Nicolet. "The Kitāb al-Maghāzī of ʿAbd al-Razzāq b. Hammām al-Ṣanʿānī: Searching for Earlier Source Material," in Nicolet Boekhoff-van der Voort, Kees Versteegh, and Joas Wagemakers (eds.), *The Transmission and Dynamics of the Textual Sources of Islam*. Leiden, 2011.

Bottini, Laura. "al-Kindī, ʿAbd al-Masīḥ ibn Isḥāq (pseudonym)," in David Thomas and Barbara Roggema (eds.), *Christian-Muslim Relations*. Leiden, 2009, 1:585–594.

Böwering, Gerhard. "Covenant," in *EQ*, 1:494f.

Brockelmann, Carl. *Geschichte der Arabischen Litteratur*. Weimar, 1898–1902; suppl. vol., Leiden, 1943–49.

Brown, Jonathan. *The Canonization of al-Bukhārī and Muslim: The Formation and Function of Sunnī Ḥadīth Canon*, Leiden, 2009.

Brown, Jonathan. "The Canonization of Ibn Mâjah: Authenticity vs. Utility in the Formation of the Sunni Ḥadîth Canon," *Revue des mondes musulmans et de la Médeterranée* 129 (July 2011): 169–181.

Brown, Jonathan. "Critical Rigor vs. Juridical Pragmatism," *Islamic Law and Society* 14 (2007): 1–41.

Brown, Jonathan. "Did the Prophet Say it or Not? The Literal, Historical, and Effective Truth of Ḥadīths in Early Sunnism," *JAOS* 129, no. 2 (2009): 259–286.

Brown, Jonathan. "How We Know Early Ḥadīth Critics Did *Matn* Criticism and Why It's So Hard To Find," *Islamic Law and Society* 15, no. 2 (2008): 143–184.

Bulliet, Richard. *Conversion to Islam in the Medieval Period: An Essay in Quantitative History*. Cambridge, 1979.

Bulliet, Richard. *The Patricians of Nishapur: A Study of Medieval Islamic Social History*. Cambridge, 1972.

Bülow, Gabriele. "Ḥadithe über Wunder des Propheten Muḥammad insbesondere in der Traditionssammlung des Buhārī," PhD dissertation, Rheinische Friedrich-Wilhelms-Universität, Bonn, 1964.

Burge, Stephen. "Myth, Meaning and the Order of Words: Reading Ḥadīth Collections with Northrop Frye and the Development of Compilation Criticism," in *Islam and Christian-Muslim Relations* 27, no. 2 (March 2016): 1–16.

Burge, Stephen. "Reading between the Lines: The Compilation of Hadīt and the Authorial Voice," in *Arabica* 58, nos. 3–4 (2011): 168–197.

Colby, Frederick. *Narrating Muḥammad's Night Journey: Tracing the Development of the Ibn 'Abbās Ascension Discourse*. Albany, 2008.

Cook, Michael. *Early Muslim Dogma*. Cambridge, 1981.

Cook, Michael. "Eschatology and the Dating of Traditions," in *Princeton Papers in Near Eastern Studies* 1 (1992): 23–47.

Coulson, N. J. "European Criticism of *Ḥadīth* Literature," in A. F. L. Beeston (ed.), *Arabic Literature to the End of the Umayyad Period*. Cambridge, 1983, pp. 317–321.

Della Vida, Levi. "Sīra," in *EI*^{1}, 7:440.

Delooz, Pierre. "Pour une étude sociologique de la sainteté dans l'Eglise Catholique," in *Archives de Sciences Sociales des Religions* 13 (1962): 17–43.

Delooz, Pierre. *Sociologie et Canonisations*. Liege, 1969.

Dickinson, Eerik. *The Development of Early Sunnite Ḥadīth Criticism: The Taqdima of Ibn Abī Ḥātim al-Rāzī (240/854–327/938)*. Leiden, 2001.

Dietrich, Albert. "Ibn Abī al-Dunyā," in *EI*^{2}, 3:684.

Dūrī, ʿAbd al-ʿAzīz. *The Rise of Historical Writing among the Arabs*. Princeton, 1983.

Ess, Josef van. *Theologie und Gesellschaft im 2. und 3. Jahrhundert Hidschra: eine Geschichte des religiösen Denkens im frühen Islam*. Berlin, 1991.

Fakhri, Majid. *Interpretation of the Qur'an: English Translation of the Meanings. A Bilingual Edition*. New York, 2002.

Fück, Johann. "Ibn Saʿd," in *EI*^{1}, 3:922f.

Fück, Johann. *Muḥammad Ibn Isḥāq*, Frankfurt a. M., 1925.

Funkenstein, Amos. "History, Counterhistory, and Narrative," in Amos Funkenstein (ed.), *Perceptions of Jewish History*. Berkeley, 1993.

Geiger, Abraham. *Was hat Mohammed aus dem Judenthume aufgenommen?* Berlin, 2005.

Gibb, Hamilton and Alexander Rosskeen, "Ta'rīkh," in *EI*[1] Suppl., 235.

Gimaret, Daniel. *Doctrine d'al-Ashʿarī*. Paris, 1990.

Goldziher, Ignaz. *Muhammedanische Studien*. Hildesheim, 1961. Trans. C. R. Barber and Samuel M. Stern as *Muslim Studies*. London, 1968.

Goldziher, Ignaz. *Schools of Koranic Commentators*. Edited and translated by Wolfgang H. Behn. Wiesbaden, 2006.

Goodman, L. E. "Rāzī vs. Rāzī—Philosophy in the Majlis," in Hava Lazarus-Yafeh (ed.), *The Majlis: Interreligious Encounters in Medieval Islam*. Wiesbaden, 1999, pp. 84–107.

Görke, Andreas. "The Historical Tradition about al-Ḥudaybiya: A Study of ʿUrwa b. al-Zubayr's Account," in Harald Motzki (ed.), *The Biography of Muḥammad: The Issue of the Sources*. Leiden, 2000.

Görke, Andreas. "The Relationship between *Maghāzī* and *Ḥadīth* in Early Islamic Scholarship," *BSOAS* 74, no. 2 (2011): 171–185.

Graetz, Heinrich, Bella Löwy, and Philipp Bloch (eds.). *History of the Jews*. 6 vols. Philadelphia, 1974.

Gramlich, Richard. *Die Wunder der Freunde Gottes: Theologien und Erscheinungsformen der Heiligenwunder im Islam*. Wiesbaden, 1987.

Griffith, Sidney. "Answering the Call of the Minaret: Christian Apologetics in the World of Islam," in Jan van Ginkel, Hendrika L. Murre-van den Berg, and Theo Maarten van Lint (eds.), *Redefining Christian Identity: Cultural Interaction in the Middle East since the Rise of Islam*. Leuven, 2005, pp. 91–126.

Griffith, Sidney. *The Bible in Arabic: The Scriptures of the "People of the Book" in the Language of Islam*. Princeton, 2013.

Griffith, Sidney. "Disputing with Islam in Syriac: The Case of the Monk of Bêt Ḥālê and a Muslim Emir," *Journal of Syriac Studies* 3, no. 1 (2000): 29–54.

Griffith, Sidney. "Excursus I: Christian Theological Thought During the First ʿAbbasid Century," in Sabine Schmidtke (ed.), *The Oxford Handbook of Islamic Theology*. Oxford, 2014, pp. 91–102.

Griffith, Sidney. "Faith and Reason in Christian Kalam: Theodore Abu Qurrah on Discerning the True Religion," In S. K. Samir and J. S. Nielsen (eds.), *Christian Arabic Apologetics during the Abbasid Period (750–1258)*. Leiden, 1994, pp. 1–43.

Griffith, Sidney. "The Prophet Muḥammad, His Scripture, and His Message According to the Christian Apologies in Arabic and Syriac from the First Abbasid Century," in T. Fahd (ed.), *La vie du prophète Mahomet: Colloque du Strassbourgh, 1980*. Paris, 1983, pp. 99–146.

Griffith, Sidney. "The Syriac Letters of Patriarch Timothy I and the Birth of Christian Kalām in the Muʿtazilite Milieu of Baghdad and Basrah in Early Islamic Times," in W. J. van Bekkum (ed.), *Syriac Polemics: Studies in Honor of Gerrit Jan Reinink*. Leuven, 2007, pp. 103–132.

Hallaq, Wael. *The Origins and Evolution of Islamic Law*. Cambridge, 2005.

Heidemann, Stefan. "The Evolving Representation of the Early Islamic Empire and Its Religion on Coin Imagery," in Angelika Neuwirth, et al. (eds.), *The Qur'an in Context: Historical and Literary Investigations into the Qur'ānic Milieu*. Leiden, 2010, pp. 149–195.

Heimgartner, Martin. *Die Disputation des ostsryrischen Patriarchen Timothy (780–823) mit dem Kalifen Al-Mahdi*. Leuven, 2011.

el-Hibri, Tayeb. *Reinterpreting Islamic Historiography: Hārūn al-Rashīd and the Narrative of the 'Abbāsid Caliphate*. Cambridge, 1999.

Hollander, Aaron. "Comparison as Collaboration: Notes on the Contemporary Craft of Hagiology," in *Religions* 11, no. 1 (2020): 31, https://doi.org/10.3390/rel11010031.

Horovitz, Josef. "Alter und Ursprung des Isnād," in *Der Islam* 8 (1918): 39–47.

Horovitz, Josef. *Earliest Biographers of the Prophet and Their Authors*. Princeton, 2002.

Horovitz, Josef. "Zur Muḥammadlegende." *Der Islam* 5 (1914): 41–53.

Horst, Heribert. "Zur Überlieferung Im Korankommentar Aṭ-Ṭabarīs." *Zeitschrift Der Deutschen Morgenländischen Gesellschaft* 103 (n.F. 28), no. 2 (1953): 290–307.

'Irāqī, Aḥmad Ṭāhirī and Naṣr Allāh Pūrjavādī. "Abū Sa'd-i Khargūshī-yi Nīshābūrī," in *Ma'ārif* 15, no. 3 (1377/1999): 2–33.

Jarrar, Maher. *Die Prophetenbiographie im Islamischen Spanien: Ein Beitrag Zur Überlieferungs- und Redaktionsgeschichte*. Frankfurt a. M., 1989.

Jeffrey, Arthur. "Ghevond's Text of the Correspondence between 'Umar II and Leo III," in *Harvard Theological Review* 37, no. 4 (1944): 269–332.

Jones, J. M. B. "The Maghāzī Literature," in A. F. L. Beeston (ed.), *Arabic Literature to the End of the Umayyad Period*, Cambridge, 1983, pp. 344–351.

Judd, Steven. "Muslim Persecution of Heretics During the Marwānid Period (64–132/684–750)." *Al-Masaq* 23, no. 1 (2010): 1–14. https://doi.org/10.1080/09503110.2011.552943.

Juynboll, G. H. A. *Encyclopedia of Canonical Ḥadīth*. Leiden, 2007. (listed on page 61, footnote 36)

Juynboll, G. H. A. *Muslim Traditions: Studies in Chronology, Provenance, and Authorship in Early Ḥadīth*. Cambridge, 1983.

Khalidi, Tarif. *Images of Muhammad: Narratives of the Prophet in Islam Across the Centuries*. New York, 2009.

Khoury, Raif Georges. "Wahb ibn Munabbih," in *EI*², 11:34ff.

Khoury, Raif Georges. *Wahb ibn Munabbih*. 2 vols. Wiesbaden, 1972.

Kister, Meir Jacob. "Notes on the Papyrus Text about Muḥammad's Campaign against the Banū al-Naḍīr," in *Archiv Orientální* 32 (1964): 233–236.

Kister, Meir Jacob. "The Sirah Literature," in A. F. L. Beeston (ed.), *Arabic Literature to the End of the Umayyad Period.* Cambridge, 1983, pp. 352–367.

Knight, Michael Muhammad. *Muhammad's Body: Baraka Networks and the Prophetic Assemblage.* Chapel Hill, NC, 2020.

Koertner, Mareike. "Scholarship or Folklore? A Comparison of the Earliest Sources of the Sira, ʿUrwa b. al Zubayr and Wahb b. Munabbih" in: Jamal Elias and Bilal Orfali, Light upon Light. Essays in Early Islamic Thought in Honor of Gerhard Bowering, Brill, Leiden, 2019, pp. 3–24.

Koertner, Mareike. "Dalāʾil al-Nubūwa Literature as Part of the Medieval Scholarly Discourse on Prophecy," in: *Der Islam*, 95(1), pp. 91–109, 2018.

Kohlberg, Etan. *A Medieval Muslim Scholar at Work: Ibn Ṭāwūs and His Library.* Leiden, 1992.

LaCapra, Dominick. *Rethinking Intellectual History: Texts, Contexts, Language.* Ithaca, 1983.

Lazarus-Yafeh, Hava. *Intertwined Worlds: Medieval Islam and Bible Criticism.* Princeton, 1992.

Lecker, Michael. "Wāqidī's Account on the Status of the Jews of Medina: A Study of a Combined Report," in *JNES* 54, no. 1 (Jan. 1995): 15–32.

Lecker, Michael. "Zayd b. Thābit, 'A Jew with Two Sidelocks,' Judaism and Literacy in Pre-Islamic Medina (Yathrib)," in *JNES* 56 (1997): 259–273.

Lecomte, "Ibn Ḳutayba," in *EI*², 3:844–847.

Leder, Stefan. "Conventions of Fictional Narration in Learned Literature," in Stefan Leder (ed.), *Story-Telling in the Framework of Non-Fictional Arabic Literature.* Wiesbaden, 1998, pp. 34–60.

Leder, Stefan. "The Literary Use of Khabar: A Basic Form of Historical Writing," in A. Cameron (ed.), *The Byzantine and Early Islamic Near East 1: Problems in the Literary Source Materials.* Princeton, 1992, pp. 277–315.

Leder, Stefan and Yāsīn Muḥammad al-Sawwas. *Muʿjam al-samāʿat al-dimashqiyya: Suwar al-makhṭūṭāt al-muntakhaba min sanat 550 ilā 750 H/1155 ilā 1349 M.* Damascus, 1996.

Lifshitz, Felice. "Beyond Positivism and Genre: "Hagiographical" Texts as Historical Narrative," in Felice Lifshitz (ed.), *Writing Normandy.* London, 2020.

Loth, Otto. *Das Classenbuch des Ibn Saʿd.* Leipzig, 1869.

Lucas, Scott. *Constructive Critics: Ḥadīth Literature and the Articulation of Sunnī Islam.* Leiden, 2004.

Madelung, Wilferd. "Abū Noʿaym al-Eṣfahānī," in *EIr*, vol. 1, Fasc. 4, p. 354f.

Martin, Richard C. "Inimitability," in Jane Dammen McAuliffe (ed.), in *EQ*, 2:526–535.

Martin, Richard C. "The Role of the Basrah Muʿtazila in Formulating the Doctrine of the Apologetic Miracle," in *JNES* 39, no. 3 (1980): 175–189.

McDermott, Martin. "Eṣfahānī, Abū'l-Šayk Abū Moḥammad ʿAbd Allāh," in *EIr*, vol. VIII, Fasc. 6, p. 583.

Melchert, Christopher. "Khargūshi, *Tahdhīb al-asrār*," in BSOAS 73, no. 1 (2010): 29–44.

Motzki, Harald. "Dating Muslim Traditions: A Survey," in *Arabica* 52, fasc. 2 (April 2005): 204–253.

Motzki, Harald. "Der Fiqh des–Zuhrī: Die Quellenproblematik," in *Der Islam* 68 (1991): 1–44.

Motzki, Harald. *The Origins of Islamic Jurisprudence: Meccan Fiqh Before the Classical Schools*. Leiden, 2002.

Motzki, Harald. "Quo vadis Ḥadīth-Forschung?" in *Der Islam* 73 (1996): 40–80 and 193–231.

Mūsā, ʿIzz al-Dīn ʿUmar. *Ibn Saʿd wa-ṭabaqātuhu*. Beirut, 1987.

Nagel, Tilman. *Allahs Liebling. Ursprung und Erscheinungsformen des Mohammedglaubens*. Munich, 2008.

Neuwirth, Angelika. "Das islamische Dogma der 'Unnachahmlichkeit des Korans' in literaturwissenschaftlicher Sicht," in *Der Islam* 60 (1983): 166–183.

Newby, Gordon. "Tafsir Isra'iliyat: The Development of Qur'an Commentary in Early Islam and its Relationship to Judeo-Christian Traditions of Scriptural Commentary," in *Journal of the American Academy of Religion* 47, no. 4S (Dec. 1979): 685–698.

Newmann, Andrew. *The Formative Period of Twelver Shīʿism: Ḥadīth as Discourse between Qum and Baghdad*. Richmond, 2000.

Nöldeke, Theodor. *Geschichte des Qorān*, edited by Friedrich Schwally. Vol. 2. Leipzig, 1909.

Nomoto, Shin and David Thomas. "Abū Ḥātim al-Rāzī," in David Thomas and Alex Mallet (eds.), *Christian-Muslim Relations: A Bibliographical History*. Leiden, 2010, 2:200–209.

Palombo, Cecilia. "The 'Correspondence' of Leo III and ʿUmar II: Traces of an Early Christian Arabic Apologetic Work," in *Millenium* 12, no. 1 (2015): 231–264.

Paret, Rudi. "Die Lücke in der Überlieferung über den Urislam," in Fritz Meier (ed.), *Westöstliche Abhandlungen. Rudolf Tschudi zum 70. Geburtstag*. Wiesbaden, 1954, pp. 147–153.

Pedersen, Johannes. "The Criticism of the Islamic Preacher," in *Die Welt des Islams* 2 (1953): 215–231.

Putman, Hans. *L'Eglise et l'Islam sous Timothée I (780–823). Etude sur l'église nestorienne au temps des premiers ʿAbbasides avec nouvelle edition et traduction du dialogue entre Timothée et al-Mahdi*. Beirut, 1975.

Raḥmān, Fazlur. *Islam*. Chicago, 1978.

Reinhart, A. Kevin. Review of *Juynbolliana, Gradualism, the Big Bang, and Ḥadīth Study in the Twenty-First Century*, by G. H. A. Juynboll, Jonathan Brown, Recep Senturk, Jonathan A. C. Brown, and Aisha Y. Musa, in JAOS 130, no. 3 (2010): 413–444.

Reynolds, Gabriel Said. “al-Hādī ilā l-Ḥaqq,” in David Thomas and Alex Mallet (eds.), *Christian-Muslim Relations: A Bibliographical History*. Leiden, 2010, 2:15–129.

Reynolds, Gabriel Said. *A Muslim Theologian in a Sectarian Milieu: ʿAbd al-Jabbār and the Critique of Christian Origins*. Leiden, 2003.

Reynolds, Gabriel Said. *The Qurʾān and Its Biblical Subtext*. New York, 2010.

Rieu, Charles. *Catalogues of Persian Manuscripts in the British Museum*. London, 1879–83.

Robinson, Chase F. “History and Heilgeschichte in Early Islam: Some Observations on Prophetic History and Biography,” in Bernd-Christian Otto, Susanne Rau, and Rüpke Jörg (eds.), *History and Religion: Narrating a Religious Past*. Berlin, 2015, pp. 119–150.

Robson, James. “al-Bayhaḳī,” in *EI*², 1:1130.

Robson, James. “The Isnād in Muslim Tradition,” in *Transactions of the Glasgow University Oriental Society* 15 (1953–54): 15–26.

Robson, James. “Muslim Tradition—the Question of Authenticity,” in *Memoirs and Proceedings Manchester Library and Philosophical Society* 93 (1951–52): 84–102.

Roggema, Barbara. *The Legend of Sergius Baḥīrā: Eastern Christian Apologetics and Apocalyptic in Response to Islam*. Leiden, 2008.

Roggema, Barbara. “Risālat Abī l-Rabīʿ Muḥammad ibn al-Layth allatī katabahā li-l-Rashīd ilā Qusṭanṭīn malik al-Rūm (The Letter of Abū l-Rabīʿ Muḥammad ibn al-Layth Which He Wrote for al-Rashīd to the Byzantine Emperor Constantine),” in David Thomas and Barbara Roggema (eds.), *Christian-Muslim Relations*. Leiden, 2009, 1:349–353.

Rondolino, Massimo. “Some Foundational Considerations on Taxonomy: A Case for Hagiography,” in *Religions* 10, no. 10 (2019): 5–13; https://doi.org/10.3390/rel10100538.

Rubin, Uri. “Exegesis and *Ḥadīth*: The Case of the Seven Mathānī,” in Gerald R. Harting and ʿAbdul-Kader Shareef (eds.), *Approaches to the Qurʾān*. New York, 1993, pp. 141–156.

Rubin, Uri. “Jews and Judaism,” in *EQ*, 3:21–34.

Sachau, Eduard. “Der Berliner Fragment des Mūsā Ibn ʿUḳba,” in *Sitzungsberichte der Preussischen Akademie der Wissenschaften* 11 (1904): 445–470.

Saleh, Walid. *In Defense of the Bible: A Critical Edition and Introduction to al-Biqāʿī's Bible Treatise*. Leiden, 2008.

Schacht, Joseph. “Dāwūd b. ʿAlī b. Khalaf,” in *EI*², 2:182f.

Schacht, Joseph. “Ibn Rāhway,” in *EI*², 3:902.

Schacht, Joseph. “On Mūsā b. ʿUqba's Kitāb al-Maghāzī,” in *Acta Orientalia* 21 (1953): 288–300.

Schacht, Joseph. *Origins of Islamic Jurisprudence*. Oxford, 1967.

Schimmel, Annemarie. *And Muhammad Is His Messenger: The Veneration of the Prophet in Islamic Piety*. Chapel Hill, NC, 1985.

Schmidtke, Sabine. "Abū al-Ḥasan al-Baṣrī and His Transmission of Biblical Material from *Kitāb al-Dīn wa-l-dawla* by Ibn Rabban al-Ṭabarī: The Evidence from Fakhr al-Dīn al-Rāzī's *Mafātiḥ al-ghayb*," in *Islam and Christian-Muslim Relations* 20, no. 2 (April 2009): 105–118.

Schmidtke, Sabine. "Biblical Predictions of the Prophet Muḥammad Among the Zaydīs of Iran," in *Arabica* 59 (2012): 218–266.

Schmidtke, Sabine. "The Muslim Reception of Biblical Materials: Ibn Qutayba and his *Aʿlām al-Nubuwwa*," in *Islam and Christian-Muslim Relations* 22, no. 3 (2011): 249–274.

Schoeler, Gregor. *Charakter und Authentie der Muslimischen Überlieferung über das Leben Mohammeds*. Berlin, 1996.

Schoeler, Gregor. "Die Frage der schriftlichen oder mündlichen Überlieferung der Wissenschaften im frühen Islam," in *Der Islam* 62 (1985): 201–230.

Schoeler, Gregor. "Mündliche Thora und Ḥadīth: Überlieferung, Schreibverbot, Redaktion," in *Der Islam* 66 (1989): 231–251.

Schoeler, Gregor. "Mūsā b. ʿUqbas Maghāzī," in Harald Motzki (ed.), *The Biography of Muḥammad: The Issue of the Sources*. Leiden, 2000.

Schoeler, Gregor. "Schreiben und Veröffentlichen: Zu Verwendung und Funktion der Schrift in den ersten islamischen Jahrhunderten," in *Der Islam* 69 (1992): 1–43.

Schoeler, Gregor. "Weiteres zur Frage der schriftlichen oder mündlichen Überlieferung der Wissenschaften im Islam," in *Der Islam* 66 (1989): 38–67.

Schoeler, Gregor and Andreas Görke. *Die ältesten Berichte über das Leben Muhammads: Das Korpus ʿUrwa Ibn az-Zubair*. Princeton, 2008.

Sezgin, Fuat. *Geschichte des Arabischen Schrifttums*. Frankfurt, 1967–2007.

Shahid, Irfan. *Byzantium and the Arabs in the Fourth Century*. Washington, DC, 1984.

Shahid, Irfan. *Byzantium and the Arabs in the Fifth Century*. Washington, DC, 1989.

Shahid, Irfan. *Byzantium and the Arabs in the Sixth Century*. Washington, DC, 1995–2009.

Sharfī, ʿAbd al-Majīd. *al-Fikr al-islāmī fī l-radd ʿalā l-naṣāra ila nihāyat al-qarn al-rābiʿ*. Tunis, 1986.

Ṣiddīqī, Muḥammad Zubayr. *Ḥadīth Literature: Its Origin, Development & Special Features*. Cambridge, 1993.

Spectorsky, Susan. "Sufyān b. ʿUyayna," in *EI*², 9:182f.

Spiegel, Gabrielle. "History, Historicism, and the Social Logic of the Text in the Middle Ages," in *Speculum* 65, no. 1 (1990): 59–86.

Sprenger, Aloys. *Das Leben und die Lehre des Mohammed*. Berlin, 1861–65.

Stetter, Eckart. "Topoi und Schemata in Ḥadīṯ," PhD dissertation, Eberhard-Karls-Universität zu Tübingen, 1965.

Storey, Charles Ambrose. *Persian Literature*. 5 vols. London, 1927.

Stroumsa, Sarah. *Dāwūd ibn Marwān al-Muqammiṣ's Twenty Chapters (ʿIshrūn Maqāla)*. Leiden, 1989.

Stroumsa, Sarah. *Freethinkers of Medieval Islam: Ibn al-Rawāndī, Abū Bakr al-Rāzī and Their Impact on Islamic Thought*. Leiden, 1999.

Stroumsa, Sarah. "The Signs of Prophecy: The Emergence and Early Development of a Theme in Arabic Theological Literature," in *Harvard Theological Review* 78, nos. 1/2 (Jan.–April 1985): 101–114.

Stülpnagel, Joachim von. "ʿUrwa Ibn az-Zubair: Sein Leben und Seine Bedeutung als Quelle frühislamischer Überlieferung," PhD dissertation, Eberhard-Karls-Universität zu Tübingen, 1957.

Sviri, Sara. "The Early Mystical Schools of Baghdad and Nīshāpūr," in *Jerusalem Studies in Arabic and Islam* 30 (2005): 450–482.

Talbani, Shamsuddin. "The Debate about Prophecy in 'Kitab aʿlām al-nubūwah': An Analytic Study," MA thesis, Institute of Islamic Studies, McGill University, Montreal, 1987.

Tannous, Jack. *The Making of the Medieval Middle East: Religion, Society, and Simple Believers*. Princeton, 2018.

Thomas, David. "Abū l-Ḥasan b. al-Munajjim," in David Thomas and Alex Mallet (eds.), *Christian-Muslim Relations: A Bibliographical History*. Leiden, 2010, 2:234–237.

Thomas, David. "Abū ʿIsā Aḥmad b. Munajjim," in David Thomas and Alex Mallet (eds.), *Christian-Muslim Relations: A Bibliographical History*. Leiden, 2010, 2:108–111.

Thomas, David. "Abū Yaʿqūb al-Sijistānī," in David Thomas and Alex Mallet (eds.), *Christian-Muslim Relations: A Bibliographical History*. Leiden, 2010, 2:381–385.

Thomas, David. "al-Bāḥilī," in David Thomas and Alex Mallet (eds.), *Christian-Muslim Relations: A Bibliographical History*. Leiden, 2010, 2:134f.

Thomas, David. "The Caliph al-Maʾmūn," in Barbara Roggema and David Thomas (eds.), *Christian-Muslim Relations: A Bibliographical History*. Leiden, 2009, 1:582–584.

Thomas, David. "al-Wāsiṭī," in David Thomas and Alex Mallet (eds.), *Christian-Muslim Relations: A Bibliographical History*. Leiden, 2010, 2:145f.

Thomas, David. "al-Zuḥayrī," in David Thomas and Alex Mallet (eds.), *Christian-Muslim Relations: A Bibliographical History*. Leiden, 2010, 2:522f.

Thomas, David and Gabriel S. Reynolds. "ʿAbd al-Jabbār," in David Thomas and Alex Mallet (eds.), *Christian-Muslim Relations: A Bibliographical History*. Leiden, 2010, 2:594–609.

Vadet, Jean-Claude. "Ibrāhīm b. Isḥāḳ," in *EI*², 3:994.

Wansbrough, John. *Quranic Studies: Sources and Methods of Scriptural Interpretation*. Oxford, 1977.

Wansbrough, John. *The Sectarian Milieu: Content and Composition of Islamic Salvation History*. Oxford, 1978.

Watt, Montgomerey. "The Materials Used by Ibn Ishaq," in Bernard Lewis and P. M. Holt, *Historians of the Middle East*. London, 1962, pp. 23–34.

Wellhausen, Julius. *Muhammed in Medina. Das ist Vaktidi's Kitab al-Maghazi, in verkürzter deutscher Wiedergabe*. Berlin, 1882.

Wensinck, Arent Jan. *Concordance et Indices de la Tradition Musulmane*. Leiden, 1936–88.

Wensinck, Arent Jan. "Muʿdjiza," in *EI*², 7:295.

Wüstenfeld, Ferdinand. *Die Familie el-Zubeir*. Göttingen, 1878.

Zaman, Muhammad Qasim. *Religion and Politics under the Early ʿAbbāsids: The Emergence of a Proto-Sunnī Elite*. Leiden, 1997.

Index of Subjects

ʿAbbāsid period
  circumstances/environment of 184, 186
  socio-political shifts during 2
ablutions 104, 115, 140
abrogation 89, 171
admonishers 19–20. *See also* preachers
ahl al-bayt (members of [Muḥammad's] household) 97
ahl al-ḥadīth
  circles 176
  movement 53, 61, 204
akhbār (reports, traditions) 42, 44, 71, 88, 130, 179
amarāt al-nubūwa 39
American Academy of Religion (AAR) 14
angel(s)
  discourse of, and *jinn* 36*n*101, 84, 113
  Gabriel and Michael 127
  removed "Satan's share" from Muḥammad's heart 194
  shade Muḥammad 107–108
  in shape of pigeon 87
  weighed Muḥammad against his community 194
animals 74, 79, 120, 131, 179
  camel(s) 138
    during *hijra* 212, 214
    and Jābir 137
    prostrate before Muḥammad 196
    protect Muḥammad 36
    seeks protection 118, 195
    speaking 190
  cows/calf 6*n*16, 80*n*52
    for idol Suwāʿ 112
    for sacrifice, voice from 112, 178
  donkey, as smarter, faster 117
  dove, in cave 31
  gazelle, and hunters 195
  goats
    milk from 115–116, 128, 129, 135–136
    poisoned 189, 201
  horse, of Surāqa 31–32, 75–77, 128, 189
  interactions with 118, 195
  lion
    fulfills Muḥammad's curse of ʿUtba 190
    stranded on island 198
  lizard 190, 196, 198
  physical transformation of 190
  pigeon, at entrance to cave 72, 77–79, 87, 90, 195
  seek protection 118
  sheep
    in account of *hijra* 33, 213
    milking of barren 31–32, 72–74, 115–116, 189, 195, 197
    poisoned, speaking 110
    prostrate before Muḥammad 196
  speech of/speaking 1, 6, 189
  wolf, speaking 7, 79–80, 91, 114, 189, 195, 198
annunciation narratives 170, 172, 180, 184–185. *See also* predictions/announcements
Anṣār 32
apologetic literature/works 150, 158
  Christian 152, 157, 167, 169, 172
  earliest Syriac 154
  Near Eastern Christian 153
apologists
  Christian 153, 155, 162, 165, 168, 169–170, 181
  Syriac anti-Muslim 154
Arabic (language) 20, 184
  churches' adoption of 151
  translations of Bible 183
Arabs 44, 93–94, 113, 159, 163–165, 180
  ask for signs of Muḥammad's prophecy 141
  political power among 165
army(ies) 115–117, 136, 189*n*19. *See also* campaigns; conquests
  victory of Muslim 134
arrangement 92, 94
  of Abū Nuʿaym's *Dalāʾil al-nubūwa* 192
  of al-Bayhaqī's works 59
  chronological 70, 179
  of Ibn Isḥāq 180
ascension (*miʿrāj*), of Muḥammad 97, 133
ascetics 20, 61
Ashʿarī school 58–59, 200*n*81
  theology of 15, 204

astronomers 36, 96
astronomy 112, 114
audience(s) 38, 65, 172
  Arabic-speaking 150
  certificate 68–69
  Christian 156, 160, 162, 174
  gender boundaries among 22
  of Muḥammad 165
  Muslim 160, 185
  popular 207
  scholarly 40
  as uneducated 80
authentication
  of accounts, narratives 11, 26
  degrees/levels of 63, 71, 84
  demands/requirements of 71, 143
  of *ḥadīth* 8, 64, 69
  parameters of 64, 66
  standards of 67, 75, 79, 84, 100, 101, 103
authenticity 67, 77*n*40, 210
  criteria of 90
authorial processes 125*n*115
authority
  doctrinal 146
  Muḥammad's prophetic 66, 149
  political 1–2, 22
authors 9, 92, 144
  of *dalāʾil al-nubūwa* works 15, 40, 41, 45, 51, 53, 55, 56, 60, 61, 63, 102
    interconnections of 51, 53, 85
authorship 40, 125, 130
awliyāʾ (saints) 200

Badr, battle of 27, 86*n*70, 97, 106, 197*n*63
Bāhila (tribe) 136
Banū ʿAbd al-Muṭṭalib 117
Banū ʿAdī 29, 214
Banū ʿAmr b. Awf 29
Banū ʿIfār 112
Banū Isrāʾīl 107
  prophet of 108–109
Banū Lihb, omen of 114, 123
Banū l-Najjār 29
Banū Makhzūm 32
Banū Mudlij 31
Banū Qurayẓa 27, 108–109, 179
Banū Saʿd b. Bakr 123
Bayān b. Samʿān al-Nahdī 148
Bedouins, accept Islam 141
Bible 26. *See also* Gospel
  Hebrew 3, 154, 162, 174, 181
  Muḥammad predicted in 177
  New Testament 3, 154, 162
  translations of 183, 210
biblical passages/texts 181, 210
  announcing Muḥammad's coming 154, 173–174
  as evidence of Muḥammad's prophetic mission 185, 209
  in Hebrew, Syriac, Greek 171
  Muslim approach to, use of 171, 176
biographical
  dictionaries (*ṭabaqāt*) 16, 144
  material, chronological 98, 192
biography(ies) 20. *See also sīra*
  comprehensive 99, 196
  of Muḥammad 4, 148, 177
blessings 132
  baraka, through Muḥammad's touch 140, 141
  of dates 135–137
  on Ḥalīma's family 120, 122, 124, 193, 205
  in *hijra* account 74
  from Muḥammad 108

campaigns/raids (*maghāzī*), of Muḥammad 70, 105. *See also maghāzī* (raids)
caregivers/genealogy, of Muḥammad 96, 97, 123, 167, 192
cave 97
  concealment of, with cobweb 31, 34, 72, 77–78, 85, 189
  of al-Ḥirāʾ 132, 139
  pigeons/dove, at entrance of 31, 72, 77–79, 87, 90, 195
  scorpion in 30
  spider in 31, 90
  of Thawr 30–31, 212
  trees in front of 78, 87, 90
chain of transmission (*isnād*) 24, 26–27, 85–86. *See also isnāds*
chapters, thematic 84, 92, 98, 106
character, of Muḥammad 126, 132, 137, 138, 169, 174, 185, 193
charlatans 6, 19, 60, 80
Christianity 2, 155, 162, 164, 168

Christian(s) 96, 160, 168
account/legend of Baḥīrā 106, 159, 165
accusations against Islam/Muslims 169
accused of falsifying scripture 171, 173
awareness/recognition of Muḥammad 106, 108, 111–112, 145
conversion to Islam 152
discourses 17, 170
doctrines 152–153, 154, 158, 172
Ibn Isḥāq's reliance on works of 183
Jacobite, Melkite, Nestorian 155
-Muslim debates/exchanges 16
and Muslims, social proximity of 149, 153, 156–157, 184
refutations 166, 173, 176, 185
scholars/learned men 150, 151, 192
tropes, in rejecting Islam 162
chronology 41, 164, 183, 187
of Muḥammad's childhood 94, 96, 99
clouds 120, 131
shade Muḥammad 118–119, 124, 189
coins/coinage 151
communication, divine 165
community(ies)
Christian and Muslim 150
construct memory of individuals 208
faith, proximity to 145
Companions (*ṣaḥāba*) 71, 89
Muḥammad traveling with 115
preserved Muḥammad's biography 18
concubines 165
conquests/raids (*maghāzī*) 20, 24, 44, 99, 134, 150, 197. *See also* campaigns; *maghāzī*
context(s) 9–10, 102
of ʿAbbāsid period 184
historical 94, 97, 109, 121
intellectual 40, 144, 184, 207
monotheistic and pagan 131
political 144, 173, 184, 207, 209
of sacred history, miracles of Muḥammad 202
social 144, 207
of socio-political shifts 2–3
contextualizations 16
historical 192
theological 98
conversion 128, 153, 168–169, 194, 196
of Abū Dharr al-Ghifārī 194
after hearing Qurʾānic recitation 205
of ʿAlī b. Rabbān al-Ṭabarī 161
of Christians, to Islam 108, 158
during *hijra* 214
to Islam 104, 108, 110, 136, 149, 151, 152, 166, 178
to Judaism 109
miracles 189
narratives/stories 99, 114, 194
of Salmān al-Fārisī 178–179, 194
of Surāqa b. Mālik 75
of ʿUmar b. ʿAbasa al-Sulamī 194
correspondence
fictional, between al-Kindī and al-Hāshimī 159
fictitious Christian-Muslim 152
between John I and Muslim official 154
between ʿUmar b. ʿAbd al-ʿAzīz and Leo III 154, 171–172, 176, 181
counter-history 158, 160, 168, 185
court, centrality/influence of 182
createdness (of Qurʾān) 49, 146, 152
criticism/critique
of *ḥadīth* 44, 64–66
of Islam 166
of *isnāds* 64
of *quṣṣāṣ* 22
culture, Muslim 25*n*49

dalāʾil al-nubūwa 2–3, 12, 39
authors of 41, 45, 51, 53, 56, 60, 61, 63, 102
as biographies of Muḥammad 11
compilations, transmission of 51
considered hagiographic 207
as discourse 186
genre of 105
methodological approaches of 85
not entertainment/popular literature 40, 207
patterns in 51, 103
and primary sources for 4
dalāʾil al-nubūwa literature 4, 7, 11–12, 23, 185
of Abū Nuʿaym and al-Bayhaqī 6, 60, 80, 100
centered on network/circle of scholars 12, 53, 61, 90
character of 1, 63
dismissal of 6, 10, 79
earliest thematic compilation of 42

dalāʾil al-nubūwa literature (*cont.*)
  framework of 90, 191
  ḥadīth-based 4–5, 13, 67, 101, 209, 210
  influences on 15
  methodological shift in/systematization of 101, 203
  scholarly origins of 15, 45, 84
  as sub-genre of *sīra* 7, 72
dalāʾil al-nubūwa works
  and *ḥadīth* scholarship 86
  majority *ḥadīth* compilations 63
  methodological approaches of 99
  organization of 15, 99
death, and final judgment 20
debate(s) 158. *See also* correspondence; exchanges
  between Abraham of Tiberias and ʿAbd al-Raḥmān b. al-Mālik b. Ṣāliḥ 155
  Christian-Muslim, on prophecy of Muḥammad 16, 184
  inter-religious 14
  on *kalām* 152
  between monk of Bēt Ḥālē and Muslim 157, 164
  polemical 16
  on prophecy 50
  on Qurʾān's rejection of evidentiary miracles 167
demographic changes/shifts 149, 152, 184
demons 133. *See also* Iblīs/Satan
dhikr circles 21
discourse(s)
  Jewish and Christian 17
  on Muḥammad's prophetic mission/legitimacy 170, 176
  Muslim, to challenge Christian doctrines 172
  on paraclete 183
  on prophecy, Muslim-Christian 184–185
  theological, on miracles 188
disputation
  narratives 153, 157
  between Timothy I and al-Mahdī 163, 176, 181
divorce 165
dreams 114, 132. *See also* visions
  of Muḥammad 127, 141, 212
drought 31, 72, 119. *See also* water
elite(s)
  Christian and Muslim 157
  political 146–147, 152
  religious and intellectual 149
eloquence (*balāgha*) 200
emigrations
  to Abyssinia 28, 33
  to Medina 28
entertainment 207
  for laymen 60
  for masses 6, 18, 20, 67, 79–80
epistemological
  boundaries of "legitimate" prophecy 145
  meaning, in inclusion 142
  notions 144
epistolary exchanges 153, 157
ethics/ethical 51
  behavior 169
  religious 53
  values 166
exchanges
  Christian-Muslim 182, 185
  direct and indirect 157
  fictional, between al-Hāshimī and al-Kindī 157–158, 161–162
  intellectual 149, 151, 153
  between ʿUmar b. ʿAbd al-ʿAzīz and Leo III 171–172
exegesis/commentaries (*tafsīr*) 20, 177
exemplary persona, construction of 10, 208–209
explanation (*bayān*) 200
expression (*lisān*) 200

fabrications/fabricators 5, 207
  of *ḥadīth* 66
  of narratives to entertain masses 5, 67, 79–80
Fadak (Jewish tribe of Medina) 110, 112
fictionalization, of debates/correspondences 158. *See also* correspondence; debate(s); exchanges
fiqh. *See* jurisprudence
folklore 79–80. *See also* legends
Followers (*tābiʿūn*) 23, 26, 37, 71, 89
food 135, 140, 213
  abundance/increase in 116–117, 132, 137, 195

food (*cont.*)
and/or water incidents/miracles 106, 116, 131–132, 133, 134, 136, 140, 189
milk, and Miqdād 128
milk of goat/sheep suffices many 115–116
fortune-tellers, in pre-Islamic Arabia 83

Gabriel (angel). *See also* angel(s)
and Aswad b. al-Muṭṭalib 35–36
Muḥammad encounters 127–128, 139
warned Muḥammad 212
gender boundaries 22
genealogy(ies)
of Muḥammad, from Christian view 167
tribal and ethnic 179–180
genres 5, 13, 209
of Christian apologetics 152, 157
and *dalāʾil al-nubūwa* works 7, 72, 105, 186
hagiographic 10, 14
literary 86, 156–157
shamāʾil al-nabī 105
God/divine
attributes 166
existence and unity (*tawḥīd*) of 1
human contact with 156
and interaction with Muḥammad 96
and protection, of Muḥammad 99, 197
gold, increase of 130, 179
Gospel 164, 166–167, 171, 180–181. *See also* Bible
Christian Palestinian Aramaic (CPA) version of 183
Greco-Arabic translation movement 149, 151

ḥadīth 3, 13, 53, 80*n*52, 89, 92, 142, 177, 179, 198. *See also isnāds*
accounts 3, 41
āḥād (transmitted from a single person) 66–67, 88–89
authentication of 8, 64
canonical collections 47, 61, 64–65, 80
collections, exhaustive *vs.* critical 67
collections/compilations 39, 40*n*3, 92, 209
collectors/compilers 40, 64, 66
criticism 44, 65–66
and *dalāʾil al-nubūwa* literature 12, 13, 39, 63, 84, 100
factual style of 82
forged and fabricated 66
al-ḥadīth fī-hi qiṣṣa 80
methodology, Sunnī *isnād*-based 60
mutawātir (accounts transmitted through numerous transmitters) 88–89
organization of 187
parameters 91
reliability of 66–67, 69, 89
scholar(s)/scholarship 4, 42, 51, 63, 67, 79–80, 90, 100, 142–143, 144
Abū Nuʿaym al-Iṣfahānī as 191
efflorescence of 42
foremost/respected 46–48, 58, 60, 61
methodological requirements of 86, 87–88, 92
paternalistic view of 65
shared understanding among 135
as source of materials 14
standards/parameters of 24, 71, 85–86, 91
studies 12, 24
transmitters 20–21, 22, 69, 71
weak (*ḍaʿīf*) 66
ḥadīth-based *dalāʾil al-nubūwa* works 13–14, 41, 61, 84, 209
hagiographic works/texts 205, 207
hagiography 7, 10
comparative 13, 14, 209, 210
and historiography 8, 11
study of 207–208
hagiology, as methodological approach 207–208
hagios (sacred, or holy) 14
Ḥanbalī school 53, 59
vs. Shāfiʿī school 58
ḥanīf (non-denominational monotheist) 96, 111
heart (of Muḥammad), opened and cleansed 99, 124, 177, 194, 197, 205
heaven 127
ascension (*miʿrāj*) of Muḥammad to 133
hegemony, social and cultural 151–152
heresy 146–147
hijra 27, 189, 214
accounts/narratives of 15, 38, 72, 74
accounts of, ʿUrwa b. al-Zubayr *vs.* Wahb b. Munabbih 32–33
comparison of accounts 211–214

historicity 11, 63, 157–158
  or truthfulness, positivist quest for 8
historiographic, *vs.* hagiographic texts 207
historiography 7–8, 101, 177
  vs. hagiography 8, 10, 11
history 20, 156
  of conquests/raids (*maghāzī*) 44
  intellectual, of Islam 15
  positivist theory of 7, 10
  rival community rewrites 158
  universal 177, 182
holy spirit (*rūḥ al-qudus*) 111–112
Hour, references to 134
human(s)
  conduct, permissible and forbidden (*ḥalāl* and *ḥarām*) 166
  contact with divine 156
  free will 146
  physical transformation of 190
  reason 50, 152
hypocrites (*munāfiqūn*) 129

Iblīs/Satan 29–30, 33, 96, 113, 194
idol(s) 96, 112–113, 192
  at Buwāna 113
  Suwāʿ 112, 113*n*37
Idrīs 95*n*102
illiterate/unschooled, Muḥammad as 111–112, 173
immigration 211–212
incarnation 154, 161
infallibility, theological concept of 201
inimitability of the Qurʾān (*iʿjāz al-Qurʾān*) 200, 203, 205
innovation (*bidʿa*) 21
inscriptions (on coins, monuments, tombstones) 148
interpretation, subjective 9
Islam 22
  as Christian heresy 154, 163
  discrediting of message 158–159
  as last divine message/revelation 162, 164–165
  legitimizing 176
  as marginal development of Judaism 163
  as part of sacred history 158, 162–163
  refuting/denying 166, 169
  as religious/spiritual challenge 151, 155
  symbolic manifestations of 151
  teachings of 165
Ismāʿīlī works 3, 209
isnāds 23, 27, 77*n*40, 85, 91, 100
  collective 25, 70–71, 91, 100
  criticism 64
  evaluation of 66
  full 64, 71, 86
  individual 68, 70–71, 73, 75
  mursal (sound chain of transmission to Followers) 89
  paradigm of, *ṣaḥīḥ* (sound), *ḥasan* (good), and *ḍaʿīf* (weak) 66
  questionable/problematic 25, 66
Isrāʾīliyyāt (stories of the prophets) 6, 20, 26–27, 80, 86, 91

Jews 96, 99, 168
  accused of tampering with scriptures 171
  announce and/or recognize Muḥammad 106–109, 111–112
  envy/enmity toward Muḥammad 108, 110, 112
  on future prophecy of Muḥammad 36, 145
  and Ibn Isḥāq 183
  scholars/learned men among 109–110, 192
  warnings of 178
jinn 73, 96, 132, 177, 192
  announce revelation 36*n*101, 113, 133
  chased by meteors/shooting stars 79, 83–84, 113, 194
  on future prophecy of Muḥammad 36
  listening to celestial discourses 83, 178
  ruses of, Muḥammad protected from 193
Judaism 2, 109, 150*n*14, 175*n*107
judges 20
jurisprudence (*fiqh*) 12, 25, 55–56
jurists (*fuqahāʾ*) 20, 23

kalām (theology) 151–153, 209
  ʿilm al- 146
khulafāʾ al-rāshidūn (rightly-guided caliphs) 149

knowledge 146
hidden, of Muḥammad 118, 129, 133–134
Neoplatonic theory of 164
of Sunna 88

al-Lāt and al-ʿUzza (deities) 107
laymen 18, 60, 63, 102. *See also* masses
masses 18, 91
preachers 18
vs. specialists 65, 88
legal rulings (*aḥkām*) 20, 89
legends 1, 4
of Baḥīrā 156, 159, 165
hagiographic 7, 34
legitimacy 185, 210
challenges to religious 2–3, 16
of Muḥammad, as prophet 101, 142, 163, 173, 176, 179
political 148, 185
of sources 146, 152, 198
light 127, 137, 138
illuminated Busra 122
as marker of prophecy 121–122, 138
themes 138–139
literary
aspects, of inimitability of Qurʾān 205
dialogue between Christian master and Muslim disciple 163
genres 86, 156–157
personae *vs.* historical figures 158
and social functions of texts 158
literature 14–15, 177
maghāzī (raids) 89, 100, 101
of merits (*faḍāʾil*), remembrance (*tadhkira*), virtue (*manaqib*) 210
popular 4–5, 12, 40

madhhab, of al-Ẓāhirī 50
maghāzī (raids) 25, 71, 91, 98, 179. *See also* campaigns/raids; conquests/raids
Ibn Isḥāq as innovator in 185
literature/works 41, 70, 89, 100, 101
scholars 36–37
Manichaeism 147
manumission, of Salmān al-Fārisī 36–37, 130, 179
marriage
of ʿAbdallāh and Āmina (Muḥammad's parents) 121, 192
of Muḥammad, to Zaynab bt. Jaḥsh 160
masses (*ʿāmm*) 5–6, 67, 79–80
laymen 60, 91–92
vs. scholars or specialists (*khāṣṣ*) 65
uneducated 18–21
materialism 169
material transformations 104, 106, 130, 179, 190
matn 71
memory 18
collective 37
construction of 14, 208
deconstruction of 158
messengers 1
Abrahamic 170
successive 164–165
methodology(ies) 1, 64, 99–100, 207
for discussing religious questions 153
and framework of *dalāʾil al-nubūwa* compilations 90
shifts in 91, 203
miracle(s) 10–11, 34, 37, 89, 100, 188, 191, 197, 202
conversion 189
evidentiary 11, 167–168, 169, 173
food and/or water 36, 90, 96, 104, 106, 189
gold, increased in weight 36
hierarchy of 199
karamāt 199
legitimate and illegitimate 11–12
of material transformation 104
of Muḥammad 87, 92, 174, 200–201, 202
muʿjiza, pl. *muʿjizāt* 188, 209
narratives 34, 132
of Qurʾān (*iʿjāz al-Qurʾān*) 202
and signs 99
as subtype of proofs of prophecy 199
as term 188, 199, 204
mīthāq (covenant) 95
monk(s)
Baḥīrā 159, 164
Baḥīrā, and encounter with Muḥammad 99, 107, 125, 156, 158–159, 178, 197
of Bēt Ḥālē, debate with Muslim 157, 164
monotheism, Muḥammad preaching of 164–165, 174, 178
monotheists 96, 112, 131, 145, 177, 179

Montanist sect 147
moon, splitting of 11, 133, 194, 204
morality 166. *See also* ethics
of Muḥammad's character, actions, teachings 169
motif(s) 36, 143
Qur'ānic, of shooting stars and *jinn* 113–114
Mozarabs 155
muḥaddith
circles of 46
and *qāṣṣ*, binary between 27
muṣannaf works 44
mushrikūn 194, 204
Muslim(s)
and Christian communities 149–150
refuting Christianity 150*n*14
mutakallimūn 15, 160–161, 169, 200*n*81
mutawātir (transmitted through numerous initial transmitters) 66–67
vs. āḥād (one transmitter) 88–89
Muʿtazilī
doctrine, opposition to 53, 61
scholars, notions of 200*n*81
works 3, 209
Muʿtazilism 43, 49

al-Naḍīr (Jewish tribe of Medina) 110, 112
narrative(s) 71–72, 82, 130*n*136
authenticated *vs.* unauthenticated 23
in chronological arrangement 179
context of 16, 109
to entertain masses 18, 67, 79–80
Qur'ān/Qur'ān-inspired 133, 194
scholarly *vs.* popular, dichotomy of 22–23
of signs of prophecy, comparisons 125
subversive retellings of 160
unauthenticated 33, 85, 87, 189
narrators 73
science of (*ʿilm al-rijāl*) 45, 90
natural phenomena 96, 106, 117, 131, 135, 140, 189, 197
as signs of prophecy 119–120
nature. *See also* stone(s); tree(s)
protective aspects of 118
and recognition of Muḥammad's prophetic status 117, 179
soil and rain interact with Muḥammad 119–120, 126
non-Muslim population (*dhimmī*) 161

oath (sworn by Christians, Jews, polytheists) 168
oral traditions 26–27
orators 20. *See also* admonishers; preacher(s)
Orientalist(s) 7, 67, 81
assumptions/dismissal of *dalāʾil al-nubūwa* literature 56, 60, 79
positivist concerns of early 63
orthodoxy, imposing/implementing 146, 148

pagan(s) 96, 112–113, 131, 145, 163, 214
Arabs 165
beliefs 164, 205
Muḥammad protected from 201–202
practices 99
testimonies 179
paraclete 185
annunciation of 172
of Gospel of John 169, 171, 180–181, 183
in Ibn Isḥāq 183
partisans of *ḥadīth* (*ahl al-ḥadīth*) 152. *See also ahl al-ḥadīth*
vs. theologians (*mutakalimūn*) 15
People of the Book (*ahl al-kitāb*) 2, 16, 25, 150, 175
permission (*ʾijāza*) 68
poetry 44, 98, 179, 192
polemic(al)
arguments 162
Christian, against Muḥammad/Muslims 155, 160, 166, 185
texts 150
politics 173
polygamy 165
polytheists (*mushrikūn*) 204
demanded signs 194
positivist
approach 7–8
concerns of early Orientalists 63
theory 10, 14
post-Enlightenment European scholars 7
power, political 2–3, 146, 148–149, 165, 169, 184

preacher(s) 20, 51, 60–61
  female 22
  al-Khargūshī as 57, 60
  qāṣṣ 19–20
  wāʿiẓ 55–56, 61
predestinarian views 146
predictions/announcements 106, 131
  of Āmina's pregnancy 123
  monotheistic 106, 112, 114
  of Muḥammad 36, 96, 135, 143, 171, 174
  from pagan entities 112
  of paraclete 172
  scriptural 112
pregnancy, of Muḥammad's mother 192
pre-Islamic traditions 27
proofs of prophecy 3, 11–12, 40, 144–145, 150
  in biblical passages 174
  definition of 103
  epistemological notions of 134
  methodological approaches to 41
  and miracles as separate 199
  notion of 13, 16, 63, 98
  as part of multi-themed compilations 53
  thematic choices of 15–16
  theme of 99, 196
prophecy 94–95
  claims to 147
  concept/notion of 147–148, 170, 210
  defining feature of 132
  discourses about 184–185, 207
  epistemological notion/paradigm of 40, 169
  future 112
  light as marker of 121
  Muḥammad's call to 37, 99
  Muḥammad's claim to 167
  nature of 3, 209
  predictions/announcements of Muḥammad's 36, 96, 106, 111–112
  and role of Ibn Isḥāq in discourse of 181–182
  seal of 31, 94, 111
  theological discourses/discussions on 3, 87, 144, 210
prophethood
  Christian understanding of 160
  Ibn Isḥāq on 180
  Islamic concepts of 2
  proofs of 144
  scholarly discourse about 1–2
prophetic mission (of Muḥammad) 149, 170
  accounts contemporaneous with 106
  and annunciation of 180
  constructing "evidence" of 209
  defending 172–173, 177
  doctrine of 148
  proof/evidence of 131, 145
  proofs of 145
  spiritual preparation for 99, 205
  veracity of 13, 50, 103, 141, 152, 190, 196, 198, 201, 204
prophets 95, 179, 210
  announced by Jesus and in Torah 108
  earlier, annunciated Muḥammad's coming 169, 170, 174
  false 190
  preceding Muḥammad 95, 97, 111, 200–201
  pre-Islamic 38
  previous/earlier 180, 202–203
  self-proclaimed 147–148
protection 120
  animals seek 118, 195
protection, divine 121, 126, 128
  ʿiṣma 22, 201, 205, 209
  of Muḥammad 32, 36, 77, 189, 201–202
provisions
  for *hijra* 33
  sufficed many 117

qadar, issue of 21
Qadarīs 146
qāṣṣ (preacher) 19, 23, 38. *See also* preacher(s)
  and *muḥaddith*, binary between 27
  as term impossible to translate 20
qibla, changing from Jerusalem to Mecca 97
qiṣṣa, pl. *qiṣāṣ* 54, 71*n*20. *See also quṣṣāṣ*
  notion of 7, 80–81
Qurʾān 20, 29, 178, 194, 200
  and abrogation of earlier scriptures 171
  on biblical scriptures 170–171
  challenge (*taḥaddī*) verses 203
  claim of, and miracles 168
  claim that Muḥammad was predicted in Bible/previous scriptures 50, 177

Qur'ān (*cont.*)
createdness of 49, 152
on earlier communities 162
on evidentiary miracles 168
as false scripture 166
as greatest of prophetic miracles 199
knowledge of, by Christian apologists 158
miracles of (*iʿjāz al-*) 202
as most glorious of signs (*ʿalāmāt*) 188, 204
as Muḥammad's main miracle 204–205
passages on *jinn* 113
as proven to be inimitable (in Muḥammad's time) 173
Quraysh 28–30, 124, 211
and boycott of Banū Hāshim 129
on intent to kill Muḥammad 212
Muḥammad sprinkling dust on heads of 86–87, 189
Qurayẓa (Jewish tribe) 110, 112
quṣṣāṣ 38
as embellishers and fabricators for masses 5
as innovation (*bidʿa*) 21
material in commentaries (*tafsīr*) 20
material in *sīra* 27, 34–35
nature of 18–19
as religious scholars 21–22

rebellions (in Kufa) 148
refutations, Christian 166, 173, 176, 185
reliability 90–92, 100, 145
epistemological 63
of *ḥadīth* 66–67, 69, 89
religion, and process of defining 22
religio-political events/matters 14, 20
religious
competition, milieu of 158
ideal, embodied perfection of 208
personae, constructing 209
topics, and theological questions 20
retreats
to cave of al-Ḥirāʾ 132
of Muḥammad to mountains 135
revelation 73, 140
and absence of witnesses to 167, 169
acts of 126, 132, 170
beginning of 27, 34, 132
and Islam as final 165
signs prior to 134
while Muḥammad sat with ʿUthmān b. Maẓʿūn 127–128
reward, and punishment 166

sacred history 8, 165, 180–181, 203
Arabia's greater 184
continuous/continuum of 95, 97, 126, 145, 158, 162–165, 169, 202, 204
sacrificial animals 96, 112. *See also* animals
on Muḥammad's prophecy 36, 189
ṣaḥīḥ movement 65–66, 67, 88
ṣarfa (divine intervention) 200*n*81
scholarly
circles, as origin of *dalāʾil al-nubūwa* works 84, 208–209
discourse 145
reputation/standing, decline in 55, 60
standards 89–90
tradition 33–34
scholars 51, 61
from circles of pious individuals 65
legal and theological orientations of 40
personal relationships between 51
religious 38, 157, 185
as self-aware class of 65
specialists (*khāṣṣ*) *vs.* masses (*ʿāmm*) 65
and storytellers (*quṣṣāṣ*), dichotomy between 15
sciences, religious 14
scriptural corruption (*taḥrīf*), doctrine of 171, 181
scripture(s) 36, 145, 165, 167
al-Bayhaqī's focus on 202
Christian 31, 192
Christians accused of altering/falsifying 173, 181
doctrine of scriptural corruption (*taḥrīf*) 171, 181
Jewish 106, 192
Muḥammad recognized/described in 106, 110, 131
pre-Qur'ānic 171, 176, 180, 184
Qur'ān's abrogation of earlier 171
secularism 10

selection(s) 160, 162, 206, 209
of accounts 40, 142, 144, 201
of Ibn Saʿd 120–121, 132–133, 134, 150, 179
of narratives 61, 101, 145, 179, 188, 191
parameters 68
processes 16, 101, 103, 135, 170
title-based 16, 39–40
of topics 96
selectivity, aspect of 33
self-image(s) 156, 158
Shāfiʿī, *vs.* Ḥanbalī legal schools 58
Shīʿī
doctrines 59
imams 59, 210
Shīʿism, Twelver 40*n*3
shooting stars (*shihāb*) 36*n*101, 113–114, 177
or "fire in the sky" 133
sign(s) 197
ʿalāma, between Muḥammad's shoulders 105
āyā 200, 204
/indicator (*ʿalāma*) 200
miraculous 167–168
Qurʾān as most glorious of 188, 200
splitting of moon 11, 133, 194, 204
signs of prophecy (of Muḥammad) 64, 67, 69–70, 73, 77, 79, 92, 99, 100, 107, 114, 115, 214. *See also* heart (of Muḥammad)
accounts/narratives of 125, 130
after revelation 73, 110
ʿalām al-nubūwa 39, 42–43, 51, 70
books on *ayāt al-nabī* 45
chapters on 71–72, 74, 91, 195
earliest compilations of 41
explicit 118
in Ibn Saʿd 4, 42–43, 63, 91, 93, 120, 132
notion of 16, 135, 142
and physical appearance 72–73, 105, 193
prior to revelation 70–71, 142, 145
in *Ṣaḥīḥ al-Bukhārī* 133
sīra 14, 24–25, 70–71, 77, 91, 185
accounts 41, 100
and *dalāʾil al-nubūwa* as part of 101
Ibn Isḥāq, as innovator in 185
of Ibn Saʿd 70, 72–73, 78, 91, 93–94
literature 3, 7–8, 209
/*maghāzī* literature 64, 144, 187
miraculous/folkloristic material added to 34–35
of Wahb b. Munabbih 72–73
sleep 167
of Muḥammad 126
social proximity 153, 156, 184
of Muslims and Christians 149
soothsayers 112, 124, 179, 192
on future prophecy of Muḥammad 36
kuhān 96
sorcery/sorcerers 83, 169
soundness (*faṣāḥa*) 200
sources 180
of Abū Nuʿaym's *Dalāʾil al-nubūwa* 192
of al-Bayhaqī 87
broad pool of 87, 91–92, 192
of *dalāʾil al-nubūwa* literature 4
Ibn Isḥāq's reliance on Christian networks 184
of Ibn Saʿd 177
quṣṣāṣ as unreliable 19
scope of 209
scriptural, of Qurʾān and Sunna 152
spaces, social 9
specialists, *vs.* laymen 88
stone(s) 120. *See also* natural phenomena; tree(s)
greeted Muḥammad 141, 179, 189
interact with Muḥammad 118
vessel, split in two 122
stories of the prophets (*qiṣaṣ al-anbiyāʾ*) 26. *See also* Isrāʾīliyyāt
storytellers 6–7, 79
as entertainment for uneducated masses 20, 80
and scholars, dichotomy between 15
as unreliable 81
student(s) 23, 58, 61, 177
of ʿAbd al-Razzāq 43
of Abū Zurʿa al-Dimashqī 55
of al-Firyābī 54
of al-Ḥumaydī 51
of Isḥāq b. Rāhwayh al-Ḥanẓalī 53
of al-Jūzajānī 46–48, 51, 55
of al-Khargūshī 60
lists of, in sources 44, 47, 47*n*45
of al-Madāʾinī 53
of Maʿmar b. Rāshid 43, 105

student(s) (*cont.*)
 of al-Rāzī 48
 of al-Ṭabarānī 54
 -teacher relations 55, 85, 103
 and teachers 44, 68–69, 70*n*18
 of al-Zuhrī 24, 41, 64
Sufi masters, lives of 210
sunna 1, 20
 ahl al-sunna, doctrine of 59
Sunna 149
 legal concept of 149
 legitimized 88
Sunnī legal theorists 63
 epistemological framework of 66
supernatural
 elements, in *sīra* of Wahb 33
 events 36, 37–38, 104
 means 114
supplication(s) (*duʿā'*)
 of Muḥammad 82, 117, 119–120
 for rain 128, 133
 related to Surāqa 76
 and response by divine/God 120, 126, 128
supremacy, religious 2
sword, transformation to 105, 130
symbolic dominance 151
symbols(ism)
 Islamic 152
 of light 139
Syriac 154
systematization
 of *dalā'il al-nubūwa* works 16
 of materials 99
 of *sīra*, process of 98

tafsīr work 56
tales, popular/imaginary 79–80
taṣnīf, Muslim tradition on 24*n*37
tawātur. *See mutawātir*
tax (*jizya*) 150
teachers 46–47, 56, 59, 61, 68–69, 105, 163
 ʿAbd al-Razzāq b. Hammām 42
 Abū l-Majad Fatayān b. Ḥaydra b. ʿAlī l-Bajalī 58
 Abū l-Shaykh al-Iṣfahānī 86
 Abū Nuʿaym al-Iṣfahānī 57
 Baḥīrā as 165
 al-Ḥumaydī 47
 Ibn Abī l-Dunyā 50
 Ibn Shihāb al-Zuhrī 183
 Isḥāq b. Rāhawayh al-Ḥanẓalī 47, 49
 al-Madā'inī 51
 Musaddad b. Musarhad 49
 al-Naqqāsh 60
 shared 45
 -student relations 55, 85, 103
 Sufyān b. ʿUyayna 43, 45
 ʿUrwa 24
 al-Wāqidī 25
teaching circles (*ḥalaqāt*) 23
testimony of faith (*shahada*) 151, 198
texts/books 8–10, 57
 critical scholarly, *vs.* unreliable popular accounts 18
 hagiographic 14
 Syriac, Armenian, Greek, Coptic 150
thematic
 arrangements 94
 categories/categorization 103, 106, 135, 140, 141
 groups 131
 structure 196
theologians
 Ashʿarī 209
 Christian 150
 mutakalimūn vs. partisans of *ḥadīth* (*ahl al-ḥadīth*) 15
theology 93, 146, 204
 Ashʿarī 15, 199, 204
 concepts/notions of 198–199
 on divine protection (*ʿiṣma*) 209
 on miracles (*muʿjizāt*) 209
 narrativized 180, 185–186, 209
 position of (re. Muḥammad's primary miracle) 200
 on prophecy 148, 210
 as religious purpose 144
 speculative 61, 204
Torah 108, 110, 171
traditions. *See also ḥadīth*
 authenticated *vs.* unauthenticated 27
 dichotomy between scholarly and unauthenticated 38
 historical (*akhbār*) 42
 oral Jewish 26
 prophetic, compilation and transmission of 51

translation movement, Greco-Arabic 149, 151
transmitters 70, 85
  authority of single 100
  criterion of 88*n*83
  relying on weak 89
  rijāl (lit., men) 145
treatises
  fictionalized, of ʿAbd al-Masīḥ b. Isḥāq al-Kindī 166
  formal 153, 157
tree(s) 120, 130, 131
  in front of cave 78, 87, 90
  greet/interact with Muḥammad 118, 179
  in miracles of Muḥammad 189
  palm tree 119, 130, 133, 141, 195, 197
  prostration, relocation of 126, 195
  seedlings (re. Salmān's manumission) 179
trials (*miḥna*) 15, 146, 152
trials/afflictions (*fitna*), of Muslims 134
trinity 154, 161, 164, 165
trope, of milking a goat to feed crowd 136. *See also* motif(s)

Umayyads 146–147
unseen (*ghayb*) 203, 205

victories, military 174
violence 169
visions 114, 132. *See also* dreams
  apocalyptic, to interpret Muslim rule 159

wāʿiẓ (preacher; admonisher) 19. *See also* preacher(s)
water. *See also* food
  miracle at Ḥudaybiyya 36, 90, 197
  provision of, by Muḥammad 35, 104, 115, 195
  scarcity 104, 115, 116

Index of People and Places

ʿAbdallāh b. Abī Bakr 29, 213
ʿAbdallāh b. Abī Bakr b. Muḥammad 37
ʿAbdallāh b. Jaḥsh 104
ʿAbd al-Ḥalīm Maḥmūd 5
ʿAbd al-Malik 24*n*37, 28, 146–147, 151
  letter to 33, 211
ʿAbd al-Maṣīḥ b. Isḥāq al-Kindī 155–156, 157–158
  fictionalized treatise of 166
ʿAbd al-Muṭṭalib 96, 109, 122–123, 193
  on future rule of Muḥammad 114, 125, 178, 193
ʿAbd al-Qays, people of 31, 191
ʿAbd al-Raḥīm b. al-Ḥaytam [?] b. ʿAbd al-Raḥīm 68
ʿAbd al-Razzāq b. Hammām al-Ḥimyarī 20, 25, 42–43, 46, 86, 105
  Muṣannaf 28, 42
Abraham 95*n*94, 95*n*102, 96, 111
Abraham of Tiberias 167, 181
Abū Aḥmad al-ʿAsāl al-Qāḍī 54*n*99
Abūl-Aswad 35
Abū Bakr al-Ṣiddīq 29, 31, 112
  encounter with Ibn al-Daghina 33
  and *hijra* 211–212
Abū l-Daḥdāḥ 68–69
Abū Dāwūd Sulaymān al-Ashaʿth al-Sijistānī 43, 47
  on letter to scholars in Mecca 65
  Sunan and *Aʿlām al-nubūwa* 48
Abū Dharr al-Ghifārī, conversion of 194
Abū Ḥāritha 153
Abū l-Ḥasan ʿAlī b. Aḥmad b. Mūsā b. al-Samsār 68–69
Abū Hāshim 200*n*81
Abū Ḥayyān al-Tawḥīdī 156
Abū Hudhayl al-ʿAllāf; "Against ʿAmmār the Christian, in Refutation of the Christians" 160–161
Abū Hurayra 26, 136
Abū l-Ḥusayn al-Baṣrī 175
Abū ʿĪsā l-ʿIṣfahānī 147
Abū Isḥāq b. Ḥamza 54*n*99
Abū Isḥāq Ibrāhīm b. al-Haytham b. al-Muhallab 51
Abū Jahl 30, 32
Abū Karib Asʿad 109
Abū l-Khayr al-Salāma b. Ibrāhīm b. al-Salāma al-Ḥaddād 68
Abū Maʿbad 32
Abū Manṣūr Muḥammad b. al-Ḥusayn b. Abī Ayyūb 203
Abū Maʿshar 25
Abū Muḥammad al-Ḥasan b. ʿAlī b. al-Ḥusayn b. Aḥmad b. Ṣafr 68
Abū Nuʿaym al-Faḍl b. Dakīn 49
Abū Nuʿaym al-Iṣfahānī = Aḥmad b. ʿAbdallāh b. Aḥmad b. Isḥāq b. Mūsā b. Mehrān 3, 4, 12, 15, 39, 54, 58–59, 84, 100, 101, 203
  approach, methodology of 87, 92
  books: *Ḥilyat al-awlīyāʾ, Akhbār Iṣfahān* 58
  Dalāʾil al-nubūwa 86, 98, 191–192, 196
  and influence of Ashʿarī theology 199–200
  on miracles 200–201
  organization/systematization of 187, 195, 199
Abū l-Qāsim ʿAlī b. al-Ḥasan b. Ṭaʿān 68
Abū Qurra, Theodore 150, 155, 166, 168
  vs. caliph al-Maʾmūn 157
  disputation of 161
  Maymar fī wujūd al-khāliq wa-l-dīn al-qawīm 161
  Treatise on the existence of the creator and true religion 164
Abū l-Shaykh = Abū Muḥammad ʿAbdallāh b. Muḥammad al-Iṣfahānī 54, 86*n*73, 191
  books: *Ṭabaqāt al-muḥaddithīn, Kitāb al-ʿAẓama, Dalāʾil al-nubūwa, Akhlāq al-nabī wa-adabuhu* 56
Abū Ṭalḥa, and Umm Sulaym, conversation of 140
Abū Ṭālib al-Makkī 21, 96, 99, 113, 115–116, 129, 178
  Baḥīrā's warning to 107
  and Muḥammad 124–125, 158, 178
Abū Usāma 211
Abū Usāma al-Fāyyiq 32

Abū Zurʿa al-Dimashqī 47
Abū Zurʿa al-Rāzī 43, 47
dalāʾil al-nubūwa work of 48
Abyssinia, emigration to 28, 33, 211
Adang, Camilla 175
ʿAffān b. Muslim 49
Aḥmad b. Ḥanbal 44, 46, 47–48
Musnad 6, 80, 83
ʿĀʾisha 23, 71
and *hijra* 29
lie surrounding 27
on Muḥammad's character 119
on Muḥammad's protection by God 128
ʿAlī b. Abī Ṭālib 30–31, 71, 147, 213
in cave, with Muḥammad and Abū Bakr 212
and Fāṭima, impoverished 117
ʿAlī b. ʿĪsā l-Rummānī 200
al-Amīn 152
Āmina 95–96, 121–123
ʿĀmir b. Fuhayra 29, 213–214
ʿAmmār al-Baṣrī 150, 155, 167–168
in intellectual milieu of Basra 160
Kitāb al-Burhān 168–169
ʿAmmār b. Muḥammad b. Makhlad 182*n*146
ʿAmr b. Umayya 113
Anas b. Mālik 71, 119
al-Andalus 175
Andrae, Tor 1, 37, 39, 79, 81
on *dalāʾil al-nubūwa* works 10–11, 80, 114, 132
Die Person Muhammeds in Lehre und Glaube seiner Gemeinde to legends and miracles 4–5
on *sīra* 7
Anthony, Sean 180, 182*n*146
on "narrativized theology" 144
al-ʿAqaba 212
Armstrong, Lyall 6, 20, 38, 80
al-ʿĀṣ b. al-Wāʾil 36
al-Ashʿarī, Abū l-Ḥasan 200*n*81
ʿĀṣim b. ʿUmar b. Qatāda 36, 37, 71
Asmāʾ bt. Abī Bakr 23, 31, 33, 213
Aswad b. ʿAbd Yaghūth 36
Aswad b. Kaʿb al-ʿAnsī 147
Aswad b. al-Muṭṭalib 36
Baḥīrā 106–107, 125, 165, 178
Christian legend/reworking of 156, 158–159, 165, 185
encounter with Muḥammad 99, 107, 125, 156, 158–159, 178, 197
al-Bajalī, Abū l-Majad Fatayān b. Ḥaydra b. ʿAlī 68
al-Bāqillānī, Abū Bakr Muḥammad 200
al-Baṣrī 150
al-Bastawī 46*n*40
Bayān b. Samʿān al-Nahdī 148
al-Bayhaqī = Abū Bakr Aḥmad b. al-Ḥusayn b. ʿAlī b. Mūsā l-Khusrawjirdī 3, 4, 12, 15, 39, 58–60, 85, 100–101, 203
Dalāʾil al-nubūwa 99, 187, 196, 198
influence of Ashʿarī theology 198, 199, 202
Kitāb al-Sunan al-kubrā 59
on scripture/miracle of Qurʾān 202
sources of 87–88
al-Bazzār; *Musnad* 83
Berkey, Jonathan 6, 80
al-Bīrūnī 156
Bishr al-Muʿtamir; *Ḥujja fī ithbāt al-nabī* 43
Brockelmann, Carl 57, 188
Brown, Jonathan A. C. 65, 67
al-Bukhārī 43–44, 47, 64–65, 92, 142
arrangement of 101
canonical *ḥadīth* collection of 6, 80, 133
and comparison with Ibn Saʿd 134
methodological approaches of 63
and requirements of authentication 143
Ṣaḥīḥ 12, 47, 64, 88, 133, 138
Bülow, Gabriele von 12, 142
Busra 107

Christ 167, 168. *See also* Jesus
Conrad, Lawrence 24*n*37
Constantine VI 172–173
Ibn al-Layth's letter to 176

al-Dāraquṭnī 46
Delooz, Pierre 10, 14, 207, 209
al-Dhahabī 27, 42, 44, 57, 187
Ḍirār b. ʿAmr 161
Dome of the Rock 148, 151

Eve 95*n*102

Fāṭima 134
al-Firyābī, Abū Bakr 49
Funkenstein, Amos 158

Gibb, Hamilton A. R. 7
Goldziher, Ignaz 5, 7, 19
Görke, Andreas 24, 27, 33–34, 35
Graf, Georg 161*n*50

Ḥabīb b. Khidma Abū Ra'iṭa 150, 155, 168
Hagar 111
Ḥājjī Khalīfa/Kātib Çelebī 24*n*37, 44, 57
al-Ḥākim Abū 'Abdallāh Muḥammad b. 'Abdallāh 55, 58
Ḥalīma 96, 123, 193
  and blessings received 117, 205
  poverty of 116
al-Hamadhānī, 'Abd al-Jabbār; *Tathbīt dalā'il al-nubūwa* 3, 41, 175
Ḥamd b. Muḥammad al-Khaṭṭābī 200
Ḥammād b. Salama 211
Hammām b. Munabbih 26
al-Ḥarbī, Ibrāhīm b. Isḥāq 48–49
  books: *Kitāb Manāsik al-ḥajj, Kitāb al-Hadāyā, Kitāb al-Hammām* 49
al-Ḥārith b. Sa'īd al-Kadhdhāb 147
al-Ḥārith b. al-Ṭulāṭila 36
Harran 182
Hārūn al-Rashīd 46, 152, 172–173, 181
Ḥasan and Ḥusayn 137
Ḥasan al-Baṣrī 21, 41
Ḥassān b. Thābit 177
al-Ḥasan al-Mu'addib 182
al-Hāshimī, 'Abdallāh b. Ismā'īl 155, 157–158
  and fictional exchange with al-Kindī 162–163
Heimgartner, Martin 163
Heraclius 183
Ḥirā', cave of 132, 139
Hishām b. 'Urwa 28, 33, 35, 211
Hollander, Aaron 208
Horovitz, Josef 7
Horst, Heribert 20
Ḥudaybiyya
  treaty of 27, 35, 106, 115
  water miracle at 36, 125, 197
al-Ḥumaydī, Abū Bakr 5, 43, 45, 47, 145, 186
al-Ḥusayn b. Fahm 70*n*18
al-Ḥusayn b. al-Ḥasan b. Muḥammad b. Ḥalīm 203

Ibn al-'Abbās, 'Abdallāh 26, 71, 168
Ibn Abī l-Dunyā = Abū Bakr 'Abdallāh b. Muḥammad b. 'Ubayd b. Sufyān b. Qays 50–51
Ibn Abī Shayba 49
  Muṣannaf 84
  Musnad 83
Ibn Abī Ṭāhir Ṭayfūr 172
Ibn 'Adī al-Jurjānī 46
Ibn Daghina 211
Ibn Ḥajar 27
Ibn Ḥanbal. *See* Aḥmad b. Ḥanbal
Ibn al-Hayyabān, Abū 'Umayr 108–109
Ibn Ḥazm; *Kitāb al-Uṣūl wa-l-furū'* 175
Ibn Ḥibbān 46
Ibn Hishām, Abū Muḥammad 'Abd al-Malik 177
  Sīra 184
Ibn Isḥāq, Ḥunayn 168
Ibn Isḥāq, Muḥammad 24, 24*n*37, 35, 71*n*20, 86–87, 178, 180, 189
  and collective *isnāds* 25
  as innovator in *maghāzī* and *sīra* 179, 185
  Kitāb al-Maghāzī 177, 179, 182*n*146
  prophetic biography of 8
  proximity to 'Abbāsid court 182
  reliance on Christian networks 183–184
  role in discourse about prophecy 180–182
  Sīra 73, 153
Ibn al-Jawzī
  Kitāb al-Quṣṣāṣ wa-l-mudhakkirūn 19, 21
  al-Wafā' bi-aḥwāl al-Muṣṭafā 176
Ibn Jurayj 24*n*37
Ibn Kathīr 24*n*37
  al-Sīra al-nabawiyya 6, 80–81
Ibn al-Layth = Abū l-Rabī' Muḥammad 173
  letter to Constantine VI 176–177, 181
  Risāla 172–173
Ibn Ma'īn 47, 49
Ibn Mājah 43
Ibn Mandah, Abū 'Abdallāh Muḥammad 54–55, 56–58, 191
Ibn Ma'rūf 70*n*18
Ibn Mas'ūd 71, 116, 195

Ibn al-Munādī 49
Ibn al-Nadīm 43
Ibn Qutayba = Abū l-ʿAbbās Muḥammad b. al-Ḥasan b. Qutayba 50–51, 176
 Aʿlām (or *dalāʾil*) *al-Nubūwa* 50, 175, 186
Ibn Rabban = ʿAlī b. Rabban al-Ṭabarī 175–176, 181
 Kitāb al-Dīn wa-l-dawla 174–176, 181
 on trinity and incarnation 161
Ibn al-Rāwindī 162*n*52
Ibn Saʿd 42–43, 45, 77–78, 101, 145–146, 189, 204
 "ʿAlamāt al-Nubūwa" 69, 93–94, 105
 on cave 77–78
 chapters and arrangement of 93–94
 and Christian-Muslim debates 17
 on Christian perspectives toward Muḥammad 162
 comparison with al-Bukhārī 134
 comparison with Wahb b. Munabbih 74
 context of 209
 and degrees of authentication 71, 78
 as earliest author of a *sīra* 25
 epistemological concept/notions of 131, 170
 Kitāb Akhbār al-nabī [attrib.] 70
 Kitāb al-Ṭabaqāt al-kubrā 4, 6, 39, 42, 69–70, 80
 methodological approach of 69–70
 on Muḥammad's prophetic mission 96–97, 170
 on proofs of prophecy 16, 144, 170
 selections of 142, 150
 on "signs of prophecy" 63, 106, 114, 132
 sources of 145, 177
 on witnesses of legitimacy of Muḥammad 179
Ibn Ṣāʿid 49
Ibn Samura al-Jaʿdī 27
Ibn Shāhīn = Abū l-Ḥafṣ ʿUmar b. Aḥmad b. ʿUthmān b. Aḥmad al-Baghdādī 55–56
Ibn Taymiyya 176
 Aḥādīth al-quṣṣāṣ 19
Ibn Urayqiṭ, ʿAbdallāh 31, 31*n*80, 214
ʿĪsā b. Ṣubayḥ al-Murdār 161
al-Iṣfahānī, Abū l-Qāsim al-Taymī 176
Isḥāq b. Rahawayh al-Ḥanẓalī 47, 49–50
Ismāʿīl 95*n*102
al-Jāḥiẓ, ʿAmr b. Baḥr 200
 Kitāb Ḥujjaj al-nubūwa 3, 41
Jarrar, Mahar 105
Jerusalem 111
 night journey to 133
Jesus 95*n*94, 96, 163–165, 175. *See also* Christ
 addressed Children of Israel 170
 announced prophet 108, 181
 good tidings of 111
 prophetic status of 176
John 1 154, 157
John of Damascus 154, 165
 on absence of witnesses to revelation 167, 169
 The Fount of Knowledge, "On heresies" 154, 163
Jones, Marsden 73*n*23
al-Jurjānī, ʿAbd al-Qāhir 200
Juynboll, G. H. A. 45*n*36
al-Jūzajānī = Abū Isḥāq Ibrāhīm b. Yaʿqūb b. Isḥāq al-Saʿdī l-Jūzajānī 46–48, 92
 Amārāt al-nubūwa 135, 139
 "Amārāt al-nubūwa" 67–68
 books: *Aḥwāl al-rijāl, al-Mutarjim, al-Jarḥ wa-l-taʿdīl, Kitāb al-Ḍuʿafāʾ, Masāʾil al-Imām Aḥmad, al-Tārīkh, Amārāt al-nubūwa* 47
 methodological approaches of 63

Kaʿba 123
Kaʿb al-Aḥbār, in Abū Nuʿaym's work 86
al-Kalbī, Hishām b. 42
Kātib Çelebī 187–188
Khadīja 23, 107, 178
Khālid b. ʿAbdallāh al-Qasrī 148
Khālid b. Sinān 147
al-Khandaq, battle of 27
al-Khargūshī = Abū Saʿd ʿAbd al-Malik b. Abī ʿUthmān Muḥammad b. Ibrāhīm al-Nīsābūrī 57–58, 84, 100–101, 187, 203
 chapter of 189–190
 influence of Ashʿarī theology 199
 methodology of 85
 on miracle (*muʿjiza*) 188, 190–191
 Sharaf al-Muṣṭafā 187–188
 Sharaf al-nabī 85, 97–98, 187, 204
 works: *Tahdhīb al-asrār, Bishāra wa-l-nidhāra, Sharaf al-Muṣṭafā* 57

al-Khaṭīb al-Baghdādī 182
Khaybar 110, 112
Khoury, Georges 25*n*49, 26
Kister, Meir Jacob 4, 39, 42, 55

LaCapra, Dominick 8–10, 207
Lecker, Michael 73*n*23
Leder, Stefan 69*n*16
  on editing of *akhbār* 125, 130
Leo III 154
  exchange with ʿUmar b. ʿAbd al-ʿAzīz 171–172, 176, 181
Levi Della Vida, Giorgio 7
Lifshitz, Felice 10, 14, 207
Liḥb 178
Loth, Otto 70*n*18
Lucas, Scott 42

al-Madāʾinī, Abū l-Ḥasan 5, 44–45, 48, 145, 186
al-Mahdī 154, 157, 161, 173–174
  and disputation with Timothy I 163, 176, 181
Mālik b. Anas 24*n*37, 183
Maʿmar b. Rāshid 4–5, 15, 24, 39, 41–42, 45, 86, 142
  vs. Ibn Saʿd 144
  al-Jāmiʿ 42, 64, 105
  methodological approach of 63
  structure and arrangement of 92, 101
  on water narratives 115, 132
al-Maʾmūn 15, 146, 152, 162*n*52
  aʿlām al-nubūwa ascribed to 43
  court of 155, 161
Mani, established Manichaeism 147
al-Manṣūr 182
al-Maqdisī = Abū Naṣr Muṭahhar b. Ṭāhir 175
al-Māwardī, Abū l-Ḥasan 175
  Aʿlām al-nubūwa 3
Maysara 107, 178
Mecca 212
  conquest of 27
  persecutions of Muslims in 28, 34
Medina 30, 212
  hijra to 28–29, 112, 212, 214
  Jewish tribes of 110
Melchert, Christopher 57, 188
Miqdād 116, 128, 197
  encounter with devil 79, 81–82
al-Mizzī 27
Moses 95*n*94, 175–176
Mughīra b. Saʿīd al-ʿIjlī 148
Muḥammad, Prophet
  and animals 36, 118, 189–190, 195–196
  annunciation narratives of 170, 172, 180, 184–185
  appearance of 72–73, 105, 193
  and ascension to heaven (*miʿrāj*) 97, 133
  authority vested in 2, 66, 110, 149
  biography of/*sīra* works 18, 34, 38, 70, 99, 177, 185, 209
  campaigns/raids (*maghāzī*) of 70, 105
  caregivers/household/genealogy of 96, 97, 123, 167, 192
  character of 126, 132, 137, 138, 169, 174, 185, 193
  Christian awareness/recognition of 106, 108, 111–112, 145
  cleansing heart of 99, 124, 177, 194, 197, 205
  conception, birth, childhood, adolescence 37, 96, 99, 114, 121–122, 142, 177, 193
  divine protection of 36, 77, 189, 193, 197, 201–202, 205
  dreams of 127, 141, 212
  early life/childhood of 96, 120, 134, 143, 180, 192, 194
  encounters with Gabriel 29–30, 35–36, 127–128, 139, 212
  encounter with Maysara 107–108, 178
  encounter with monk Baḥīrā 125, 156, 159, 164–165, 178, 197
  encounter with Surāqa b. Mālik 75–76, 78, 91, 128, 133, 195
  encounter with Umm Maʿbad 73–75, 78–79, 91, 189
  evidentiary events/miracles 3, 11, 40, 78, 101, 103, 115, 131, 139, 167–168, 169, 173, 195
  as false prophet 163, 166
  feeding Khadīja in paradise 136–137
  as good tidings of Jesus 111, 177
  hidden knowledge of 96, 106, 116, 118, 129, 131, 133–134, 143
  and *hijra* 75–76, 195, 213–214

Muḥammad, Prophet (*cont.*)
as illiterate 111–112, 173
and interaction with divine/God 96
and Jews 36, 107–110, 112, 125
and legends 4, 7, 34, 159, 165
legitimacy of 2, 101, 142, 173, 176, 179
marriage to Zaynab bt. Jaḥsh 160, 165
miracles of 35–36, 87, 92, 104, 116–117, 174, 189, 201
and nature-related events (trees, stones) 117–119, 124, 126, 132, 141, 179, 189
popular veneration of 1, 7, 81
as prayer of Abraham/Abrahamic messenger 111, 170, 177
preaching of monotheism 164–165, 174, 178
predicting/announcing prophecy of 36, 96, 106, 111, 135, 143, 171, 174
in previous scriptures 3, 50, 106–110, 112, 114, 131, 167, 170–171, 174, 176, 184, 192
removal of "Satan's share" 99, 194, 197
in sacred history 95, 97, 126, 145, 163, 165, 202–203, 204
as seal of prophets/prophecy 31, 94, 111
soothsayers recognized 36, 93, 96–97, 112, 120, 179, 192–193
sprinkling dust on Quraysh 86–87, 189
states of 96, 126
supplications of 82, 117, 119–120, 128, 133
threats to 107, 125, 212
veracity of prophetic mission 13, 50, 103, 141, 152, 190, 196, 198, 201, 204
and wedding celebration/gatherings 193–194, 202
Muḥammad b. ʿAbd al-Raḥmān 28*n*61
Muḥammad b. Aslam 48
Mukhtār al-Thaqafī 147
al-Muqammiṣ, Dāwūd b. al-Marwān al-Raqqī 150, 175*n*107
Mūsā b. ʿUqba 24, 25, 71*n*20
account of, *vs.* Wahb b. Munabbih 76–78
Maghāzī of 75
Musaddad b. Musarhad 49
Musaylima b. Ḥabīb 147, 190
Muslim b. Ḥajjāj 43, 47, 64–65, 67
canonical *ḥadīth* collection of 6, 80
Ṣaḥīḥ 83, 88
al-Mutawakkil 161

Nafiʿ, on goat feeding army 136
Nagel, Tilman 5
Najrān, delegation from 108
al-Naqqāsh, Abū Bakr Muḥammad b. al-Ḥasan b. Muḥammad b. Ziyād 54
books: *Kitāb Akhbār al-quṣṣāṣ, Kitāb Ḍidd al-ʿaql, Kitāb Qirāʾāt bi-ʿilaliha, Kitāb al-Ishāra fī gharīb al-qurʾān* 53–54
al-Naẓẓām 200*n*81
Negus 28
Nesṭūr 107
Newmann, Andrew 40*n*3
al-Nisāʾī 43, 47
Noah 95*n*94, 95*n*102
Nöldeke, Theodor 39
Nonnus of Nisibis 155, 163

Palombo, Cecilia 154*n*29
Peter the Venerable 156

Qāḍī ʿIyāḍ 7
al-Shifāʾ 5, 80
al-Qāsim b. Ibrāhīm 161
al-Qāsim b. Sallām 49
Qatāda b. Diʿāma 41
Qatāda b. al-Nuʿmān, account of eye 130, 197
Qubāʾ 32, 97

Rayy 182
al-Rāzī, Abū Ḥātim 43–44
al-Rāzī, Abū Ḥātim Muḥammad b. Idrīs 47
al-Rāzī, Fakhr al-Dīn 175
Renan, Ernest 7
Rondolino, Massimo 13, 208

Ṣafīya 23
Sajāḥ 147
Salmān al-Fārisī 130
conversion of 178–179, 194
manumission of 36–37, 130, 179
Sāmūl 108
al-Sawwās, Yāsīn Muḥammad 69*n*16
Schacht, Joseph 77*n*40
Schimmel, Annemarie 11
on *dalāʾil al-nubūwa* as miracle narratives 132

Schmidtke, Sabine 53
Schoeler, Gregor 24, 27, 33–34, 73*n*23, 77*n*40
Sergius 163
al-Shāfiʿī 43, 65, 100, 149
on Sunna 88
al-Shāshī, Abū Bakr Muḥammad b. ʿAlī 55
al-Sijistānī, Abū Yaʿqūb; *Kitāb Ithbāt al-nubūwa* 3
Spiegel, Gabrielle 9–10, 207
Storey, Charles Ambrose 57, 188
Stroumsa, Sarah 2–3, 175*n*107
Sufyān b. ʿUyayna 43, 45
al-Sulamī, ʿUmar b. ʿAbasa 194
Sulaymān b. Ibrāhīm al-Ḥāfiẓ 54*n*99
Surāqa b. Mālik 31–32, 72, 75–77, 78–79, 91
conversion of 75
encounter with 34, 75–77, 128, 133, 195
and horse of 32, 75–76, 128, 189
al-Suyūṭī; *Taḥdhīr al-khawāṣṣ min akādhīb al-quṣṣāṣ* 19

al-Ṭabarānī, Abū l-Qāsim 54, 191
al-Ṭabarī 24*n*37, 47, 162*n*52
tafsīr of 20, 84
Tārīkh al-rusul wa-l-mulūk 8
Ṭalḥa b. ʿUbaydallāh, gift from 214
al-Ṭayālisī; *Musnad* 83
Thābit b. Bunānī 71
Thawr, cave of 30–31, 212
Theodore bār Kōnē 154, 163, 165
Tihāma 113
Timothy I 154, 165, 173–174
and disputation with Muslim scholar/al-Mahdī 157, 161, 163, 176, 181
al-Tirmidhī, Abū ʿĪsā 43, 47–48, 64, 142
arrangement of 92, 101
"Bāb mā jāʾa fī ayāt nubūwat al-nabī wa-mā qad khaṣṣa Allāh bihi" 49
al-Jāmiʿ al-ṣaḥīḥ 48, 83
methodological approaches of 63
and requirements of authentication 143
Ṭulayḥa 147

Uḥud, battle of 27, 37, 97, 104, 197
ʿUkāsha b. Miḥṣan, and sword 130
ʿUmar b. ʿAbd al-ʿAzīz 151, 154, 172
and Leo III 171–172, 176, 181
ʿUmar b. al-Khaṭṭāb 117
conversion after hearing recitations 205
ʿUmayr b. Saʿd al-Ansārī 157
Umayyad Mosque 151
Umayyya b. Khalaf 30
Umm Maʿbad al-Khuzāʿīya 31–32, 72–74, 78, 91, 116, 189
ʿUrwa b. al-Zubayr 15, 23–25, 37–38, 71, 86
account of 35, 211–214
and *hijra* 28, 33
Usāma b. Fāyiq 30
ʿUtba 190
ʿUthmān b. Maẓʿūn, and Muḥammad's revelation 127–128

Wahb b. Munabbih 15, 23, 25–26, 26*n*50, 38, 189
account of, *vs.* that of ʿUrwa 211–214
account of *hijra* 72, 77
cobweb at entrance to cave 87
episode of Surāqa 75–76
and Isrāʾīliyyāt/*Kitāb al-Isrāʾīliyyāt* [attrib.] 26
Kitāb al-Mubtadaʾ wa-qiṣāṣ al-anbiyāʾ [attrib.] 26*n*50
used in Abū Nuʿaym's work 86
al-Wāqidī, Muḥammad b. ʿUmar 25, 42, 73, 86–87, 122*n*83
Warāqa 178
al-Warrāq, Abū ʿĪsā Muḥammad b. Hārūn 161
Wellhausen, Julius 73*n*23

Yaḥyā b. ʿAdī 162*n*52
Yamāma, people of 190
Yaʿqūb 111
Yāqūt al-Ḥamawī 27
Yathrib. *See* Medina
Yazīd b. Rūmān 35
Yemen, king of 108–109

al-Ẓāhirī = Abū Sulayman Dāwūd b. ʿAlī b. Khalaf al-Iṣbahānī; *Aʿlām al-nubūwa* 50
Zayd, and divorce of Zaynab 165
al-Zubayr 23
al-Zuhrī, Ibn Shihāb 24, 28, 33, 41, 45, 71, 86, 183
on miracles 35–37
al-Zuhrī, Ibrāhīm b. Saʿd 183

Index of Scriptures

Bible

Deuteronomy 18:18 174
Isaiah 171–172
Isaiah 21:6–9 174
Isaiah 21:7 172, 181
John 14:16 167*n*76
John 15:26–16:1 180

Qur'ān

2:4 162*n*53
2:41 162*n*53
2:75–79 171*n*90
2:89 170*n*85
2:91 162*n*53
2:97 162*n*53
2:129 95*n*99
3:3 162*n*53, 170*n*85
3:81 95*n*94, 162*n*54, 171*n*88
4:46 171*n*90
4:47 162*n*53, 170*n*85
4:163–165 202*n*87
5:13 171*n*90
5:46–48 162*n*53
5:67 128*n*125
5:110 202*n*89
6:92 162*n*53
6:109 168*n*79
7:157 171*n*87, 181
8:17 86*n*70, 189*n*19
8:30 29*n*69, 212
8:39 212
10:94 162*n*53
15:16–18 83*n*66
15:17–18 36*n*101, 113*n*41
16:90 128*n*123
16:103 171*n*89
17:1 133*n*139
17:13–18 133*n*140
17:59 168*n*82
17:88 200*n*80
17:101 202*n*89
29:48 171*n*89
33:7 95*n*94
33:37 160*n*46
34:10 202*n*89
35:31 162*n*53
37:6–10 36*n*101, 83*n*66, 113*n*41
46:12 170*n*85
46:28 178*n*129
46:30 170*n*85
51:1–2 133*n*141
54:1 11*n*41
61:6 170*n*86, 172, 174, 181
67:5 36*n*101, 83*n*66, 113*n*41
72:1 178*n*129
72:8–9 36*n*101, 113*n*41
72:8f. 83*n*66
81:15–29 97*n*106

Printed in the United States
by Baker & Taylor Publisher Services